Great Cities of the Ancient World

OTHER BOOKS BY L. SPRAGUE DE CAMP

FICTION

The Arrows of Hercules
The Bronze God of Rhodes
The Carnelian Cube
  (WITH FLETCHER PRATT)
The Castle of Iron
  (WITH FLETCHER PRATT)
The Clocks of Iraz
Conan
  (WITH ROBERT E. HOWARD AND LIN CARTER)
Conan of Cimmeria
  (WITH ROBERT E. HOWARD AND LIN CARTER)
Conan of the Isles
  (WITH LIN CARTER)
Conan the Adventurer
  (WITH ROBERT E. HOWARD)
Conan the Avenger
  (WITH BJÖRN NYBERG AND ROBERT E. HOWARD)
Conan the Buccaneer
  (WITH LIN CARTER)
Conan the Freebooter
  (WITH ROBERT E. HOWARD)
Conan the Usurper
  (WITH ROBERT E. HOWARD)
Conan the Wanderer
  (WITH ROBERT E. HOWARD AND LIN CARTER)
Divide and Rule
The Dragon of the Ishtar Gate
An Elephant for Aristotle

The Fallible Fiend
The Fantastic Swordsmen
  (ANTHOLOGY)
Genus Homo
  (WITH P. SCHUYLER MILLER)
The Glory That Was
The Goblin Tower
The Golden Wind
A Gun for Dinosaur
The Hand of Zei
The Incomplete Enchanter
  (WITH FLETCHER PRATT)
Lest Darkness Fall
A Planet Called Krishna
The Reluctant Shaman
Rogue Queen
The Search for Zei
Solomon's Stone
The Spell of Seven
  (ANTHOLOGY)
Swords and Sorcery
  (ANTHOLOGY)
The Tower of Zanid
The Tritonian Ring
Wall of Serpents
Warlocks and Warriors
  (ANTHOLOGY)

Great Cities of
the Ancient World

L. SPRAGUE DE CAMP

Doubleday & Company, Inc., Garden City, New York
1972

ISBN: 0-385-09187-7
LIBRARY OF CONGRESS CATALOG CARD NUMBER 75–168288
COPYRIGHT © 1972 BY L. SPRAGUE DE CAMP
ALL RIGHTS RESERVED
PRINTED IN THE UNITED STATES OF AMERICA
FIRST EDITION

To my friend and colleague,
Alan E. Nourse, M.D.,
my traveling companion
through thick and thin
to a number of these cities.

ACKNOWLEDGMENTS

Grateful acknowledgment is made to the following for permission to quote these copyrighted selections:

To Cassell & Co., Ltd., for the quotation from *The Tomb of Tut-Ankh-Amen*, by Howard Carter and A. C. Mace, © 1923 by Cassell & Co., Ltd.

To Dodd, Mead & Co. and Miss D. E. Collins for the excerpt from *Lepanto*, by Gilbert Keith Chesterton, in *The Collected Poems of G. K. Chesterton*, © 1932 by Dodd, Mead & Co.

Doubleday & Co., Inc., for the quotation from *The Battles That Changed History*, by Fletcher Pratt, © 1956 by Doubleday & Co., Inc.

Doubleday & Co., Inc., the Macmillan Co. of Canada, and Mrs. George Bambridge for the excerpt from *Cities and Thrones and Powers*, by Rudyard Kipling, in *Rudyard Kipling's Verse: Definitive Edition*.

The Dowager Lady Dunsany for the quotation from *The Madness of Andelsprutz*, by Lord Dunsany, in *A Dreamer's Tales*.

Harvard University Press, for quotations from the Loeb Classical Library.

Harcourt, Brace, Jovanovich for the excerpt from *Four Preludes on Playthings of the Wind*, in *Smoke and Steel*, by Carl Sandburg, © 1920 by Harcourt, Brace, Jovanovich, Inc.; renewed 1948 by Carl Sandburg. Reprinted by permission of the publishers.

Indiana University Press for excerpts from *Martial: Selected Epigrams*, © 1963 by Indiana University Press, and *The Satires of Juvenal*, © 1958 by Indiana University Press, both translated by Rolfe Humphries.

Glenn Lord for the excerpts from *Babylon*, by Robert E. Howard, in *Always Comes Evening*, © 1957 by Glenn Lord, and *Oh, Babylon, Lost Babylon*, by Robert E. Howard, hitherto unpublished.

The Macmillan Co., Inc., for the quotations from *The Wonder That Was India*, by A. L. Basham.

The Macmillan Co., Inc., and Cambridge University Press for the quotations from *The Cambridge Ancient History*.

The Macmillan Co., Inc., the Macmillan Co. of Canada, the Mac-Millan Co., Ltd., and Mrs. W. B. Yeats for the excerpt from *Sailing to Byzantium*, by W. B. Yeats.

The University of Michigan for the quotation from *Heliodorus: An Ethiopian Romance*, translated by Moses Hadas, © 1957 by the University of Michigan.

W. W. Norton & Co., Inc., for the quotations from *The Greek Way*, *by Edith Hamilton*, © 1930 by W. W. Norton & Co., Inc., and *Power*, by Bertrand Russell, © 1938 by Bertrand Russell.

Penguin Books, Ltd., for quotations from the translation by E. R. A. Sewter of *Fourteen Byzantine Rulers*, by Michael Psellus, © 1966 by E. R. A. Sewter.

Routledge & Kegan Paul, Ltd., for quotations from the translation by Elizabeth A. S. Dawes of *The Alexiad*, by Anna Comnena.

Rutgers University Press for quotations from *Byzantium: Greatness and Decline*, by Charles Diehl, © 1957 by Rutgers University Press.

For the use of photographs, permission is gratefully acknowledged to Henry Angelo-Castrillon, Istanbul; the Arab Information Center, New York City; Werner Braun, Jerusalem; the Commissioner of the Archaeological Department of Ceylon, Colombo; George F. Dales, Philadelphia; Paul E. P. Deraniyagala, Colombo; the Deutsches Museum, Munich; the Directorate General of Antiquities of Iraq, Baghdad; the Institut Français d'Archéologie, Beyrût; Kathleen M. Kenyon, Oxford; Ellen Kohler, Philadelphia; the Lebanon Tourist Information Office, New York City; Alan E. Nourse, North Bend, Wash.; David O'Connor, Philadelphia; Dündar Ozar, Izmir; and Donald N. Wilbur, Princeton. Photographs not otherwise credited are by the author. The maps and the imaginative reconstructions of scenes in ancient cities were prepared especially for this volume by Rafael Palacios and Roy G. Krenkel respectively.

For help with this book—obtaining source books and pictures, reading and criticizing parts of the manuscript, answering questions, and helping and entertaining my wife and myself in the course of our travels to the places described, I am earnestly grateful to Henri Abdelnour, Isaac Asimov, L. D. C. Austin, Robin Banerjee, Boubaker Ben Yahia, Lionel Casson, K. C. Chacko, John D. Clark, Arthur C. Clarke, Gerard B. Crook, Paul E. P. Deraniyagala, S. U. Deraniyagala, Ahmed El-Shaboury, Mohamed Ezzat Abdel Wahab, Samuel Freiha, Edward M. James, Ragnar H. Johansen, Raja and Viola Kassab, Erle Leichty, Labib Majdelany, Samuel Moskowitz, Dündar Ozar, K. D. P. Perera, James E. Sax, T. B. E. Senevirratne, Mohamed Sobeih, the Maharajkumar Virendrasingh, Victor W. von Hagen, Donald N. Wilber, Samuel T. Winter, and Irving Wolman.

CONTENTS

LIST OF ILLUSTRATIONS

LIST OF MAPS

Great Cities of the Ancient World

INTRODUCTION

CITIES AND THRONES AND POWERS
  STAND IN TIME'S EYE,
ALMOST AS LONG AS FLOWERS,
  WHICH DAILY DIE:
BUT, AS NEW BUDS PUT FORTH
  TO GLAD NEW MEN,
OUT OF THE SPENT AND UNCONSIDERED EARTH
  THE CITIES RISE AGAIN.[1]

Kipling

1. The harbor at Alexandria in the days of the Ptolemies—showing the Pharos and a portion of the Heptastadion.

THIS book will tell about several great cities of ancient times—fourteen of them, of which I have visited all but Nineveh. I mean to describe their physical plan and appearance, narrate some of their history, and tell about life in them during the days of their glory. I have chosen them on a basis of size, importance, and the extent of our knowledge about them.

So many cities have risen and fallen in the 5,000 years of recorded history that I could easily have doubled the length of my list. I had, however, to draw the line somewhere. Some cities I might have described were left out because their most flourishing periods came after the time I was concerned with, making them medieval rather than ancient. This was the case with Baghdad, Cuzco, Damascus, Delhi, Hangchow, Kyoto, Polonnaruva, and Tenochtitlán. Others were omitted because not enough is known (or at least *I* do not know enough) about them. Still others were never quite important enough, or I had already written about them elsewhere,[2] or some combination of these reasons. Hence, no chapters on Angkor Wat, Anshan, Cádiz, Knossos, Meroê, Persepolis, Susa, Tikal, and Troy.

But first, let me tell a little about how cities arose, long before any reached the size and splendor implied by the sobriquet "great." In this book, I use the system of writing dates employed in *The Ancient Engineers* and other previous works. It is a combination of the systems used by the historians of science Joseph Needham and the late George Sarton. Years A.D. and B.C. are shown by an Arabic numeral preceded by + or −; e.g. −623 means 623 B.C. whereas +59 is A.D. 59. The plus sign is, however, omitted from dates after +1000. Centuries are indicated by Roman numerals, again with + or −; e.g. +XVIII means the eighteenth century of the Christian Era.

1

THE COMING OF THE CITY

FOR THERE CAME THE SOUL OF CAMELOT THAT HAD LONG AGO
FORSAKEN USK; AND THERE WAS ILION, ALL GIRT WITH TOW-
ERS, STILL CURSING THE SWEET FACE OF RUINOUS HELEN; I
SAW THERE BABYLON AND PERSEPOLIS, AND THE BEARDED FACE
OF BULL-LIKE NINEVEH, AND ATHENS MOURNING HER IM-
MORTAL GODS.[1]

Dunsany

First was the hunting band. Then the farming village appeared. Lastly came the city.

Ten thousand years ago, the world's entire human population was a few hundred thousand Stone Age primitives, who roamed in hunting bands of seldom more than fifty souls. Of such a band, perhaps a dozen would be active male hunters. While these men hunted and fished, the women searched for fruits, nuts, edible roots like the carrot, and edible tubers like the potato. Such hunting bands usually dwelt in temporary camps; for, after they had hunted an area for a while, the game was largely killed off or frightened away, and the people had to pack up and move to a new hunting ground.

The Agricultural Revolution began about —8000 (that is, 8000 B.C.) during the Neolithic Era or New Stone Age. Once men learned how to tame animals and to grow small fields of edible grains, they became food producers instead of food gatherers. With a supply of food assured, they could settle in permanent villages instead of wandering the face of the earth. In fact, they were compelled to settle down; no farmer, in moving, could take with him the field he had laboriously fenced, leveled, plowed, seeded, weeded, and harvested. Because a fertile tract (at least, until primitive farming methods exhausted the soil) could support 20 to 200 times as many farmers as it could hunters, the population in farming regions multiplied many times over.

Around the northern end of the Arabian Desert sweeps a curve of hills and mountains. Here arose the earliest villages of mankind: Tepe Sarab, Jarmo, Hassuna, Amq, and Jericho. The first four bear the names of nearby modern places, because we do not know what the earliest villagers called them. In time, Jericho grew into a sizable town. As far as is known, it is the oldest still-inhabited settlement on earth, where men have lived continuously for over 8,000 years.

The Agricultural Revolution, which made village life both possible and compulsory, probably began in this mountainous arc because here dwelt the beasts and plants that, of all the earth's hundreds of thousands of species, have proved the easiest and most useful to tame. These are the ox, the goat, the sheep, the pig, and the grasses wheat and barley.

There are, of course, many other useful plants and animals. The dog had already been domesticated in food-gathering times. Later, men tamed the cat and the ass in northeast Africa, the horse in eastern Europe, the camel in southwest Asia, the elephant and the chicken in India, the reindeer in Siberia, and the llama in South America. During these millennia, men (or perhaps their women) domesticated such plants as rice, maize, bananas, and other fruits and vegetables. Other species did not turn out well and were abandoned. Most of the food that men consume today is still derived from wheat, rice, and maize, and from the ox, the goat, the sheep, and the pig.

Having a fixed abode meant building a permanent house to replace the tents, lean-tos, caves, and other primitive shelters, portable or improvised, used by the hunting band. Early houses were made of whatever suitable local material lay ready to hand: stone around the rocky shores of the Mediterranean, wood in the forests of northern Europe, clay on the muddy Euphratean plain. Stone and clay encouraged the building of round houses; timber, of rectangular dwellings. Round huts, with cylindrical walls of stone or of clay reinforced by reeds or withes, often had roofs integral with the rest of the structure. They were made by curving the walls inward to form a dome. In other cases, the roof was a separate conical structure of poles and thatch, resting atop the cylindrical wall.

For several thousand years, peasant villages spread slowly out from the mountainous arc where they started. They moved west to Egypt and east to India. Since there were no roads, there was little travel. Because such new ideas as did take root spread with glacial slowness, life went on with little change for century after century.

About —4000, another revolution took place. Some villages flowered into cities. Below the eastern end of the mountainous arc lies the country we call Iraq, across which the mighty Euphrates and Tigris rivers wind their way to the Persian Gulf. They approach each other near Baghdad, swing apart, and finally join before they reach the sea. The earliest known true cities—Nippur, Eridu, Isin, Shuruppak, Uruk, Larsa, and Ur—arose in southern Iraq, in or near the leaf-shaped peninsula formed by the junction of the Tigris and Euphrates rivers. This land was known as Sumer or Shumer—the plain of Shinar of Genesis. Civilization (literally, cityfication) spread northward to central Iraq (Babylonia) and thence to northern Iraq (Assyria).

Now, a city is not just an oversized village. A farming village cannot grow forever because, after a time, it would harbor more farmers than were needed to till the surrounding fields. Latecomers would have to walk so far each day to work their plots that they would decide to found a new village in a more convenient place.

Cities, on the other hand, can grow to hundreds of times the size of a village precisely because most of the city-dwellers are not farmers. They are specialists who make their livings in other ways. They produce articles that farmers come to the city to get in exchange for their foodstuffs. Cities could not have existed at the beginning of the Agricultural Revolution because, with the rudimentary farming and stock-raising methods of the time, each peasant had all he could do to raise enough food, eked out by hunting and fishing, to supply himself and his family.

During the four or five thousand years between the rise of villages and the development of cities, however, agricultural methods improved. Such advances as the ox-drawn plow (in place of the hoe) and breeding better strains of wheat and cattle enabled a peasant—at least in a good year—to raise a surplus with which to trade.

These early farmers also had a motive for trading. Like all pioneers, the earliest villagers had to be jacks-of-all-trades. A specialist, who spends his life practicing one craft, can turn out a better product than the average rustic villager who has to be his own smith, carpenter, mason, mechanic, well-digger, surveyor, and wainwright. Even the most primitive food-gathering cultures had a couple of specialists: the tribal priest or wizard, and the tribal chief or war leader. Now, more and more specialists appeared. Instead of making their own shoes, houses, weapons, tools, carts, and boats, farm folk bartered with the specialists in the city who could make these things better than the peasants could.

We do not know much about the birth of the earliest cities, because the early Sumerians left no written records. From what little evidence has been salvaged from the ruins of these cities, however, and from the way cities are known to have started in later times, we can make some plausible guesses.

Sometimes, no doubt, a village simply grew into a city as an increasing number of specialists set up shop there. Sometimes a city grew out of a ceremonial center: a shrine, a temple, a palace, or a graveyard. Wherever people gathered for religious or political meetings, tradesmen settled in to sell them things. Yet some ceremonial centers, like the British outdoor Neolithic temple at Stonehenge, failed to grow into cities.

Another nucleus of a city was the stronghold or castle. When a strong man raised a wall to protect his people and his wealth, other folk would settle nearby, putting up with the war lord's demands for the sake of having a refuge to flee to. The stronghold was often set upon a mountaintop or crag, as at Athens and Siena, or upon an island, as at Paris and Stockholm. A headland, a peninsula, and the inner side of a sharp bend in a river were other sites favored for the protection they afforded.

Cities also sprang up at commercial centers where villagers gathered for periodical fairs, or where trade routes crossed or joined, or where goods were unloaded from transport of one kind and loaded on that of another. Thus Vienna lies at the crossing of several important trade routes, and Palmyra in the Syrian desert flowered because it was a convenient stopping place for caravans. Other favored sites are the mouth of a major river, as at New York and Shanghai; the site farthest downstream on a river where a bridge can be built, as at Rome and London; the highest point on a river where ships can navigate, as at Montreal; or a place with a fine natural harbor, as at Naples and San Francisco.

Furthermore, cities tend to grow wherever natural or man-made wonders exist to be seen. The tourist trade has been a lively source of profit for thousands of years. In classical times, tourists came to Memphis in Egypt to see the Pyramids, the Sphinx, and other wonders, just as they come to Cairo to see the same sights today. An ideal city would be a political, religious, military, commercial, manufacturing, artistic, and educational center all in one, set around a good harbor and enlivened by a few beguiling tourist attractions. Many of the world's great modern cities do, in fact, combine most of these features.

The earliest cities were probably independent political units of the kind the Greeks called a *polis*, which we awkwardly translate as "city-state." Although this kind of polity flourished for thousands of years and gave the world many of its most creative minds, it has now almost wholly vanished.

The polis ruled enough land around it to feed its folk and, whether republic or monarchy, ran its affairs as an independent nation. Every native dweller regarded himself as a citizen of Larsa, or Tyre, or Athens, or Rome as the case might be and looked upon everyone else as a foreigner. He would fight like a fiend to defend his city but would seldom join forces with the people of another polis for defense against a common foe. Since groups of city-states were always divided among themselves by murderous hatreds, a strong outsider was likely to conquer them sooner or later, one by one.

The first cities were organized along the same lines as the peasant societies whence they had sprung. People were grouped into families, clans, and tribes, and each tribe had its own section of the city. Usually the city had a king, who might be a high priest who left the fighting to someone else or who might be a general who left religion to someone else. Or he might combine the military and religious functions.

Power shifted back and forth among the leading groups: the king and his supporters; the senate, a gathering of the heads of the richest families; the priesthood; and the assembly, a gathering of all the armed men. Poor men, women, and slaves, having neither wealth, supernatural powers, nor armed might, did not count for much. Sometimes the senate got rid of the king, or at least reduced him to purely ritual functions, and ran the resulting "republic" to suit itself.

Government was rather loose and informal. No ruler could afford to be very tyrannical, because it was too easy for his subjects to flee to a neighboring polis. The earliest kings dressed and lived much like their subjects. A visitor to a small polis was not surprised to find His Majesty thatching or painting his own palace, while the queen wove him a royal robe on her own loom and screamed at the royal children when they got out of hand.

When a polis grew large and powerful, its government usually became more autocratic and centralized. Then the king might set out to conquer his neighbors. In Iraq, for nearly 2,000 years, one ambitious king after another founded a short-lived empire. Such conquerors had an advantage peculiar to Iraq, which is mostly semi-desert and needs irrigation to flourish.

In early Sumerian times, irrigation was on a small scale; each polis dug its own canals regardless of what its neighbor was doing. When kings conquered large empires, however, they put all the canals under one management, because this was more efficient and enabled the land to support more people. This larger taxable population furnished the king with additional wealth and power and made it easier for him to extend his conquests still further. Since circumstances favored large-scale organization, as fast as one of these watershed empires fell, another arose in its place.

With the rise of large kingdoms and empires, starting around —3000, cities reached a new size and complexity. Each king lived in a royal capital, surrounded by his court, his host of officials, and his army. Because these folk worked full-time for the king, they had to be furnished by others with essential goods and services. In addition, to honor the gods and the powerful priesthoods, the king built imposing temples. These in turn required people to construct and maintain them and to serve the gods in them, and still more people to supply these attendants with goods and services.

To guard the wealth that they wrung from their subjects, kings surrounded their cities with walls, built storerooms, and hired men to guard their hoards of gold and silver, their bins of grain, their jars of wine and oil, their chests of fair raiment, their armories of weapons, and their other property. Writing and arithmetic were invented to keep track of these treasures.

Of these innovations, the building of walls was one of the earliest and perhaps the most important; for, without walls, men might never have reached the city-building stage of culture at all.

A village usually contained little worth stealing. Hence, when threatened by armed marauders, most villagers ran away and hid until the danger had passed. If the strangers destroyed their houses, these could be rebuilt without too much difficulty.

A city, on the other hand, contained all sorts of attractive goods, well worth stealing and also well worth defending. With a massive wall and an ample supply of food and water, a city could withstand a siege by an army several times the size of its own, since one man atop a wall was worth several at its foot. So marked was the distinction between walled and unwalled settlements that some archaeologists define a city as a settlement surrounded by a wall. But Jericho seems to have had a solid wall of stone while it was still a farming village; perhaps that is why it has outlasted all the other ancient cities of the world.

A city wall was made of whatever local material best served the purpose. In Sumeria and Babylonia, there is practically no stone or hardwood. In fact, the most abundant natural resource of these lands is mud. Hence, in Mesopotamia, walls were made of clayey mud. At first the mud was simply scooped up and piled in handfuls. Then it was found that a neater, straighter wall, without visible weak spots to invite attack, could be made by molding the clay into bricks and making the wall of these.

Early Sumerian bricks were patted into shape by hand on a flat surface and hence had bulging, biscuit-shaped topsides. By —3000, a capital Sumerian invention, the brick mold, made it possible to turn out bricks of uniform size, flat on all six surfaces.[2] With such bricks, men could build a more solid and even wall, less vulnerable to hostile men and wet weather. The mold-made brick was perhaps the first step in the age-long evolution of standardized, interchangeable parts. One might almost say that the Industrial Revolution began with the brick mold.

About the same time—the late fourth or early third millennium B.C.—people developed a brick of a new kind. The brick of the old kind—mud brick or sun-dried brick—is made by forming a piece of clay in a mold and drying it in the sun for a period that may range from a few days up to five years, depending on how strong a brick is wanted. Although such a brick is fairly strong when dry, it soon softens and crumbles when wet.

The newer kind of brick, developed around —3000, was burnt or kiln-dried brick. As a result of chemical changes in the clay during baking, burnt brick is not only much stronger than mud brick but also keeps its strength and hardness when wet. Such brick, however, was costly in lands like Egypt and Mesopotamia, where fuel for the kilns was scarce. Therefore, it was used only on the outsides of the most important buildings. The interiors of these buildings and the whole of ordinary buildings were made of mud brick.

To ward off the rains of the wet season, builders put roofs with overhanging eaves on top of their mud-brick houses. Even this precaution could not maintain such a house indefinitely. After a certain time—perhaps a few decades, perhaps a few generations—the house decayed to such an extent that the owner gave up trying to repair it, knocked it down, and built a new house on the ruins. Moreover, burglars easily dug through the soft mud-brick walls with simple picks and shovels.

Where there was considerable rain, even buildings faced with burnt brick had to be carefully maintained. Otherwise, cracks appeared in the facing, just as they do in a modern stuccoed house when it settles unevenly. If these cracks were not promptly repaired, the rains dissolved the sun-dried brick within and the building crumbled into a shapeless heap of mud.

Where stone was to be had, city walls were made of stone— preferably the largest stones that could be moved with the techniques of the time. Even before mortar was invented, men could build a good, solid wall of small stones, which would stand up to the weather better than a wall of mud brick. But then, all an enemy had to do was to pry out a few stones with his spear, and down came a whole section of the wall.

Therefore, many early fortifiers made their walls of very large stones. They trimmed the stones to fit roughly together and stopped up the chinks by pounding in small stones. The sheer weight of the large stones kept the foe from pulling them out, especially if the defenders on top of the wall were raining missiles upon him. Such walls are called "cyclopean" because the ancient Greeks, seeing the ruins of rough walls made of huge stones, built several centuries earlier, thought that the large stones must have been put in place by the mythical one-eyed giants called Kyklopes.

To protect a city, any wall had to be at least 30 feet high and 15 feet thick. If the wall were much lower than this, a numerous enemy could overrun it with scaling ladders. And if the wall were too narrow on top, the defenders could not move along it fast enough to gather at threatened points.

A wall meant more safety, and greater safety fostered the growth of population, partly by natural increase and partly by immigration. As populations waxed, the crowding that ensued made it necessary to use the space inside the wall more efficiently. Therefore, in lands where round houses of stone or clay had prevailed, the round house gave way to the rectangular house; for an oblong house could occupy the whole of a small rectangular lot, whereas a circular house left wasted space at the corners.

As wealth accumulated and houses grew larger, a house of a new type, the courtyard house, came into use among prosperous householders in the hot-dry belt that stretches from Morocco to western India. In this belt, the surrounding country, where it is not true desert, is at best semi-desert or "poor steppe," relying either on irrigation or on a short annual rainy season for its crops. Here the courtyard house has remained popular ever since. It took the form of a hollow square or rectangle, presenting blank brick walls to the outer world. Within, all its rooms opened on an unroofed interior court, which might contain a garden, a fountain, or similar amenities.

This house let its dwellers enjoy the pleasures of the outdoors while preserving their security against robbers and their privacy against strangers and tax collectors. There has lately been a move to imitate it in American Suburbia. If the worst fears of contemporary Americans about the increase in crime should be realized, it is not hard to imagine a greater vogue for the courtyard house in the future as a measure of defense.

As villages evolved into cities, the spaces between houses developed into streets. Since the houses in early villages were ordinarily set every which way, the first streets were narrow, winding lanes. When a village grew into a city, the streets were still crooked alleys, save when some ruler ruthlessly drove a straight, wide avenue through this ancient tangle. Some great modern cities, like Rome and Damascus, keep this archaic cow-path plan in their older parts. Many of their meandering streets have been trodden continuously for thousands of years.

On the other hand, when some ruler decided to create a new capital and commanded that a city be built from scratch, the new city was often laid out on an orderly grid plan, with straight streets crossing at right angles. Sometimes the entire city had a neat square or circular shape. Alas! more than one ruler, in picking the site of his new metropolis, failed to consider such vital factors as trade routes and water supply. Hence, after he died, his former subjects moved back to the tangled old city, leaving the new one to crumble. This happened to Akhetaten in Egypt, Samarra in Iraq, and Fatehpur Sikri in India.

Man has reached the beginnings of civilization a number of times, in widely scattered places. The first foundations were laid in Sumeria, between —4000 and —3000. During the next few centuries, civilization also arose in Egypt and in what is now West Pakistan. It appeared in China and around the eastern Mediterranean about —1500, and it arose in Mexico, Guatemala, and Peru around the beginning of the Christian Era. Lastly, civilization began to make an appearance in Dahomey, Benin, and other Negro kingdoms of West Africa a few centuries ago.

All the Old World centers of civilization were more or less interconnected, so that each has influenced those that came later. Whether the New World civilizations of South and Middle America influenced each other and whether either was influenced by the civilizations of the

Old World are still disputed questions. It is likely, although not firmly proved, that the Middle American and the Andean centers of civilization arose independently of each other and of the Old World, save for a few isolated culture traits like the bow, which diffused from the Old World to the New in the early Christian Era.

Everywhere that men have become civilized, they have built cities. These cities changed very slowly over the centuries from the days of ancient Sumeria to +XVIII (that is, the eighteenth century of the Christian Era). Although there were improvements in building, paving, lighting, water, and sewerage, the changes were extremely gradual. Paris of the year 1500 was not too different from Babylon of —1500. A clever man from one city could have learned to live in the other, once he had overcome the barriers of time, language, and custom.

Ever since late +XVIII, however, with the beginning of the In-dustrial Revolution, city life has been subject to faster and faster changes. A modern metropolis like New York or Tokyo differs more strikingly from Paris of 1500 than that Paris differed from Babylon of —1500.

This growth of cities is, in the strictest sense of the word, "civili-zation." Sometimes people say "civilized" when they mean kind, honest, or polite. But civilized men are not necessarily kinder, more honest, or more courteous than uncivilized men. In fact, many civilizations (Sume-ria, Egypt, Carthage, China, Mexico, and Dahomey) went through an early stage of development wherein they practiced human sacrifice on a huge and gory scale. But civilized men do have cities, metals, writing, and arithmetic. They are organized in larger masses and possess tech-nical skills beyond those of uncivilized men. They therefore have power that uncivilized men lack. They are not necessarily more or less virtuous than uncivilized men; men of both kinds have their own laws and customs, their vices and virtues, and each has the problem of coping with individuals who flout the rules. In short, civilization is a matter, not of virtue, but of power.

So let us get on with our fourteen ancient cities. Of these, the one that first reached immortal splendor, of which imposing remains abide, was that city of many names in Upper Egypt, where Luxor now stands: Waset, or Egyptian Thebes.

II

THEBES OF THE HUNDRED GATES

I MET A TRAVELLER FROM AN ANTIQUE LAND
WHO SAID: TWO VAST AND TRUNKLESS LEGS OF STONE
STAND IN THE DESERT . . . NEAR THEM, ON THE SAND,
HALF SUNK, A SHATTERED VISAGE LIES, WHOSE FROWN
AND WRINKLED LIP, AND SNEER OF COLD COMMAND,
TELL THAT ITS SCULPTOR WELL THOSE PASSIONS READ
WHICH YET SURVIVE, STAMPED ON THESE LIFELESS THINGS,
THE HAND THAT MOCKED THEM, AND THE HEART THAT FED:
AND ON THE PEDESTAL THESE WORDS APPEAR:
'MY NAME IS OZYMANDIAS, KING OF KINGS:
LOOK ON MY WORKS, YE MIGHTY, AND DESPAIR!'
NOTHING BESIDE REMAINS. ROUND THE DECAY
OF THAT COLOSSAL WRECK, BOUNDLESS AND BARE
THE LONE AND LEVEL SANDS STRETCH FAR AWAY.[1]

Shelley

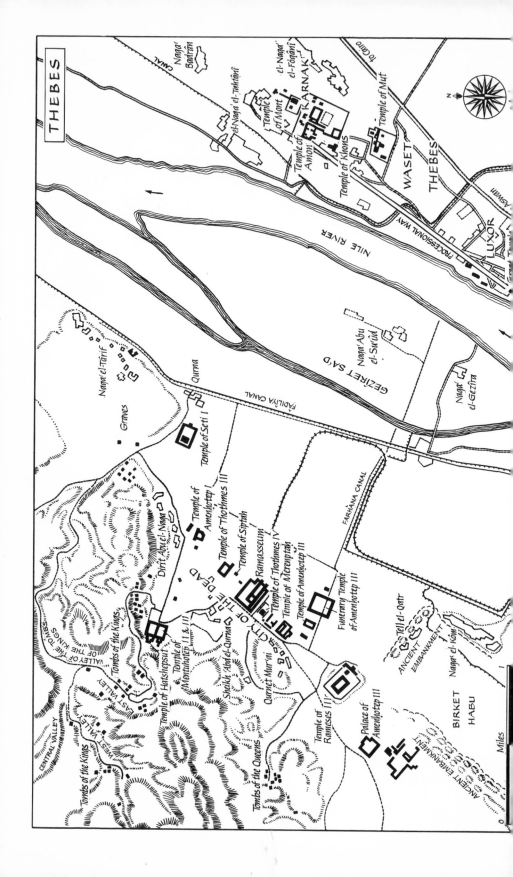

IN Upper Egypt, two-thirds of the way from the shores of the Mediterranean to the Sudanese border, the Nile, on its way from inner Africa to the sea, makes several short, sharp bends. It turns first west, then east, then west again, before straightening out to continue in a long, gentle arc to the Delta. Through these bends, the Nile serpents its leisurely way, dividing to flow around countless islands and sand bars.

On either side of the Nile, a flat alluvial plain, green with the produce of irrigation farming, stretches away for several miles. These plains give way to a series of steep bluffs, rising several hundred feet above the valley floor. Sometimes these bluffs close in upon the river until they frown vertically down upon it; again, they recede many miles into the shimmering distance.

Behind the bluffs on either side lies a stretch of broken country, carved into gullies and ravines during that time, ten or fifteen thousand years ago, when Upper Egypt had the rainfall that it almost totally (save for a rare downpour) lacks today. Beyond the ravines, the land flattens out into one of the world's driest deserts: a vast expanse of sand and bare rock, almost lifeless save where ground water rises close enough to the surface to support a rare oasis.

On both banks of the Nile, in the midst of these bends, stood one of the ancient world's great cities, which for many centuries was the capital of Egypt. This was a city of many names. Some dwellers called it simply "the City"—in Egyptian, a word something like Neut or Newet, which appears in the Bible as No.[2] Others more formally added the name of the city's patron god, Amon; hence Neut-Amon, "the City of Amon." Still others called it Waset or Opet.[3] A name like Tabé seems also to have been current. This got into Greek as Thêbai, the name of a city-state in Boiotia; in Latin, Thebes. Hence the modern form Thebes—albeit the Egyptian Thebes did not at all resemble its Greek namesake.

The Greeks had heard of the wealth of Waset-Thebes as far back as —VIII. In Homer's *Iliad*, when Achilles is sulking because King Agamemnon has ranked him out of a woman he captured on a raid and is spurning the gifts Agamemnon sends him, he says:

Not if he gave unto me ten times, or even if twenty,
All he possesses or all that he may obtain in the future—
Even Orchomenos' wealth, or that of Egyptian Thêbai,
Where in the storerooms are hoarded the most magnificent treasures—

Thêbai the hundred-gated, through each of whose portals there sally
Fighters in number two hundred, each with his horses and chariot—
Even if presents like grains of sand or of dust he proffered,
Nay, Agamemnon's gifts should not even then beguile me . . .[4]

The allusion to the "hundred gates" is a puzzle. No real ancient
city ever had 100 gates in its wall. So many weak spots in its defense
would invite a sack.

When, in +XIX, many European travelers began to reach the upper
Nile Valley, they found on the site of Waset-Thebes the world's most
amazing display of ruined temples. On the east bank, the ruins stretched
along the river for nearly two miles. Grouped in two main clumps,
one brooded over the village of Karnak; the other, farther south, arose
amid the town of Luxor. The name of the latter comes from the Arabic
al-Quṣûr,[5] "the castles." This name refers to the many huge pairs of
stone pylons that once served as gates in the walls of temple courtyards.

On the west bank of the Nile, the ruins spread over an even
larger area. They extended over three miles along the bank of the Nile
and stretched nearly as far back from the river, into the gullied bad-
lands where the valley floor rises to the plateau of the desert.

Nineteenth-century archaeologists knew that ancient cities had
walls. At Thebes, however, they found no sign of walls—just a vast
congeries of ruined temples, statues, and royal tombs dug into the
hillsides. All the tombs, it seemed, had been entered and looted in
ancient times.

Hence a belief grew up that Thebes had never had any wall at
all. Homer's "hundred gates," it was said, were simply the pylons of
the temple inclosures, of which so many still remained standing. And
no walls have been discovered from that day to this. Some archaeologists go so far as to say that no ancient Egyptian cities had walls,
and that, therefore, these settlements should not be deemed real cities
at all.

This, however, cannot be right. There are records in ancient
Egyptian history of sieges, in which the walls of the beleaguered
cities played their part. For instance, in −VIII, the rule of Egypt
was divided among a host of petty sovrans. The Kushite king Pi'ankhi,
whom the Greeks called an Ethiopian and who to us would be a
Sudanese, ruled the South. A conflict arose among the lords of the
Delta, which gave the energetic Pi'ankhi a pretext for intervening in
Lower Egyptian affairs. One kinglet besieged another in Herakleopolis,[6]
which held out until Pi'ankhi sent an army to relieve it. Then the
redoubtable black king came down in person and squelched the dynasts
one by one. He proclaimed:

2. Temple of Amon, Mut, and Khons at Luxor.

Then they fought against Tateḥne, great in might. They found it filled with soldiers, with every valiant man of the northland. Then the battering ram was employed against it to overturn its walls: a great slaughter was made of them, one knows not the number, but among them was the son of the prince of Ma, Tefnakhte . . . [Pi'ankhi] had made for him a camp to the west of Hermopolis[7] and besieged it daily. A mound was built to lift up the archers to shoot and the slingers to hurl stones and kill men among them each day . . .[8]

Obviously, some Egyptian cities had substantial walls. That Thebes had a wall, too, is indicated by the boast of Amenhotep II that he hanged the corpses of six rebellious Asian kings, whom he personally executed, on the wall of Thebes. True, no trace of this wall has been found; but perhaps the Theban wall was comparatively feeble, or perhaps all traces of it have disappeared as later builders carried off its stones or bricks. We know that men of later generations have utterly demolished other imposing structures of ancient Thebes.

Luxor is a sleepy resort town with a jumble of buildings old and new. A horse-drawn carriage still brings the train-borne visitor from the railroad station to the Winter Palace Hotel, the best-known although not the only hostelry. In this place of faded Victorian charm, in the evening, white-haired retired British gentlefolk sit listening to a chamber-music concert. Or one can sit on the terrace overlooking the Nile, watching the lateen-rigged sailing barges waft past, each equipped with a collapsible mast for passing under the Nile bridges. The Nile is a marvelous artery for sailing craft. Because it flows north, while most of the year the wind blows from north to south, one can either drift north with the current or sail south with the wind.

A few blocks north of the Winter Palace stand the towering remains of the Temple of Luxor. The lotus capitals of its splendid colonnades of lotus-topped columns, over 50 feet high, are purely ornamental. Much early Egyptian masonry imitated earlier wooden construction. For example, some columns were ribbed in imitation of the bundles of reeds once used, in the lack of good timber for posts, to hold up houses. But the lotus is only a water lily, whose stem has no more strength than a piece of wet spaghetti.

Amenhotep III built the original temple here about −1400 and dedicated it to three deities: the god Amon, Amon's wife Mut, and their son, Khons the moon god. Amenhotep's successors, especially the

3. Hypostyle Hall of the Great Temple of Amon at Karnak. (Courtesy of David O'Connor.)

4. Hypostyle Hall of the Great Temple of Amon at Karnak.

vainglorious Rameses II, modified the temple. Tearing down and rebuilding continued through the later centuries. One chamber was rebuilt in the time of Alexander the Great, with reliefs showing Alexander before Amon and other gods. The largest court of all, that of
Rameses II, now harbors a small mosque named for a local Muslim
saint, Abû 'l Ḥaggâg.[9]

Like other Egyptian temples, the Temple of Luxor belonged to
the class of religious buildings that may be called "houses of a god."
That is, they were primarily shelters for a statue of the god. When
he felt like it, the god could occupy the statue and animate it. Such
temples normally comprised two parts, more or less concentric: an inner
part containing the statue, to which only the priests had access, and
an outer part—usually an open-air court—where the worshipers gathered.
In highly developed temples of this sort, there might even be more
subdivisions. For instance, there might be a central sanctuary or Holy
of Holies, containing the statue, to which only priests of the highest
rank were admitted; then a temple building housing ordinary priests;
then a sacred area or *temenos* open to initiated members of the con-
gregation; and, outside all the rest, an area open to the general public.

5. Hypostyle Hall of the Great Temple of Amon at Karnak, from the northeast.

Other kinds of religious edifice were the "high place"—an elevation, natural or artificial, whence the priests shouted their prayers up to the gods in Heaven; the shrine, sheltering the bones or other relics of some saint or god; and the meeting house of the worshipers. A single building has often combined two or more of these functions.

A mile and a half northeast of the Temple of Luxor and a third of a mile back from the river, a long succession of Egyptian kings built the Great Temple of Amon at Karnak. Roughly rectangular in plan, it is over a third of a mile long and over 100 yards wide. Although it is not a thing of great beauty—its plan is too irregular and it has suffered too much damage—it is one of the most impressive examples of ancient sacred architecture in the world. Its sheer size makes its plan hard to grasp and tires the visitor's feet. Its complexity baffles the writer and makes it easy for the wanderer to get lost in its maze of ruins.

The Great Temple of Amon was not built all at one time and

then preserved as it stood. Kings of the Twelfth Dynasty began erecting small shrines and temples in the area around the year —2000. These were slowly transformed into an impressive temple with a surrounding court, which we call the Temple of the Middle Kingdom and which has now been largely destroyed.

In —XVI, kings of the Eighteenth Dynasty began extensive additions to their already sumptuous temple. An account of all the courts, colonnades, halls, rooms, reliefs, statues, pylons, and obelisks would fill a book by itself. Since these additions were often made without regard for the over-all design, the site became a chaotic jumble of structures. Additions continued down through the rule of the Kushite kings of —VIII and —VII.

The largest pair of pylons—and the best preserved, even though they were never quite finished—were those of the Kushite king Taharqa. These pylons, the others like them, and their attached walls all have a pronounced batter. That is, each face slopes back, so that the wall tapers as it rises. In building a wall of soft mud brick, the Egyptians learned that battered walls did not crumble so quickly as walls with vertical sides. Having become extremely conservative after the first few dynasties, the Egyptians kept on building battered walls even after they had taken to building in stone, although stone walls did not require batter.

The outstanding feature of this temple, however, is the Great Hypostyle Hall, built by successive kings of the Nineteenth Dynasty—Rameses I, Seti I, and Rameses II. ("Hypostyle" means "upheld by columns.") The area of this hall, 338 by 170 feet, could comfortably contain the entire Cathedral of Notre Dame de Paris.

From a floor paved with broad stone slabs rises a forest of the largest stone columns on earth. To step out of the glare of the fierce Egyptian sun into the shade of this colossal mass of masonry is to get the sensation of having entered some enchanted cavern. There are 134 of these columns, arranged in 16 rows. Of these, the columns of the two central rows are larger than the rest: 11.75 feet in diameter and 80 feet high, counting the 11-foot papyrus-plant capitals that crown them. Massive stone lintels across the tops of the capitals support a stone roof, restored in modern times. The space between the high roof of the nave and the lower roofs of the sides form a clerestory. This is occupied by a stone lattice, of which some parts remain, to let in enough light to see by.

The columns, lavishly decorated with painted reliefs, are not solid. If they had been, not even the Romans of 1,500 years later, who raised fifty-four 65-foot solid granite columns at Ba'albakk in Lebanon, could have handled such weights; even less could the Egyptians of the

6. Hypostyle Hall of the Great Temple of Amon at Karnak, in the time of the Ramessid pharaohs, —XII. (Drawing by Roy G. Krenkel.)

Nineteenth Dynasty have done so. The Karnak columns are built up of pairs of half-disks, 3.5 feet thick.

To raise such ponderous stones to such heights, the Egyptians had no sophisticated hoisting devices, as did the Romans later. Lacking even tongs, pulleys, and iron tools, they probably used the laborious but simple methods by which they had built the pyramids. They piled up gently sloping ramps of earth, sledded the stones up these by main force, and shoveled the dirt away.

From the point of view of architecture, Karnak was a mighty achievement but in many ways an unsophisticated one. The rows of huge, crowded columns used up so much of the space inside the temple that a man in one part of the hall could not see what was going on in another. Not until Roman times, when the arch, the vault, and the dome came into common use, could builders leave so large an interior space uncluttered by supports for the roof.

Outside the main mass of the Great Temple of Amon are lesser temples, stretching off into the distance on both sides. To the southeast, a series of walled courts bounded by four pairs of huge pylons extends away from the central part of the Great Temple. Farther southeast, an avenue of stone rams leads from this complex to a large temple of Mut and a smaller temple of Rameses III; farther east yet stands a small temple of Khons. Northwest of the Great Temple, one finds a complex of several small temples, with avenues of stone rams. All these temples, large and small, have their main axes northwest-southeast instead of being aligned with the major compass directions. The reason is that they all face the Nile, which here flows from southwest to northeast.

So vast is this mass of sacerdotal masonry and so complex its history that a day spent here gives only a brief, confusing glimpse. If one spends a week prowling the grounds with a good guidebook, one begins to know one's way around. For people seriously interested in the history, art, architecture, and archaeology of such sites, there is no equal to the old Baedeker's *Handbooks for Travellers*, mostly published in the 1920s and available today only from rare-book dealers.[10]

The ruins of Waset-Thebes on the west bank are more widely scattered than those on the east, and no single monument surpasses in grandeur the Temple of Luxor or even compares with Karnak. Nevertheless, the west bank includes many handsome and impressive structures.

Passing from northeast to southwest, we first come upon the mortuary temple of Seti I at Qurna, built around −1300. Not much is now left, save the partly ruined walls of the central sanctuary and the graceful row of lotus-topped columns before it.

Passing by several smaller ruined temples, we approach the Great Temple of Dayr al-Baḥri. This is the mortuary temple of Queen Hatshepsut—that formidable lady who, after the death of her husband-half-brother Thothmes II about −1490, managed to run the kingdom for twenty years as regent for her resentful stepson Thothmes III. When Thothmes came to the throne at last, he mutilated his stepmother's monuments, causing her figure to be hacked out of all the reliefs and paintings in which it appeared.

This temple—creamy white against the tawny cliffs of crumbled sandstone—stands in a bay at the foot of the bluffs that rise from the valley floor. It consists of a series of terraces, each upheld by a colonnade of plain, square columns of severely modernistic appearance, and joined ramps, which have been restored in modern times.

The next main structure, as we proceed southeast, is the Ramesseum. This is the mortuary temple of Rameses II, the able, vigorous, long-lived, and colossally self-conceited king who ruled the Two Lands around —1300. Rameses dotted the land of Egypt with gigantic statues of himself, displaying idealized versions of his lanky form and long, hooked nose.

In the Ramesseum, as at Qurna, only the central core of the ancient building remains. Although the outer parts (including a mass of brick storehouses) have disappeared, the walls and columns that remain still make an impressive total. The walls and pylons are carved with reliefs and records of the battle of Rameses II against the Hittites at Qadesh in Syria. While Rameses described the event as a glorious victory for him, modern military scholars suspect that the battle was really indecisive and that the Hittites gave as good as they got.

The most memorable feature of the Ramesseum owes its interest less to the egotistical Rameses than to what an English poet made of his monument over three millennia later. The Ramesseum included several colossal statues of its builder; the head of one, in black granite, lies in the sand next to the remains of the temple.

Another statue fell in ancient times and broke into three huge pieces and smaller fragments. When new, this statue must have weighed around a thousand tons. Now it lies with its face obliterated, hardly recognizable as the remains of a human statue. There is no doubt of its identity, though, because Rameses' name appears on the fragments.

In +I, the historian Diodoros the Sicilian described the Ramesseum as the "tomb of Osymandyas." This name is a Hellenization of one of Rameses' names, User-ma-Ra'. Diodoros' account, together with the reports of later travelers, inspired Percy Bysshe Shelley to compose his celebrated *Ozymandias,* quoted at the beginning of this chapter. True, the site of the Ramesseum does not look at all like the scene depicted by Shelley; but then, the poet had never been to Egypt.

Half a mile south of the Ramesseum stand two colossal seated statues of Amenhotep III, the so-called "Colossi of Memnon." Memnon was a legendary Ethiopian prince who led a contingent of Kushites to the relief of Troy but was there slain by Achilles. (The story is not in

7. Great Temple of Amon at Karnak, from the southeast.

8. Great Temple of Amon at Karnak—Festal Temple of Thothmes III.

9. Pylons of Ptolemaios II at the Temple of Khons, Karnak.

Homer, who alludes only briefly to Memnon, but appears elsewhere in
the Trojan cycle of legends.) When, in −VII and −VI, the kings of
the Twenty-sixth or Saïte Dynasty hired Greek mercenaries, these soldiers, knowing little and caring less about authentic Egyptian history,
bestowed upon the statues the name of the only Homeric hero they had
heard of who had come from these southerly parts. They also told a tale
that the northern statue gave forth a musical sound as the rays of the
dawning sun struck it. Other ancient travelers testified to the reality of
this sound, but nobody in modern times has heard it.

In antiquity, the colossi stood before a huge mortuary temple of
Amenḥotep III; but this temple has almost entirely vanished, leaving the
statues towering by themselves in the midst of a spacious plain. Most
of the demolition was by later kings who wanted the stone for their own
projects. The statues' faces are gone, together with pieces from their
bodies and limbs; but they still make an imposing spectacle. The southern
and taller now stands 64 feet high, counting 13 feet of pedestal. Several
smaller figures of the king's womenfolk, in high relief, stood beside or
between his knees.

The last of the main ruins, as we continue southwest from the
Ramesseum parallel with the Nile, is the temple of Rameses III at

Medîna Habu, intermediate in size between the Temple of Qurna and the Ramesseum but better preserved than either.

Then there are the tombs. A thousand years before the Eighteenth and Nineteenth dynasties, Egyptian kings had built pyramids, in which were stored their mummies and a choice selection of their wealth. But all the pyramids were sooner or later robbed, especially in times of disorder, and this fact no doubt became known to the later kings. The latter resorted to what they hoped would be a more secure system of interment. Instead of building an artificial mountain at vast expense, they had their men tunnel into a real mountain to excavate burial chambers for themselves and their treasures, hoping that their servants would succeed in hiding the entrance after their master was laid to rest.

Alas, the underground tombs were looted just as promptly as the pyramid tombs had been. The underground scheme worked only once, in the case of Tutankhamon, a son-in-law and successor of the heretic pharaoh Ikhnaton.[11] Tutankhamon reigned briefly around −1360. After he was buried, a later king, Rameses IV, had his tomb dug into the same hillside over the entrance to Tutankhamon's tomb, which was thus buried by the talus and forgotten until Howard Carter and Lord Carnarvon opened it in 1922. Carter described his sensations upon entering the tomb chamber:

> The effect was bewildering, overwhelming. I suppose we had never formulated exactly in our minds just what we had expected or hoped to see, but certainly we had never dreamed of anything like this, a roomful—a whole museumful it seemed—of objects, some familiar, but some the like of which we had never seen, piled one upon another in seemingly endless profusion.
>
> Gradually the scene grew clearer, and we could pick out individual objects. First, right opposite to us—we had been conscious of them all the while, but refused to believe in them—were three great gilt couches, their sides carved in the form of monstrous animals, curiously attenuated in body, as they had to be to serve their purpose, but with heads of startling realism. Uncanny beasts enough to look upon at any time: seen as we saw them, their brilliant gilded surfaces picked out of the darkness by our electric torch, as though by limelight, their heads throwing grotesque distorted shadows on the wall behind them, they were almost terrifying. Next, on the right, two statues caught and held our attention; two life-sized figures of a king in black, facing each other like sentinels, gold kilted, gold sandalled, armed with mace and staff, the protective sacred cobra upon their foreheads.
>
> These were the dominant objects that caught the eye first.

Between them, around them, piled on top of them, there were countless others—exquisitely painted and inlaid caskets; alabaster vases, some beautifully carved in openwork designs; strange black shrines, from the open door of one a great gilt snake peeping out; bouquets of flowers or leaves; beds; chairs beautifully carved; a golden inlaid throne; a heap of curious white oviform boxes; staves of all shapes and designs; beneath our eyes, on the very threshold of the chamber, a beautiful lotiform cup of translucent alabaster; on the left a confused pile of overturned chariots, glistening with gold and inlay; and peeping from behind them another portrait of the king.[12]

This dazzling wealth of precious things has since been on display in the Cairo Museum. If a poor little royal nonentity like Tutankhamon—who died at about eighteen—could command such funerary riches, one can imagine the fantastic hoard of a really important king, a Senusert or an Amenhotep.

The custom of burial in underground tombs continued through the New Empire, until the hillsides west of Waset-Thebes were pocked by scores of excavations, in which were laid the mummies of kings, queens, grandees, and officials. The tombs are all empty now, save for a few sarcophagi; but many are decorated with colorful paintings. To keep the flames of lamps from smudging the walls with soot during decoration, the artists relied upon sunlight reflected from outside by mirrors. This system works in the brilliant sunlight of Upper Egypt and is still employed by tourist guides to show off the tombs of their distant forebears.

When I visited Luxor with my wife some years ago, we did the standard excursions to the temples of Luxor and Karnak, Queen Hatshepsut's temple, the colossi of Amenhotep III, and King Tutankhamon's tomb. In addition, I asked the tourist agency for a car and a driver to visit monuments off the tourist track: the Temple of Seti I at Qurna, the Ramesseum, and the Temple of Medîna Habu. I asked the agency not to send a guide, because I knew more about the things I was to see than most guides, who have only a few well-rehearsed speeches. These they recite like recording devices and get hopelessly confused if the traveler breaks in with an unexpected question.

I picked up the car on the west bank and set out. At each stop, the driver disappeared into the nearest mud hut and came out with a *fallah* pal who tried to sell me tea and cookies. For reasons of health I did not wish tea and cookies and got gracefully out of the situation by saying: "*Ana ramadhâni* [I'm keeping Ramadan, the Muslim Lent]." Then they were all smiles of respect and sympathy.

I paid off the driver, boarded one of the launches that served as

10. Temple of Seti I at Qurna.

ferries across the Nile, and scrunched down in the fantail amid a swarm of locals, from children to graybeards. Soon they were asking about my wives and children, and a young teacher came aft to help when I ran out of Arabic.

At last somebody asked whether I were a Muslim or a Copt[13] (a member of the Egyptian Christian Church, closely allied to the Greek Orthodox). This was a tricky question, since there are many Copts around Luxor, and a good deal of mutual hostility lingers between the religious communities. I racked my brains for a tactful reply. As we landed, Allâh sent me an inspiration; I said: *"Fi fikri kull id-dîn kuwayyis* [In my opinion, all religion is good]." Again, broad smiles all around, and we parted fast friends.

The city of Waset-Thebes arose from obscurity during the Old Kingdom—the age of the pyramid-builders—in the centuries before —2000. At the end of the Sixth Dynasty, around —2200, the Old Kingdom dissolved into feudal chaos. For a century or so thereafter, Egypt was divided among a multitude of quarreling petty sovranties. One of these states ruled most of Upper Egypt under a dynasty later called the Eleventh. About —2050, Mentuḥotep[14] II of this dynasty united Egypt again, founding the Middle Kingdom, which lasted for 300 years. Under these kings, Thebes grew from a village called Yat into a city.

For a capital, Thebes was not ideally located. It had no natural defenses. Commercially it was negligible, not being at an important trade-route junction or transshipment point. For administration it was awkwardly distant from the populous Delta and the sensitive Palestinian frontier. It was twenty-three days' travel from Memphis—the capital under the Old Kingdom—and more than thirty from the Mediterranean.

Nonetheless, Waset-Thebes remained Egypt's capital on and off for several centuries. Ancient rulers cared little for the commercial advantages of a site. Merchants were people of low status, and the laws of economics were not even dreamed of. A king was more likely to be interested in the religious sanctity of a place, or its fortifiability, or the existence of a group of local landowners on whom he could count for support and whose tenant farmers could be enlisted to fill out his army.

At the same time, even the kings who counted Waset-Thebes as their main capital spent much time in other parts of the kingdom. Memphis continued in use as a second capital. The first king of the Twelfth Dynasty, Amenemhat I, built a new capital city, Ithtowi, north of the Fayyûm—a fertile depression west of the Nile above Memphis.

After the Twelfth Dynasty came another time of disorder, with scores of ephemeral kings. Around —1750, the Middle Kingdom was brought low by Asian invaders from the northeast, whom the Egyptians called Hyksôs[15] or "foreign princes." It is not known for sure who the Hyksôs were. Various theories identify them with the horse-taming Aryan barbarians—then spreading the Indo-European languages from Iberia to India—or with nomadic Semites from the Arabian desert, or with a mixture of the two. Some think that they were Hurrians or Mitannians from Asia Minor.

Despite the spells of Egyptian sorcerers—who made figurines of the enemy and ceremonially broke them—the Hyksôs conquered most of Egypt. They made their capital at Avaris[16] at the eastern end of the Delta. They introduced to Egypt the horse, the vertical loom, and the well sweep. The last-named device, also called the *shadûf*, consists of a counterweighted boom, mounted on an axle supported by two posts, and a bucket hung from the long end of the boom.

Although the Hyksôs became largely Egyptianized during their stay, the Egyptians never became reconciled to the rule of these vile foreigners. The Hyksôs never established firm control of all Egypt, and native rulers persisted in Thebes. After two centuries of Hyksôs rule, the Theban kings drove the Hyksôs back to Palestine and founded the Eighteenth Dynasty, celebrated for its imperialistic conquests. The long fight against foreign rulers had militarized the Egyptians and given them a taste for foreign adventures; hence the name "New Empire" for the ensuing period. Although Palestine and Syria were not annexed outright, their kings were reduced to tributary clients of the Egyptian monarchs.

During this dynasty, Egyptian kings took to calling themselves *per-'o*, "great house," whence the modern "pharaoh." The custom is

11. Mortuary Temple of Queen Hatshepsut at Dayr al-Baḥri.

paralleled by the modern journalese term "the White House" for the President of the United States.

Under the Eighteenth Dynasty king Amenḥotep III, Egypt achieved its greatest prosperity. Coming to the throne in —1397, Amenḥotep reigned for thirty-seven years. An easygoing man, he was devoted to building, to hunting lion and aurochs (wild cattle), and most of all to his first and chief wife, Queen Tiy. Aside from leading one Nubian campaign early in his reign, Amenḥotep III stayed home and let his generals handle the few military problems that arose. His realm extended from the upper Nile to the upper Euphrates.

With the wealth of the world flowing into his coffers and the kings of Babylonia, Assyria, and Mitanni (an important kingdom in eastern Syria and southeastern Asia Minor) flattering and courting him, this fun-loving pharaoh can hardly be blamed for taking life easily. In every direction, Egypt was supreme. Eastward, Babylon had sunk from her preëminence of half a millennium before and, under the rule of the foreign Kassites, was a minor power. Assyria's time of imperial might

12. Mortuary Temple of Queen Hatshepsut at Dayr al-Baḥri.

was still to come. Northward, Mitanni was allied with Egypt although threatened by the rising power of Khatti—the Hittite kingdom. To the west, the turbulent Libyans were quiet. To the south, the swarthy Nubians were fast becoming Egyptianized.

During this golden age, the products of most of the civilized world flowed into Egypt. The oldest-known glass vessels, then rare and precious, appear in Egyptian tombs. Likewise, Egyptian influence flowed outwards. It even appeared in the sophisticated art of distant Crete. And over all this wealth, power, and land reigned the genial golden emperor, the third Amenḥotep.

Amenḥotep ruled from awkwardly-placed Thebes, which in his day was not one city but two. The settlements on the two banks of the Nile were independent and largely autonomous. Each had its own mayor, bureaucracy, and police. Each mayor (a deputy vizier appointed by the king) could appeal to the vizier, the most powerful man in the kingdom after the king himself. The two towns sneered at each other and told jokes at the other's expense in the manner of Minneapolis and St. Paul, or Fort Worth and Dallas.

The two halves of Thebes differed. The town on the east bank was much like other Egyptian cities. It clustered along the monumental avenue, a mile and a half long, with which Amenhotep connected the two great temple complexes: Luxor, which he began, and Karnak, already in existence. He also laid out a park along this avenue and built more avenues lined with stone rams to connect the various temples.

Inland from the processional avenue and the two temple clusters, Thebes was doubtless much like the other cities that have flourished during the last few thousand years in the hot-dry belt. I say "doubtless" because nothing remains to show the street plan or even the outline of ancient Thebes. Although the laying out of streets on a grid plan began soon after the time of the golden emperor, there is no reason to think that Thebes was so planned. We can, therefore, be fairly sure that Thebes was a tangle of narrow, crooked alleys lined with blank-walled, mud-brick houses. There were substantial dwellings for the prosperous and hovels for the poor.

Probably, the citizens were grouped by kinship and by occupation to a much greater extent than in a modern city. Hence a given block might be occupied solidly by one clan or extended family, and there might be a Street of Coppersmiths, a Street of Weavers, and so on. Since occupations tended to concentrate in given families much more than they do today, grouping by kinship implied grouping by occupation and vice versa.

There was, however, no zoning in the modern sense. The mansion and the mud hut jostled each other, and hovels crowded in on temples and palaces. The crowding, the noise, the dust, the flies, and the filth were probably much as they have been in recent times in this arid belt. Because of the heat and the dryness, however, Waset-Thebes probably stank less than the cities of medieval Europe, whose sanitation was equally primitive.

The other half of Waset-Thebes—the City of the Dead on the west bank—was a more specialized urbanism. It was devoted to the dwellings of the gods, the kings, and the nobles—living and dead—and their dependents and servants. Hence it consisted of palaces, temples, tombs, and the houses of those who worked therein.

In the time of Amenhotep III, the Ramesseum had not yet been built; but most of the other structures, whose ruins amaze us today, were in place, looking far more impressive than now. Seeing their battered remains, it takes a powerful mental effort to picture the temples as they were in their days of glory, with their surfaces covered with whitewash and stucco, brightly painted reliefs on their walls and columns, gilded statues of gods and kings, stelae (inscribed monolithic monuments) glittering with gold leaf and precious stones, and the sun flashing from the miniature pyramids, sheathed in the gold-silver alloy electrum, on the tops of the obelisks. Attached to the temples were the rectories of the priests and the storehouses in which was kept the wealth that the temples reaped from their lands and their worshipers.

Near the river rose the palace of Amenhotep and the villas of the nobles. For Queen Tiy, Amenhotep built an annex to his palace with an artificial lake a mile long and a quarter of a mile wide. On this lake, the king and his court sailed in processions of barges for the amusement of the common folk, whose lives were cheered the year round by a series of gaudy religious festivals, ceremonies, and parades.

A visitor to Amenhotep's palace ascended from the river landing up an avenue lined with stone jackals. After a detour around the vast mortuary temple, then under construction,

> . . . appeared the palace of the king, of rectangular wooden architecture in bright colours; very light and airy, and having over the front entrance a gorgeous cushioned balcony with graceful columns, in which the king showed himself to his favourites on occasion. Innumerable products of the industrial artists, which fill the museums of Europe, indicate with what tempered richness and delicate beauty such a royal chateau was furnished and adorned. Magnificent vessels in gold and silver, with figures of men and animals, plants and flowers rising from the brim, glittered on the king's table among crystal goblets, glass vases (made by the sons of the craftsmen who produced the earliest known glass vessels), and grey glazed bowls inlaid with pale blue designs. The walls were covered with woven tapestry which skilled judges have declared equal to the best modern work. Besides painted pavements depicting animal life, the walls also were adorned with blue glazed tiles, the rich colour of which shone through elaborate designs in gold leaf, while glazed figures were employed in encrusting larger surfaces. The ceilings were a deep blue sky across which floated soaring birds done in bright colours. Ceiling, walls, and floor merged in a unified colour scheme . . .[17]

The mansions of the nobles, scattered about the west bank, were more modest imitations of that of the king. Like the king, the magnates, as far as their resources allowed, filled their houses with costly art objects, domestic and imported. All these fine buildings were made of wood and mud brick, just as were the huts of the poor. In nearly rainless Upper Egypt, wood and mud brick last better than they do in most places. Nevertheless, all the thousands of structures built of them in the days of Egypt's glory have almost completely vanished.

The buildings that have endured are the tombs (including the pyramids) and the temples, and these the Egyptians made of stone.

They thought they knew what they were doing. A tomb was called a "house of eternity" and a temple, a "house of a million years." A private house, they reasoned, had to stand for a man's lifetime only; he would not care if it crumbled after his death. On the other hand, tombs and temples, being meant for all time, were made to endure.

Besides the temples, the palaces, and the mansions, the plain of west-bank Thebes and the hills behind it were pocked with hundreds of tombs. Not only were the kings and their kinsmen buried there, but Egyptians of humbler rank, as well, had themselves interred, reasoning that their lot in the life to come would be better if they took advantage of the magical aura radiating from the sepulchers of the divine kings.

In addition, the City of the Dead included a constellation of mud-hut villages. Here dwelt the swarms of workers who ministered to the wants of gods and priests, kings and magnates, living and dead. There were thousands of skilled workers: masons, brickers, plasterers, carpenters, smiths, jewelers, painters, sculptors, embalmers, and members of all the other trades needed to build and maintain the temples, the palaces, and the tombs. Ordinarily the kings paid these workers in grain and

13. "Round the decay of that colossal wreck . . ." Broken remains of a colossal statue of Rameses II at the Ramesseum, near Shaykh 'Abd-al-Qurna.

14. "Half sunk, a shattered visage lies . . ." Head from a statue of Rameses II at the Ramesseum, near Shaykh 'Abd-al-Qurna.

garments. When the kingdom was hard up, payments fell behind, and the starving workers took to robbing the very tombs that they or their forebears had built.

Meanwhile, across the river in Waset-Thebes, life flowed on through the dusty, unpaved, narrow streets in the immemorial pattern that has molded the pre-industrial city from ancient Sumer on down. Sweating multitudes toiled at their trades, relieved by an endless succession of religious festivals. People bought and sold by barter, schemed to get their sons into the bureaucracy, and touched noses instead of kissing. Doubtless Thebes had a well-developed underworld, since crime has flourished in cities from ancient times on down.

Poor men and women still went about in simple kilts and loincloths, as they had done for many centuries. If the work was arduous, they went altogether naked. The ancient Egyptians and Greeks, while highly civilized folk, had none of the Judaean nudity tabu that has since spread over most of the world in the wake of Christianity and Islâm. They therefore went nude whenever they felt like it.

The dress of the rich, however, had changed since the Old Kingdom. In place of the simple linen kilt, worn in pyramid-building days by all Egyptian men from the king on down, the prosperous Egyptian now wore an elaborate combination of pleated skirt and robe, topped off with a shoulder-length wig over his shaven skull. Women's dress had likewise been elaborated. A common garment among women was a long sheath dress that left one or both breasts bare.

Foreign fashions had begun to reach Egypt along with foreign products and the foreigners themselves. No longer was Egypt the hermit kingdom of former times. Besides the traders and the itinerant workers who trickled in from Asia during the Eighteenth Dynasty, the conquests of Thothmes II and Amenhotep II had filled the land with Asian captives.

While a certain amount of slavery always existed in Egypt, the institution never—save perhaps briefly, during the Eighteenth Dynasty —played a very large part in that land. To be sure, forced labor existed. So did caste barriers and the concentration of wealth in a small ruling class, but not much slavery in the strict sense. We think of the ancient world as living on the labor of slaves, because the ancient empires most familiar to us, the Athenian and the Roman, *did* at times make very large use of slaves. This fact led Karl Marx into the error of lumping all ancient societies together as "slave societies."

Slavery was originally a humane institution. In prehistoric times, when prisoners were captured in war, they were normally killed, because nobody knew what else to do with them and they might be dangerous to their captors if turned loose. Slavery gave the captors a motive for keeping the prisoners alive and healthy.

In the case of Egypt, the slaves brought in during the conquests of the Eighteenth Dynasty were either enrolled in the army or parceled out among the magnates as serfs, settled on the land, and put to work sowing and reaping as they had done at home. In a few generations they were assimilated, but their influx made Egypt a more heterogeneous and cosmopolitan place than it had been in earlier centuries.

Another change in the class structure of Egypt had been a weakening of class barriers as a result of the growth of the empire and the consequent enlargement of government. Social mobility increased as the kings, not finding enough capable noblemen to run things, gave more and more important posts in the bureaucracy to promising commoners. This was no democracy. The king was, if anything, even more absolute than before; in theory all the land in Egypt belonged either to the king or to the temples. But a kind of rough-and-ready equality among his subjects came into being.

Women occupied a better position in Egypt than in most ancient societies. A woman could be the head of a family, with all the rights and obligations of such. In Egypt, in fact, women came the nearest to equality with men that they ever attained before modern times.

Three features of life in Waset-Thebes would strike a modern time-traveling visitor with especial force. One was the lack of money. Goods were priced in weights of gold, silver, copper, or grain, but most sales and purchases were by simple barter. The lack of any standard medium of exchange, together with the primitive state of arithmetic, must have made every transaction extremely complex, tedious, and time-consuming. But then, no ancient people had anything like our split-second time-consciousness.

Another feature was the complete lack of public sanitation. We can guess that Waset-Thebes saw the usual running conflict between the municipal government, which wanted all citizens to dump their human waste in some prescribed place outside the city, and the citizens, who found it more convenient to dump it anywhere away from their front doors when they thought nobody was watching. This conflict was a regular feature of city life down to the development of modern sewer systems in +XIX.

Third, literacy was very restricted. Outside of the priests and nobles, it was mainly confined to a class of professional scribes, educated for that purpose in temple schools. After all, there was little for the ordinary

15. Colossal statues of Amenhotep III ("Colossi of Memnon") near Medîna Habu.

man to read, even if he had been able to do so. There were no street signs, no newspapers or magazines, no advertisements—even signs over shops—and no public notices. Outside of temple and governmental business, letter-writing must have been extremely rare. Most folk lived in a small, static circle of kinsmen, friends, and fellow-workers, dwelling nearby. Knowing few if any people who lived at a distance, they would not have occasion to write them. If some rare emergency made it essential for a man to send a letter, he could hire a scribe to write it for him, and the recipient at the other end could hire another scribe to read it to him.

Literacy would have been hard to spread, even if anybody had wanted to spread it. The Egyptian language had a difficult writing system, with over 700 symbols. It began—as most systems of writing have begun—with simple pictures. But pure picture-writing can present only the simplest and most concrete messages, like "John caught a fish."

In time, some pictures came to represent consonantal sounds, either singly or in pairs. Thus pictures could represent words for abstract ideas like "thought" or "good" and operative words like "become" or "about."

Long *î*, *â*, and *û* were represented by the signs for the similar consonants, so that a picture of a feather might mean a sound like the *i* of "police" or the *y* of "yet." But, as in unpointed modern Hebrew and Arabic, the Egyptians did not represent short vowels. Hence the pronunciation of ancient Egyptian names is uncertain. Some scholars transliterate Egyptian letter for letter, resulting in such baffling combinations as YMHTP and DHWTYMS.[18] Others insert vowels where needed to make the names pronounceable: usually *e*, save where there is reason to think that the sound might have been something else. Thus the fact that YMHTP was rendered into Greek as *Imouthês* suggests that the original name had a back vowel (*o* or *u*) before the *t* sound and a front vowel (*i* or *e*) after it. Hence the spelling "Imhotep."

Modern renderings of Egyptian names would probably sound to an ancient Egyptian somewhat as the English of a foreigner, who had never heard English spoken and who tried to guess the pronunciation from the spelling alone, would sound to us. Since Egypt spoke many local dialects, and since pronunciation changed from century to century, no system would suit all ancient Egyptians if they were alive to criticize. This is why for some kings I use the more familiar Greek forms of their names, e.g. Thothmes instead of Tehutimose or Dhutmose, and why I often give several alternative spellings in the notes for a given name. J. B. Hurry, in his book *Imhotep* (1928), listed thirty-four ways to spell the name of the man in question.

In addition, many of the little pictures of the hieroglyphic system retained their picture values. To distinguish among ambiguous spellings,

16. Mortuary Temple of Rameses III at Medîna Habu.

other little pictures called "determinatives" were added to many words to make sure the reader knew what class of things the meaning of the word belonged to. Since it was impractical in ordinary handwriting to draw all those beautiful little men, animals, birds, insects, implements, and other objects that make up the hieroglyphic system, scribes of the First Dynasty devised a cursive system, the hieratic. Each picture was represented by a squiggle that only vaguely resembled the original hieroglyph but could be quickly drawn. Several centuries after the reign of Amenhotep III, a still less pictorial system, the demotic, came into use as well.

The system remained extremely complex, erratic, and arbitrary, with many redundancies and ambiguities—even more, perhaps, than the spelling of our own English tongue. Perhaps the scribes were just as pleased to leave it in that state. If writing had been made easy, anybody could have learned it and there would have been nothing in it for the scribes. After all, only a few years ago the Soviet Union backed down on a modest program of spelling reform when leading Russian intellectuals loudly opposed making reading and writing too easy.

Modern pseudo-science and cultism have often tried to make the ancient Egyptians into a race of profound and solemn mystics, preserving the wisdom of the ages or of the lost Atlantis. From all we can learn about them, however, they were not very different from their modern descendants. It is dangerous to generalize about any whole people or nation, because individuals vary so widely. This is all the more so in ancient Egypt, because its history covered such an enormous span of time, during which customs, costumes, technics, beliefs, and outlooks changed from century to century.

It is fair to say, however, that if there ever was such a thing as a typical ancient Egyptian, he was something of a genial, materialistic extrovert, fond of beer, games, jokes, parties, and picnics. His modern descendants, whatever their shortcomings, have perhaps the keenest sense of humor in the world; and enough ancient Egyptian writings have come down to hint that this saving virtue goes back in that land for thousands of years.

About —1375, Amenhotep III died and was succeeded by his son. Amenhotep IV: a queer-looking youth with a potbelly, spindleshanks, thick lips, and a long chin. At first under the thumbs of his mother, Queen Tiy, and his beautiful wife Nefertiti,[19] the new king turned out to have a burning interest in religion but none in war or politics.

After a few years, Amenhotep IV turned his back on Amon, the king of the gods in the Theban pantheon, and became a zealous partisan of Aten, the sun god of Heliopolis.[20] Amenhotep promoted his sun god to be not only chief of all the gods of Egypt but also the chief god of the universe, an idea quite startling at the time.

Having been brought up on monotheism, Judaeo-Christians have long made much of this king as "the first monotheist." They have described his religion as "purer" or "loftier" than the swarming polytheistic cults of Egypt. It is well, however, to remember that polytheists have seldom or never burned anybody for heresy. The massacre of unbelievers is a monotheistic specialty.

In any case, Amenhotep IV tried to secure for his sun cult a monopoly of supernaturalism in Egypt. When the priests of Amon opposed him, he mutilated the monuments of Amon and changed his name to Ikhnaton in honor of his new deity. Finding that he did not have the power utterly to suppress the cult of Amon of Thebes and destroy its priests and temples, he built a new capital, Akhetaten,[21] on the east bank of the Nile halfway between Thebes and Memphis. There he spent the rest of his reign, absorbed in theological speculations. He ignored the frantic pleas from his officials in the Asian provinces, who wrote to tell that their lands were being overrun by brigands from the desert called *Khabiru*.

One of the most vociferous complainants was King Abdi-Khiba[22] of Urusalim, a small fortified town on a rocky ridge in southern Palestine, better known to us as Jerusalem. The name probably meant "founded by [the god] Salim." Abdi-Khiba denounces other Palestinian chieftains for raiding his caravans, plotting against Egyptian rule, and going over to the Khabiru, all the while loudly protesting his own loyalty. The other shaykhs made similar complaints against Abdi-Khiba.

Ever since these letters, in the form of clay tablets inscribed in the Akkadian (Assyro-Babylonian) language, were dug out of the ruins of Akhetaten in 1887, speculation has been rife as to whether the Khabiru were the Hebrews, and whether this invasion was the conquest of Canaan by the Israelites under Joshua. There is no simple answer to this question, but several facts must be taken into account. One is that "Hebrew" comes, with many modifications, from the Hebrew *'Ibhri*, "from across [the Jordan River]." This does not look quite so much like "Khabiru" as does its modern English corruption "Hebrew."

Moreover, *'Ibhri* seems originally to have meant a man from any of several northern Semitic-speaking peoples, including not only the Israelites but also the Ammonites, the Moabites, and the Edomites. Genesis lists all these peoples, together with the Ishmaelites (Arabs), Aramaeans (Syrians), Midianites, and Chaldaeans as descendants of Eber (Hebrew, *'Ebhêr*), the eponymous ancestor of the Hebrews. As for Joshua, as nearly an anyone can time his half-mythical conquest, it seems—if we can take it at all as serious history—to have occurred at least a century after the reign of Ikhnaton.

After Ikhnaton died about −1360, the priests of Amon regained their power. Following several short reigns—including that of the boy-king Tutankhamon—a usurping general named Horemheb[23] recovered the lost Asiatic provinces. Thebes became the capital once more. Then another general succeeded Horemheb as Rameses I and founded the Nineteenth Dynasty. Thereafter, Waset-Thebes declined.

For a time a dynasty, the Twenty-first, ruled from Tanis,[24] while the real power in the South was held by the High Priest of Amon at Thebes. Then Libyans from the west conquered Egypt and resigned from Herakleopolis as the Twenty-second Dynasty. After a time of trouble, with several rival dynasties, the black Kushites came up from beyond Nubia and reigned as the Twenty-fifth. The terrible Assyrians drove out the last of these, Taharqa, and in −663 sacked Waset-Thebes. They slaughtered the people and carried off two obelisks.

Trouble at home forced the Assyrians to withdraw, leaving an Egyptian named Psamtek[25] to reign as a puppet. As soon as the Assyrians were out of the way, Psamtek made himself king in fact and began the Twenty-sixth Dynasty, ruling from Saïs[26] in the Delta. Later, Egypt was conquered by Persians, Macedonians, Romans, Arabs, Turks, French, and British, regaining independence only in the last quarter-century.

But, after the Ethiopian conquest, Thebes was never again the capital. Lacking natural advantages, it never recovered from the Assyrian sack. It slowly decayed and lost population, becoming a mere congeries of temples with a few villages scattered among them.

Under the Christian Roman Empire, Christian monks mutilated statues and reliefs of Egyptian gods and kings on the ground that they were images of detestable demons. When the Muslim Arabs conquered Egypt in +641, they continued the destruction, holding all works of art to be graven images forbidden by Allâh. But the pharaohs of the New Empire had wrought on such a vast scale that not even the iconoclasm of generations of ignorant fanatics could wholly erase the glory of their works. So Waset-Thebes remains to this day one of the grandest displays in existence of the wonders of the ancient world.

III

JERUSALEM THE GOLDEN

KING SOLOMON DREW MERCHANTMEN,
    BECAUSE OF HIS DESIRE
FOR PEACOCKS, APES, AND IVORY,
    FROM TARSHISH UNTO TYRE:
WITH CEDARS OUT OF LEBANON
    WHICH HIRAM RAFTED DOWN,
BUT WE BE ONLY SAILORMEN
    THAT USE IN LONDON TOWN.[1]
                            Kipling

17. Jerusalem: the Old City, looking west from the Mount of Olives.

A CITY may become great, not because of the material advantages of its site, but because of the ideas associated with it.

For almost 400 miles, the Canaanite coast runs north and south in a nearly straight line. The coastal plain is shaped like an hourglass drawn out long and thin: broad in Syria in the northern third of the coast; shrinking to a mere ribbon in the central or Lebanese third; and widening again along the southern third in the land that has been called Israel, Judaea, Syria Palaestina, the kingdom of Jerusalem, and Palestine. East of the coastal plain rise rocky hills. These culminate in the huge ridge of Mount Lebanon, which parallels the coast for a hundred miles in the middle of the stretch.

The climate is Mediterranean, with a cool rainy season from November to March and hot, dry, rainless weather the rest of the year. In ancient times, the land supported considerable wildlife, including auroch, deer, gazelle, oryx, ostrich, lion, leopard, bear, wolf and hyena; most of these have now been exterminated. Although a land of modest natural endowments, with thin soil and scrubby vegetation, Canaan nevertheless seemed a "land flowing with milk and honey"[2] to dwellers in the dismal deserts to the east and south, who for thousands of years have seeped into the coastal plain.

In —XI the weak Rameseses of the late Twentieth Dynasty reigned in Egypt but had lost control of Palestine. At this time, men who called themselves *Kĕna'anîm* or Canaanites dwelt in all of Canaan save the southern coast. Calling their country *Kĕna'an*, they spoke dialects of a language, Canaanitish, which belongs to one of the world's great linguistic families. We call this family "Semitic" after Shem, one of Noah's sons.

The Semitic languages form a compact family, resembling one another as closely as, say, Italian, French, and Spanish resemble one another. They have a logical structure, in which a basic idea is represented by a cluster of consonants—usually three—and inflections are made by varying the quality and position of the vowels. Thus in Arabic, the group KTB includes all words having to do with books and writing. Hence *kitâb*, "book"; *kutub*, "books"; *kâtib*, "writing"; *aktib*, "I write"; *maktûb*, "it is written"; and so on.

In —XI, some Canaanites had built cities on the central and northern parts of the coast and had become noted as traders and mariners. The Greeks later called them *Phoinikes* or Phoenicians, and the Romans, *Poeni* or *Punici*, Punics; but they referred to themselves as Canaanites.

In the hinterland lived other Canaanites. Some were settled farmers; others, semi-nomadic shepherds. They included Amorites, Aramaeans, Ammonites, Israelites, Moabites, Edomites, Kenites, and Amalekites. Beyond these, where the hills leveled off and the steppe gave way to desert, roamed true, camel-raising nomads: the Ishmaelites or Arabs.

Along the southern Canaanite coast lived the non-Semitic *Pelishtîm* or Philistines, from whose name comes the word "Palestine." Their origin is doubtful, but there is cause to suspect that they came from southwestern Asia Minor. They built five cities: Ashdod, Ekron, Gath, Askalon, and Gaza, and ruled the southern coastal plain.

The Philistines were skilled ironworkers, iron having been lately discovered in Asia Minor. They were also redoubtable warriors. Their heavy infantry bore iron spears and swords. They were armored with cuirasses of bronzen scales and bronzen helmets with towering horsehair crests, like those the Greeks adopted later. So equipped, they scattered the ragged, unarmored war bands of Semitic shepherds armed with slings and with bronze-bladed knives and spears.

Then as now, people moved in a never-ending stream from poor to rich land and from country to city. Plagues, assisted by wars, famines, and conflagrations, killed off the city-dwellers faster than they reproduced themselves, and these losses were made up by migration from the countryside. Nomads from the desert crowded into the semi-desert of the Canaanite hills, driving before them the semi-nomads, who in turn fell upon the sedentary farmers of the lowlands.

In —XI, a confederacy of twelve semi-nomadic Canaanite tribes, the Israelites, had taken over most of the southern hill country. These did not call themselves Canaanites but applied the term to other Semitic-speaking tribes. Nevertheless, they spoke a dialect of the same tongue. Like their kinsmen the Edomites, the Moabites, and the Ammonites, they were called *'Ibhrîm*, Hebrews, because they came from across the Jordan River. Their chief god, they explained, had given them the land. This excused their ferocious massacres of the cities they took. Racially, they showed the same mixture of the Mediterranean and Armenoid types of the white or Caucasoid race that has prevailed around the eastern Mediterranean from earliest historical times to the present.

Towards the end of —XI, eleven of these tribes were spread over southern Canaan, save for the coastal plain. Judah, the largest tribe, held the largest area, in the South. Levi had no special territory, having become a priestly caste among the other tribes. The Israelites disputed the coastal plain with the Philistines, but the latter's armor and chariots usually enabled them to rout the light-armed hillmen.

Since religion played a large part in the story of the Israelites, it would be interesting to know more about their religion at this time. In

18. Nineteenth-century Jerusalem from the Pool of Hezekiah. (From Louis Charles Lortet: *La Syrie d'aujourd'hui*, Paris: 1884.)

fact, however, we know very little about it. The chief god of their pantheon was a bloodthirsty storm god called Yahveh, who punished the chiefs of the Israelites when they did not thoroughly enough exterminate the peoples whom Yahveh had marked for doom. Like the chief gods of other early peoples, Yahveh was surrounded by a court of subordinate gods. We know very little about these; but Eve, for example, may have been a serpent goddess.

In late —VII or early —VI, before the Babylonian Captivity, an Egyptian king set up a military colony of Judaean mercenary soldiers at Elephantinê, on the upper Nile near modern Aswân,[3] to keep out the Kushites. It would seem that these Israelites continued to practice a Yahvism of the old, polytheistic form, unaffected by the monotheistic reforms that the priests and prophets put into practice before and during the Captivity. At Elephantinê, Yahveh was provided with a couple of female colleagues: the goddesses Ashima and Anath. Anath was a fierce Canaanite war goddess, somewhat like the Greek Athena. The evidence from Elephantinê confirms the idea that Yahveh began as a local variant of a widespread west-Semitic storm god, otherwise called Hadad, Rimmon, or Resheph, since in some places Anath was Resheph's consort.

The western Semites once practiced human sacrifice in emergencies, as when they faced defeat in war. Then they burned their children on the altars of their gods in place of the usual offerings of sheep and other

19. Wall of Süleyman the Magnificent at Jerusalem, with an Arab cemetery in the foreground. (Courtesy of Ellen Kohler.)

animals. The story of Abraham and Isaac (Genesis xxii, 1–13) suggests that the Israelites once practiced such sacrifices, too, but that a reformer arose to denounce and abolish the custom.

The Israelites' attitude towards their gods was like that of their neighbors. Each "people" had its own company of gods, whose jurisdiction was confined to the national territory. In a foreign land, the writ of one's own gods no longer ran, so that one had to learn to flatter, bribe, and plead with the gods of the foreigners.

About 500 years after the time (around −1100) of which I am writing, the Yahvist priesthood told the faithful a marvelous history of their people. In the first six books of the Old Testament, they narrated how their ancestors had been enslaved in Egypt, had escaped and wandered in the desert, and had finally conquered Canaan under the leadership of Yahveh and a war chief named Yehoshua or Joshua.

In fact, this was a self-serving fiction compiled by the priests to bolster their own power and prestige. Authentic Israelite history only starts in −XI, because then the Israelites began to read and write. Everything earlier—Adam and Noah, Abraham and Moses—is more or less fictional, and these fictions came from many sources. Some, like the story of the Flood, are Babylonian myths picked up during the Babylonian Captivity.

For that matter, the Babylonian Flood legend is not the original. The oldest-known form of this legend is Sumerian. A fragmentary Sumerian tablet from Nippur tells how the gods decided to destroy mankind by a flood. One soft-hearted god, Enki, warned the pious king of Shuruppak, Ziusudra, of the catastrophe in time for Ziusudra to build a raft and thus save himself, his family, and his livestock.

The legend later spread far and wide, so that Ziusudra became the Babylonian Utnapishtim, the Greek Deukalion, and the Hebrew Noah. It is not hard to see why this tale was popular with the priesthoods of many lands. For one thing, the flood is the commonest kind of disaster in river-valley civilizations. For another, how better to frighten the worshipers into paying for a new roof to the temple when the old one has begun to leak?

Besides all the myths and legends, there are also, doubtless, fragments of authentic history buried in the early parts of the Old Testament. But, without outside evidence, there is no trustworthy way to filter them out.

The story of the Israelites from —XI to —VI is, in a sense, the story of the self-promotion of the Yahvist priesthood to supreme power. This was done, first, by elevating Yahveh to the rank of sole god to the Israelites. The subordinate deities were demoted to angels like Gabriel or mortals like Eve. Then Yahveh was proclaimed superior to all the gods of the other nations. Finally, Yahveh was made the sole god of the universe. The other gods were declared to be evil spirits or not to exist at all.

Furthermore, the Israelites were described as having been pious monotheists from the very beginning, back in the legendary days of Moses and Joshua. This is not so. The priests were not clever enough to edit out of their holy books all allusions to the Israelites' early polytheism. Thus in Genesis, the Creator is called 'Elôhîm, "gods," and refers to himself as "we."[4] Theologians have explained this as an "honorary" plural, like a king's calling himself "we." But, since the "plural of majesty" only began with bad King John of England about 1200, this explanation will not hold water.

Finally, the priests edited the written history of Israel, from the beginning of the monarchy on down, in line with their own interests. Kings who favored the Yahvist priesthood, no matter what their murders and perfidies, were "good" kings. Kings who let competing cults flourish, regardless of their other achievements, were "bad."

This monopoly of the supernatural, for which the Yahvist priests struggled and schemed so long and which they finally achieved, is of advantage to any priesthood in terms of their own wealth, power, and glory. Other priesthoods have asserted similar claims with similar motives. They need not have been hypocrites: men are wont to believe that whatever is to their advantage is also right, good, and true.

Despite the massacres inflicted upon them at Yahveh's command by the Israelites ("But of the cities of these people . . . thou shalt save alive nothing that breatheth: but thou shalt utterly destroy them . . ."[5]) the other Canaanites were not really wiped out. The distinctions among these groups were never so sharp as the Yahvists pretended. There was always a good deal of shifting about by capture in war, enslavement and liberation, adoption, and voluntary migration—say, when some family, on the losing side of a feud, fled to a foreign land and settled. Moreover, some Canaanites kept their independence for centuries in enclaves, surrounded by Israelites.

One of these tribes was called the Jebusites. Their capital was a small town on the boundary between Judah and Benjamin, one of the smallest Israelite tribes. We have met Abdi-Khiba of Urusalim, an earlier king of the Jebusites. The Israelites called the town Yerûshâlayim or (in English) Jerusalem.[6] According to the half-legendary Book of Joshua, another king of Jerusalem, Adonizedek, was captured by Joshua, along with four other kinglets. After suitably humiliating his royal captives, Joshua "smote them, and slew them, and hanged them on five trees."[7]

Jerusalem stood on a barren limestone plateau, two-thirds of a mile across, bounded on the east, south, and west by steep-sided valleys but sloping gently to the north. Another valley divided the southern part of the plateau into two ridges: a smaller, lower extension in the east and a larger, higher one in the west. The plateau thus had the shape of a mitten, with the thumb forming the south-pointing Eastern Ridge and the pouch for the fingers the Western.

The eastern valley was called the Valley of Kidron. The western, which turned sharply east south of the city to join the Kidron, was the Valley of Hinnom. Since "of Hinnom" is gai-Hinnom in Hebrew, the name came into Latin as "Gehenna." The central valley, sundering the thumb of the mitten from the fingers, was formerly almost as deep as the other valleys but has now been largely filled in. Josephus, the Jewish historian of Roman times, called this depression the Tyropoeon, doubtfully translated as "Vale of Cheesemongers."

Beyond the valleys, low hills rise all around Jerusalem, save to the southeast. Thither a gap in the hills lets the viewer glimpse in the distance the ramparts of the plateau of Moab.

King Abdi-Khiba's city—really a village a mere 11 acres in extent—stood on the Eastern Ridge: the thumb of the mitten, also called Zion,[8] Ophel, or Mount Moriah. In later centuries, when Jerusalem had spread over the Western Ridge, writers like Josephus assumed

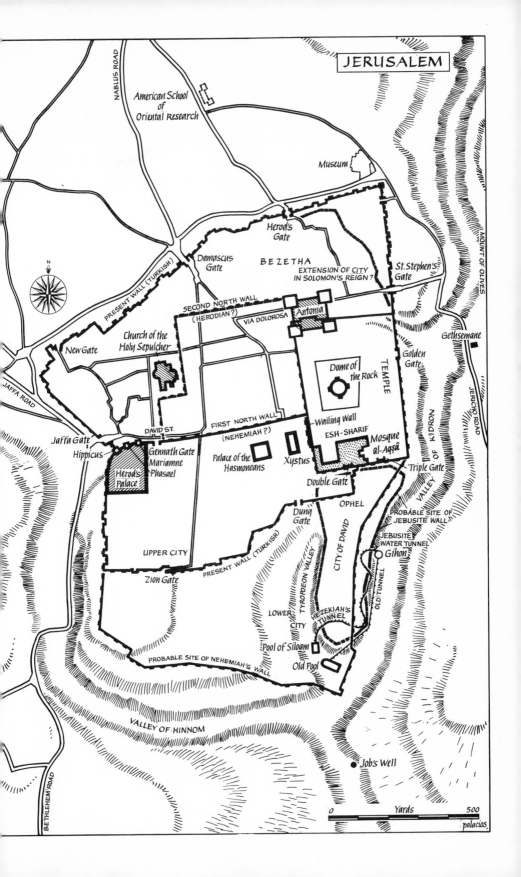

JERUSALEM

NABLUS ROAD

American School of Oriental Research

Museum

Herod's Gate

Damascus Gate

BEZETHA

EXTENSION OF CITY IN SOLOMON'S REIGN?

St. Stephen's Gate

MOUNT OF OLIVES

N

PRESENT WALL (TURKISH)

SECOND NORTH WALL (HERODIAN?)

VIA DOLOROSA

Antonia

New Gate

Church of the Holy Sepulcher

Gethsemane

Golden Gate

JAFFA ROAD

Dome of the Rock

TEMPLE

JERICHO ROAD

DAVID ST.

FIRST NORTH WALL (NEHEMIAH?)

Wailing Wall

ESH-SHARIF

Jaffa Gate

Hippicus

Gennath Gate
Mariamne
Phasael

Palace of the Hasmoneans

Xystus

Mosque al-Aqsā

Triple Gate

VALLEY OF KIDRON

Herod's Palace

Double Gate

Ophel

PROBABLE SITE OF JEBUSITE WALL

Dung Gate

CITY OF DAVID

JEBUSITE WATER TUNNEL

UPPER CITY

Gihon

Zion Gate

PRESENT WALL (TURKISH)

TYROPOEON VALLEY

OLD TUNNEL

LOWER CITY

HEZEKIAH'S TUNNEL

PROBABLE SITE OF NEHEMIAH'S WALL

Pool of Siloam

Old Pool

VALLEY OF HINNOM

BETHLEHEM ROAD

Job's Well

0   Yards   500

palacios

that the original city had been on the Western Ridge. Therefore they called this part "Zion" and named things there after Old Testament worthies: "David's Tower," "Hezekiah's Pool," and so forth.

This glib identification of modern sites with ancient events has gone on ever since, because the locals can thus profit at the expense of credulous visitors. Today one can learn the precise spot where Jesus did this or that, and where Muḥammad stood before he ascended to Heaven, and other pseudo-historical disclosures. (At least, one could before the Old City came under its present Israeli rule, and I doubt if this condition has changed.) The tradition of the famous Way of the Cross or *via dolorosa* dates only from about 1300, in the Turkish period. It is probably wrong in any case, since it assumes that Pilatus held court in the Antonia fortress, whereas he more likely held it in Herod's palace.

In sooth, the Jebusites settled on the Eastern Ridge for good reasons. It was easy to defend. The slopes, steeper then than now, provided natural defenses on three sides, and the Jebusites dug a ditch and raised a wall across the vulnerable northern side of their ridge.

For another thing, Zion had a water supply, which the Western Ridge lacked. A source of water was needed, since without it a beleaguered city could be forced to surrender in a few days. Later, cities could sometimes manage by means of rain cisterns, but in Jebusite days the waterproof plaster needed to make such cisterns had not yet been invented. There are no real rivers near Jerusalem, although thousands of years ago the valleys of Kidron and Hinnom may have run with perennial streams.

At the foot of the slope in the Kidron Valley bubbled the spring of Gihon. Now, to take advantage of the slope of Zion, the Jebusites had to build their wall well up on the slope. But that put the spring outside the wall. So they dug a tunnel from the spring under the city, and the water flowed through this tunnel into a pool in a cave. They drilled a vertical shaft from this cave up to the surface, so that housewives could descend by a sloping tunnel to the top of this shaft and lower their jars on cords down the shaft to the pool and haul them up filled.

South of the Eastern Ridge, the valleys of Kidron and Hinnom joined and wandered away to the southeast. Another spring, En-rogel, lay in this combined valley, a quarter-mile from the city. While useful in peace, it was too far to be effective in sieges. In later times Gihon and En-rogel were renamed, with the usual motives, "The Spring of the Virgin" and "Job's Well" respectively.

The Jebusite wall ran around the Eastern Ridge. Its exact location is known in one place only, where its remains were discovered a few years ago by the diggers of the British School of Archaeology in Jerusalem. This is on the east side of Zion near the spring of Gihon. The wall stood a little over halfway from the top of the slope to the bottom and dates back to around −1800. This does not make Jerusalem the oldest city in the world; Jericho, fourteen miles to the northeast, was settled several thousand years earlier. But it still gives Jerusalem a respectable antiquity.

To provide more level space for homes, the Jebusites built stone terraces on the slope between the top of the ridge and the wall. What with the 45° slope and the weakness of the construction, however, these terraces collapsed from time to time as a result of the erosion of heavy winter rains or from minor earthquakes and had to be rebuilt.

During −XI, the Israelites became dissatisfied with their perennial war with the Philistines. Even the presence of their divine talisman, the Ark of the Covenant, had not saved them from a disastrous defeat at Aphek. Worse, the foe had captured the Ark itself. This was a large box, containing—so said the priests—the stone tablets on which Moses had inscribed the laws given him by Yahveh.

At this time the Israelites formed a loose confederacy, each tribe ruled by a chieftain or "judge." Since these judgeships do not seem to have been hereditary, the judges were probably elected. Many Israelites, however, thought that the nation needed a tighter organization. Why not, said some, have a king like other nations?

The prophet Samuel chose a handsome youth named Saul[9] to be king, doubtless thinking to rule through him. Saul, however, developed a mind of his own, whereupon Samuel quarreled with his protégé. Samuel threatened Saul with doom because, he said, Saul had disobeyed Yahveh's orders to exterminate the Amalekites and destroy all their property. The Israelites had looted the property, and Saul had spared the Amalekite king Agag, so that Samuel had to butcher Agag himself.

Meanwhile, Saul had fallen in with a young Judahite named David, notable for good looks, energy, ambition, shrewdness, and a total lack of scruples. The second half of 1 Samuel is devoted to the relations of Saul and David, but we cannot be sure what really happened. The story was put together in late −VI by priestly editors, working from many older documents like the Book of Jasher.[10]

These documents, however, gave incomplete and contradictory accounts. Some of the original writers glorified Saul and denigrated David. Some favored David and tried to make Saul look bad. Some, favoring the Yahvist priesthood, opposed all kings. The documents were sometimes transcribed in helter-skelter order. While the books of Judges, Samuel, and Kings begin authentic Israelite history, they are

20. Qubbit aṣ-Ṣakhra or Dome of the Rock on the site of Solomon's Temple at Jerusalem. (Courtesy of Kathleen M. Kenyon.)

hardly history in our sense. They are heavily fictionized, as is shown by their reporting of private conversations that could never have been written down and preserved.

This is not to sneer at these priestly historians. They were among the first men in the world—outside of China, at any rate—to try to compose continuous narratives of their people's past. Like most pioneers, they did things that to later generations seemed to have been blunders.

Having, however, given the authors of Judges, Samuel, and Kings credit where due, we should not be blind to their limitations. For example, 1 Samuel tells two inconsistent stories of how David met Saul. In the first, David is hired as a harper to cheer up Saul's fits of melancholy and also serves as his armor-bearer. In the second, during a campaign against the Philistines, David slays the giant, Goliath of Gath, with a slingstone. Impressed, King Saul asks David who he is, which he would hardly have done if David had already served as his musician and armor-bearer. We can be fairly sure that the Goliath tale, at least, is a fiction, concocted by some propagandist for David. Elsewhere, 2 Samuel says that "Elhanan the son of Jaare-oregim, the Bethlehemite, slew Goliath the Gittite [that is, of Gath]."[11]

When David became popular and formed a close friendship with one of Saul's sons, Saul became suspicious of an impending palace revolution. Hearing that Saul meant to kill him, David fled, became a bandit chief, and then worked as a mercenary captain for King Achish of Gath—an unlikely post if he had really slain Gath's national hero. He told Achish that he was raiding Israelite villages. Later, he told the Israelites that he had raided, not his fellow-Israelites, but the other Canaanites. Since David "left neither man nor woman alive"[12] in these raids, there was none to gainsay him.

In time, Saul and his older sons fell in battle with the Philistines. David hurried back to Judah and was made king of that tribe and presently of all Israel. The nation seems not to have been really united. Instead, there was a "kingdom of Judah" iin the South, including Judah and little Benjamin, and a "kingdom of Israel," including the remaining tribes, in the North. David was king of both, but each kingdom kept its own laws and governmental machinery. The Stuart kings of England and Scotland were in a like position.

David was distinguished not so much for his murders and treacheries —in which he was probably no worse than most kings of the time— but for his adroitness in dodging the blame for these acts. Most of his dirty work was done by his ruffianly general, Joab the son of Zeruiah. When the deed had been done, David would piously exclaim: "I and my kingdom are guiltless . . . Let it rest on the head of Joab . . ."[13]

When David decided to get rid of the seven younger sons of Saul, instead of killing them himself he turned them over to the Gibeonites, who, having a grudge against the house of Saul, hanged the lot. Then David proclaimed: "Is there any yet that is left of the house of Saul, that I may show him kindness?" Not surprisingly, there were no volunteers. David did locate one grandson of Saul, Mephiba'al, but let him live because as a cripple he was considered harmless.[14]

When David became king, one of his first tasks was to capture Jerusalem. Standing in the midst of the Israelite lands and bestriding two minor trade routes, independent Jerusalem hindered the efficient governing of the two kingdoms. Moreover, since it was neither a Judahite nor an Israelite town, it would make a suitable capital for the ruler of the twin kingdoms.

The Jebusites looked down upon David's army from their stout walls and boasted that even an army of lame and blind men could hold the place.[15] David called for volunteers to crawl through the tunnel from the spring of Gihon and climb up the shaft to the surface. Joab led the party. Archaeology shows that David also made a breach, later crudely patched, in the wall. Presumably he timed his attack on the wall to coincide with the emergence of Joab's band from the water shaft, to take the defenders in the rear.

David did not entirely kill off the Jebusites, for later one of them named Araunah owned a threshing floor north of the city. David bought this property for fifty shekels of silver[16] as a site for the grand Temple of Yahveh that he planned but did not live to build.

Whatever David's flaws, he was certainly an efficient and energetic ruler. He conquered the Amalekites, the Edomites, the Moabites, the Ammonites, and the Aramaeans or Syrians to the north. Usually these peoples were left under their own kings, who paid tribute to Jerusalem. David's realm stretched from the Egyptian border to the upper Euphrates. He got the Ark back from the Philistines, although he could never quite bring these mighty warriors under his sway. He built a stone-and-timber palace at the northern end of the Jebusite city, for which the king of Tyre, glad to keep on good terms with so formidable a neighbor, sent him materials and workmen.[17]

When David was dying, he called in his son Solomon and urged the latter, when he became king, to kill various people who had once vexed David but whom David had sworn not to harm. As soon as David was dead, Solomon sent his hatchet man, Benaiah, to slay them. He also had Benaiah kill Solomon's older brother Adonijah, who had hoped to become king, and Joab, who had supported Adonijah.

When David finally died in —973, after a forty-year reign, he left an empire that, for the moment at least, compared in size and power with those of Egypt, Babylonia, and even swiftly growing Assyria. It was not fated to last, but David could not have foreseen that.

When the dying David heard that his son Adonijah was intriguing for the succession, he hastily sent Solomon on the royal mule to the spring of Gihon, along with Zadok the priest, Nathan the prophet, Benaiah the captain of the royal guard, the mercenaries, and such other officials and partisans as could be rounded up. At Gihon, where the Ark was kept in a tent, Zadok anointed Solomon with oil and presented him with the royal insignia. Solomon thus became the "anointed one" (in Hebrew, the *mashiah* or messiah) chosen by Yahveh as king. Trumpets blew, and all present shouted: "God save King Solomon!"[18]

So—after the minor unpleasantness of killing the people on the new king's black list—began a reign to which the Israelites' descendants looked back fondly as a time of peace and prosperity, when "Judah and Israel dwelt safely, every man under his vine and under his fig tree . . ."[19] And in fact the new king, if not above murdering a kinsman or two, proved able. Although unwarlike and luxurious, he was commercially enterprising at a time when most Israelites were backward in matters of trade. He exploited the copper mines of Ezion-geber at the head of the Red Sea, near modern Elath.

Solomon also formed a partnership with King Hiram[20] of Tyre, to send trading fleets down the Red Sea from Ezion-geber and westward from Tyre to distant Spain.[21] Hiram furnished the ships and the sailors; Solomon, soldiers and trade goods. In their lighter moments, Hiram and Solomon sent each other riddles, with bets that the recipient could not solve them.[22]

It is also written that the queen of Sheba,[23] in southern Arabia, came to visit Solomon to quiz him on his celebrated wisdom and to exchange gifts with him. The Bible does not name the lady, nor say how old she was, nor claim that she was beautiful, nor state that she and Solomon had a love affair. All these romantic details were added by later fictioneers. For all that anybody knows, the queen may have had the face of a camel and the heart of a pawnbroker. The lavish gifts she exchanged with Solomon may have been a barter deal arrived at after a hard-nosed oriental haggle.

For that matter, the whole story looks more than a little suspicious. Queens do not usually set out on 1,400-mile camel rides over scorching deserts merely to trade wares and witticisms with distant kings of whom they have heard. She might of course have sent a caravan, the tale of which grew in the telling. Since authentic Sheban history only begins about −800, a century and a half after the alleged visit to Solomon, there is no way to confirm or refute the tale.

Anyway, the twin kingdoms prospered. At least, Solomon himself prospered, since it was the practice for a king to arrogate to himself a monopoly of trade in any commodity that looked particularly profitable. During Solomon's reign, Jerusalem grew to an area of half a square mile, covering the whole of the East Ridge.

Solomon also launched a grandiose building program, buying materials from King Hiram and hiring Phoenician workmen more skilled than any to be found among the rustic Israelites. The foreman was a Tyrian of half-Israelite parentage, called Hiram in Kings and Huramabi in Chronicles. His original Canaanitish name was probably Ahîrômabi, and he continues a shadowy existence to this day as the "Hiram Abif" of Masonic ritual. The Israelites seem never to have learned the skilled technics of the Phoenicians, for their later masonry long remained crude.

The main edifice was the Temple, designed as a proper housing for the Ark and for Yahveh, who in some mysterious way was connected with the Ark. On the site of Araunah's threshing floor, north of the city on Zion, Phoenician engineers cleared an oblong space corresponding closely to the present court of the Ḥaram ash-Sharîf. In the midst of this court now stands the handsome mosque called the Qubbit aṣ-Ṣakhra, or Dome of the Rock, and miscalled the Mosque of Omar. The mosque may in fact occupy the exact site of the Temple. There is no way to be sure, since not a stone remains from the original Temple to mark its site.

Temple of Solomon — Jerusalem

21. Temple of Solomon at Jerusalem, −X to −VI. (Drawing by Roy G. Krenkel.)

The Bible gives many details of the Temple. But, being no architect, the writer was not precise enough to make an accurate reproduction possible.

Standing on a broad stone platform or terrace, the Temple was a rather plain building, whereof the main part, the nave, was rectangular, 60 by 20 cubits in plan and 30 cubits high. In other words, assuming a 20-inch cubit, it was about 100 feet long (half the length of the Parthenon), 33 feet wide, and 50 feet high. Its long axis ran east and west, and the entrance was at the east end.

Along each side of the nave ran a smaller, three-story rectangular structure, containing rooms for the priests and their paraphernalia. Folding wooden doors let into the nave from the east entrance. The space before these doors, forming the *ulâm* or porch, was flanked by a pair of freestanding bronze pillars with ornate capitals.[24]

Inside, the nave was divided into the main chamber or *hêkhâl* and the *dĕbhîr* or Holy of Holies. The *hêkhâl* housed costly cult objects like a golden altar for burning perfumes, a table on which was placed the god's daily ration of "shewbread," candelabra, lamps, cups, basins, and other sacred accessories. The interior was lined with wooden paneling. This wood, like that of the main doors, was carved with reliefs of cherubim[25] (winged angels or guardian spirits) and palm trees, and gilded.

The *děbhîr* was a dark, cubical room at the far end of the *hêkhâl*, entered only by the High Priest and then only once a year. It contained the Ark, flanked by a pair of gilded wooden cherubim thrice the height of a man. Evidently the Yahvists did not, at this time, observe the strict tabu against graven images that they later adopted.[26]

Outside were other structures. The altar of burnt offerings was a raised platform. The "sea of bronze" was a huge bronzen basin, about 17 feet across (the same size as Mount Palomar's 200-inch telescope mirror), resting on the backs of twelve bronzen oxen. There were also smaller bowls on wheels for the priests' ceremonial ablutions. Presumably there were smaller buildings providing living quarters for the priests and their servants, but nothing is known of these.

South of the Temple grounds, a lower terrace supported another complex of buildings. These included Solomon's palace, a "House of the Forest of Lebanon," a "Hall of Pillars," a throne room for audiences and judgments, and a separate house for the most aristocratic of Solomon's hundreds of wives, a daughter of the king of Egypt. (At least, Pharaoh said she was his daughter; but great kings sometimes cozened their vassals in such matters.) The House of the Forest of Lebanon and the Hall of Pillars, we may guess, were used for governmental purposes. Since nothing is left of these structures and no plans have come down, their arrangement is unknown, although many books contain drawings that purport to show their layout.

Having built his Temple, Solomon staged a grand dedication. Israelites came from all over to feast for a week, to see the king sacrifice, and to hear him pray and deliver a sermon. Solomon had already installed the priest Zadok,[27] who had supported him against his brother Adonijah, as High Priest of Yahveh. Zadok displaced old Abiathar, a surviving member of the house of Eli, which had long held the High Priesthood and which claimed descent from Aaron. Abiathar was exiled, and the family of Zadok kept their grip on the office for centuries.

It is unlikely that worship in Israel was so strictly monotheistic as the later Yahvists believed. Probably the subordinate gods still shared in the use of the Temple. Moreover, Solomon himself was religiously tolerant—an attitude that strikes most of us as praiseworthy but that filled post-exilic Yahvists with horror. The priestly historians blamed this lapse on Solomon's wives. As a result of the influence of these women, he "went after Ashtoreth the goddess of the Sidonians, and after Milcom the abomination of the Ammonites," and "built a high place for Chemosh the abomination of Moab."

Over a century after Solomon's death, a small shrine to one of the Canaanite gods was flourishing just outside the east wall of Jerusalem. Here, in the 1960s, Dr. Kathleen Kenyon's diggers exposed a pair of *mazzeboth* or standing stones (like those of Stonehenge and Brittany), which served as cult objects in such places. There was also a cave in which were placed the vessels in which offerings had been made and which, therefore, were tabu for ordinary use. The style of this pottery shows a date of about −800, in the reign of King Jehoash, of whom the author of 2 Kings complains: "But the high places were not taken away: the people still sacrificed and burnt incense in the high places."[28]

Worshiping in "high places" was an old Semitic custom, probably based upon the simple notion that the gods in heaven could better hear one's prayers if one got up as close to them as one could. It was generally done in Palestine before the erection of Solomon's Temple. Once the Temple was up, the local clique of Yahvist priests, headed by Zadok, urged the secular arm to close these outlying places of worship and centralize all Yahvistic ritual at the Temple. They had a simple motive for wanting all sacrifices offered at Jerusalem, since their diet was largely made up of those parts of the sacrificed animals (the more edible parts, naturally) not burned on the altar.

Despite all the flattering things that people have said about Solomon, many subjects disliked his rule. The tributary Edomites and Syrians broke away. Solomon's building projects, like those of Rameses II, bore hard upon the people, since the work was done by forced labor.[29] Solomon probably favored his native Judah, angering the men of the kingdom of Israel. Running out of metal to pay Hiram for building materials, he ceded twenty northern towns to the Tyrian king, who nonetheless complained that Solomon had shortchanged him.

The resentments accumulated under Solomon's reign came to a boil in −933, when Solomon died. His son Rehoboam was made king of Judah and went to Shechem to be made king of Israel as well. When the Israelite leaders asked him to oppress them less harshly than had his late father, Rehoboam rashly replied: "My father chastised you with whips, but I will chastise you with scorpions."[30]

Israel promptly revolted and chose as its king Jeroboam, a leader of the anti-Judah faction. For two centuries there were two Israelite kingdoms: Judah (including the remnant of Benjamin) in the South, and Israel, with the nine remaining tribes (other than the Levites) in the North. Tribal distinctions had pretty much broken down. The two little kingdoms fought each other as often and as zestfully as they fought the Syrians, the Moabites, and other neighboring peoples.

22. Temple of Herod the Great, in a scale model of the Herodian city on the grounds of the Holyland Hotel in Jerusalem. (Courtesy of Werner Braun.)

During these two centuries, the Yahvist priesthood—or at least the stricter faction among them—became more and more exclusive, more strictly monotheistic, and more hostile to all competing cults. The oldest existing, strictly monotheistic Israelite religious writings are the sermons of the prophets Hosea and Amos, written in —VIII. Some kings followed Solomon's policy of religious pluralism, but others lent ear to the monopolistic claims of the Yahvists.

In late —VII, after the kingdom of Israel had fallen, the strict Yahvists persuaded King Josiah of Judah to command "Hilkiah the high priest . . . to bring forth out of the temple of the Lord all the vessels that were made for Baal, and for the grove, and for all the host of heaven, and he burned them without Jerusalem . . ."[31] Josiah attacked the cults of the heavenly bodies and of the neighboring gods Chemosh, Milcom, and Ashtoreth. He broke up their altars, chopped down their sacred groves, destroyed their statues, and burned the chariot of the sun god. He sent the sacred prostitutes packing and slaughtered the priests of the competing cults.

In late —VIII, Israel lay in the path of the Assyrian colossus. After several times yielding tribute, revolting, and being reduced to subjection again, Israel was finally crushed in —722. The Assyrian king, Sargon II, deported 27,000 Israelites, who had formed the ruling classes

of the northern kingdom. He settled them "in Habor"—that is, along
the river Khabur, which flows south across the steppe of eastern Syria
to join the Euphrates. Since nothing was ever heard of these deportees
again, they have become the subject of a pseudo-scientific cult. By
arguments even sillier than those of most such visionaries, this cult
claims to identify the "Lost Ten Tribes of Israel" with various modern
peoples like the British, the Irish, the American Indians, the Japanese,
the Malays, the Papuans, and the Masai of Africa.

23. Courtyard of the Church of the Holy Sepulcher, in nineteenth-
century Jerusalem. (From John Carne: *Syria, the Holy Land, Asia
Minor, etc.*, Lon.: 1836.)

In fact, there never was any mystery about what happened to the missing Israelites. Those who stayed in Palestine became the Samaritans, practicing a form of Yahvism which the priests of Judah scorned as corrupt and heretical. Those deported lost their national identity under the rigors of Assyrian rule and merged with the Mitannians and Aramaeans among whom they were settled. All the modern Syrians are probably in part their descendants.[32]

While the two kingdoms lasted, there was a distinction between "Israelite" and "Judahite." When independent Israel vanished, this distinction vanished with it. Thereafter the people of Judah called themselves Hebrews, Israelites, or Yĕhûdhîm (Judahites, Judaeans, or Jews) indifferently, and so they have done ever since.

Although during these times it was the capital of a much smaller realm, Jerusalem continued to grow. Its exact boundaries are not known, because extensive quarrying inside the city, in Hellenistic and Roman times, destroyed much of the archaeological evidence of earlier occupations. Its population may have been somewhere in the 10,000–20,000 range, compared to a mere few thousand as a Jebusite city. Around —700, King Hezekiah (who subdued the Philistines at last) built new walls and a new aqueduct from the spring of Gihon to a new reservoir, the Pool of Siloam. Kathleen Kenyon, who commanded the British dig of the 1960s, believed that this reservoir was outside Hezekiah's wall but was in a man-made cave and so not accessible to the foe. Later, the roof of the cave fell in, exposing the Pool.

By timely submission, flattery, and bribery, the kings of Judah preserved a precarious independence from the Assyrian colossus until Assyria fell in —612. The Chaldaean kings of Babylonia, however, proved just as menacing. If less bloodthirsty than the Assyrian monarchs, Nabopolassar and his son Nebuchadrezzar[33] II were just as masterful. After Nebuchadrezzar had bullied King Jehoiakim into paying him tribute, a couple of ill-timed revolts brought the Babylonians down upon Judah. Jerusalem was destroyed and much of its population deported to Babylonia. In —586, King Zedekiah saw his sons executed before he was blinded and led away in chains. Babylonian rule was mild only in comparison with Assyrian, not by modern standards.

So ended Solomon's Jerusalem, Temple and all. But such is the strength of an idea that, even with no great natural advantages, Jerusalem rose again. Under the ineffectual successors of Nebuchadrezzar the Great, the Neo-Babylonian Empire weakened, and Cyrus the Persian overthrew it in —538.

The Persian kings were shrewder than their Babylonian and Assyrian predecessors in running a huge and motley empire. Cyrus told his new Jewish subjects that those who wished might go back to Judaea, taking with them the Temple accessories that the Babylonians had carried off. Some remained in Babylon, where they had prospered; others took part in the Return. There, in an ironic rehearsal of the Zionist movement, they met the hostility of the people—Edomites and Samaritans—then dwelling in Judaea. These saw no reason to welcome a swarm of immigrants who were to them just obnoxious foreigners. But firm Persian rule kept the locals from resisting the influx by force.

During the Exile, the Yahvist priesthood had consolidated its power. Its theologians had worked out a creed of austerely strict monotheism. It had imposed upon the faithful a complex program of ritual and a stringent body of tabus. Thus the priests erected social barriers between the Jews and the Gentiles among whom they lived. Despite some apostasy from Judaism and some biological mingling, these barriers proved so effective that they have preserved the Jews as a distinct ethnic and cultural group, even when scattered about the world in a multitude of little enclaves, for over two thousand years. No other dispersed folk approaches this record.

The century after the Return saw another flourishing Jerusalem on the East Ridge. Nehemiah, the Jewish governor under King Artaxerxes,[34] built new walls. The section on the eastern side of Zion was nearer the crest of the ridge than it had been in the Jebusite site, since it had proved impossible to keep the terraces on that steep slope from collapsing. Instead, the city was extended westward, down the gentler western slope of the East Ridge into the Tyropoeon. A new Temple had also been built, although aged critics, who had seen the original, said it was but a poor, shoddy imitation of Solomon's.

With Alexander the Great, Judaea passed from Persian to Macedonian rule. At the breakup of Alexander's empire, Judaea became a bone of contention between the Seleucids, ruling from Syria to Iran, and the Ptolemies, ruling Egypt. The Jews divided into two factions: the Hellenizers, who, charmed by Greek culture, wished to adopt some of its features; and the orthodox, who scornfully rejected all such foreign ways.

The brilliant but eccentric Seleucid king, Antiochos IV Epiphanes, tried to convert the Jews forcibly to Graeco-Roman culture and stirred up a revolt among the orthodox. Then in −163 he fell sick and died on a campaign against the rising power of Parthia. This enabled the orthodox Jews to make good their revolt and set up an independent kingdom, which flourished for a century. This victory is still celebrated as Ḥanûkkâh. The rulers of the new kingdom were the Hasmonaean or Maccabaean Dynasty—the descendants of the priest Mattathias Maccabaeus, whose sons had led the revolt against Antiochos. Fratricidal murders and civil wars amongst the Hasmonaeans gave the Romans an excuse to reduce Judaea to a client kingdom.

During this time, Jerusalem spread north and northwest, past the Temple to the main part of the plateau and out on the West Ridge. We do not know how far it had spread in these directions on any particular date, because this area is now solidly built up. A thorough archaeological exploration would mean tearing down a goodly part of the present city with all its holy places. It is known that the rulers built several walls, each inclosing more than its predecessor as the city grew.

In —39, during the Second Triumvirate of Antonius, Octavianus, and Lepidus, the Roman Senate gave the kingship of Judaea to Herodes or Herod, an Idumaean (Edomite) adventurer and politician. The Edomites had been forcibly converted to Judaism by one of the Maccabaean kings, but the stricter Yahvists still viewed Herod and his line as detestable Gentiles.

Herod was a man of great ability, but a cruel, gloomy, and murderous tyrant whose victims included his favorite wife, three of his sons, and assorted in-laws, friends, and hangers-on. Although he probably never committed the Slaughter of the Innocents with which he is charged in the Gospel according to St. Matthew, he did other acts about as reprehensible. Even though a modern historian may say that "Herod was not a royal ogre as he appears in the Jewish and Christian tradition,"[35] he still came pretty close to it.

Fond of display, hoping to ingratiate himself with his subjects, and (like Antiochos IV) an admirer of Rome and the Romans, Herod the Great spent vast sums on refortifying Jerusalem and rebuilding the Temple. His new Temple, standing on a platform twice the size of that of Solomon's Temple, was the most magnificent ever. The foundation of the terrace on which it stood, made of enormous blocks of well-cut stone, comprises the famous "Wailing Wall." One or two causeways on arches across the Tyropoeon joined the Temple area to the West Ridge, now fully built up. The population of Jerusalem may have risen to 25,000 or 30,000.

In +66, enraged by the oppressions of a succession of rapacious and tyrannical Roman governors—including Pontius Pilatus of New Testament fame—and stirred to frenzy by a series of messianic prophets and cultocrats, the Jews revolted, trusting Yahveh to make good the difference between their forces and those of Rome. The war ended in a hard-fought siege of Jerusalem. The city was held by three mutually hostile armed bands, who under fanatical leaders fought one another as zealously as they fought the Romans. Yahveh failed to intervene, and in +70 the city fell. The Romans burned Herod's splendid Temple, razed the city, and massacred the people. A second rising in +132 was crushed with even greater severity.

On the ruins of Jerusalem, the Romans built a new city, Aelia

Capitolina, which they forbade the surviving Jews of Palestine to enter. They also forbade Jewish religious practices such as circumcision. But in time these laws were repealed or forgotten; the Jews trickled back, and the old name of Jerusalem reasserted itself.

The rise of Christianity further complicated the status of Jerusalem. About +330, Constantine, the first Christian Roman emperor, ordered the Bishop of Jerusalem to find the Holy Sepulcher. He also sent his aged mother, Helena, on a pilgrimage to Jerusalem. Having just had his wife, his illegitimate son, and a nephew killed, Constantine doubtless felt the need of working up some spiritual capital. In any case, a rock-cut tomb was shortly found in the northwestern part of the city, and this was proclaimed the tomb of Christ. Later monkish historians also told how Helena discovered the True Cross in an old cistern. The authenticity of these discoveries was attested by suitable visions and miracles.

Constantine then ordered a set of sacred buildings to be erected over the Holy Sepulcher. After countless changes, additions, fires, repairs, destructions, and rebuildings, this complex evolved into the present Church of the Holy Sepulcher. It is an irregular mass of heterogeneous structures, jammed in among other buildings, so that there is no place whence the visitor can get a good look at the church as a whole. Possession of the Holy Sepulcher is divided amongst a multitude of squabbling Christian sects—the Roman, Greek, Armenian, Syrian, Coptic, and Abyssinian churches.

Esthetically, the Holy Sepulcher is far less pleasing than Caliph 'Abd-al-Malik's splendid mosque, the Qubbit aṣ-Ṣakhra, on the spacious platform where once stood Herod's Temple. The dome of the Qubbit was originally covered with sheets of gilded brass. Later this was replaced by lead, and this a few years ago by sheets of gilded aluminum, which makes a brave if anachronistic show. (I am sorry to report, however, that the roof of the Qubbit leaks. When I was there in February, 1967, it snowed for the first time in Jerusalem in forty years, and I toured the mosque wading in stocking feet in an inch of icy water.)

In +IV, following Helena's visit and the building of the Church of the Holy Sepulcher, pilgrimages to Jerusalem became popular among Christians throughout the Roman Empire. Such a pilgrimage combined the pleasures of tourism with the virtuous feeling of performing a religious duty. These pilgrimages have continued down to the present, supporting a goodly part of the Holy City's population.

Ever since, Jerusalem has had its ups and downs. It was sacked by the Persians in +614. It surrendered in +638 to the Arabs of the caliph 'Umar (or Omar) ibn-al-Khaṭṭab, a wise, farsighted, and humane little mulatto. Although on the whole 'Umar treated the Jerusalemites

24. Interior of the Church of the Holy Sepulcher, in nineteenth-century Jerusalem. (From John Carne: *Syria, the Holy Land, Asia Minor, etc.*, Lon.: 1836.)

well, he confiscated the Church of the Virgin Mary, built on orders of the Roman emperor Justinian at the southern end of Solomon's temple platform, and made a mosque of it.

Thereafter called the Masjîd al-Aqṣâ, this building has undergone much repair and reconstruction, especially after its partial destruction by earthquakes in +VIII. Therefore little of Justinian's masonry is left. It has also come to be regarded as one of Islâm's holiest shrines, to which miraculous stories are attached. On August 21, 1969, it was further damaged by a fire set by a young Australian divinity student, Michael D. W. Rohan. An adherent of a Fundamentalist sect, the Church of God, Rohan said that God, having appointed him king of Judaea, had told him to burn the "temple of Satan" to make room for the rebuilding of Solomon's Temple. Most Arabs, the world's most accomplished wishful thinkers, preferred to believe that the blaze had been set by their foes the Israelis.

In 1099, the Crusaders took Jerusalem and killed every Jew and Muslim, without distinction of age or sex, whom they found in the city. Saladin's Muslims soon got the city back, happily without another massacre. In 1517, it became part of the empire of the Osmanli Turks, whose sultan Süleyman the Magnificent had new walls built around the city in 1537. On the east and west, these walls followed the lines of the walls of Hasmonaean and Roman times. On the north and south, however, Süleyman's walls were about a quarter of a mile north of the ancient ones, as if the whole town had been pushed a quarter-mile northward. Those walls still stand.

I need not tell the later history of Jerusalem: the conflicts of Turk and Briton, of Arab and Jew. The older parts of the city are much as they were in Süleyman's time, while most of the growth of recent years has been to the northwest. Its site is no more strategic nor commercially valuable than it was in Jebusite days; but men still struggle for its possession. Truly, man does not live by bread alone, but also by myths and legends, ideals and traditions. Were this not so, history would perhaps be less exclusively a "register of the crimes, follies, and misfortunes of mankind"[36]; but it might also be less fascinating.

IV

NINEVEH, THE BLOODY CITY

THE ASSYRIAN CAME DOWN LIKE THE WOLF ON THE FOLD,
AND HIS COHORTS WERE GLEAMING IN PURPLE AND GOLD;
AND THE SHEEN OF THEIR SPEARS WAS LIKE STARS ON THE SEA,
WHEN THE BLUE WAVE ROLLS NIGHTLY ON DEEP GALILEE.[1]

Byron

25. Nineveh: Mound of Quyunjiq in +XIX. (From John P. Newman: *The Thrones and Palaces of Babylon and Nineveh*, N.Y.: 1876.)

26. Excavations at Nineveh, in +XIX, under direction of Hormuzd Rassam. (From John P. Newman: *The Thrones and Palaces of Babylon and Nineveh*, N.Y.: 1876.)

T HERE was a man of the Ionian city of Knidos, at the southwestern tip of Asia Minor, named Ktesias. About —415, Ktesias went to the court of Artaxerxes II Memnon of Persia to practice the family trade of medicine. There he made himself so agreeable to the young king that Artaxerxes appointed him his personal physician. Ktesias served in this capacity through the revolt of Artaxerxes' brother Cyrus. This civil war ended in the death of Cyrus at the battle of Cunaxa (—401) and the epic retreat of the ten thousand Greeks, whom Cyrus had hired as mercenaries in his bid for the throne, through Kurdistan and Armenia to the Black Sea.

During his seventeen years at the Persian court, Ktesias gathered reams of data on the Persian Empire, which he later put into a book. He also collected tales of India and of the empires before the Persian: the Babylonian, the Median, and the Assyrian.

Ktesias was an industrious but uncritical compiler. Whereas most of his information on Persia, drawn from the royal archives, was fairly sound, his material on other lands included the wildest yarns. About India, he heard tales of a fountain of liquid gold and of a beast called the *martichora*, with a man's face and a tail from which it shot stings like arrows.

Ktesias also heard that the Assyrian Empire had been founded by King Ninus, who built a city named after him on the Euphrates River. Ninus also married the Syrian demigoddess Semiramis, who succeeded him, founded Babylon, and invaded Africa and India. The thirtieth Assyrian king after Ninus was an effeminate called Sardanapalus. Beaten by the Medes, Sardanapalus burned himself up in his palace with all his concubines, eunuchs, and treasure.[2]

For centuries, historians solemnly wrote of Ninus and Semiramis and Sardanapalus as if they were serious history. Actually, the Assyrian capital had vanished so utterly that nobody knew its site for sure. Called Ninua by its builders and Nineveh by the Hebrews, it had stood, not on the Euphrates at all, but on the Tigris River. Marching northwest along the left bank of the Tigris, twenty miles beyond the river Zapatas (the modern Zab), Xenophon's Ten Thousand Greeks passed a huge field of ruins. They were told that it was the Median city of Mespila, none suspecting that it was in sooth once-mighty Nineveh.[3]

For over 2,000 years, Nineveh was practically lost to human knowledge—almost as lost as Plato's Atlantis, which never really existed at

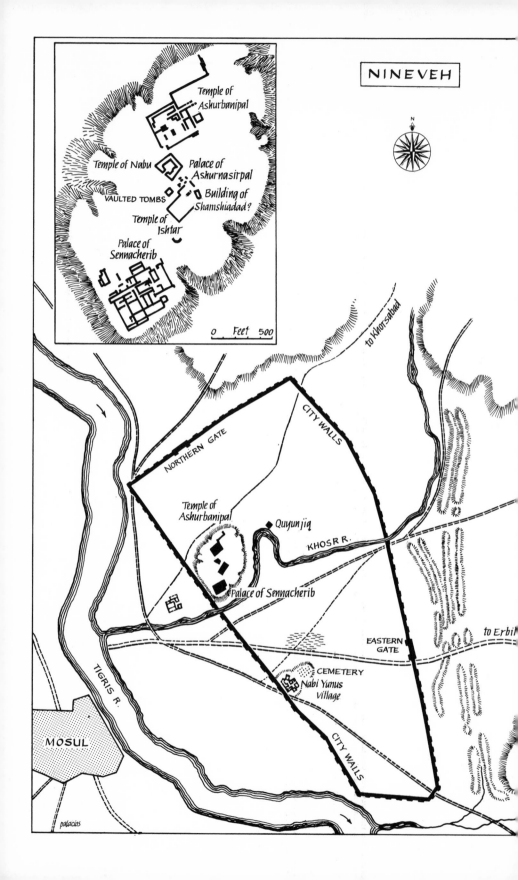

NINEVEH

Temple of
Ashurbanipal

Temple of Nabu

Palace of
Ashurnasirpal

VAULTED TOMBS

Building of
Shamshiadad?

Temple of Ishtar

Palace of
Sennacherib

0   Feet   500

to Khorsabad

CITY WALLS

NORTHERN GATE

Temple of
Ashurbanipal

Quyunjiq

KHOSR R.

Palace of Sennacherib

EASTERN
GATE

to Erbil

CEMETERY
Nabi Yunus
Village

TIGRIS R.

MOSUL

CITY WALLS

palacios

all. True, Nineveh was mentioned in the Old Testament and in the surviving fragments of Ktesias' *Persika*. But its whereabout was not definitely known.

In Roman times, a new town grew up on the right bank of the Tigris. Called Mespila, which Xenophon had been told was the name of the ruin field, it evolved into medieval and modern Mosul. In +XIX, Turkish misgovernment had rendered Mosul one of the less pleasant places for Europeans to visit. One wrote:

> Mosul town is an evil city. By night robbers stalk untouched from house to house, and the time of rest and darkness is made fearful by the cracking of pistols and confused cries of strife. By day, drunkenness and debauchery are openly indulged in. The population is rotted by the foul distemper, corrupted and rendered impotent by drink, stupefied and besotted by vice . . . Tales are whispered of dark and hideous sorceries and incantations . . .[4]

The rediscovery of Nineveh began in 1808, when a young Englishman with a genius for languages, Claudius James Rich, took up the post of Resident in Baghdad for the East India Company. In his spare time, Rich rode about the countryside. In 1811, he spent ten days on the site of Babylon—which, unlike Nineveh, had never been lost. The mound marking the site of the city was still called "Babil," an obvious cognate of the Hebrew "Babel" and the Greek "Babylon."

Rich did some tentative digging and the next year published a memoir of his survey. Twenty-odd years later, this memoir, together with a later and fuller account of Rich's travels published by his widow, came to the notice of Paul Émile Botta, a French naturalist. Botta had already traveled in the Near and Middle East. Realizing that here a whole new scientific field awaited an enterprising man to open it up, Botta pulled wires to get himself appointed French consul at Mosul.

Mosul lies in the northern part of the modern nation of Iraq, which has an ameboid shape something like a bloated letter Y. The stem of the Y extends southeast to the Persian Gulf; the left fork reaches across the Arabian desert to touch the kingdom of Jordan; the right fork stretches north into the Kurdish hills.

In very ancient times the southernmost part, around the Persian Gulf, was called Sumer. Later it became known as Kaldi—in Latinized Greek, Chaldaea. The next section to the northwest, around modern Baghdad, was Babylonia. Still farther north, around modern Mosul, lay Assyria. To the northeast, where the land rose in a series of long mountain ranges paralleling the stem of the Y, lay Elam, corresponding to the provinces of Luristan and Kuzistan in modern Iran.

The two great rivers, the Tigris[5] and the Euphrates,[6] rise in Turkey and flow to the south. The Tigris, farther east, flows directly into Iraq; the Euphrates, to the west, cuts across Syria before entering Iraq. Both meander southeastward across the vast flat plain, approaching to within twenty miles of each other near Baghdad. Then they diverge again for another 300 miles. Hence the Greek name for Iraq: Mesopotamia, the "Land Between the Rivers." At last they join and flow together for fifty miles into the Persian Gulf. Some believe that in ancient times, when the Persian Gulf extended farther to the northwest, the rivers entered it separately, and that silt from these streams has since filled up the head of the gulf.

Assyria gets more rain than most of Iraq—12 to 15 inches a year, enough to support a modest growth of trees on the hills. Being higher and farther north, it escapes the scorching heat that paralyzes most of Iraq in summer. Whereas Assyria has plenty of stone—mostly limestone—the rest of Iraq is almost stoneless.

In the hills north of Mosul live the Kurds. These descendants of the ancient Medes speak a language closely akin to Persian. Although they have a better claim to nationhood than many groups, the Kurds are presently divided among Turkey, Iraq, and Iran, forming a restless minority in all three nations. One sees them in Baghdad—big, stout, ruddy men wearing a kind of baggy jump suit and a large turban with fringed ends.

Having settled in Mosul, where should Botta dig? Within 50 miles were several promising sites. Across the Tigris from Mosul rose the twin mounds of Quyunjiq and Nabi Yunus.[7] Fourteen miles north of this was the mound of Khorsabad. Twenty-five miles down the Tigris from Quyunjiq was Nimrûd, on the left bank; an equal distance farther south, on the right bank, was Qal'at Sharqât. Botta excavated at Quyunjiq in 1843. Getting small results, he shifted to Khorsabad, where he soon dug up the remains of a splendid palace.

At the same time a young Briton, Austen Henry Layard, turned his attention to the ruin fields of Assyria. Layard had started out on an overland journey to India but had gotten sidetracked in Iraq and Iran, where he spent a couple of years in wild adventures among the tribesmen. He was repeatedly held up and robbed and had narrow escapes from being shot or speared.

In 1845, Layard had been working at minor diplomatic jobs for the British ambassador to Turkey, in Istanbul. The ambassador furnished a small subsidy for Layard to start digging in the mounds of the Mosul region. Layard became fast friends with Botta, since both had to cope with the Turkish pasha of Mosul. This was a fat little pockmarked scoundrel with one eye and one ear, who ran his pashalik with

27. The site of Nineveh, viewed across the Tigris from Mosul. (Courtesy of Lionel Casson and the Pontificio Istituto Biblico, Rome.)

all the dastardly villainy of the wicked oriental potentate of old-fashioned adventure fiction. Layard wrote:

> The pashaw was accustomed to give instruction to those who were sent to collect money, in three words—"Go, destroy, eat"; and his agents were not generally backward in entering into the spirit of them. The tribes, who had been attacked and plundered, were retaliating upon caravans and travelers, or laying waste the cultivated parts of the pashawlik. The villages were deserted, and the roads were little frequented and very insecure.[8]

Convinced that Layard was on the track of a treasure and determined to get his own hands on it first, this Mohammed Keritli Oglu once ordered his men secretly to take gravestones from a nearby Muslim cemetery and place them about the site of the dig. Thus he could forbid Layard's excavation on the ground that it was desecrating the graves of True Believers.

After visiting several Iraqi ruin fields, Layard settled down to serious digging at Nimrûd. Here he soon uncovered statues of winged, human-headed bulls—a type of Assyro-Babylonian protective genie—and other antiquities as spectacular as those that Botta had been finding at Khorsabad. He also dug at Quyunjiq and Qal'at Sharqât.

Presently Botta went back to France. His replacement, Rouet, adopted an attitude of nationalistic rivalry towards Layard. During the next few decades, this grew into an unseemly scramble on the part of French and British diggers in Iraq to see which could forestall and outwit the other.

In 1851, Layard left Iraq for the last time, to go on to a distinguished career in politics and diplomacy. His successor was a Christian native of Mosul, Hormuzd Rassam, who for several years had been Layard's assistant. Rassam was an interesting man. Being himself a Moslawi, he accomplished things with his fellow-Iraqis that no foreigner could have done. On the other hand, his temperament was that of an adventurer rather than that of a scientist.

Rassam entered the nationalistic game with zest, giving the French archaeologists Place and de Sarzec cause to complain that he had invaded their diggings when they were not looking and made off with finds that should have been theirs. The method of all these early archaeologists was glorified treasure-hunting. Any detailed account makes a modern archaeologist wince. They drove tunnels into ruins at random, paying no heed to stratigraphy or architectural plans, in hope of finding some nice piece of portable loot that would look good in a distant museum. Thus they made the task of later and more scientific archaeologists, who try to recover every last detail of the lives of the former dwellers, hard or impossible.

True, these early diggers—who had to cope with sizzling heat, freezing cold, dust, sandstorms, mud, flies, scorpions, vipers, corrupt officials, brigandish tribesmen, superstitious workers, and lean purses—did recover an extraordinary lot of antiquities. But another host of relics perished because, in the absence of modern methods of preservation, the finds crumbled to pieces as soon as they were exposed to air or were roughly pried up by inexpert diggers. Many were destroyed by natives, either for reasons of religious fanaticism or for the childish pleasure of breaking things.

Many pieces were lost in transit. Cases sent by Layard to Britain via Bombay were broken open by Bombay's curious Britons, who stole what pleased their fancy and disordered the rest. In 1855, the French sent 300-odd cases of material down the Tigris in a convoy of boats and rafts. At Kurnah, a little above the Persian Gulf, the convoy was held up by Arab bandits, who vented their disappointment at finding no loot but stones and bricks by capsizing the boats and sending the entire cargo to the bottom.

In the 1880s, when the locals learned that infidels would pay for these relics of the Days of Ignorance (as Muslims call the times before Muḥammad) a thriving trade in bootleg antiquities sprang up in that part of the world and has flourished ever since. Rassam, now elderly

28. Tell Nabi Yunus (Hill of the Prophet Jonah) on the site of Nineveh. The curious conical or pyramidal structure to the left of the minaret covers a building of the sect of the Yezidis or Satan-worshipers of northern Iraq. (Courtesy of the Arab Information Center, New York.)

but still running the British digs, continued his old plundering tactics. He scattered gangs of men about the country and left them unsupervised for months at a time, hoping that one gang or another would come upon another site rich in loot. At last he retired to England with his English wife and spent his last years writing memoirs.

At this time, thanks largely to the development of a meticulous methodology by German savants, archaeology was at last becoming scientific. But Rassam's uncontrolled workmen simply stole most of their finds and sold them to the relic-bootleggers. Archaeology, however, was still in its childhood, and its practitioners had to learn by doing. If, in their haste and ignorance, the early diggers lost much irretrievable information, there is one consolation. Iraq has so many of these mounds, each marking the site of a former town, that they could keep all the world's archaeologists busy for generations to come.

Meanwhile, several scholars, including the Göttingen professor Georg Friedrich Grotefend and the fearless, adventurous, hard-riding British empire-builder Major Henry Creswicke Rawlinson, had solved the secret of the cuneiform writing used by the ancient Mesopotamians. To write, these peoples marked thin slabs of wet clay with the ends of sharpened reeds until they looked as if they had been trampled by a host of little birds. Then they baked these slabs to brick-hardness.

As in Egypt, the system started out as simple picture-writing, evolved towards a phonetic system, and got stuck before the process was completed. Therefore Akkadian cuneiform remained a confusing mixture of hundreds of ideographic and phonetic signs, the latter representing whole syllables. Later, the Ugaritians of Syria and the Persians adopted the cuneiform method of writing but devised true alphabets, which reduced the number of symbols to a mere thirty-two.

As tons of inscribed clay tablets reached European museums in the mid-nineteenth century, they were read and translated. Thus the nagging doubts as to which ancient cities the mounds represented were soon resolved. It transpired that ancient Assyria had had four different capitals at different times. The oldest, Ashur, was represented by the mound at Qal'at Sharqât, 50-odd miles downstream from Mosul. Layard had dug there but found little, since Ashur—unlike the other three capitals—lay in the stoneless plain and was therefore built almost entirely of brick. The archaeological techniques of the time could not distinguish softened sun-dried brick from the surrounding soil.

Another city, which had been the capital off and on under several Assyrian kings, was Kalakh (the Calah of Genesis). Kalakh stood farther

29. Excavations at the site of Nineveh; the town of Nabi Yunus in the background. (Courtesy of the Directorate General of Antiquities of Iraq.)

north, where now rose the mound of Nimrûd. Nineveh was Quyunjiq, across the Tigris from Mosul. The capital at Khorsabad was Dûr Sharrukîn, which Sargon[9] II had built in —VIII.

Ashur, the oldest Assyrian capital, goes back at least to —3000. At one time it seems to have been under Sumerian rule. Later, around —2500, it was an independent city-state. Then the Semites, ceaselessly flowing out of the desert, became dominant in Assyria.

Racially, the Assyrians seem always to have been predominantly of the Armenoid type of the white race. This type, which has prevailed in Asia Minor from the earliest historical times on down, is stocky and muscular, with a medium swarthy complexion, abundant dark curly hair and beard, a large hooked nose, and a broad skull. This is the type shown in Assyrian sculptures, even though the Assyrians were probably not all so much alike as the reliefs might give us to think.

During the second millennium B.C., Assyria grew into a powerful kingdom, which often fought the more cultured and populous Babylonia for mastery of Mesopotamia but which was oftener tributary to Babylonia. Tiglathpileser[10] I, who reigned around —1100, first conquered an empire extending west to the Mediterranean and north to Lake Vân. This lake was the center of the kingdom of Vân or Urartu, the biblical Ararat.

Tiglathpileser's empire, however, did not long endure. A new wave of Semitic invaders, the Aramaeans, overran Syria and occupied much of Babylonia. For a century or more, the Assyrians had all they could do to maintain themselves against the invaders.

During this period, Assyrian history is sketchy. But it seems that the Assyrians, who had always been warlike, survived the invasion only by becoming the fiercest militarists of their day. In late —X, Assyrian power revived, and in —883 Ashurnasirpal II ascended the throne and set forth conquering and to conquer. He and his successors proudly recorded what they had done to those so perverse as to resist them:

> I destroyed them, tore down the wall, and burned the town with fire; I caught the survivors and impaled them on stakes in front of their towns . . . Pillars of skulls I erected in front of the town . . . I fed their corpses, cut into small pieces, to dogs, pigs, vultures . . . I slowly tore off his skin . . . Of some I cut off the hands and limbs; of others the noses, ears, and arms; of many soldiers I put out the eyes . . . I flayed them and covered with their skins the wall of the town . . . The heads of their warriors I cut off, and I formed them into a pillar over against their city; their young men and maidens I burned in the fire . . . Three thousand captives I

30. Assyrian *lamassu*, or guardian spirit in the form of a winged, human-headed bull, from the palace of Sargon II at Khorsabad, now in the Iraqi National Museum, Baghdad.

burned with fire; I left not a single one alive to serve as a hostage . . .[11]

Other ancient kings played rough, too, but without quite such fiendish gusto. Most Egyptian and Babylonian kings preferred to boast of their justice, piety, and public works, rather than of their cruelties and atrocities.

Such tactics failed to endear the Assyrians to their subjects. Hence the death of an Assyrian king was usually the signal for a frantic revolt of the subject peoples, and the new king spent the first few years of his reign reconquering his sire's dominions. To discourage such revolts, Assyrian kings deported sections of the revolting population to other parts of the empire. That is how the ruling classes of the kingdom of Israel were resettled on a tributary of the upper Euphrates. This policy worked for a while.

King Shamshiadad V died in −811, and his widow Sammuramat ruled for three years as regent for her son Adadnirari III. The legends of Semiramis, which Ktesias passed on to the Greek world, are based upon the regency of Sammuramat, who was an important lady even if she never invaded India or did any of the other fantastic things credited to her.

After Adadnirari III came several kings, under whom the rebels made good their revolts. The empire shrank until another great conqueror took the throne in −744. This was Tiglathpileser III, who conquered the kingdom of Damascus, killed King Rezin, and deported the Damascenes. When Tiglathpileser had restored the Assyrian Empire to much its former size, his son Shalmaneser[12] V attacked Israel, whose King Hoshea had rebelled. Shalmaneser died either during the siege of Samaria or just after its fall. Either he or his successor, Sargon II, then deported the leading Israelites.

Sargon II extended Assyrian rule far out into the Arabian Desert and built a new capital north of Nineveh. He fittingly named it after himself—Dûr Sharrukîn or Abode of Sargon. Posterity played a joke on him by renaming it Khorsabad after a Persian king, Khusrau[13] the Great, who reigned 1,250 years later.

Sargon fell in battle with northern hillmen in —705 and was succeeded by his son Sennacherib.[14] The new king abandoned Dûr Sharrukîn, save as a military outpost, and moved back to Nineveh. For centuries, Assyrian kings had moved their capital restlessly back and forth among Ashur, Kalakh, Nineveh, and now Dûr Sharrukîn, building palaces here and there and then abandoning them to crumble.

Sennacherib determined to make Nineveh a proper imperial capital once and for all, rivaling Babylon in glory. Here the other sides of the Assyrian character appear. When not busily burning, blinding, beheading, or skinning their prisoners, they executed considerable works of art. Most of these took the form of reliefs in the royal palaces, showing scenes of war and hunting. They also turned out a respectable literature.

They were enterprising traders. A set of letters on clay tablets, found near Lake Vân, comes from the files of an Assyrian merchant doing business there. One letter is from the man's wife, who complains that she and her mother-in-law have quarreled over the size of the offering for the temple, and the mother-in-law has locked her out, and will the husband please come home at once? While this merchant was, doubtless with no small effort and risk, trying to make an honest shekel abroad, his women were fighting at home. *Plus ça change . . .*

Furthermore, the Assyrians were gifted and energetic inventors and engineers. They were pioneers in the military art, being among the first to adopt such innovations as iron weapons and squadrons of cavalry. They invented wheeled war machines like the belfry—the *helepolis* or movable siege tower—with a battering ram on the ground floor and a tower above. The tower was made as tall as the wall to be attacked, so that, when it was pushed up to the wall, the attackers could swarm up the tower by ladders and invade the top of the wall. The earliest known representation of a pulley is from an Assyrian relief of about —1500, in which the device is used to make it easier to haul water up from a well.

When Sennacherib had finished rebuilding Nineveh, the city was surrounded by a huge stone wall, pierced by fifteen gates. The wall inclosed an irregular quadrangle, about one mile from east to west and three miles from north to south. In the midst of this oblong rose two hills, on which stood the temples and palaces. The rest of the area was occupied not only by the dwellings of the common folk but also

31. Eastern wall of Nineveh at the Shamash Gate, restored. (Courtesy of the Directorate General of Antiquities of Iraq.)

by public gardens and the orchards of private citizens. For his private garden, where storks clattered and tame lions prowled, Sennacherib designed an improved swape or well hoist, with a copper bucket and posts of timber instead of dried mud. For the wells of the city, he devised an endless chain hoist with a bronze chain and several score pots attached to the chain by ropes.

To water all his fine plantings, Sennacherib undertook a vast scheme of waterworks. He personally toured the countryside near Nineveh, striding over plains and toiling up hills, to choose the sites for his constructions. Ten miles north of Nineveh, he dammed the river Tebitu,[15] which descended from the north to flow through the middle of Nineveh and empty into the Tigris. From the reservoir thus created, he brought a canal down to the city. Since the grade of the canal was less than that of the river, the canal water arrived at Nineveh high enough to be used for irrigation without hoisting.

To take care of the overflow during the high-water season in spring, Sennacherib installed, northeast of the city, a municipal canebrake, of the sort often maintained in Babylonia. As in Egypt and Babylonia, swamp reeds were often used as structural materials. A bundle of them tied together served as a pillar to hold up a house of light construction. Sennacherib made this marsh into a game preserve, loosing deer, wild boar, and game birds to breed there.

Besides planting reeds and timber trees, Sennacherib imported from India another novelty: the cotton tree. His inscription announced that: "The mulberry and the cypress, the product of the orchards, and the reeds of the brakes which were in the swamp I cut down and used as desired, in the building of my royal palaces. The wool-bearing trees they sheared and wove the wool into garments."[16]

Sennacherib's first canal sufficed for several years. When the city outgrew it, the king dug another canal to the northwest, where it tapped another stream. When Nineveh outgrew these schemes, too, Sennacherib undertook his most ambitious project. He went more than 30 miles from the city, to the watershed of the Atrush or Gomal River. Thence a canal was dug overland to the headwaters of the Tebitu, carrying water downstream to Nineveh.

32. Nineveh in the days of Sennacherib and Ashurbanipal. (Drawing by Roy G. Krenkel.)

Where the canal crossed a tributary of the Atrush-Gomal, near modern Jerwan, Sennacherib built an aqueduct. This was a remarkable piece of construction for its time. It was made of cubes of stone, about 20 inches on a side. In the actual channel, a layer of concrete or mortar under the top course of stone prevented leakage. The aqueduct crossed the stream on a 90-foot bridge of five pointed corbeled arches.

Sennacherib prided himself on completing this canal and aqueduct in a year and a quarter. As work neared completion, he sent two priests to the upper end of the canal to perform the proper religious rites at the opening. Before the ceremony, however, a minor mishap occurred. The sluice gate or spillway at the upper end of the canal gave way, and the waters of the Atrush-Gomal rushed down the channel without awaiting the king's command.

The pious Sennacherib at once looked into the occult meaning of this event and decided that it was a good omen. The very gods, he thought, were so impatient to see the canal in use that they had caused the breach in the sluice gate. So King Sennacherib went to the head of the canal, inspected the damage, gave orders for its repair, and sacrificed oxen and sheep to the gods. "Those men," he wrote, "who had dug that canal I clothed with linen and brightly colored woollen garments. Golden rings, daggers of gold I put upon them."[17]

This was no doubt a delightful surprise to the engineers and workmen, who had probably been shaking in their sandals ever since the mishap for fear that the Great King would order all their heads chopped off. He was, indeed, quite capable of it.

33. Shamash Gate of Nineveh, restored. (Courtesy of the Directorate General of Antiquities of Iraq.)

Like all great Mesopotamian cities of the time, Nineveh had a Processional Way—a broad, straight avenue, paved with slabs of stone or brick. Along this way, wagons bearing the images of the gods were wheeled in religious processions. At Ashur, the Processional Way had a pair of grooves in the pavement for the wheels of the sacred wagons, to assure the gods a smooth, safe ride. This may be deemed the world's first railroad. After all, it would not do to have a god's wagon get stuck or upset. The god would not like it, and there is no telling what an angry god might not do.

Sennacherib set up posts along the Processional Way in Nineveh, reading: ROYAL ROAD. LET NO MAN LESSEN IT. Further, he decreed that any violator should be slain and his body impaled on a stake before his house. It is tempting to look upon Sennacherib's posts as the first no-parking signs; but their real import was probably to keep householders from extending their houses out into the road. In medieval European cities, for the same reason, an official was caused to ride along the streets from time to time with his lance athwart his saddle bow, to make sure that no property owner was encroaching on the public right of way.

Sennacherib's empire included Babylonia, Chaldaea, Syria, and Phoenicia. Palestine was usually tributary. Sennacherib campaigned in Judaea at least once. He beat an Egyptian army and besieged Jerusalem but let King Hezekiah buy him off with a whopping tribute.

Something happened on this campaign to upset Sennacherib's plans, but it is not known what. The Bible says that "the angel of the Lord went out, and smote in the camp of the Assyrians." Herodotos says that mice ate the Assyrians' bows, quivers, and shield handles so that they could no longer fight.[18] Sennacherib himself says nothing of any reverse, but one would hardly expect him to. Some have thought that the Assyrians suffered a plague; others, trying to reconcile the contradictory stories, have inferred that Sennacherib invaded the land twice. But all this is surmise.

Like his predecessors, Sennacherib ruled most of the subject territories through native kings, whom the Assyrians had conquered but left in power on condition that they pay tribute and furnish troops to the King of Kings. The Assyrian kings tried to govern Babylonia through such puppet kings, since Babylonia was too big for them to rule directly unless they were willing to move thither. Moreover, the Assyrians had the same kind of grudging respect for Babylonia, whence they had derived most of their culture, that the Romans later had for Greece.

The puppets, however, often revolted. In the —690s, Sennacherib deposed one restless Babylonian king and put one of his own sons,

Ashurnadinshum, in his place. The leaders of the anti-Assyrian faction fled south into the marshes of Chaldaea, where they thought they would surely be safe.

They failed to reckon, however, on Sennacherib's engineering genius. He called upon the tributary Phoenician cities for ships. These ships, built in sections, were hauled overland and assembled on the Euphrates. They sailed down the river to Chaldaea, where they helped to rout the anti-Assyrians.

But not for long. The Babylonians soon rose and drove out Ashurnadinshum. When the wrathful Sennacherib recaptured Babylon in −689, he massacred the people and sacked and burned the world's greatest city. He dug canals through the city, dammed the Euphrates, and sent the river coursing through these canals. He dumped the temples into the canals and made a vast, muddy morass of the former metropolis.

Later, Sennacherib had second thoughts and began to restore the city. His son and his grandson continued the work, and in time Babylon again became the largest city in the world.

During the twenty-four years of Sennacherib's reign, the Ninevites prospered. There was plenty of work to be done on Sennacherib's fine new buildings and waterworks, and life was enlivened by religious festivals and by the spectacle of captured kings being paraded through the city before having their heads cut off. The Assyrians showed the beginnings of religious fanaticism, making sacred rites of the execution of captives. Assyrian religion seems to have been a rather gloomy form of polytheism. The pantheon was much the same as that of Babylonia, with Ashur—who gave his name to the original capital city and to the empire—substituted for Marduk as king of the gods. The world was thought to swarm with evil spirits, and the science of omens was tediously elaborated.

The kings practiced some form of poor relief. Married women were compelled to go veiled, but other women were forbidden to do so. Voluntary abortion by a woman was a capital crime, since it might deprive the king of a sturdy future soldier. As among the Israelites, sexual deviation was a problem; that is, it existed to some extent but was viewed as sinful and severely punished.

In −681, two of Sennacherib's sons conspired against him. The great engineer-king was lured into a temple in Nineveh and beaten to death with statuettes of the gods. Another son, Esarhaddon,[19] defeated the murderers, who fled to Vân, and took the throne himself. One of the grimmest of a line of singularly grim monarchs, Esarhaddon began one inscription: "I am mighty, I am omnipotent, I am a hero, I am gigantic, I am colossal!"[20] He somehow neglected to add: "I am also modest."

34. Chamber, excavated by Rassam's tunnelings at Nineveh, where Ashurbanipal's library was found. (From John P. Newman: *The Thrones and Palaces of Babylon and Nineveh*, N.Y.: 1876.)

Besides rebuilding Babylon, Esarhaddon invaded Egypt, trounced the armies that opposed him, and sent Taharqa, the last king of the Ethiopian Dynasty, fleeing back to his native Kush. Although Esarhaddon took the title of "King of Egypt," threats nearer home soon forced him to withdraw the Assyrian army from Egypt.

The steppes that stretch from the Ukraine to Turkestan—an area vaguely known to the ancients as "Scythia"—were boiling over in one of their periodical eruptions. A nomadic horde, the Gimirrai or Cimmerians, had broken into Asia Minor in the reign of Sargon II, who defeated them in a great battle. The Cimmerians, who shaved their faces and wore caps that stood up in tall points, then turned their attention westward against the kingdom of Lydia, which appealed to Assyria for help.

Esarhaddon died on a second expedition against Egypt and was succeeded by his son Ashurbanipal, who again drove the Kushites out of Egypt. Ashurbanipal was as tough, energetic, and cruel as most Assyrian kings. One of his reliefs shows a pretty scene of Ashurbanipal and his queen enjoying a victory banquet, with musicians and fan-wavers, and the head of a rebel Elamite king hanging from a nearby tree.

Ashurbanipal was, however, a more cultured and intellectual man than his predecessors. He sent out a host of scribes to copy and translate the writings gathered in the temple libraries throughout his empire. Thus he accumulated a royal library of tens of thousands of clay

35. Nergal Gate at Nineveh, restored. (Courtesy of the Directorate
General of Antiquities of Iraq.)

tablets, which preserved voluminous records of the arts and sciences of
Babylonia. Hormuzd Rassam's greatest find occurred in 1853, when
he came upon this library in the mound at Quyunjiq and shipped
25,000 tablets to the British Museum. Layard had found another section
of the royal archives at Nimrûd three years earlier. These two hauls
account for much of our modern knowledge of Assyria and Babylonia.

Following the usual custom, Ashurbanipal set up his brother Shamashshumukin as king of Babylonia. Shamashshumukin revolted in —652,
but Ashurbanipal defeated him and shut him up in Babylon. The city
succumbed to famine, and Shamashshumukin lit a fire in his palace and
threw himself into it. Ktesias' "Sardanapalus" seems to be a combination
of Ashurbanipal, Shamashshumukin, and some later Assyrian kings, all
rolled into one and liberally fictionized.

Ashurbanipal's armies also beat the Elamites and the Cimmerians.
The latter horde broke up, and some settled in northeastern Asia Minor,

where their descendants became the Armenians. At least, their language evolved into Armenian, although the people themselves doubtless mingled with the folk they found already settled in Armenia and disappeared as a distinct ethnic type. The Cimmerians' place as a barbarian menace was soon taken by the Scythians, a nomadic folk akin to the Medes and the Persians.

Ashurbanipal's last years were filled with foreboding, as is shown by a remarkable inscription credited to him:

> I did well unto god and man, to dead and living. Why have sickness, ill-health, misery and misfortune befallen me? I cannot away with the strife in my country and the dissensions in my family. Disturbing scandals oppress me alway. Misery of mind and of flesh bow me down; with cries of woe I bring my days to an end. On the day of the city-god, the day of the festival, I am wretched; death is seizing hold of me and bears me down. With lamentation and mourning I wail day and night, I groan, "O god, grant even to one who is impious that he may see thy light . . ."[21]

Poor old Ashurbanipal died in −633. There followed several short, disorderly reigns of undistinguished kings, who fought one another for the throne while more and more of the subject peoples revolted. The Assyrian Empire dissolved with startling swiftness.

In −612, an alliance of Scythians, Medes, and Babylonians conquered Assyria. In assailing Nineveh, the Medes took advantage of a flood on the Tigris to mount battering rams on rafts. The allies captured the capital and blotted it out. A ferocious yell of triumph went up from the Assyrians' victims: "Woe to the bloody city! . . . Nineveh is laid waste: who will bemoan her? . . . Thy shepherds slumber, O king of Assyria: thy nobles shall dwell in the dust: thy people is scattered upon the mountains, and no man gathereth them."[22]

Two centuries later, when the Ten Thousand passed that way, Nineveh was a mere field of ruins, and the scourge of Assyria was fading from the memories of men.

V

TYRE IN THE MIDST OF THE SEA

I HAVE SEEN OLD SHIPS THAT SAIL LIKE SWANS ASLEEP
BEYOND THE VILLAGE WHICH MEN STILL CALL TYRE,
WITH LEADEN AGE O'ERCARGOED, DIPPING DEEP
FOR FAMAGUSTA AND THE HIDDEN SUN
THAT RINGS BLACK CYPRUS WITH A LAKE OF FIRE . . .[1]

Flecker

36. Aerial view of modern Tyre, with the Northern Harbor at the left. (Courtesy of the Institut Français d'Archéologie, Beyrût.)

O<small>UR</small> knowledge of the ancient world has come down in spotty, capricious form. Some rulers have set up monuments inscribed with their deeds; others have not, or the monuments have perished. Almost all our knowledge of the Khmer kingdom of Cambodia and of the Kushite kingdom of the Sudan, for instance, comes from such monuments.

In other cases, the whims of fate have determined whether the history of a land should survive. Many ancient Egyptian manuscripts, though writ on fragile papyrus, have been preserved by Egypt's extreme aridity. The Mesopotamians wrote on tablets of clay, which were then baked brick-hard. Although awkwardly heavy—if there had been postmen in Babylon, they would have had to make their rounds in oxcarts laden with tons of written bricks—these durable tablets have come down in vast numbers. Many writings of the Greeks and the Romans survived because people were sufficiently interested in them to copy and recopy them down to the time when printing made duplication easy. And Jewish piety has preserved the histories of the minor kingdoms of Judah and Israel in rich (if not always trustworthy) detail.

In other great nations, such as the Persian, Seleucid, and Parthian empires in Iran, or the empires of pre-Muslim India, either not much was written, or what was written has mostly perished. In India, for example, people wrote on paper made from palm fronds, which soon disappeared in that land of climatic extremes, swarming insect life, and many destructive invasions.

As a result, beginning students of ancient history get the impression that during the Golden Age of Greece, for instance, the Greeks were the only people in the world who were really alive. It seems as if everyone else was standing around like waxworks, in suspended animation. Of course, that is not true. During the Golden Age of Greece, all along the Main Civilized Belt from Spain to China, teeming multitudes toiled. Everywhere princes preened; politicians plotted; priests prayed; merchants haggled; warriors swaggered; thinkers pondered; lovers sighed; drunkards reeled; poets declaimed; prophets ranted; sorcerers conjured; charlatans beguiled; slaves shirked; thieves filched; and people joked, quarreled, sang, wept, lusted, blundered, yearned, schemed, and carried on the business of living in quite as lively a fashion as the Greeks were doing.

But, because the Greeks put their experiences down in writing, and because luck has saved a small part of these writings, we know a lot about the Greeks. We know much, for instance, of the little brawls of their tiny city-states. On the other hand, we know almost nothing about the score of thunderous battles by which Darius the Great and his generals put down the many rival claimants to the Persian throne, although these battlefields may have seen as brilliant feats of generalship and as gallant deeds of dought as the fields of Leuktra and Koronea.

One folk whom time has buried in near-oblivion is the Phoenicians—the Canaanites who dwelt in a necklace of city-states along the Mediterranean coast between Mount Lebanon and the sea. Although they seem to have once possessed a considerable literature, only a few scraps of this have come down, and that by having been translated into Greek or Latin. To judge by these fragments, Phoenician writing does not appear to have amounted to much, but it might look more impressive if we had more of it. Josephus tells us that the Phoenician cities, especially Tyre, had kept extensive historical records. He quotes briefly from the Phoenician histories that two earlier historians, Dios and Menandros, had composed by examining these records.[2]

The histories of Dios and Menandros have otherwise perished. So have the many other local histories composed around the Mediterranean in classical times, with but a few exceptions like Aristotle's *Constitution of Athens* and less than half of Memnon's history of Herakleia Pontika.

The Phoenician religion never became a widespread and long-lived cult like Judaism. Neither did the Phoenician dialect of the Canaanite tongue become a general medium of discourse, as did Greek, so that an educated man had to know it. Without such extraneous supports, Phoenician records and literature perished for good and all in the fall of Phoenician cities. Sidon was destroyed by the Persians in −345, Tyre by Alexander in −332, Carthage by the Romans in −146, and Beyrût by Tryphon, the Seleucid king, in −140. So all the Phoenician history we have is what can be pieced together from a few inscriptions and casual mentions in Egyptian, Hebrew, Mesopotamian, Greek, and Latin writings.

From these scanty materials, we can compile a fairly continuous if sketchy history of the greatest Phoenician city of Canaan: Tyre. The modern Arabic-speaking Tyrians call their town Şûr. The ancient dwellers also called it Şûr, or perhaps Tsûr. The Greeks made that into Tyros, whence our modern name.

Archaeology furnishes a few clues only to the story of Tyre. The reason is simple. The land supplies abundant limestone for building. In fact, Mount Lebanon is practically one vast, solid mass, 100

37. Nineteenth-century Tyre, seen from the mainland. (From John Carne: *Syria, the Holy Land, Asia Minor, etc.*, Lon.: 1836.)

miles long, of elephant-gray limestone. Therefore, since time immemorial, Lebanese houses have been built of this material.

When a Tyrian house was demolished or was cast down by some catastrophe, the stones, being much more durable than mud brick, were not wasted. Instead of being allowed to lie where they had fallen to serve as a foundation for a new house, as was often done in lands where brick prevailed, they were thriftily gathered up and built into new walls, not only in Tyre itself but also as far away as Beyrût. Hence the present town of Tyre contains a few remains from medieval and Roman times but nothing identifiable as from the days of the famous King Hiram.

Archaeology has been more useful in elucidating the form of the harbors of ancient Tyre, since in this case the stones, being under water, were less easily salvaged. In the 1930s a French priest, Antoine Poidebard, explored these harbors. Père Poidebard lacked many scientific accessories of modern underwater archaeology, such as aqualungs, research submarines, and underwater television, but he made the most of what did exist. He reconnoitered the harbors by taking photographs from an airplane and by sending down Lebanese sponge divers. The actual work was done by a diver in the suit of the time, with bronze helmet and lead-soled shoes.

Poidebard supervised the work by peering down from the surface with a simple waterglass. One difficulty was that of finding an engineer

38. Nineteenth-century Tyre, showing the Northern Harbor. (From Louis Charles Lortet: *La Syrie d'aujourd'hui*, Paris: 1884.)

not subject to seasickness. Poidebard needed an engineer to run his apparatus, and bouncing around in a small boat on the Mediterranean chop gives a touch of *mal de mer* to any but the toughest old salts.

Like many other peoples, the ancient Tyrians averred that their city had been founded by the gods. In +1, a Hellenized Phoenician, Philon of Byblos, published a translation into Greek of the *Theology* of Sanchouniathôn of Berytos (our Beyrût or Beyrouth). Sanchouniathôn had lived long before; some said "at the time of the Trojan War,"[3] but that was guessing. Around +300 the Christian scholar Eusebius, in his *Preparation of the Gospel*, included excerpts from Philon's work, which tell us most of what we know about the Phoenician cosmogony.

In Philon's account, some of the Canaanite names were translated into Greek equivalents; some were transliterated and more or less mangled. The tale tells how:

> By Genos the son of Aeon and Protogonos were again begotten mortal children, whose names were Phos, Pur, and Phlox. These found out the method of generating fire by rubbing together pieces of wood, and taught men the use of it. These begat sons of vast bulk and height, whose names were given to the mountains which they occupied. Thus, from them were called Mount Cassius, and Libanus, and Antilibanus, and

Brathu. Of these men were begotten [through intercourse with] their mothers, Memrumus and Hypsuranius; the women of those times without shame having intercourse with any man they might chance to meet. Then Hypsuranius dwelt in Tyre, and he invented huts constructed of reeds and rushes, and [found out the use of] papyrus. And he fell into enmity with his brother Usous, who first invented a covering for the body, of the skins of the wild beasts which he could catch . . .[4]

And so on, through the inventors of ships and iron and fishhooks and sails and bricks and other useful things.

Herodotos said that the Phoenicians "dwelt anciently upon the Red Sea,"[5] which would put them in or near the land called the Negebh by the Hebrews. Later, he said, they migrated to Canaan. Some modern scholars agree with Herodotos. But, since any such migration took place before the Phoenicians began to keep written records, there is no solid evidence for or against the tale. All we know for sure is that, by the middle of the second millennium B.C., the Phoenicians were well settled on the Canaanite coast, where they became active as mariners and traders. The archaeological site that has so far yielded the oldest Phoenician traces is Byblos,[6] where they go back almost to −2000.

Furthermore, the Phoenicians developed their own system of writing from the Egyptian and perhaps from other systems then current in the Near East. They made the further advance of strictly limiting their signs to one letter per sound. In other words, they invented the alphabet, although the precise details of how they did this are obscure.[7]

Like the Hebrew and Arabic[8] alphabets derived from it, the Phoenician alphabet did not represent short vowels. Because of the peculiar structure of the Semitic languages (see Chapter III) this was no great handicap. The fact that there were only 20-odd symbols to learn, instead of 700-odd as in Egyptian, meant that for the first time literacy could become widespread among the masses instead of being the monopoly of a small class of professional scribes.

When the Greeks borrowed the Phoenician alphabet, around −1000, consonantal signs alone were not enough, because their Indo-European language did not have the Semitic consonantal structure. If an Arabic-speaker sees the symbols for K, T, and B, he knows that the word has something to do with writing and can probably guess the vowels from the context. If, however, an English-speaker sees the symbols for L, T, and R, without an indication of vowels, he cannot tell whether the word meant is "liter," "litter," "later," "letter." "latter," "lottery," "looter," "altar," "Altair," "ultra," and so on. Like most Semitic languages, however, Phoenician was much richer than Greek in the throaty sounds loosely called "gutturals" (velars, uvulars, pha-

ryngeals, and glottals). So the Greeks used some of the otherwise superfluous Phoenician letters for gutturals to represent their vowels.

The first hard historical facts that we have about Tyre come from
the Tell-el-Amarna letters, from the files of Ikhnaton of Egypt, who
reigned from −1375 to −1360. At this time, Egypt had ruled the land
of Canaan, which had been reduced to vassalage by Thothmes III a
century before. But now Egypt was fast losing its grip on this province
under the feckless rule of the visionary Ikhnaton. At least two factions,
both claiming loyalty to Egypt, struggled for supremacy in Phoenicia.
Abimilki, the governor of Tyre, wrote a series of letters, of which
seven have survived, pleading for help to withstand a siege by Governor
Zimrida of Sidon and the Amorite adventurer Aziru, leaders of the
opposing faction. One letter begins.

> To the king, my lord, my sun, my god, thus saith Abim-
> ilki, thy servant: "Seven times and seven times do I pros-
> trate myself at the feet of the king, my lord. I am the dust
> beneath the feet of the king, my lord, and upon that which he
> treadeth. O my king and my lord, thou are like unto the god
> Shamash and to the god Rimmon in heaven. Let the king give
> counsel to his servant! Now the king, my lord, hath appointed
> me the guardian of the city of Tyre, the Royal Handmaid, and
> I sent a report in a tablet unto the king, my lord; but I have
> received no answer thereunto . . ."[9]

A modern king—even so self-conceited a one as Louis XIV—
might if so addressed think that the speaker was being a little effusive;
but such language was usual in Abimilki's time. Abimilki's letters explained, over and over, that he needed wood, water, and soldiers. Even
twenty soldiers would have been a great help. Alas! it would seem that
no help came, for a later letter from King Ribadda of Byblos indicates
that the Tyrians eventually revolted and slew their governor. If poor
Abimilki was the first victim of a dilatory correspondent, he was not
the last. Over 3,000 years later, the British lost the American Revolutionary War in part because that paragon of incompetence, Colonial
Secretary Lord George Germain, being in haste to get away for a week-
end, could not be bothered to sign the letter that ordered Sir William
Howe to march up the Hudson to join St. Leger and Burgoyne. Some
things change but little with the ages.

After Abimilki's downfall, we have the names of a few kings of
Tyre but practically no hard historical facts about the city for the next
400 years. In later −XIV and in −XIII, under Seti I and Rameses II,
Egypt recovered its dominion in Canaan. Then, however, Egyptian rule

39. Tyre in the times of Hiram the Great. (Drawing by Roy G. Krenkel.)

faded away again, and no other imperial power arose for several centuries to take its place.

During these centuries of freedom from outside control, the peoples of this region developed a number of small, independent states: the realms of the Edomites, the Moabites, the Israelites, the Philistines, the Phoenicians, and Aramaeans, and others. The land was in constant turmoil from invasions and immigration. The Israelites and the Aramaeans pushed in from the east; the Philistines arrived by sea from the west.

About −970, Hiram the son of Abiba'al came to the throne of Tyre and reigned with great success for thirty-four years. We already know of his long and profitable partnership with Solomon. Besides his construction work for Solomon, he rebuilt the temples of Tyre, doubt-

40. Tyre: Ruins of the Roman and Byzantine periods; columns of the Roman market in the background. (Courtesy of Lionel Casson and the Pontificio Istituto Biblico, Rome.)

less in a style like that which his workmen had bestowed upon Solomon's Temple. He enlarged Tyre by adding made land on the eastern side of the main island and laid out a forum on this extension.

If we knew more about Hiram, we might well deem him a greater king than Solomon. Five miles southwest of Tyre, in a small valley, a huge, plain sarcophagus (long since broken into and emptied) stands on a massive stone pedestal. This goes by the name of Qabr Hirâm, the Tomb of Hiram. The tradition that attributes this tomb to Hiram may be as worthless as those that assign scores of sites in Jerusalem to incidents in the lives of biblical worthies. Still, nothing actually rules out the possibility that the great Hiram may after all have slept his last sleep in this monument.

After Hiram, Tyre flourished for another 400 years as the largest and richest of the Phoenician cities. During this time, we know the names of the kings but very few facts about their reigns. Such information as we have is mostly in connection with the Israelite kingdoms and is related in the Bible and Josephus.

In early —IX, the priest Ithoba'al murdered the then king of Tyre, a descendant of Hiram, and seized the throne. To strengthen his shaky position, he married his daughter Jezebel to King Ahab of Israel. Jezebel worshiped the chief god of Tyre, called Ba'al, "lord," or Melqarth,[10] "ruler of the city." (He may also have had a "true name," kept secret from everyone but the priests and therefore lost to history.)

Jezebel tried—whether for ideological or for political reasons—to foster the worship of Ba'al in Israel. The Yahvist priesthood, however, was not prepared to allow the slightest competition if it could help it. Poor Ahab found himself in the middle, between the strong-minded queen on the one hand and the fanatical priesthood, led by the prophet Elijah, on the other. This strife continued for years, with the gangsters of each faction murdering members of the rival faction as opportunity offered.

Ahab, who seems to have had some statesmanlike qualities, kept the balance through an unquiet reign of twenty-two years. In —853, he was mortally wounded in a battle with the Syrians. He was succeeded by an older son and, when that young man died, by a younger son, Jehoram.

Meanwhile, Ahab's and Jezebel's daughter Athaliah had married the king of Judah. When he died, she ran the kingdom through her compliant son, Ahaziah.

When Jehoram of Israel was wounded in another battle with the Damascenes, a Yahvist general named Jehu usurped the throne and had Jezebel thrown out of a palace window. The old lady had put on cosmetics to show that she could die like a queen; hence the term "painted Jezebel." The pejorative connotation of the phrase is due to the fact that her side lost, while the winners—the Yahvists—wrote the history.

Jehu lured the two kings to a parley and had them killed. Then he massacred the kinsmen and supporters of the late King Ahab. In Judah, the dowager queen Athaliah tried to keep power by slaughtering the males of the house of David, but after a few years the prophet Jehoiada fomented a conspiracy to murder Athaliah and put Jehoash, a princeling who had escaped her attentions, in her place. The Melqarthists were slain or driven out, and so ended Tyrian influence in the Israelite kingdoms.

The Canaanite coast has the typical Mediterranean climate, with wet, windy winters, in which spells of heavy rain alternate with long, clear stretches. Then comes a long, hot, dry, cloudless summer, with mild winds. The climate has often been compared to that of southern California. Thunderstorms occur, but only rarely; hence lightning and thunder were regarded as omens throughout the ancient Mediterranean lands. Nobody would bother to read omens from lightning and thunder in places where they occur almost daily.

As I explained in the first chapter, an ideal site for a commercial city is either at the junction of trade routes or at a transshipment point— that is, where goods are unloaded from one conveyance and reloaded on another. This applies whether the conveyances are asses, camels, trucks, trains, or ships, and whether the ships are propelled by sails or by engines.

Tyre had both advantages. It bestrode the coastal trade route from Egypt to Asia Minor and, at the same time, it was the transshipment point for goods moving between Syria and Cyprus, Crete, Rhodes, and other parts of the Inner Sea. The trade route from Damascus to the coast wound around the southern end of Mount Lebanon, passing Mount Hermon and following the Litani River to the sea a few miles north of Tyre.

Tyre grew up, however, not at the mouth of the Litani, but farther south, where a rocky island rose from the sparkling sea 1,000 yards offshore. To be exact, the original town, later called Palaityros or "Old Tyre," grew up on the shore facing the island. The new city was built on the island, and thither the king and the important people soon moved.

When they took to seafaring, the Phoenicians learned that the safest place to store goods in transit was a fortified offshore island, near enough to the shore to make the boat trip easy but far enough out so that no hostile army or sudden swarm of raiding nomads could get to it by wading. They must needs build boats or rafts, and the islanders' navy could easily break up such craft. Hence trading cities arose not only at Tyre but also at Arados,[11] 120 miles to the north at the other end of Phoenicia. Here a similar island stands a mile and three-quarters from the mainland. Where no island was to be had, a cape or peninsula, as at Sidon[12] and Beyrût, would do.

Another advantage of an offshore island was that the shoreward side of the island provided a lee for anchorage. The Canaanite coast is quite straight, not deeply indented like the coasts of Greece and Norway. It therefore has but few good natural harbors.

The island of Tyre had a trapezoidal shape, measuring about 1,000 yards from north to south and half that from east to west. There was a cluster of islets south of the main island, on the largest of which was built the temple of Melqarth. One of Hiram's works was to join this islet with the main island. An older temple of Melqarth at Palaityros continued in use.

The main island was surrounded by a massive, well-built stone wall. Inside the city, limitations of space caused architects to build apartment houses of several stories. Writing at the beginning of the Christian Era, Strabon the geographer said that the houses of Tyre were even taller than those of Rome, which were limited by law to 70 feet.[13] Several times in its history, Tyre suffered from earthquakes, which brought these skyscrapers tumbling down with frightful havoc. But each time the Tyrians dug themselves out of the ruins and rebuilt their city.

Using the local pudding stone from the mainland, the Tyrians built up the reefs under the adjacent waters into an elaborate system of

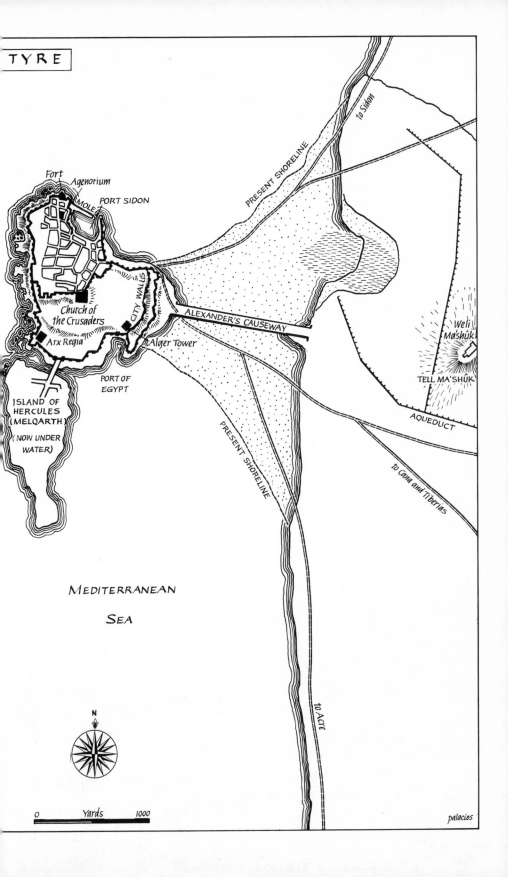

TYRE

Fort
Agenorium
MOLE
PORT SIDON
PRESENT SHORELINE
to Sidon
Church of
the Crusaders
CITY WALLS
Arx Regia
ALEXANDER'S CAUSEWAY
Alger Tower
PORT OF
EGYPT
Weli
Mashúk
TELL MA'SHÚK
AQUEDUCT
ISLAND OF
HERCULES
(MELQARTH)
(NOW UNDER
WATER)
PRESENT
SHORELINE
to Cana and Tiberias
MEDITERRANEAN
SEA
to Acre
N
0   Yards   1000

palacios

breakwaters, thus providing the city with two good all-weather harbors. Poidebard found that the stones of these breakwaters had been set as headers—that is, with their long axes perpendicular to the wall—to make the most of their strength.

In accordance with the usage of the time, these harbors were named for the destinations towards which they looked. Thus the harbor on the northeastern side of the island was called the Sidonian Harbor, while that on the southeast was called the Egyptian Harbor.

Tyre was not merely a transshipment point. Like other Mediterranean lands, Phoenicia produced wheat, barley, olives, and wine, with a surplus in good years for export. It also grew oats, beans, vetch, figs, pomegranates, and nuts.

More important yet was timber. In those days, vast forests of the cedar of Lebanon, *Cedrus libani*, covered Mount Lebanon and the adjacent hills. The tree grows to enormous size if left alone for a few centuries, and the timber was much sought after for large buildings in Egypt and Mesopotamia, which had little good building timber of their own.

As a result of thousands of years of improvident cutting, the cedar of Lebanon is now restricted to a few groves in its homeland. It is in no danger of extinction, however, because it has been planted as an ornamental tree in many other parts of the world, where it thrives.

41. Tyre: Ruins of the Roman theater, with columns of the Roman market in the background. (Courtesy of the Lebanon Tourist and Information Office, New York.)

I can see several out my window, in southeastern Pennsylvania, as I write. The Phoenicians also sold the timber of other trees, notably pine, fir, and terebinth, and the pitch distilled from pine for coating ships.

Another Phoenician resource was its red and purple dyes. The famous "Tyrian purple"—actually a deep crimson—was obtained from a shellfish. This was a gastropod (that is, a mollusk with a single, spirally-twisted shell, like a snail) of the family Muricidae. The murices are peculiar not only in their fantastically spiny shells but also in having an internal sac into which they secrete the chemical muricine, which furnishes the dye. Since the animals are not very large, an average murex furnishes one good-sized drop of dye; but several productive species, especially *Purpura haemostoma*, dwelt in the waters of the Canaanite coast. The Phoenicians sent divers to gather the murices, boiled them, and extracted the sacs. Travelers through Palaityros complained that the old town stank from the dye works, but Tyrian purple colored the stripes on the tunics of Roman knights and senators.

In addition, the Phoenicians sold textiles dyed with a paler shade of red, from insects found on a species of oak. This is the "crimson" of the Old Testament. Other good, fast dyes were few, and brightly-colored garments were costly. People whose ideas of the ancient world have been formed by the movies may think of an ancient crowd as a colorful spectacle. In fact, such a crowd would probably look rather drab, with a preponderance of undyed garments in natural whites, grays, beiges, and browns.

Plinius the Elder to the contrary notwithstanding,[14] the Phoenicians did not invent glass. Glass had been known in Egypt and in Mesopotamia for over 1,000 years before the Canaanites took up its manufacture in the early first millennium B.C. Glass was at first made as a colored paste with which to coat beads, to make them look like precious stones. Since the glass industry was in its infancy, such beads must have been fairly costly in themselves. Later, the Egyptians and the Mesopotamians began to make small bottles to hold cosmetics and even some larger vessels.

Then the Phoenicians and their neighbors, the Syrians and the Israelites, took up glassmaking. The Phoenicians in particular, using the excellent sand from the mouth of the Belos River, developed commercial lines of bowls and other vessels. In early Achaemenid times, glass was so precious that only the Persian King of Kings and his grandees could afford to drink from goblets of glass. A few centuries later, thanks to Syro-Phoenician glassmakers, nearly everybody could afford this luxury, instead of drinking from vessels of metal or pottery. All this glass was cast, built up, or ground; glass blowing was not invented until —I.

The Phoenicians exported these materials to pay for their imports: silver, iron, tin, and lead from Spain, slaves and bronze vessels from Ionia, linen from Egypt, and sheep and goats from Arabia. To keep this traffic flowing and to handle the many commodities for which they acted as carriers and middlemen, their mariners set up trading ports here and there about the Mediterranean. They preferred offshore islands, as at Motya at the western end of Sicily, and at Gades[15] at the mouth of the Cilbus in southwestern Spain (or, as we should say, at Cádiz at the mouth of the Guadalete). Or they chose an easily-defended peninsula, as at Carthage.

In time, many of these trading posts grew into colonies. The Phoenicians had little xenophobia and no apparent objection to mixed marriages. Such a tolerant attitude helped their colonies to grow. Nevertheless, their numbers were small in proportion to the vast area they covered. Their ships went out into the Atlantic, where they sailed north to pick up British tin to alloy with copper to make bronze. Whether they actually got to Britain or only to some intermediate place of exchange is a disputed question.

They also sailed south to trade with the natives of Negro Africa. Since the Africans were understandably fearful of being kidnapped for slaves, the Phoenicians worked out a method of silent barter to reassure them. As Herodotos described it:

> There is a country in Libya, and a nation, beyond the Pillars of Herakles, which they are wont to visit, where they no sooner arrive but forthwith they unlade their wares, and, having disposed them after an orderly fashion along the beach, leave them, and, returning aboard their ships, raise a great smoke. The natives, when they see the smoke, come down to the shore, and, laying out to view so much gold as they think the worth of the wares, withdraw to a distance. The Carthaginians upon this come ashore and look. If they think the gold is enough, they take it and go their way; but if it does not seem to them sufficient, they go aboard ship once more, and wait patiently. Then the others approach and add to their gold, till the Carthaginians are content. Neither party deals unfairly with the other: for they themselves never touch the gold until it comes up to the worth of their goods, nor do the natives ever carry off the goods till the gold is taken away.[16]

The Phoenicians developed the art of barter to so high a degree that they tended to stick to it even after money came into general use. This conservatism finally cost them much of their commercial preëminence.

42. Tyre: Excavation of Roman and Byzantine houses. (Courtesy of the Lebanon Tourist and Information Office, New York.)

The greatest Tyrian colonizing effort came about as a result of a domestic feud. According to tradition, which may or may not be true, Carthage was founded by Tyrians in −814. King Pygmalion[17] of Tyre had a sister, Elissa, who was married to her uncle, a rich and aristocratic priest of Melqarth named Acherbas. Elissa was a great-niece of Jezebel, who married King Ahab of Israel. Pygmalion murdered Acherbas in hopes of seizing his fortune. Elissa fled to the West with several shiploads of her partisans, including the High Priest of Ashtarth[18] and eighty virgins who had been destined for temple prostitution. Founded by so large a group at the start, Carthage grew to overshadow its parent city.

The Phoenician religion was much like the other West Semitic polytheisms, with a chief god ruling a bureaucracy of subordinate, departmental gods. These included such deities as Resheph, the god of lightning; Asherah, the sea goddess; Eshmun, the healing god; and Ashtarth, the fertility goddess. Ashtarth was the western version of the Mesopotamian Ishtar. There was also a group of godlets, the Pataikoi or Pataecian gods, who ruled ships and navigation. Their statuettes were mounted on Phoenician ships.

Besides the usual round of festivals and animal sacrifices, Phoenician religious practices included some usages strange to us but widespread in the ancient world. One was temple prostitution. Young women (and boys, too, for clients whose tastes ran in that direction) were expected as a matter of pious duty to spend time in a temple, accepting the sexual solicitations of all comers. We may assume that the temple kept the money earned by these devotees; we may even suspect that this income was the basic reason for the practice, whatever theological justifications the priests advanced for it. In later times, women might be excused from such service at the price of having their heads shaven.

The other egregious feature of Punic worship was the sacrifice of children in times of peril. For example, when between −310 and −307 Carthage was besieged by the Sicilian Greeks under the *tyrannos* or dictator Agathokles, the Carthaginians, like many other folk, thought that the gods were punishing them for neglecting their religious duties.

> In their zeal to make amends for their omission, they selected two hundred of the noblest children and sacrificed them publicly; and others who were under suspicion [of having escaped previous sacrifices by subterfuge] sacrificed themselves voluntarily, in number not less than three hundred. There was in their city a great bronze image of Cronus [Ba'al Hammon], extending its hands, the palms up and sloping toward the ground, so that each of the children when placed thereon rolled down and fell into a sort of gaping pit filled with fire.[19]

This story has been confirmed by archaeological research at Carthage. In 1920, in the precinct of Tanith (the Carthaginian name for Ashtarth), in a section of the town called "Salammbô" after the heroine of Flaubert's novel of that name, were discovered thousands of urns containing the charred bones of children. The Punics reasoned: How better to convince the gods of one's sincere devotion to them than by giving up to them one's dearest possessions?

No positive evidence, either literary or archaeological, has been found to show that such sacrifices obtained at Tyre. It would be surprising if they did not, since they were general among other Phoenicians and were practiced in the Tyrian colony of Carthage down into Roman times. The Romans detested the Phoenicians for the custom and,

43. Byzantine gardens excavated at Tyre, with a monumental Roman arch in the background. (Courtesy of the Lebanon Tourist and Information Office, New York.)

after they had conquered Punic Africa, gradually stamped it out. In view of the Romans' notion of public games suitable for amusing the mob, however, a modern man will not accord them much moral superiority over the despised Punics.

So Tyre throve. To the rustic Israelites, looking down with awe and envy from their barren hills, Tyre seemed a glittering stronghold of wealth, beauty, luxurious refinement, delicate craftsmanship, and commercial acumen. The prophet Ezekiel, even while prophesying the fall of Tyre to Nebuchadrezzar's Babylonians, rhapsodized:

> And say unto Tyrus, O thou that art situate at the entry of the sea, which art a merchant of the people for many isles, Thus saith the Lord God; O Tyrus, thou hast said, I am of perfect beauty. Thy borders are in the midst of the sea, thy builders have perfected thy beauty. They have made all thy ship boards of fir trees of Sennir: they have taken cedars from Lebanon to make masts for thee. Of the oaks of Bashan they have made thine oars; the company of the Ashurites have made thy benches of ivory, brought out of the isles of Chittim. Fine linen with broidered work from Egypt was that which thou spreadest forth to be thy sail; blue and purple from the isles of Elishah was that which covered thee.[20]

44. Tyre: Roman monumental arch of +II. (Courtesy of Middle East Airways.)

The period of independence for the petty states of Canaan, which began with the collapse of Egyptian power in the land around −1200 and reached its climax with the monarchies of Solomon and Hiram, did not long endure. In −876, the mighty and merciless Ashurnasirpal of Assyria made his grand tour of the western lands, extorting tribute from all the states, including Tyre, in his path. His successors continued to collect this tribute, while Elissa fled from her brother to found Carthage.

In the next century, −VIII, Tyre and Sidon were united for several decades under a single rule. An energetic king named Luli or Eluleus ruled not only Tyre and Sidon but Cyprus as well. Finding Luli not submissive enough, Shalmaneser V, Sargon II, and finally Sennacherib in turn besieged Tyre. None, however, took the city.

To strengthen their defenses, the Phoenicians had lately invented a warship of a new kind, better than anything that could be brought against it. This was the diere or bireme. Whereas earlier galleys had been simply oversized rowboats, with twenty-five or so rowers in single file on each side, the new ship had rowers in pairs, in a staggered arrangement. The ship also had a ram at the bow, strong bracing to take the shock of ramming, and a solid deck over the rowers' heads for the sailors and marines. Since the ship employed twice as much muscle power for a unit of length, it was much faster than the older, single-banked type.

Although not especially warlike—they were businessmen, not soldiers—the Phoenicians defended their cities with fanatical courage and stubbornness. These qualities, as well as their naval might, enabled the Tyrians to hold out against the Assyrian army, the strongest of its time. At the end of Sennacherib's siege, however, Luli appears to have given up his claim to the rule of Tyre and Sidon and to have retired to Cyprus, while the Assyrians appointed a governor for the Phoenician cities.

Sennacherib's death led to the usual revolt of the subject provinces of the Assyrian Empire. In restoring his realm, Esarhaddon attacked both Tyre and Sidon. Tyre held out; but Sidon, not being on an island, was not so fortunate. Esarhaddon took the city and captured its king, Abimilkut. He cut off Abimilkut's head and that of another local kinglet, Sanduarri. He paraded a couple of his eminent captives through Nineveh with the heads of the late kings hanging by cords from their necks.

Ashurbanipal, the last strong Assyrian king, besieged Tyre in −668 but failed to capture it, although the Tyrians agreed at the last to terms and gave up tribute and hostages. Assyria fell, but the Neo-Babylonian Empire took its place. For thirteen years, from −585 to −572, Nebuchadrezzar II besieged Tyre, which finally submitted on terms like those with Ashurbanipal. So long a siege gravely damaged Tyre's commerce, so that Sidon took its place as the leading Phoenician city.

During this depressed period, the Tyrians ousted their king and set up a republic, like those with which the Greek city-states had been experimenting for the past two centuries. This lasted only seven or eight years before the royalist party again got control and installed the kings once more. Then Babylon fell to Cyrus, and Phoenicia became the fifth satrapy of the Persian Empire. The Phoenician kings became puppets with little power. Of most of them, not even the names are known.

On the whole, the Phoenician cities did fairly well under Persian rule. The Persian Empire was neither so bad as Greek historians were wont to consider it nor so good as some of its modern apologists say; but it was a decided advance in several respects upon its predecessors. Phoenician ships furnished the backbone of the Persian navy in the Mediterranean and were involved in the Graeco-Persian wars, and the Phoenician cities suffered when this navy was defeated in these wars. The Phoenicians revolted against the harsh rule of the able but cruel and gloomy Artaxerxes III Ochus in −352. Betrayed by their own king and facing the downfall of their city, the Sidonians burned up themselves and their families.

The destruction of Sidon led to the revival of Tyre. This lasted until Alexander the Great, during his conquest of the Persian Empire, attacked Tyre in —332. He wanted Tyre in order to secure his rear against the Phoenician-Persian navy before plunging into the illimitable distances of Asia. The Tyrians sent him gifts and offered the kind of conditional submission that had worked with the Assyrian and Chaldaean kings. When, however, they learned that Alexander insisted on entering the city with his army, they defied him.

Characteristically, Alexander showed much more originality than the kings who had besieged the place before. He demolished Palaityros and dumped the materials into the sea to build a causeway out to the island. The six-month siege was a tremendous operation, with vast ingenuity and heroism on both sides. When the city fell, most of it was burned. In revenge for the murder of his heralds, Alexander crucified 2,000 young Tyrians and enslaved 30,000 of the people. Eight thousand had perished in the siege. More thousands either had escaped to Carthage or were given refuge on the ships of the Sidonians, who were serving under Alexander. These figures suggest a total population on the order of 100,000.

Since the causeway now joined Tyre to the shore, Tyre no longer enjoyed its insularity. Moreover, storms and currents piled up sand on both sides of this causeway, so that Tyre became a cape or peninsula, a mile wide at the base. The city revived as people moved in—some strangers and some refugees who had fled from Alexander. But it was no longer the Tyre of Hiram.

During the Persian rule, the Phoenician nationality had dissolved away. The Phoenician dialect of Canaanitish had died out, to be replaced by the related Aramaic tongue, which also took the place of Hebrew in Judaea. At the same time, Greek culture began to charm the Phoenicians, as it did other Near Eastern peoples. Little by little, the Phoenicians absorbed Hellenic influence and thus became just one more set of semi-Hellenized Syrians.

Even the Phoenicians' commercial supremacy withered. Greek art, manufacture, and commerce, advancing rapidly, drove the Punic traders from the Aegean. They could not compete with the beautiful new Greek artifacts. Neither could they hold their own in an economy dominated by money. They were reduced to mass-producing cheap copies of Greek and Egyptian art objects and bartering these gimcracks to the eager barbarians on the fringes of civilization, from Scythia to Portugal and from Senegal to Britain. During the following Hellenistic and Roman periods, the very name of "Phoenician" dropped out of use.

During the Hellenistic Age, Tyre was snatched back and forth between the Seleucids and the Ptolemies. Under Rome, Tyre developed considerable intellectual life. It gave birth to several philosophers and the noted geographer Marinus, the main source of the more famous

45. Qabr Ḥiram or Tomb of Hiram, near Tyre. (From Louis Charles Lortet: *La Syrie d'aujourd'hui*, Paris: 1884.)

Claudius Ptolemaeus. In +193, when Septimius Severus and Pescennius Niger were fighting for the emperorship, the Tyrians chose the side of Severus and were massacred by Niger's troops, although Niger was finally defeated and slain.

With the Christian Era, religious partisanship and theological fanaticism were added to all the other causes of strife among men. Such conflict had been known before, as in Israel between Yahvists and Melqarthists, in Iran between Zoroastrians and Mithraists, or in India between Hinduists and Buddhists. But such conflicts had been few and minor. The Christian Era ushered in an age of holy war that convulsed the world for over a millennium and a half.

In early +VII, for instance, Tyre saw a frenzied conflict between the Jews and the Christians, since the Jews regarded the Christians as detestable heretics, while to the Christians the Jews were the murderers of their demigod. The Jews besieged the city and demolished the churches outside the walls, while the Christians inside cut off Jewish heads and threw them over the wall, 100 heads for each church.

A few years later, the town passed into the rule of Muḥammad's Arabs. At first the conquering Arabs treated their Jewish and Christian subjects with tolerance. Later the Muslims imposed many petty harassments and humiliations upon the infidels, such as making them wear distinctive dress and forbidding them to ride horseback or to hold offices of trust and honor with the government. Hence most of the *kafirîn* (unbelievers) in time accepted Islâm.

46. Medieval castle, the Qal'at al-Baḥr, at Sidon (Ṣaidâ), showing the drums of classical columns built into its walls.

The Crusaders under King Baldwin of Jerusalem besieged but failed to take Tyre in 1111–12; when the defenders one night destroyed the besiegers' siege engines by incendiary missiles, the Westerners panicked and fled to Acre despite Baldwin's efforts to rally them. They tried again in 1124, and this time the city surrendered on terms. A Turkish general, Tuktagin of Damascus, had tried but failed to break the siege; now he came to arrange terms. True to their ancient traditions, the Tyrians made the best bargain they could. Those who wished to leave might do so with their movable possessions; the rest might remain by paying a ransom. To make sure that the terms were kept, the Christian and Muslim armies formed two long lines facing each other, and the Tyrians marched out between them.

Saladin besieged Tyre unsuccessfully in 1187–88. In 1291, the city fell to Khalil, the son of Sultan Qalâ'un of Egypt. Khalil destroyed the city even more thoroughly than Alexander had done.

For the next 500 years, Tyre, almost uninhabited, lay in ruins. In +XIX came a minor revival. But the Damascus-Beyrût railway, passing directly over the saddle on Mount Lebanon instead of around its southern end, finished Tyre as a major port. Today it is merely a prosaic little Lebanese coastal town, with a population around 10,000. When I was there in 1960, there was not much to see, save some excavated building foundations of Roman and Byzantine times, since nearly all the ancient masonry aboveground had disappeared or had been reused.

Furthermore, one was not allowed to take photographs; a mere 15 miles from the Israeli border, Tyre was in a "military zone." The historically-minded visitor would have preferred Sidon, which at least had the visible remains of an ancient harbor and a ruined thirteenth-century castle, the Qal'at al-Baḥr, with the marble drums of classical columns built into its walls.

In the subsequent decade, however, excavations by the Lebanese Antiquity Service have exposed much more of the ancient city. The Roman hippodrome has been dug out, and a chariot race was recently staged in it, the proceeds being used for charity. Lebanese soldiers in Roman costume drove one-horse chariots instead of the two-horse or four-horse vehicles of classical times; but then, well-trained chariot horses are extremely hard to come by nowadays.

If peace ever comes to that part of the world and the excavations continue, Tyre may well become a tourist attraction comparable to Ephesos. In any case, as a symbol of the peaceful, civilizing influence of commerce, Tyre will live on in literature and imagination as long as some men would rather trade goods than take them by force or fraud.

VI

BABYLON, THE GATE OF THE GODS

FOR I HAVE SEEN THE LIZARDS CRAWL
THROUGH HIGH BELSHAZZAR'S HALL
WHEN GHOSTLY SHADOW PETALS FALL,
IN BABYLON, DEAD BABYLON.
AND MANY A GOLDEN-GIRDLED SPIRE
LIKE MOLTEN MOONLIGHT VEINED WITH FIRE
THAT FELL BEFORE THE AGE'S IRE
IN BABYLON, FAR BABYLON.[1]

Howard

47. Remains of the ziggurat of Ur, in southern Iraq, with the excavated ruins of the city of Ur in the foreground. This is the best-
preserved of the many ziggurats of ancient Mesopotamia. (Courtesy
of the University Museum of the University of Pennsylvania.)

W HEN a site has sufficient natural advantages for a city, the city that arises there will be practically immortal. No matter how often or how thoroughly it is destroyed, it will arise again, either on the same site or on one nearby. Babylon is a case in point.

A French writer once called central Iraq—anciently Babylonia— "the beige country."[2] So it is: vast, flat, and everywhere the same dreary beige or dun or tan. Even the houses, made of local brick, are of this same sad hue. In ancient times, before modern structures and motor vehicles invaded the land, the monotony must have been even more pronounced.

This drab, featureless plain is not utterly flat. Besides the two great rivers that wind across it, it is broken at wide intervals by mounds or hillocks, marking the sites of former towns or cities. In the days before sewers and municipal trash and garbage disposal, such a city tended to rise with the centuries, because more material was brought into it than was taken out. This material was eventually mixed with the dirt of the streets, which rose in consequence.

Within the past century, one could guess the age of an Iraqi city house by its level. If its floor was on the street level or higher, it was new. As it aged, the street level rose before it, so that one had to reach its front door by steps going down. In time it would be demolished and a new and higher house erected on its rubble. When the city was abandoned, the mound remained, like an artificial hill. In Arabic-speaking lands, such mounds are called "tells."[3]

Besides the tells, the plain was once (and to an extent still is) crossed here and there by a canal between a pair of spoil banks, carrying the water of the Tigris or the Euphrates to irrigate the vast checker-work of farms. Along these banks, date palms grew in endless rows. Farmers raised water from the canals to their fields by means of bucket hoists and treadwheels.

With the best of care, such a canal would remain serviceable only about 1,000 years. The plain was therefore crisscrossed by the remains of abandoned canals, each marked by a pair of low, parallel ridges remaining from the original spoil banks. Traces of such ridges can be seen to this day.

The country is almost completely without stone, save for some cliffs, which furnish a poor limestone, near Uruk in the South. Hence kings had to import stone, at no small expense, for such things as statues and door sockets.

Like most parts of the hot-dry belt, Babylonia has a short wet season in winter, with usually mild temperatures. Snow and frosty days do visit the land, but not often. Then there is a very hot, dry summer. The beige-colored soil is a fine powder, which when wet becomes the most slippery, gooey mud on earth. Having slithered and staggered through this gumbo, I could imagine the brave soldiers of Cyrus and Alexander and Trajan trying to fight in it and falling down with a terrible clatter.

The rest of the year, the soil dries out to a fine powder, easily stirred up by the freakish weather of a Babylonian spring. Then one may encounter a blinding mixture of dust, rain, or hail in any proportion. In 1836, the British government sent two paddle-wheel steamers, the *Tigris* and the *Euphrates,* up the Euphrates River on a surveying expedition. On a fair, bright, calm day, a vast black cloud suddenly boiled up in the southwest. As a survivor described it:

> As the cloud neared us, the sky assumed an appearance such as we had never before witnessed, and which was awful and terrific in the extreme. A dense black arch enveloped the whole of the horizon, and the space beneath the arch was filled up with a body of dust, of a brownish orange colour, whirling round, and at the same time advancing towards us with fearful rapidity . . . At this moment the hurricane came upon us—a warm dry wind laden with the fragrance of the aromatic plants of the wilderness, followed in a few moments by a tremendous blast of wind with some rain in large drops. The crash broke upon us like heaven's own artillery, and the hurricane seemed as if bent upon hurling both steamers at once to the bottom of the foaming river.[4]

The sandstorm did capsize the *Tigris,* with a loss of twenty lives.

In summer, the Babylonian temperature runs up daily well over 100° F. Onesikritos, a savant who went with Alexander to India, noted that at Susa, northeast of Babylon, "when the sun is hottest, at noon, the lizards and snakes could not cross the streets in the city quickly enough to prevent their being burnt to death in the middle of the streets," and that "barley spread out in the sun bounces like parched barley in ovens."[5]

Climate and soil conspired to make the people of the plain of Shinar unwarlike. The weather was too hot for fighting in summer; the mud was too slippery in winter. In spring the men were busy harvesting wheat and barley; in autumn they were occupied picking dates. And the canals needed constant attention to keep them from silting up or shifting their beds. There were only short periods in the spring and the fall when warfare was practical. Hence, lacking practice at the bloody art, the Babylonian never became a great warrior.

48. Babylon: Scale model of the outermost part of the Ishtar Gate, at the entrance to the site.

True, in times when the land was divided amongst small city-states, these fought each other often enough; but in dealing with fighters from the outer world, the Babylonians usually came out second best. During two or three short periods, under exceptional kings, the men of the Euphratean plain became the masters of empire. These empires, however, proved ephemeral, and for most of the last 4,000 years the Land Between the Rivers has been ruled by foreigners—Elamites, Kassites, Persians, Macedonians, Parthians, Romans, Arabs, Turks, and Britons.

In the midst of the plain of Shinar, for 3,000 years or more, stood one of the most famous cities in the entire world, and one of the greatest of ancient times. This was Bâb-ilû,[6] the Gate of the Gods, which we (after the Greeks) call Babylon.

After Nebuchadrezzar carried off the Jews, Hebrew prophets fiercely denounced Babylon and delighted in predicting its doom: "And Babylon, the glory of kingdoms, the beauty of the Chaldees' excellency, shall be as when God overthrew Sodom and Gomorrah. It shall never

be inhabited . . . but the wild beasts of the desert shall lie there . . .
For thou hast trusted in thy wickedness . . . Thy wisdom and thy
knowledge, it hath perverted thee . . . Therefore shall evil come upon
thee . . . Stand now with thine enchantments, and with the multitude
of thy sorceries . . . And Babylon shall become heaps, a dwellingplace
for dragons, an astonishment, and a hissing, without an inhabitant."[7]

Actually, Babylon is not known to have been any wickeder than
other great cities, and the Babylonian Captivity seems to have been
milder than the Assyrian. Unlike the "Lost Ten Tribes of Israel,"
the Judaeans were at least allowed to keep their national identity. Nonetheless, in Hebrew writing, "Babylon" became a symbol for depravity.
When the author of Revelation wished to denounce Nero's Rome without courting martyrdom, he pretended to revile Babylon: "Babylon is
fallen, is fallen, that great city, because she made all nations drink of
the wine of the wrath of her fornication."[8]

In the middle of −V, Herodotos visited Babylon, then under Persian
rule. Thirty-odd years before, King Xerxes had punished Babylon for a
rebellion, but it was still "the biggest and most populous city in the
whole world—and all built of mud, without marble or stone."[9] Herodotos
wrote a lucid if sometimes inaccurate description:

> The city stands on a broad plain, and is an exact square,
> fifteen miles in length each way, so that the entire circuit
> is sixty miles. While such is its size, in magnificence there
> is no other city that approaches it. It is surrounded, in the
> first place, by a broad and deep moat, full of water, behind
> which rises a wall fifty royal cubits in width, and 200 in
> height . . .
>
> The city is divided into two portions by the river which
> runs through the midst of it. This river is the Euphrates,
> a broad, deep, swift stream, which rises in Armenia, and empties
> itself in the Red sea. The city wall is brought down on
> both sides to the edge of the stream; thence from the corners
> of the wall, there is carried along each bank of the river a
> fence of burnt bricks. The houses are mostly three and four
> stories high; the streets all run in straight lines, not only
> those parallel to the river, but also the cross streets which
> lead down to the waterside. At the river end of these cross
> streets are low gates in the fence that skirts the stream, which
> are, like the great gates in the outer wall, of brass, and open
> on the water.
>
> The outer wall is the main defence of the city. There
> is, however, a second inner wall, of less thickness than the
> first, but very little inferior in strength. The centre of each

division of the town was occupied by a fortress. In the one stood the palace of the kings, surrounded by a wall of great strength and size: in the other was the sacred precinct of Zeus Belus, an enclosure a quarter of a mile square, with gates of solid brass; which was also remaining in my time. In the middle of the precinct there was also a tower of solid masonry, a furlong in length and breadth, upon which was raised a second tower, and on that a third, and so on up to eight. The ascent to the top is on the outside, by a path which winds round all the towers. When one is about half way up, one finds a resting-place and seats, where persons are wont to sit some time on their way to the summit. On the topmost tower there is a spacious temple, and inside the temple stands a couch of unusual size, richly adorned, with a golden table by its side. There is no statue of any kind set up in the place, nor is the chamber occupied of nights by any one but a single native woman, who, as the Chaldaeans, the priests of this god, affirm, is chosen for himself by the deity out of all the women of the land.

49. Excavations on the site of ancient Babylon.

50. Babylon in the time of Nebuchadrezzar the Great. (Drawing by Roy G. Krenkel.)

They also declare (but I do not believe it) that the god comes down in person into this chamber, and sleeps upon the couch . . .

Below, in the same precinct, there is a second temple, in which is a sitting figure of Zeus, all of gold. Before the figure stands a large golden table, and the throne whereon it sits, and the base on which the throne is placed, are likewise of gold. The Chaldaeans told me that all the gold together was 800 talents' worth. Outside the temple are two altars, one of solid gold, on which it is only lawful to offer sucklings; the other a common altar, but of great size, on which full-grown animals are sacrificed. It is also on the great

altar that the Chaldaeans burn the frankincense, which is offered
to the amount of 1,000 talents' worth, every year, at the
festival of the god. In the time of Cyrus there was likewise
in this temple the figure of a man, eighteen feet high, entirely
of solid gold. I myself did not see this figure, but I relate
what the Chaldaeans reported concerning it. Darius, the son
of Hystaspes, plotted to carry the statue off, but had not the
hardihood to lay his hands upon it. Xerxes, however, the son
of Darius, killed the priest who forbade him to move the
statue, and took it away. Besides the ornaments which I have
mentioned, there are a large number of private offerings in
this holy precinct.[10]

In +XIX, Layard, Rassam, and several French archaeologists dug
tentatively into the vast ruins of Babylon but found little of interest.
Serious, productive work there began with the methodical excavations of
a German society, the Deutsch-Orient Gesellschaft, from 1899 to 1912.
The group was headed by the cheerfully extroverted Robert Koldewey.
As a result of this and later excavations, it has been possible sometimes to
confirm Herodotos and sometimes to correct him.

The Gate of the Gods goes far back into the mists of prehistoric
times, when the dwellers in the land still used tools of flint and built
their houses of bundles of reeds, as the Marsh Arabs of lower Iraq still
do. This reed construction explains the otherwise puzzling direction
given to Utnapishtim, the Babylonian Noah, by Enki, the god of
wisdom, in warning him of the impending Flood. Enki tells Utnapishtim
to pull down his house and make a raft of the materials. This would
not work with a house of brick, but if the house were of bundles
of reeds it makes sense.

The first known mention of Babylon is in an inscription of Sargon
of Akkad, in −XXIV, although archaeology shows that the site was
inhabited thousands of years before Sargon's time. Babylon formed
part of Sargon's may-fly empire. Afterwards it became again one of
the many little independent city-states of the plain of Shinar.

The three most powerful such *poleis* were then Babylon, Isin, and
Larsa. Babylon's early and long-lasting importance flowed from its location on the Euphrates at the point where the Two Rivers approached
each other closest before diverging again. Goods that originated on one
river and were bound for a destination on the other naturally flowed
through Babylon before or after the dry-land part of their journey.

Around −1800 the conquering king of Larsa, Rimsin, bade fair to
build another mighty empire. But an equally able king, Khammurabi,[11]
arose in Babylon. With skilled generalship and Machiavellian craft,

Khammurabi defeated Rimsin, conquered far and wide, and ruled Assyria through a puppet king. His writ ran from the Persian Gulf to the upper Euphrates. That he campaigned at least once in Syria or Palestine is implied by the brief, cryptic allusion in Genesis xiv, 1 to "Amraphel king of Shinar" (presumably Khammurabi of Babylon), who warred with some allied kings against Sodom and Gomorrah in the legendary days of Abraham.

Khammurabi also busily built and restored temples. He was constantly writing his governors about the upkeep of irrigation canals:

> Unto Governor Sididdinam say: Thus saith Khammurabi. Thou shalt call out the men who hold lands along the banks of the Damanum canal, that they may clear out the Damanum canal. Within the present month shall they complete the work . . .[12]

He also caused the thirty-third year of his reign to be known as the year in which he "redug the canal called 'Khammurabi-spells-abundance-for-the-people, the Beloved-of-Anu-and-Enlil'; thus he provided Nippur, Eridu, Ur, Larsa, Uruk, and Isin with a permanent and plentiful water supply . . ."[13] after these cities had been threatened with destruction by the drying up of the Euphrates.

In the early years of this century, Khammurabi became famous as a lawgiver. In 1901, a 6-foot stone stela, on which his code of laws was inscribed, was found at Susa, whither it had been taken after Khammurabi's time by Elamite raiders. Later Mesopotamian finds showed that Khammurabi was by no means the first king to codify the laws of the land. His code was merely more detailed and better thought out than the earlier ones.

The code contains some provisions that strike even a modern as enlightened: for instance, that a man who had been robbed might, if the robbers were not caught, claim compensation from the local authorities who had failed to protect him. For a given crime, a nobleman was subject to a heavier penalty than a commoner; after all, he ought to have known better. This is the opposite of the system in Merovingian France, where, other things being equal, penalties were lighter as the rank of the criminal was higher, but heavier as the rank of his victim was higher.

On the other hand, many of Khammurabi's provisions show primitive, tribalistic thinking. Some, for example, ordained that, if a man caused the death of another man's son or daughter, his own son or daughter should be slain. For several offenses, including witchcraft, the case was decided by a water ordeal. The accused was thrown into the Euphrates and adjudged guiltless if he survived. That was at least better than the water ordeal used in witchcraft cases in Reformation Europe, in which the accused had to drown to prove his innocence.

In Khammurabi's code, death was dealt out with a lavish hand, not only for such admittedly serious crimes as robbery and kidnapping but also for such felonies as being a careless and spendthrift wife. Khammurabi's laws remind one of those of Georgian Britain, which had the death penalty for over 200 offenses, including such quaint crimes as associating with Gypsies or trespassing with intent to kill rabbits. Since we know the reasoning behind the ferocity of eighteenth-century British laws, we can at least guess at that behind Khammurabi's code. Georgian Britain had practically no police force—merely a few unpaid watchmen and constables, or the worthless substitutes whom citizens hired to take their places at this irksome duty.

Since fear of royal tyranny led Britons to oppose any regular police force, the government tried to make up for its lack by decreeing ferocious punishment. Whether punishment deters crime is a subject on which there are heated and emotional arguments but little hard knowledge. We can, however, be sure that no punishment has much effect unless it is consistently applied. In eighteenth-century Britain, only a tiny fraction of the criminals were ever caught. The rest, knowing that their chances of hanging were no worse than many other hazards of everyday life, pursued their careers undisturbed.

We can guess that similar factors operated in Babylon. For crime is a normal concomitant of city life; at least, it always has been. To find a crimeless society, one must go to a backward peasant village, where population and custom remain static for generations. Such a society needs no policemen, because everybody knows everybody else and keeps an eye on everybody else. If a young man gets out of line, his kinsmen come down hard upon him. If he proves an incorrigible evildoer, they either expel him from the community or kill him.

Rulers of early cities tried to keep order in the same way, by public opinion and familial discipline. But, as cities grew, this became harder and harder. Whereas a villager knows nearly everybody whom he sees in the course of a day, a man in a large city is surrounded by strangers. In such a crowd, it is easy for a malefactor to lose himself. Furthermore, there are more valuable articles lying around, waiting to be stolen, in a city. Hence, in a city, both the opportunity to commit crimes and the temptation to do so are greater than in a village.

Between the lack of street lighting and the feeble state of law enforcement, it is likely that all great ancient cities were crime-ridden to a degree that makes the modern American metropolis look like a paradise of law and order. At night, rich men who had to move abroad hired bodyguards, who bore arms and torches or lanterns, while other honest citizens stayed home behind bolted doors. That Babylon had a police force of some sort is shown by a clay letter of Khammurabi's time, which one Etilpimarduk sent to a shaykh named Shumma-Anum:

51. Ruins of the Ishtar Gate of Babylon, from the ancient ground level.

Idinishtar, the Chief of Police, hath thus spoken: "Etirum of the police of my house hath deserted and is living in Dilbat with Shumma-Anum, the shepherd. I have sent to arrest this Etirum, but Shumma-Anum, the shepherd, hath not surrendered this Etirum to the man whom I sent to arrest him."[14]

We can infer that Idinishtar was police chief for all Babylonia. Further details of his force—how many there were, how paid, and what their duties were—have not come down to us.

Like other ephemeral empires of that age, Khammurabi's realm was a one-man affair, which Khammurabi could hold together by intelligence and energy far beyond the ordinary. When he died, in the absence of an equally able successor, his empire soon broke up. The subject city-states revolted. In —1595, King Mursilis of Khatti— the Hittite kingdom—led a great raid down the valley of the Euphrates, which took and sacked Babylon. After that, a barbarous, horse-using people from the eastern hills, the Kassites, seized Babylon and ruled it for over four centuries.

Then the Elamites ousted the Kassites, and a nationalistic revival among the Babylonians ousted the Elamites. For a while, the kings of Babylonia fought the kings of Assyria for hegemony of the Land Between the Rivers. Then the great Aramaean invasion of —XI and —X swamped both nations.

When Babylonia recovered, it was only to fall under the domination of Assyria, then beginning its time of mighty and merciless sway over nations near and far. Sennacherib punished the Babylonian revolt of —689 by the utter destruction of the city. As a result, the excavations of Koldewey and his colleagues have revealed very little about Khammurabi's Babylon. The tumbled ruin field that now marks the site is made up almost entirely of the remains of later periods—of the rebuilding by Esarhaddon and Ashurbanipal and the brief golden age that followed the fall of Assyria.

Nabopolassar,[15] the founder of the last and greatest Babylonian dynasty, was a Chaldaean—that is, he came from the south, around the head of the Persian Gulf. The last king of Assyria, Sinshariskun, appointed Nabopolassar governor of the southern provinces. For several years, Nabopolassar supported Assyrian interests in the South. Then the weakness of the crumbling Assyrian Empire became so plain that in —627 Nabopolassar declared his independence and seized Babylon.

For several years more, indecisive war raged between the Assyrians and the Babylonians. Then Nabopolassar obtained the help of the Medes and the Scythians. Sinshariskun—no feeble "Sardanapalus" —fought hard, but the odds were too great. In —612, the allies took Nineveh and wiped it out; Sinshariskun perished in the fall. Some Assyrians fled west to Ḥarrân in Syria, where with Egyptian help they held out for several years. When Nabopolassar and his son Nebuchadrezzar II drove the Egyptians out of Syria and Palestine, these Assyrian remnants disappeared from history.

Nabopolassar and his dynasty thus came to rule much the same area as that of the former Assyrian Empire. This new empire is sometimes called the Neo-Babylonian Empire, because its capital was at Babylon, and sometimes the Chaldaean Empire, because of the nationality of its ruling house. Being a usurper, Nabopolassar was careful to keep on the good side of the powerful priesthood, who might otherwise have stirred up revolts against him, and Nebuchadrezzar followed his sire's example. Hence they lavished vast sums on temples, in Babylon and elsewhere. Under the energetic rule of Nabopolassar and Nebuchadrezzar, Babylon reached its greatest size and splendor.

We cannot make more than an educated guess at the population of any ancient city. Although we may know its area quite accurately from the remains of its walls, the density of the population in that area varied enormously. A given lot might be occupied by the private house of a prosperous bourgeois, with his family and servants—perhaps ten or twenty people. Or the same lot might bear a tenement house of several stories, sheltering hundreds. The lot might support a house of one kind in one generation and of the other the next.

When estimates of the populations of great ancient cities are compared, however, we note a curious thing: before the Christian Era, all the greatest cities, like Babylon, seem to have reached a maximum in the range of 200,000 to 300,000 souls.[16] This can be understood when we think of the factors that limited the size of a city. Such a city had to be fed, and there were no trains of refrigerator cars to rush food thousands of miles to the city. Everything had to be brought in from the surrounding countryside by oxcart or donkeyback. The larger the city grew, the farther the food had to be brought and the costlier it became. In time, a point was reached where an unskilled workman, finding himself starving, decided that he had been better off in the village whence he had come to seek his fortune and left for home. When enough of the poor did this, the population stabilized.

Moreover, even if the transportation of food allowed the city to surpass a quarter of a million, and no foe sacked it and slaughtered its people, two other factors could be counted upon sharply to reduce the population from time to time. These were plague and fire. Every great city had one or the other, and usually both, at least once a century. A plague would kill off a tenth or a quarter of the population (the Great Plague of London slew about one-seventh) and send thousands fleeing into the country or back to villages where they had kinsmen, until the disease abated. A conflagration would wipe out a goodly fraction of the city and cause an exodus of those whose means of livelihood had been destroyed.

Nabopolassar was already mature when he revolted against his Assyrian overlords. In —605 he died, full of years and glory. His son Nebuchadrezzar, who reigned for forty-three years, was the outstanding soldier, statesman, and builder of his time. The indign tales told about him in the biblical Book of Daniel—how he demanded of his wise men the interpretation of a dream that he himself had forgotten, and how he went mad and ate grass—should not be taken seriously. They were the Judaean scribes' revenge on the man who had thrice sacked Jerusalem and deported thousands of Jews to Babylonia.

In Nebuchadrezzar's Babylon, the inner city was a slightly distorted rectangle, about a mile and a half from east to west and four-fifths of a mile from north to south. The Euphrates flowed diagonally through the city from north to south, dividing it into the larger Old City on the east and the smaller New City on the west. Moats carried the divided waters of the Euphrates around the inner city, making two triangular islands of it.

An enormous double brick wall surrounded the inner city. First, along the moats ran a quay wall of burnt brick, which protected the walls proper from being undermined by the water. Above and behind this quay wall rose an outer wall, about 26 feet thick, also of burnt brick. The height of this wall is not exactly known, since only the foundations have survived; but the wall was probably two to three times as tall as it was thick.

Behind the outer wall was a space of about 39 feet, and then rose another wall, of mud brick. This inner wall was thinner (about 23 feet thick) but loftier. Square towers, 28 feet on a side, straddled the inner wall. They stood at intervals of about 144 feet (or 172 feet measured from center to center). The outer wall probably had such towers, too, but if so their remains have not endured.

Koldewey found that the space between the two walls had been filled with rubble up to the general level of the ruins at the time of his excavations. How far up this rubble filling was carried is uncertain. Some writers assume that the interspace was filled all the way to the top of the outer wall. This is possible; but it is equally likely that the rubble filling was carried little if any higher than the general ground level, since the inner wall would thus be harder for attackers to scale. Medieval fortified cities with two such lines of walls, like Carcassonne, left the interspace at ground level. This space was called "the lists" and became a favorite site for tournaments. In time the word was applied to any field used for such a mock battle.

Nebuchadrezzar's walls were of a type that builders of cities and castles had standardized several centuries before and continued to build, with little change, down to the coming of cannon 2,000 years later. The form of this wall was fixed by the availability of stone and brick on the one hand and the size and shape of the wall's human defenders on the other.

The main wall was a solid structure, which attackers could not easily break down and atop which defenders could move about freely. Along the outer rim of the main wall ran a much smaller wall called a parapet. This was a mere foot or two thick and 6 feet high. Its upper edge formed a square zigzag pattern called a battlement or crenelation. The crenels, or notches in the battlement, were sufficiently low and wide so that an archer could shoot through them at foes on the ground below. The merlons, or toothlike projections, were high and wide enough so that the archer could duck behind them when not actually loosing his shaft.

Along the east bank of the Euphrates, several square miles of suburbs formed a huge right triangle surrounding the inner city. A pair of crenelated walls protected this area, also, including Nebuchadrezzar's summer palace at the north end. Apparently this outer vallation was not continued to form a complete square on the west side of the Euphrates, although Herodotos assumed that it was. That is probably why he gave "the entire circuit" of the walls of Babylon as five times that of the actual length of the main wall—that of the inner city—which is between 11 and 12 miles. Since he wrote his account many years after he had visited the place, it is not surprising, among so many walls, that he got some of his dimensions confused.

Additional walls lined the riverbanks and the fortified areas of the Old City. Furthermore, 75 miles northwest of Babylon, the great Median Wall, 68 miles long, stretched from the Tigris to the Euphrates. Altogether Babylon was about as impregnable, when held by a determined garrison, as a city could be made with the technics of the time.

Eight fortified gates pierced the double wall surrounding the inner city. The central portal on the northern side was the famous Ishtar Gate, the grandest structure of its kind ever built. This colossal entranceway comprised a rectangular tower of brick. Along its long axis, perpendicular to the wall, it measured about 155 feet; parallel to the wall, its dimension was about half this. Its height is not known for sure, since the upper parts long ago disappeared. But, from pictures of similar gates, we can guess it at about 70 feet.

Cutting through this tower was a lofty vaulted passage, which could be closed off by two pairs of huge wooden doors. On the northward side of the gate proper, flanking the approach, stood two tall, slender towers. North of these, as a first line of defense, rose two smaller towers.

There are two "replicas" of the Ishtar Gate, which give an idea of how it—or at least a part of it—looked when new. One is in the Vorderasiatisches Museum in Berlin; the other, at the entrance to the site of Babylon in Iraq. The beholder should bear in mind that these are really scale models rather than replicas, since they are only about two-thirds the size of the original. Moreover, they include only the two northernmost towers and the arched gateway connecting them. They therefore represent only a small fraction of the whole structure.

The entire Ishtar Gate was finished with enameled bricks, blue on the towers and green and pink on the connecting walls. On each tower, in low brick relief, were a number of brightly-colored bulls and dragons, repelling evil spirits by their frowning glare. They alternated vertically: a horizontal row of bulls, then one of dragons, then one of bulls, and so on—presumably—up to the top. As the gate was originally built, the foundations, including the bottom six rows of animals, were belowground. During Nebuchadrezzar's reign, the level of the roadway was

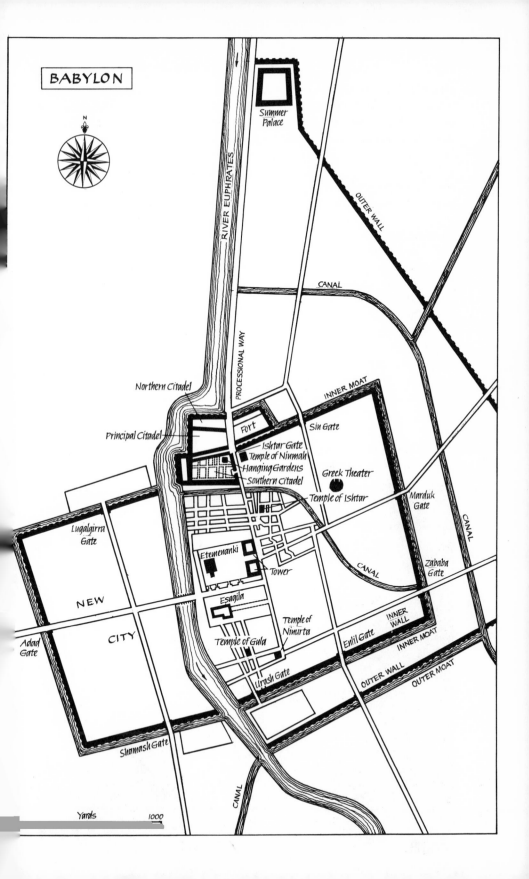

raised at least twice, so that four more rows of animals were hidden from view. The German excavations went all the way to the bottom of the foundation, so that the dragon-haunted walls that the tourist sees today were wholly underground in Nebuchadrezzar's day.

The bull was the symbolic beast of Adad, the weather god; the dragon or *sirrush*, that of Marduk, the Babylonian Jupiter. The sirrush was a composite animal, combining the body and forelegs of a cheetah with the head, neck, and scales of a serpent and the hind legs of an eagle or similar bird of prey. The head bore a curly crest and other appendages.

The discovery of these lifelike reliefs led to speculations, early in this century, that the sirrush was the Babylonians' idea of some dinosaur surviving in tropical Africa or some such suitable habitat. Greater knowledge both of dinosaurs and of Africa have slain that romantic possibility. Koldewey inferred from the story of Bel and the dragon in the apocryphal Book of Daniel that perhaps the priests kept a monitor lizard in a cage and passed it off on their credulous worshipers as a baby sirrush.[17]

The traveler who approached the Ishtar Gate from the north, walking south along the east bank of the Euphrates, found himself treading

52. Ishtar Gate of Babylon, from the level to which Koldewey excavated the foundations.

Babylon's Processional Way, paved with massive stone blocks set in asphalt. On each side rose the high brick wall of an outer fortification. These buildings, besides probably serving as guardhouses, were also museums in which were stored the statues and inscriptions from other lands that Babylonians had carried off in their foreign wars. The brick walls on either side were decorated with life-sized lions in brightly enameled brick relief. There were sixty lions on each side; red-maned yellow lions alternated with yellow-maned white lions. The lion was the symbolic animal of Ishtar, the goddess of love.

In one of my novels, my two heroes arrive at the Ishtar Gate in the Persian period. After examining the decorations,

> Myron and Bessas strolled about this vast structure, avoiding the traffic that streamed in and out. They ignored the cripples who, having been convicted of misdemeanors, had been deprived of eyes, hands, or feet by Xerxes' judges, and who now squatted and begged about the great gate . . .
>
> Finished at last, the twain strolled through the Ishtar Gate and south along Processional Way . . . The travelers dodged chariots, ox carts, and camel trains. Some of the camels, to cure them of the mange, had been shaved all over and painted black with the mineral pitch of Id, so that they looked like animals made of asphalt.
>
> The swarming Babylonians, in long tunics and knitted caps with dangling tails, were leavened by a sprinkling of trousered Persians and other Aryans, shaven Egyptians, Syrians in tall spiral hats, cloaked and skirted Arabs, robed Judaeans, booted Sakas in pointed hoods, turbaned Carduchians, felt-capped Armenians, Greeks in broad-brimmed hats, and men in the garb of even more distant lands. Beggars whined, catamites smirked, hawkers cried their wares, and pimps extolled the beauty and cleanliness of their girls. Persian soldiers strolled in pairs, arrogantly shouldering other folk out of the way.[18]

The Processional Way—whose proper name was "The Street Whereon May No Foe Ever Tread"—continued south through the Ishtar Gate and into the inner city. As the traveler emerged from the Ishtar Gate, he passed the Temple of Ninmakh,[19] the goddess of the underworld, on his left. At the same time he might glimpse greenery over the wall on his right. For here stood the famous Hanging Gardens, rated by later Greek writers as one of the Seven Wonders of the World. (Sometimes the walls of Babylon were so classed as well.) The Hanging Gardens were a splendid roof garden, planted with trees and shrubs atop a princely pleasure house. The roof that upheld the garden was waterproofed by layers of asphalt and sheets of lead. The word "hanging," which classical writers employed,[20] gives the false impression that the gardens were somehow suspended, as by cables. "Raised or "elevated" would give a more realistic picture.

Some of these writers credited the gardens to the legendary Semiramis, which is nonsense. There might, however, be a factual basis for the tale that Nebuchadrezzar built the Hanging Gardens to please his favorite wife, the princess Amytis, who in the flat Euphratean plain pined for the hills of her native Media. These writers also claimed that Semiramis had built Babylon in the first place, and that she even constructed a pedestrian tunnel under the Euphrates, connecting her palaces on opposite sides of the river.[21] The story is pure fiction, since, even if Semiramis could have built such a tunnel, she could not, before the invention of pumps, have kept it from filling up with water. It is a pity that the tale is untrue; the tunnel would have made a priceless prop for adventure stories laid in ancient Babylon.

Of Nebuchadrezzar's stately pleasure dome, only the basement survives; so nobody really knows how the Hanging Gardens looked when new. When Koldewey dug up the basement, he found the remains of fourteen large stone barrel vaults. The arched vault had been known for centuries in Babylonia and Egypt but had been used only on a small scale, for graves and drains. As far as is known, Nebuchadrezzar was the first to put it into large-scale use in major buildings. The purpose of these vaults, carefully constructed of costly imported stone, is not known. They may have been used for storage of supplies against a siege, or as summer reception rooms or banquet halls. Being partly underground, they would be cooler than most places in the baking Babylonian summer.

In the basement, Koldewey found a peculiar structure:

> . . . a well which differs from all other wells known either in Babylon or elsewhere in the ancient world. It has three shafts placed close to each other, a square one in the centre and oblong ones on each side, an arrangement for which I can see no other explanation than that a mechanical hydraulic machine stood there, which worked on the same principle as our chain pump, where buckets attached to a chain work on a wheel placed over a well. A whim or capstan works the wheel in an endless rotation. This contrivance, which is used to-day in this neighbourhood, and is called a *dolab* (water bucket), would provide a continuous flow of water.[22]

If Koldewey is right, the chain bearing the buckets extended up through the building to the roof garden. Servants, heaving on the windlass bars, kept water flowing from the well to the king's precious plants.

West of the Hanging Gardens, filling the space between this edifice and the river, stood a building with brick walls of the extraordinary thickness of 70 feet. This was evidently a fortress or keep for a last-ditch stand.

If our traveler continued south on the Processional Way, he would pass on his left apartment houses up to four stories high. On his right arose the most conspicuous structure of Babylon: the towering, rainbow-hued ziggurat[23] Etemenanki, the Cornerstone of the Universe.

Long before, to make them more impressive and to ease the drainage problem, the Mesopotamians had taken to raising their temples on pyramidal platforms of brick. These pyramids grew and grew until two types of structure evolved. The first was the temple proper: a massive, pillared hall on the ground or on a low platform. The other was the ziggurat: a lofty pyramid of brick, with setbacks, staircases, and a shrine on top. The only ziggurat that survives in anything like its original form stands at Ur in the South, amid what is now a desolate wilderness. When a ziggurat began to crumble, a pious ruler often enlarged it by simply adding another layer of brickwork to the outside.

There are several theories about the purpose of ziggurats: that they were places for the gods to alight on their visits to earth, and so on. The theory that most persuades me is that these towers were used like the Palestinian "high places" mentioned in the Bible, or the large wooden pillars on the grounds of Syrian temples. In Syria, a priest would climb to the top of such a pillar to shout his prayers up to the gods. The pillar brought the petitioning priest nearer to Heaven, so that gods could hear him better.[24] I suspect that ziggurats likewise furnished Mesopotamian priests with an elevated platform whence to address the powers above with the needed audibility.

The most famous ziggurat was that raised in Babylon in honor of Marduk. Genesis xi, in the myth of the Confusion of Tongues, calls this structure the Tower of Babel. The Babylonians thought that it had been originally built by the gods themselves.

After several destructions and rebuildings, Nabopolassar began the final version of Etemenanki during the last years of his reign. He made his sons haul bricks like common workmen to show their piety. If he had not been elderly, he would probably have hauled some himself, as Ashurbanipal of Assyria had done years before to start the rebuilding of Esagila, the temple of Marduk. A relief shows Ashurbanipal in the unkingly pose of bearing a basketful of bricks on his head, as it shows his predecessor of the third millennium B.C., the Sumerian king Ur-Nanshe of Lagash. The modern ceremony of breaking ground for a public work, with a puffing politician turning the first spadeful of earth, descends in a straight line from this royal hod-carrying of ancient Mesopotamia.

Etemenanki reached its final form under Nebuchadrezzar the Great, around −600. Then it towered skyward for nearly 300 feet and was covered with enameled bricks in colorful patterns, as if clothed in the skin of some monstrous reptile.

Like other cities that grew from villages, Babylon probably started out with the usual cow-path tangle of crooked alleys. At least as early as Khammurabi, however, the kings had been trying to straighten out the maze by driving broad avenues, crossing at right angles, straight through the tangle. The result in most cities so improved was that inside the large rectangles formed by the avenues, the streets kept their original plan. Since we do not have a complete street plan of Babylon, we cannot (despite Herodotos' words about its grid plan) be sure of its layout. From what we do know, it seems likely that the city had a few straight avenues at right angles, named for the gods—Marduk Street, Shamash Street, and Adad Street—and tangles of alleys between.

Turning right on Adad Street where it crossed the Processional Way and walking towards the river, our imaginary stroller found himself between two sacred inclosures: Etemenanki, the great ziggurat, on his right and Esagila, the Temple of Marduk, on his left. As enlarged and rebuilt by the Chaldaean kings, the temple was an L-shaped building, which occupied a square about 500 feet on a side.

This temple housed an 18-foot golden statue of Marduk. Although Herodotos says the statue was of solid gold, we may doubt this. Such statues were designed to be borne through the city in carriages during religious festivals, and a solid gold statue of that size would have weighed over fifty tons. Besides being immovable, it would have cost the equivalent of about 100 million dollars. It is not likely that so much gold was available for such purposes. Probably the statue was wood, covered with gold foil.

From the many representations in Babylonian art, we can form an idea of this statue. The bearded, benign-looking king of the gods wore a long robe and a tall crown topped by a circle of feathers, somewhat like those of a Sioux war bonnet. In his left hand he held a scepter and a ring, while his right hand grasped a scimitar. At his feet lay his pet *sirrush* or dragon.

The two great temene of Marduk contained many other buildings besides the temple and the tower. There were living quarters for the priests and for pilgrims from out of town, paddocks for animals to be sacrificed, and so on.

53. *Sirrush* or Marduk's dragon from the Ishtar Gate of Babylon, in the Iraqi National Museum, Baghdad.

Passing between these two inclosures and through a fortified river gate, the traveler reached another wonder of Chaldaean Babylon: the bridge over the Euphrates. Except for Sennacherib's aqueduct at Jerwan, this was the oldest stone bridge of which there is any record. But, whereas Sennacherib merely crossed a brook, Nabopolassar's bridge spanned one of the world's great rivers. Built when the world's few bridges were flimsy affairs of tree trunks, reeds, or inflated goatskins, this bridge was almost as celebrated in the ancient world as the Hanging Gardens. For centuries it was the only structure of its kind in the world.

Since the Euphrates has long since shifted its channel westward, cutting through the former New City, Koldewey was able to dig up the bases of the piers of the bridge. When new, the bridge was around 400 feet long and rested on seven boat-shaped piers of baked brick, stone, and timber. The superstructure was of timber. According to Herodotos, it was a drawbridge; one or more of the wooden platforms, which crossed from pier to pier, were taken up at night to keep gangs of thieves from using the bridge in their getaway. This may be so, but another possible reason for the removable sections would be to let sailing ships pass.

The Euphrates bridge had a shortcoming shared by most large ancient bridges. The massive piers took up half the width of the river

54. Statue of a lion attacking a man, excavated on the site of Babylon.

at that point, seriously impeding the flow of the water. At floodtime there was danger that the swift current, speeded up still more by this constriction, might scour away the river bottom around the piers until they collapsed, or that débris might gather on the upstream side. Nevertheless, this bridge may be counted the most signal technological advance of the Chaldaean Empire.

Another novel gives a fictional view of the river that flowed under the bridge:

> He took us out on the river wall, so we could look up and down the Euphrates as far as the hazy air permitted. North of this spot, the river makes a sharp bend, passing around the citadel. Thence it flows slowly southward past the sacred enclosures.
>
> Below us, long lines of wharves and quays spread out to north and south along this bustling waterway. There were great sluggish barges piled with produce and moved by poling. There were sharp-nosed little sailing vessels with overhanging bows and sloping masts. There were timber rafts, heaped with

brushwood for fuel, drifting down from the Assyrian mountains.

Strangest were bowl-shaped vessels of stitched hides, perfectly round, floating downstream piled with melons and other
cargo, each with a hobbled ass reposing on its side atop the
load. The boatman keeps this curious vessel in midstream by an
occasional stroke with a square-bladed paddle until he reaches
his proper wharf. Then, with much splashing and spinning, he
forces the bowl-boat to shore. When he has unloaded, the boatman sells the wooden framework of the boat along with his
cargo, rolls up the leathern covering, ties it upon the ass, and
sets out upstream again.[25]

Physically, the Babylonians were probably much like the present-
day folk of the territory: of predominantly Mediterranean type, black
of hair and eyes, and slighter on the average than the Assyrians, whom
they otherwise resembled. Their complexions, when shielded from the
sun, range from pale to swarthy, like those of southern Europeans; but
outdoor exposure soon turns them a deep bronze.

The people of Babylon led lives much like those of dwellers in
other great cities of antiquity, getting and begetting, plying their trades,
quarreling with their in-laws, taking time off for festivals and fun,
entertaining their friends and being entertained, watching for chances
to increase their wealth or to rise in the social scale, trying to keep out
of trouble, and doubtless complaining that their children were disgrace-
fully lacking in manners and morals. As Aristophanes wrote a little later:

Come listen now to the good old days when the children, strange to tell,
Were seen not heard, led a simple life, in short were brought up
    well.[26]

The rich dwelt in courtyard houses; the poor, in windowless little
mud-brick boxes of huts. People who could afford it and who liked to
keep up appearances probably whitewashed their houses, as they still do
in Iraq. Since a main purpose of a Mesopotamian house was to keep out
the sizzling heat of the summer sun, windows would have been more
a liability than an asset. The people probably slept on their roofs in
summer. The architecture of the apartment houses of three and four
stories, mentioned by Herodotos, is not known, but it was probably
somewhat like that of similar multi-story houses built of mud brick
today in the Hadhramaut, on the southeastern coast of Arabia. Palaces
had toilets connected by drains with the river or with cesspools, and
water jars with clay dippers for flushing the appliances after use. Ordinary private houses lacked such amenities.

In hot weather, men wore kilts and short-sleeved, knee-length tunics. For cold weather, they wore over their tunics ankle-length robes, like a modern bathrobe, and knitted caps with dangling tails. The women's dress was simply a dress. To greet a friend, one touched the end of one's walking stick to one's nose.

Barley, in the form of bread, biscuits, cakes, and beer, furnished much of Babylon's diet. The Babylonians also had a fair choice of greens and fruits: onions, lentils, peas, beans, cucumbers, cabbages, lettuce, apples, pomegranates, figs, quinces, apricots, and dates. The last-named were also made into date wine. For protein they relied largely on fish and mutton, but sometimes they also had beef, goat, and pork. Beer and wine were sucked through a tube to keep out the solid matter, which seems to have been considerable.

Coined money had not yet been invented, but people paid large bills with lumps of silver of standard weights and used barley for small change. Banking was well developed, and the temples seem to have acted as banks. From the Persian period, a century after Nebuchadrezzar's reign, we have the voluminous business files of the banking firm of Murashu Sons. This was a Judaean family who settled in Nippur, prospered, and stayed there after the Return.

When not busy gaining a living by honest means or otherwise, the Babylonians enjoyed the many religious festivals. These seem to have been their main amusement, albeit they also attended boxing matches. The New Year's festival, for instance, took place in March or April, depending upon the vagaries of the lunar calendar. The images of the gods were loaded into boat-shaped sacred wagons and wheeled along the Processional Way.

First came Marduk. Behind him rode the king in his chariot, with a driver and a man to hold the royal umbrella. Then came the wagon of Marduk's consort, the goddess Sarpanitum; then the sun god Shamash, and so on. Reaching the northern outskirts of the city, the images were transferred to boats and taken to the Garden Temple up the river. Here the consummation of the marriage of Marduk and Sarpanitum was celebrated, and ten days later the whole procession returned to Babylon.

Eastern Semites like the Babylonians do not seem to have been given, at least not at the time of which I speak, to human sacrifice, as were their western kinsmen of the land of Canaan. When not busy with ritual, banking, or politicking, the shaven priests of Babylon dabbled in science. We owe our fashion of dividing hours into sixty minutes, for example, to the Babylonian method of dividing a circle. They studied the stars and invented the constellations and the zodiac. True, their interest in the heavenly bodies was not what we should call scientific, since it was concerned with omens and prognostications. But scientific discoveries did flow from it. Thus a Babylonian of later

55. Babylon's modern incarnation: Baghdad on the Tigris.

times, Kidinnu[27] of Sippar (−IV), is supposed to have discovered the precession of the equinoxes.

United with Babylonian astronomy was another, less welcome legacy from Babylonia to us: the pseudo-science of astrology. To us the difference between the two is plain, but the Babylonians drew no such distinction; all was equally the science of the stars. Their astrology, however, was strictly a state matter, concerned with kings, their families, and their kingdoms. The casting of horoscopes for private persons, as is done for the credulous today, was probably the idea of some later individualistic Greek.

Lacking instruments and having only primitive ideas of the form of the universe (the earth was a floating island surrounded by a revolving sky-bowl), these astrologer-priests were always being surprised. If clouds covered the moon, that counted as an eclipse. The astrologer Balasi mournfully reported:

The moon is seen out of season,
Crops will be small.
On the twelfth day the moon is seen together with the sun.
Contrary to the calculated time,
The moon and sun appear together,
A strong enemy will devastate the land.[28]

Poor Balasi did not realize that he had erred in his figures. Instead, he thought some sinister irregularity had taken place in the heavens.

Astrology was based upon two Babylonic ideas: the zodiac, and the divinity of the heavenly bodies. The zodiac was originally just the constellations through which the sun passed in the course of a year. Taurus, which the sun then occupied at the time of the vernal equinox, was called *Mulmullu*, "the Bull," perhaps as a symbol of spring plowing or of fertility. The other divisions of the zodiac were named by similar analogies and associations of ideas: the Twins for the bright stars Castor and Pollux, the Archer for the hunting season, and the Sea Goat, the Fishes, and the Jar (Aquarius) for the wet winter months.

The signs of the zodiac were rectangular patches of sky, 18° by 30°, occupied by the constellations for which they were named. In the last 2,000 years, the precession of the equinoxes has shifted all the constellations into the adjacent signs. Hence today, the constellation Aries occupies the sign Taurus, and so on around the circle, making nonsense of the whole idea.

Then somebody inferred that the sun, the moon, and the five visible planets were the abodes of gods and named them for their divine tenants. Again, this was done by association of ideas. Thus red Mars was named for the war god Nerigal and white Venus for Ishtar, goddess of love. The Babylonians credited the planets with the influences that one would expect of their respective deities. By primitive logic, a planet was deemed strongest when rising or near the zenith and weakest when setting or retrograde—that is, apparently moving backward among the stars. When Mars was strong, wars were expected.

These notions—that the zodiac and the divine planets corresponded to any physical reality—were exploded centuries ago. But, though bereft of its logical basis, astrology continues to thrive. Truly, there is no idea so absurd that it cannot find a following among men.[29]

In −562, the great Nebuchadrezzar died, and several short reigns with violent ends followed. In −556, the army and the priesthood agreed upon a scholarly Syrian gentleman with military and diplomatic experience, Nabuna'id or Nabonidus, for king. Nabuna'id recovered Syria from the Medes but then gave his Babylonian backers some unwelcome surprises. He tried to promote the Syrian moon god Sin at the expense of Marduk. He seized the oasis of Têma',[30] an important caravan station in the Arabian Desert, and began to build it up as a new capital in lieu of Babylon. He stayed a number of years in Têma', indulging his passions for religious speculation and archaeology; he prided himself on a collection of inscriptions going back to Sumerian times. He left his son Belshazzar[31] to run Babylon.

Meanwhile, the face of politics to the north had drastically changed. One of the subject peoples of the Median Empire, the Medes' kinsmen the Persians, had an able and aggressive young king named Cyrus.[32] At first allied with Nabuna'id, Cyrus overthrew and conquered the Median Empire, then all of Asia Minor. His power grew with astonishing speed, and in —539 he descended upon Babylonia. Babylon, disaffected from its Syrian scholar-king, gave up with only token resistance, and Babylonia became part of a vast Persian Empire.

Thenceforth the mighty city slowly but surely declined. It still throve for several centuries. In fact, under the Persians, Babylonian savants made some of their greatest advances in astronomy and mathematics.

In —482, Babylon revolted against King Xerxes. The Persian sent his best general, who swiftly retook the city and tore down part of Nebuchadrezzar's walls to make them useless for defense. Xerxes carried off the 18-foot statue of Marduk and melted down the gold for his treasury. He is also said to have demolished the temples. Later historians wrote of the temple Esagila and the ziggurat Etemenanki as ruins and blamed Xerxes.

When Herodotos visited Babylon thirty-odd years after the revolt, however, he found both Esagila and Etemenanki standing. So the later historian Diodoros was probably right when he said that the Persians merely robbed the temples of their golden decorations and accessories, and that the ruin of the buildings was due to the action of time. Probably Xerxes demolished no temples—to tear down the ziggurat would have been extremely costly, and the Persian kings were a thrifty lot—but seized all the gold in sight. Later, when grinding Persian taxation caused Babylon to decay, the priests could no longer keep their buildings in repair. Thereupon they dissolved into mud, as do all such structures when left to the elements.

A century and a half after Xerxes, when Alexander the Great entered Babylon, he "commanded the Babylonians to rebuild all the temples which Xerxes had destroyed."[33] Alexander doubtless believed that Xerxes had destroyed Esagila and Etemenanki, since it had become the vogue among Hellenes to blame Xerxes, the enemy of Greece, not only for the misdeeds he had committed but for many that he had not. Alexander ordered the mountainous piles of brick left from the crumbling of Etemenanki cleared away to make a space for reconstruction. This was done; but then Alexander died and the work stopped for good and all.

During the wars of Alexander's Successors, Babylon was captured and sacked in —311 by Demetrios the son of Antigonos, later called Poliorketes, "city-taker," who became king of Macedonia. Seleukos, the Successor who founded the Seleucid Empire, gave up trying to repair decaying Babylon and instead built a new capital, Seleuceia, on the right bank of the Tigris. As Seleuceia waxed, Babylon waned. By the beginning of the Christian Era, Babylon was deserted, save for a few little villages scattered about the ruins, where peasants pried up the ancient bricks of Khammurabi and Nebuchadrezzar to build their huts.

When the Parthians drove the Seleucids out of Babylonia, they built their own capital, Ctesiphon, across the Tigris from Seleuceia. In its turn, Seleuceia decayed as Ctesiphon grew. Still later, the Abbasid caliphs fixed their capital at Baghdad, an ancient small town a few miles up the Tigris from Ctesiphon.

And so, even if poets lament its downfall:

> The sobbing desert winds still whisper how
> The golden city of the gods' desire
> Fell in the smoke and crumbled in the fire,
> And lizards bask upon her columns now.
> And rhymers sing of ages gold and gone,
> But Babylon had faded with the dawn.[34]

one might say that Babylon never really died but was reborn in successive bodies. For each of its successors filled the same function: that of the main transfer point for goods originating on one of the Two Rivers and bound for a destination on the other. In this sense, there will always be a Babylon.

VII

MEMPHIS OF THE WHITE WALL

LOOK ON THE PYRAMIDS, AND HEAR THE TWAIN
RECOUNT THEIR ANNALS OF THE LONG-GONE PAST:
COULD THEY BUT SPEAK, HIGH MARVELS HAD THEY TOLD
OF WHAT TIME DID TO MAN FROM FIRST TO LAST.[1]

The Arabian Nights

56. Step pyramid of King Joṣer at Ṣaqqâra.

Fɪʀsᴛ there was a broad, sandy plain west of the Nile, four miles wide and dotted with palms and acacias. At its western end, the plain sloped upwards in tawny bluffs to the Libyan Desert. There were a few tiny, widely scattered clusters of huts of mud and reeds, in which lived Stone Age men just emerging from the food-gathering stage of culture and becoming growers and herders. They had much ado to keep the lions from eating their half-tame flocks.

Thousands of years passed, and a great city grew up on the plain. For many centuries, off and on, this city was the capital of Egypt— or, as its folk then called it, the land of Khem. The dwellers in the city built a multitude of structures besides their dwelling houses: temples, palaces, courts, tombs, colossal statues, and above all the immense stone pyramids, which stretched in a 70-mile chain, parallel to the Nile and passing to the west of the great city, along the edge of the desert. These pyramids were the tombs of the kings who had reigned in the city. Around them, a multitude of smaller pyramids served as the tombs of their women. About the pyramids of each group was a walled inclosure and other structures, including mortuary temples where a corps of priests conducted daily services for the welfare of the dead kings' souls, and great stone causeways leading down to the Nile. The city was a little north of the center of the 70-mile chain.

More thousands of years have passed, and the great city has utterly vanished. Again, the sandy plain stretches from the Nile to the tawny bluffs, with clusters of mud huts and a scattering of palms and acacias. The lions have gone, but some of the city's monuments remain. Most of the pyramids have survived, some merely a bit dilapidated and some eroded down to mere hillocks of rubble. The colossal statues have all fallen and been buried, but some have been dug up again. One has been erected before the railroad station of a newer city, 12 miles north of the old and across the Nile. The new city is Cairo—in Arabic, al-Qâhira, albeit the dwellers commonly call it Maṣr, "Egypt."

The old city, which vanished, was Memphis. Its origin is lost in the mist of prehistory and pseudo-history that precedes the authentic history of every ancient people. About −450, Herodotos visited Egypt and was told:

> The priests said that Min was the first king of Egypt, and that it was he who raised the dyke which protects Memphis from the inundations of the Nile. Before his time the river flowed entirely along the sandy range of hills which skirts

Egypt on the side of Libya. He, however, by banking up the
river at the bend which it forms about eleven miles south of
Memphis, laid the ancient channel dry, while he dug a new
course for the stream half-way between the two lines of hills.
To this day, the elbow which the Nile forms at the point
where it is forced aside into the new channel is guarded with
the greatest care by the Persians, and strengthened every year;
for if the river were to burst out of this place, and pour over
the mound, there would be danger of Memphis being completely overwhelmed by the flood. Min, the first king, having
thus, by turning the river, made the tract where it used to run,
dry land, proceeded to build the city now called Memphis,
which lies in the narrow part of Egypt; after which he further
excavated a lake outside the town, to the north and west, com-
municating with the river, which was itself the eastern boundary.
Besides these works he also, the priests said, built the temple
of Hephaistos which stands within the city, a vast edifice, very
worthy of mention.[2]

Herodotos' "Hephaistos" was Ptaḥ,[3] the Egyptian god of property, the patron god of artists and artisans, and the tutelary deity of
Memphis. Ptaḥ's priests said that Ptaḥ had created the universe. The
priests of several other gods claimed the same achievement for their
deities, too; but the Egyptians never let a little holy inconsistency
bother them.

Later, when Egypt had fallen under Macedonian rule, the priest
Manetho[4] of Sebennytos, having become a powerful official under the
first two Ptolemies, composed a history of Egypt in Greek. No doubt
he made the rounds of the temples, collecting data from their ancient
and voluminous records. Manetho's work has perished but, in the early
centuries of the Christian Era, several Church Fathers made excerpts
from it and outlines of it to buttress their own arguments about Old
Testament chronology. Some of this material, abridged and recopied,
has come down.

Manetho started his account with dynasties of gods, demigods,
and spirits, who were supposed to have reigned over Egypt. Then:

> In succession to the spirits of the Dead, the Demigods,
> —the first royal house numbers eight kings, the first of whom,
> Mênês of This, reigned sixty-two years. He was carried off
> by a hippopotamus and perished.[5]

This Min or Mênês,[6] probably called Mena in Egyptian, was the
later Egyptians' Founding Father. In the last century, archaeology has
brought to light lists of kings from several tombs, the Turin papyrus,

the fragmentary Palermo stone, and other pieces of evidence. From these, a little more has been learned about the First Dynasty and its founder, although much remains tantalizingly vague.

It now appears that, prior to —3100, Egypt was divided between two kingdoms. The northern kingdom, or Lower Egypt, comprised the Delta, a flat, muddy, swampy area, shaped like an equilateral triangle 160 miles on a side. The name of the Greek letter "delta" (Δ) referred to the shape of the tract. The king of Lower Egypt, called the Bee King, wore a low crown of red felt.

The southern kingdom, or Upper Egypt, consisted of a narrow, 600-mile strip of land along the banks of the Nile. This ribbon ran from Nubia to the apex of the triangle formed by the Delta. At the northern end of the strip, the Nile splits into a dozen branches, which spread out fanwise over the Delta. The king of Upper Egypt, called the Reed King, wore a tall, bottle-shaped crown of white felt. Lower Egypt, with its high water table and occasional winter rains, was the more productive part of the land; but Upper Egypt produced the tougher warriors.

The names of a few kings who reigned during this time of division are known, but nothing beyond the names—not even the order in which they reigned. About —3100, the kings of Upper Egypt conquered Lower Egypt and ruled the whole country. Whether as a result of Egyptian conservatism or in an effort to reconcile the northerners to foreign rule, the realm was still called the Two Kingdoms. The king thenceforth wore a double crown, combining the low red felt headpiece of Lower Egypt with the high white one of Upper.

We know the names of several kings who reigned at this time: Ip, Narmer, Aha, and Zer among others. Some are known from their tombs, which were found at Abydos,[7] 100 miles downstream from Waset-Thebes. Others are known from artifacts bearing their names. Historians differ as to whether Aha and Mena were one and the same man or whether, instead, the "Mênês" of later accounts is a composite of several real kings.

The kings of Khem fixed their capital on the Nile, a few miles above the vertex of the Delta. The new city was on the boundary between Upper and Lower Egypt, somewhat as Jerusalem lay between Israel and Judah. At first the new city was called He-ku-Ptaḥ,[8] the Abode of the Soul of Ptaḥ, whence the Greek name Aigyptos and our own "Egypt." The founders provided the town with the celebrated White Wall, the first recorded engineering work of ancient Egypt. It is a plausible guess that the wall was originally made of brick, with a coating of gypsum plaster, and that in later times the brick was replaced by limestone. From this wall, the city was sometimes called Yaneb-ḥej, the City of the White Wall.

57. Buildings surrounding the court of Joser's pyramid at Ṣaqqâra.
Note the flutings on the columns to the right, imitating bundles of
reeds.

About —2400 the first king of the Sixth Dynasty, Pepi[9] I, founded
a new quarter of the city, which he named Men-nofer-Mirê, "the
Beauty of King Mirê (himself) Abides." In time this was worn down
to Men-nofer[10] and then to Menfe or Menfi, which the Greeks made
into Memphis and which became the name for the entire city.

In the midst of the city rose the citadel, the White Castle of later
writers, although we know not when this improvement took place.
It was an artificial hill surrounded by 40-foot limestone walls.

While no pyramids were erected in Memphis, they formed such a
feature of the local landscape that we can hardly discuss Memphis
without bringing in the pyramids. The Egyptians of the Old and Middle
kingdoms got into the extraordinary habit of building pyramids in the
following way.[11]

Most peoples believe in life after death. This belief may have
originated in the dreams of primitive men about persons whom they

knew to be dead. Once this belief had been launched, mankind's bent
for wishful thinking and dislike of personal extinction kept it afloat.
Most ancients did not make much of this belief, deeming the afterlife
a dim and shadowy thing, like a dream.

The Egyptians, however, took their beliefs in the afterlife seriously
and developed elaborate doctrines about it. One tenet held that the afterlife could be enjoyed only so long as the body was kept intact. Hence
arose the practices of mummifying corpses and of building massive
tombs, designed to foil tomb robbers forever. The robbers were drawn
by the jewels and precious metals buried with kings and nobles, who
thought that, in the afterworld, a dead man's spirit needed the spirits
of the things he had used in life to keep him happy.

Under the first two dynasties, Egyptian kings and nobles were
buried in a tomb called a mastaba.[12] This was a rectangular structure
of brick, with inward-sloping walls. After a king or a noble was laid
to rest in his mastaba, heavy stone slabs were dropped down vertical
shafts to seal off the passage to the burial chamber. The kings of the
Third Dynasty built larger mastabas and began using stone instead of
brick, since the craft of stonemasonry had now advanced enough to
make this possible.

The third king of the Third Dynasty was Joser,[13] who reigned
in —XXVII. Joser's prime minister was the great engineer, architect,
and physician Imhotep,[14] who invented the pyramid.

First, west of Memphis at modern Ṣaqqâra, Imhotep built for
his master a stone mastaba of unusual size and shape. It was square
instead of oblong like its predecessors, over 200 feet on a side and 26
feet high. Not yet satisfied, Joser and Imhotep twice enlarged this
mastaba.

Before the second enlargement was completed, the king again
changed his mind. He (or Imhotep) decided not only further to enlarge
the structure but also to make it into a step pyramid, like four square
mastabas of decreasing size, one atop the other. After more changes of
plan, the structure became a step pyramid of six stages, 200 feet high on
a base 358 by 411 feet. The main body of the pyramid was made of
blocks of limestone locally quarried. To the outside, Imhotep added a
facing of marble from quarries across the Nile at Troyu.[15]

Beneath the pyramid lay a burial chamber, whence many corridors
branched out, presumably to hold the wealth that Joser hoped to take
with him. Around the pyramid was a walled inclosure, 885 by 1,470
feet, containing Joser's mortuary temple. Here a permanent staff of
priests was supposed to perform rituals forever to promote the king's
welfare in the afterlife. The temple compound included living quarters
for these priests, tombs for royal relatives, and other structures, all of
golden-buff limestone.

Joṣer's immediate successors began similar step pyramids, but these either were abandoned at an early stage or have been so plundered for stone that little is left of them. Three large pyramids built a few decades after Joṣer, however, survive south of Ṣaqqâra. That at May-dûm, 32 miles south of Ṣaqqâra, was begun as a step pyramid with seven steps and was then enlarged to one of eight steps. Finally, the steps were filled in and the structure converted to a true, smooth-sided pyramid. Nowadays the last addition has fallen away from the upper part of the pyramid, leaving the top of the step pyramid protruding from a pile of débris.

The other two pyramids of this group stand at Dahshûr, only a few miles south of Ṣaqqâra. The southernmost of this pair was begun as a true pyramid; but, halfway up, the angle of inclination of the sides decreases sharply. Hence this pyramid is called the Bent or Blunted Pyramid. Perhaps the king for whom it was built expired during its construction, and his successor hastened and cheapened the work by completing the pyramid with a top lower than had been planned.

The other pyramid at Dahshûr was the first large true pyramid, originally planned as such, to reach completion. It still stands, huge, silent, and solitary, in the desert near the new road from Cairo to the Fayyûm. It is usually credited to King Seneferu,[16] the first king of the Fourth Dynasty, but the authorship of the other two pyramids of this trio is doubtful.

The second king of the Fourth Dynasty, Khufu (the Cheops of Herodotos, and Manetho's Souphis), built the largest pyramid of all on a hill five miles west of Giza, a town on the west bank of the Nile just above Cairo. It measures 756 feet square and once rose to a height of about 480 feet, although the top 30 feet are now missing because so much stone has been removed from the outside. The medieval Muslim rulers of Egypt plundered all the pyramids thus for building stone.

Khufu's Great Pyramid is made of about 2,300,000 blocks of stone weighing an average of 2.5 tons each. This is an estimate, since to get a more accurate figure would require taking the entire pyramid apart to count and weigh the stones. Barring the Great Wall of China, it was the largest single human construction of antiquity.

The size of this pyramid, the accuracy of its workmanship, and its peculiar internal architecture have given rise in modern times to the pseudo-scientific cult of pyramidology (see note 11 for this chapter). The sides of the base come to within 7 inches of forming a perfect square, and the sides are oriented to the main compass directions with an error of less than one-tenth of a degree. Such accuracy is amazing when we consider the very simple means the Egyptians had for surveying and measuring. Their secret was not the hidden wisdom of the lost Atlantis, but the fact that they had plenty of manpower, plenty of time, and the will to make careful, intensive use of what means they had. They operated according to the Russian peasant proverb: "Measure seven times before you cut once."

Khufu's pyramid also has strange internal features. In all the other pyramids, the king was buried in a chamber cut into bedrock below the center of the base. This chamber was excavated before construction of the pyramid began. The purpose was to confront a prospective tomb robber with such an enormous job of tunneling that he would be deterred at the outset.

Such a chamber was excavated for the Great Pyramid. Then this chamber was abandoned and a large room, misleadingly called the "Queen's Chamber," was built into the structure. This Queen's Chamber had been roofed but not completely floored when Khufu decided to go higher yet. So work was stopped on the Queen's Chamber and the architects changed their plans to allow for a third and still higher room, the so-called "King's Chamber." As construction had already risen above the Queen's Chamber, the passage to the new chamber was partly bored through the masonry already in place. Maybe Khufu was a claustrophobe who hated the thought of all those millions of tons of stone lying on top of his final resting place.

When Khufu died, his attendants placed his mummy in a wooden coffin. They carried this coffin up the passages to the King's Chamber and put it into a plain granite sarcophagus, which must have been installed during the building of the pyramid because it is too wide to go through the passage to the King's Chamber. On their way out, the workmen knocked out a series of props. This allowed huge granite plugs to fall into place, blocking the passage.

The fourth king of this dynasty was Khafra—Herodotos' Chephren and probably a younger son of Khufu, although these relationships are uncertain. On the same hill near Giza, Khafra built the Sphinx, a colossal lion with Khafra's own head on its shoulders. It is partly carved from an outcrop and partly built up of limestone blocks. The rest of the outcrop was quarried away for pyramid stones, so that the Sphinx lies in a depression formed by this quarry. Khafra also built a pyramid which, though slightly smaller than Khufu's, looks taller because it stands on higher ground. This pyramid has none of the complex interior corridors and chambers of the Great Pyramid—only a single underground burial chamber.

After Khafra, other kings continued the custom down to the Twelfth Dynasty. The last Egyptian pyramids were built about —1600, by which time seventy-odd of these sepulchers dotted the land of Khem. Most of the later ones, however, were filled with rubble instead

58. Sphinx and King Khufu's Great Pyramid at Giza.

of the costlier cut stone. Hence they eroded away to mere mounds after subsequent builders stole their marble facings.

The pyramids were not, as is often thought, built by hordes of slaves. Although Egypt was a land of vast class differences, slavery did not—as I have explained—play much part in its history. But forced labor was common. It was the standard ancient method of building roads, canals, temples, and other public works, because tax-gathering machinery was not yet effective enough to make the hiring of voluntary workers practical.

For the pyramids, there was probably a small permanent staff of skilled workmen. A set of barracks of rough stone and dried mud, whose ruins have been found near Khafra's pyramid, may have housed this staff. In addition, the king conscripted tens of thousands of peasants to help with the heavy work during the season of the annual flood of the Nile, when these men would otherwise have been idle. The conscripts were probably paid in food and were organized in gangs with such heartening names as "Vigorous Gang" and "Enduring Gang." The kings also freely pressed their soldiers into service for such work.

While it is unlikely that the workers were constantly lashed with whips, as the slaves of legend are supposed to have been, we need not think that building a pyramid was all sweetness and light, either. Egyptian tomb paintings show the foremen carrying yard-long limber rods, and these were probably not mere symbols of office. An occasional whack with a stick has been a customary part of bossing a gang of Egyptian workers from ancient times almost to the present day. The architect Nekhebu, in boasting on his tomb of his many virtues and kindnesses, mentions that he never struck a worker hard enough to knock him down. Although such treatment would cause a *badawi* from the desert to go for his dagger, the Egyptian worker prided himself on taking such treatment with a grin and a joke.

Despite all the effort and ingenuity expended on the pyramids, none fulfilled its purpose. Robbers looted every one, despite the granite plugs, false passages, and other precautions of their builders. The Great Pyramid held out until +XI, when the greedy caliph al-Ma'mûn got past the granite plugs by boring through the softer limestone around them. Caring nought for relics of the Days of Ignorance, he smashed the lid of the sarcophagus and tore Khufu's mummy to bits for its gold.

With the end of the Sixth Dynasty about −2200, the Old Kingdom collapsed in a welter of quarreling local sovranties. Kings of the Seventh and Eighth dynasties continued to reign in Memphis, but their writs did not run beyond the immediate neighborhood. This feudal era, the First Intermediate Period, endured until the kings of the Eleventh Dynasty, in −XXI, reunited the land. The Middle Kingdom, as we call it, lasted about three centuries. Then followed the Second Intermediate Period, when the Hyksôs ruled Egypt.

Not much is known of Memphis during these times. In the Middle Kingdom, the capital was at Waset-Thebes. The Hyksôs ruled from Avaris,[17] near the Isthmus of Suez at the eastern end of the Delta, although experts disagree as to just where it was.

With the New Empire—the time of the conquering Amenhoteps and Thothmeses and Rameseses—Memphis saw extensive building. Even though the capital returned to Waset-Thebes, Memphis continued as the second capital and the main administrative and military center. The kings of the Eighteenth and Nineteenth dynasties adorned the city with new temples and with colossal statues. Rameses II was especially active in planting statues—of himself, of course.

After the fall of the New Empire and the confusion of the invasions by Libyans, Ethiopians, and Assyrians, the Saïte kings of −VII and −VI added still more statues. Herodotos listed eleven colossi, of which he said six had been made on the orders of "Sesostris," two of "Rhampsinitis," and three of the Saïte king Amasis.

"Sesostris" was a fictional Egyptian hero-king who played the same part in Egyptian legend that Semiramis did in Mesopotamian legend, conquering everything and everybody and building all the monuments otherwise unaccounted for. He is a fictionized composite of several real kings, deriving his name from the Middle Kingdom monarch Senuṣert[18] III and his deeds mainly from those of Rameses II. "Rhampsinitis" is derived from Rameses, but there is no clear indication of which of the three kings of that name is meant. In any event, the two colossi that have been dug up at Memphis in modern times are both statues of Rameses II.

If Herodotos—a keen and conscientious observer—says he saw eleven colossal statues, he probably saw eleven colossal statues. On the other hand, when his priestly guides regaled the eminent tourist with tales of long ago, Herodotos had no way of sifting truth from falsehood. Even if their stories had all been truthful and accurate—which they certainly were not—Egyptian history covers such a huge span of time that he could hardly help getting some dynasties mixed up. In fact, he put the pyramid-builders of the Fourth Dynasty about 2,000 years too late.

Herodotos did his best to look, listen, and take notes, and he collected far more sound facts than does the average modern tourist. But he was in a position somewhat like mine, when I visited Cairo some years ago. My wife and I were shown about by a young man who, whenever he did not know the provenience of some relic of antiquity, attributed it to Rameses II. He became quite hurt when, in the Egyptian Museum in Cairo, I insisted on reading the captions on the exhibits myself and learning to which kings these objects really belonged.

Taharqa,[19] the last of the black pharaohs, was an energetic and stubborn man, and—as the British found out in the Mahdist wars of 1883–1900—there is nothing wrong with the Sudanese fighting spirit. In retaliation for Egyptian help to the Tyrians against Assyria, Esarhaddon sent an army in —675 to conquer Egypt. The army retreated, and the Assyrians told their Babylonian subjects that they had been forced to flee by a great storm. Perhaps.

Then Esarhaddon led an invasion in person. He forced an entry to the Delta in —674 and three years later crushed the Egypto-Kushite army. Taharqa escaped to Kush.

At this time the Assyrians far outclassed all the other peoples they fought, as later the Persians, the Greeks, the Macedonians, and the Romans did in their turn. Throughout ancient times, there was usually one nation that had, by some innovation in weapons or tactics or methods of organization and drill, drawn so far ahead of its rivals that it took the rivals centuries to catch up.

Esarhaddon went back to Assyria and died, whereupon Taharqa

stormed up from the South, slaughtered the Assyrian garrisons, and re-covered Egypt. During these changes, the local magnates, having no love for either set of foreigners, intrigued with the Ethiopians when the Assyrians were in power and with the Assyrians when the Ethiopians were in power. In —667, Ashurbanipal re-invaded the land, beat Taharqa in the Delta, and reconquered the country. Taharqa fled back to Kush and stayed there.

Beset by mounting troubles at home, Ashurbanipal decided to try to rule Egypt indirectly, through an Egyptian puppet, rather than directly. Accordingly he made a prince of Saïs, Necho,[20] his viceroy. Necho served the Assyrians loyally. He perished when Taharqa's nephew and successor Tanutamon[21] tried again to regain Egypt and occupied Memphis. But Tanutamon fled before Ashurbanipal, who appointed Necho's son Psamtek viceroy in his father's place.

When he saw that the Assyrians were in no position to interfere, Psamtek cautiously promoted himself to king of an independent Egypt and ruled from Saïs as Psamtek I, the founder of the Twenty-sixth or Saïte Dynasty. He had a long and prosperous reign of fifty-four years. When he died in —610 he was succeeded by his equally durable son Necho.[22] Necho's reign saw two signal enterprises.

One was a ship canal to connect the Red Sea with the Mediterranean. Ever since the First Dynasty, canals for irrigation purposes had been a major preoccupation of Egyptian kings and their servants. Among the first duties of a provincial governor were the digging and repair of canals. These canals were used to flood large tracts of the country during the Nile's high water, which occurs in the autumn as a result of summer rains in the lands to the South. Senuṣert III, who reigned in —XXI, was so vigorous a canal-builder that he became known as "the king who built the canals" and was remembered as the legendary "Sesostris."

Necho's canal did not run north and south through the Serbonian Swamp, between Egypt and Sinai, as does the present Suez Canal. Instead, it ran east and west, from the easternmost branch of the Nile, near modern Zagazig, to Lake Timsâḥ, the mid-point of the present Suez Canal. Thence it turned south and followed more or less the course of the Suez Canal, skirting the Bitter Lakes to the head of the Red Sea. Necho gave up the project, we are told, when an oracle warned him that he was laboring for the benefit of "the foreigner."

Necho's other project was to commission a group of Phoenicians to sail down the east coast of Africa, round the southern tip of the continent, up the west coast, and back home through the Mediterranean. It took them over two years; for, when they ran low on food, they beached their ships, sowed wheat, waited for it to grow, and harvested it before sailing on. It was an amazing achievement.

Herodotos, who repeated the story, refused to believe it on the ground that, according to the Phoenicians, the sun was to their north at noon when they were rounding the southern part of Africa.[23] But this very statement, which Herodotos disbelieved, is precisely what leads us to credit the story today. Since the earth is round, the sun *does* appear to the north to people in the Southern Hemisphere at noon. In Herodotos' day, the theory of the earth's roundness had not yet become generally known, let alone widely accepted. So Herodotos had no reason to expect the sun to behave in this outlandish fashion.

Under the Saïte Dynasty, prosperous Egypt enjoyed an Indian summer as an independent state. The illusion was rife that the land had once again recovered its ancient power and glory and would continue forever thus. Necho even tried an invasion of Syria, to recover the Asiatic provinces of the New Empire. But Nebuchadrezzar routed the Egyptian army and sent it fleeing back to Egypt.

The motif of Saïte Egypt was "back to the good old days." There was a self-conscious revival of the styles of the Old Kingdom in art and literature, as if Egypt's ancient might and security could be thus recovered. Notables had themselves sculptured wearing the simple linen kilt of pyramid-building days, much as European sculptors of late +XVIII and early +XIX, during the classical revival, portrayed eminent subjects like Voltaire and George Washington in Roman togas. For everyday wear, however, most upper-class Egyptians continued to wear their long, pleated robes and round wigs, just as Voltaire and Washington adhered to their knee breeches and powdered perukes.

For all this archaism, some things had changed beyond recall. For one thing, a new element had entered the military picture. This was the Greek mercenary infantryman, who appeared in growing numbers in the armies of Chaldaean Babylonia and of Saïte Egypt. These soldiers were effective out of proportion to their numbers, for one reason because of their armor. Bronze helmets and cuirasses (usually leather jacks studded with bronzen scales or buttons) had been used for many centuries to some extent throughout the Near East but, perhaps because of cost, had usually been limited to officers and to small élite forces. The new Greek suit was not only technically more advanced but also more generally used.

Greek traders had also taken to the new medium of exchange, coined money, with enthusiasm. The charm of Greek artifacts and the acumen of Greek merchants reduced the Phoenicians, who had long dominated the eastern Mediterranean, to second place in those waters.

Psamtek I encouraged Greeks to settle in Egypt. When they aroused the hostility of the xenophobic Egyptians, Necho ordered the Greeks to live in a single enclave, in the town of Naukratis, ten miles south-

59. Mortuary temple of King Khafra at Giza.

west of Saïs. Here they throve, for traders came from all over Egypt to deal with them. The Greeks found the Egyptians a very odd people indeed. Herodotos said of them:

> Not only is the climate different from that of the rest of the world, and the rivers unlike any other rivers, but the people also, in most of their manners and customs, exactly reverse the common practice of mankind. The women attend the markets and trade, while the men sit at home at the loom; and here, while the rest of the world works the woof up against the warp, the Egyptians work it down; the women likewise carry burdens upon their shoulders, while the men carry them upon their heads . . . They eat their food out of doors in the streets, but relieve themselves in their houses, giving as a reason that what is unseemly, but necessary, ought to be done in secret, but what has nothing unseemly about it, ought to be done openly . . .
>
> In other countries the priests have long hair, in Egypt their heads are shaven; elsewhere it is customary, in mourning, for near relations to cut their hair close; the Egyptians, who wear no hair at any other time, when they lose a relative, let their

beards and the hair of their heads grow long. All other men pass their lives separate from animals, the Egyptians have animals always living with them. Others make barley and wheat their food, it is a disgrace to do so in Egypt, where the grain they live on is spelt, which some call zea. Dough they knead with their feet, but they mix mud, and even take up dung with their hands. They are the only people in the world— they at least, and such as have learnt the practice from them— who use circumcision. Their men wear two garments apiece, their women but one . . . When they write or calculate, instead of going, like the Greeks, from left to right, they move their hand from right to left . . .[24]

Herodotos assumed that the Greek way of doing things was the right one. Actually, the Greeks had their own share of customs that "reverse the common practice of mankind." To this day, a Greek waves his hand in greeting with the back of the hand outward and the palm towards himself. If you ask a Greek a question, and he shakes his head and says "*nai*," he means "yes."

In the Saïte period, Memphis reached the form it retained with little change for several centuries. It was a city about four by eight miles, with the long axis north and south, parallel to the nearby Nile. A good part of the area inside the main wall may have consisted of cultivated fields and gardens.

Not counting the pyramids, the nearest of which (at Ṣaqqàra) rose just west of the city, the most conspicuous feature of Memphis was the Great Temple of Ptaḥ. The Greeks identified Ptaḥ with their own Hephaistos, the divine smith. This temple occupied an area about as large as that of the Great Temple of Amon at Karnak. Like that temple, it had been subjected to the additions, alterations, and rebuildings of many generations of kings. One of the Rameseses had furnished this temple with a propylaeum or ornamental entrance facing west; Psamtek I added another facing south. A number of colossal statues stood around these entrances. If later generations had not demolished this temple, it might present almost as imposing an appearance today as that at Karnak.

South of the Temple of Ptaḥ was the foreign quarter. North of the temple lay the sacred Lake Ater, a depression made by excavating clayey soil to make the Temple of Ptaḥ and the mound of the White Castle, which rose farther north yet. A number of other temples are known to have existed—of Apis, Hathor, Neit, Amon, and other deities— but no details of their construction have survived. In some cases we do **not** even know where they stood.

Theriolatry—that is, animal worship—had become increasingly important in Egypt. Every nome or province had some totem animal, be it a jackal, a baboon, a hawk, a pike, an ibis, a lion, a ram, a wolf, or a crocodile. The animal was held sacred as incorporating some divine attribute, and to kill the creature in the nome whereof it was the totem was a capital offense. In late Ptolemaic times, when Egyptians feared the growing might of Rome, an Egyptian mob nonetheless lynched a member of a Roman embassy because the man had accidentally slain a cat.[25]

The most spectacular relic of this cult of sacred beasts is at Memphis, where the temple of the Apis bull once stood. This bull, supposed to incarnate the god Apis, was kept in utmost taurine luxury. When an Apis bull died, the carcass was mummified. The mummy was placed in a great granite sarcophagus. The sarcophagus was sledded down into a catacomb beneath the temple and stored in one of the side chambers of this tunnel. Although the temple has vanished, the catacomb still exists. Twenty-one sarcophagi—the world's largest coffins—survive, although all have been emptied. They are monolithic boxes of granite, averaging 13 feet long, 7 feet wide, and 11 feet high, and weighing around 65 tons.

Saïte, Persian, and Ptolemaic Memphis was a more polyglot, heterogeneous city than anything Egypt had seen. One modern archaeological find is a collection of pottery heads, probably made by Greeks during the Persian period, showing the different national types to be seen in Memphis. There are Persians with their heads swathed in bashlyks. There are Scythians, with caps that rise to a conical point and are prolonged down into a pair of tails, which can be tied under the chin. There are Italians, Greeks, Egyptians, Babylonians, Negroes, and even Indians.

I once wrote a fictional description of Memphis in the reign of Ptolemaios I, about 225 years after the end of the Saïte period. The general picture of the city, however, had changed but little in that interval, so I shall quote it. It follows the descriptions of ancient Greek travelers and the findings of modern archaeology. The narrator is supposed to be a Greek on a mission from his native Rhodes to the court of Ptolemaios. "Manethôs" is the Hellenized Egyptian priest Manetho, a character in the story.

> Memphis was by far the largest city I had ever seen. A colossal wall of pearly limestone incloses the city proper, which stretches back from the waterfront across a spacious plain for thirty furlongs and along the river for sixty. Within the wall, many temples rise from the enormous spread of brown brick houses, and around them tower the upper parts of an army of gigantic statues . . .
> The foreign quarter of Memphis is noisily colorful. Here one is jostled by men in Hellenic cloaks, men in sleeved robes,

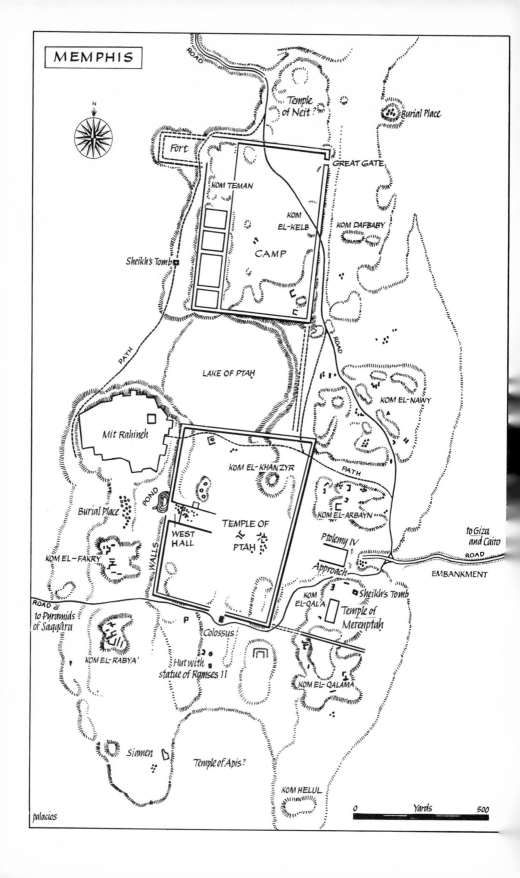

men in leather jackets, and men with naked upper bodies. Legs in kilts, and legs in trousers, and bare legs stride past; the blue eyes and lank pale hair of the Kelt mingle with the shiny black skin and tribal scars of the Ethiop. Atop the hurrying figures bob Libyan ostrich plumes, tall spiral Syrian hats, Arabian head-cloths, Persian felt caps, and Indian turbans.

Here a liquid-eyed Iberian with black side whiskers under his little black woolen bonnet tries to make an assignation with a slender Indian girl in gauzy muslins and jingling silver gim-cracks; there a curly-haired, scar-faced Etruscan quarrels with a booted, bearded, bowlegged Scythian; they shout insults with hands on knives until a Greek soldier from the garrison parts them with a threatening growl. A stocky, turbaned Kordian orders his horoscope from a curly-bearded Babylonian; a slim, hawk-faced Nabataean and a fat Phoenician goldsmith haggle over a bracelet, with much waving of arms, invocation of strange gods, and crashing of gutturals . . .

We left our comrades at the inn. Having helped Manethôs to buy a pair of paper shoes, I parted from him and bent my steps in the direction he had indicated, towards a flat-topped hill in the center of the city. On this akropolis stood the camp of the garrison and the palace of King Apries of former times. Manethôs told me that the hill on which the citadel rests is all man-made.

The palace, dating back before the Persian rule, is one of those rambling old edifices of which nearly every part has been demolished and rebuilt at one time or another, so that a chaos of architectural plans and styles results. Next to the room where I waited, workmen were noisily knocking down a wall. Lizards, fleeing the destruction of their homes, darted out of cracks in the wall of the waiting room and scuttled across the floor, paus-ing only to snap at a passing fly . . .

Next morning all in our party wished to see the sights of Memphis. We therefore followed Manethôs through the nar-row, winding, dusty streets, past block after block of blank brown walls. Striding ahead with an ivory-handled walking stick, he led us first to the small temple of Hathor in the foreign quarter. He pushed through the crowd of beggars—many blind, for blindness is a common affliction in Egypt—at the entrance to the sacred precinct. He left us in the courtyard (naturally, as we were not purified initiates) and disappeared into the temple proper. Soon he came out again, his visage glum.

"No luck," he said. "Next we shall try the great temple of Phtha."

This is the largest temple in Memphis, standing amid green groves in a spacious temenos in the midst of the city, south of the citadel where I had met with misfortune. About the main entrance, on the south side of the precinct, stand six colossal statues, two of them thirty cubits high and four of them twenty. I have been told that they represent either King Sesostris or the second King Rhameses, surnamed Osymandyas, and his family. In addition, there is an enormous statue, nearly thirty cubits long, lying on its back.

I burnt to examine these statues closely, to see what I could learn about the construction and erection of colossi. However, as soon as we appeared at the principal gate of the temenos, we were set upon not only by beggars but also by a swarm of would-be guides, who clamored:

"You want see sights, yes? Come with me! You want guide? Show you temple, pyramid, tomb? Ride camel? Me clever guide, know all secrets of ancient Memphis! Speak all languages! See dancing girl? Buy jewelry? Need passionate woman? See, here medicine for virility, made from black Ethiopian lotus! Make you good for ten stands a night! Want pretty boy? I get you rare drug, make you dream of heaven! Have fortune told? Come see orgy of Seth-worshipers! Buy antiquities from tombs of old kings? . . ."

I asked Manethôs: "How do you say 'no' in Egyptian?"

"Say *enen*. If they persist, add *rhou-ek*, which means 'run away!'"

I said *enen* and *rhou-ek* until our tormentors gave up and assailed other visitors, such as a lordly Persian couple behind us. For folk from many nations travel to Memphis to see its wondrous sights, and a class of Memphites has grown up to guide, guard, entertain, exploit, and prey upon these travelers.

We followed Manethôs into the temenos of Phtha, who to the Egyptians is the creator, the god of property and stability, and the tutelary deity of Memphis. Inside the temenos a swarm of concessionaires sold religious goods, such as little copper statues of Phtha to bury at the corner of one's lot to keep away evil spirits . . .

We trailed off southward to the temple of Apis, where dwells the sacred bull in a chamber. This chamber opens on a court surrounded by a colonnade whose columns are twelve-cubit statues. Then we marched northwest to the temple of Ammon. Gaining no advantage there, we went on to northward, along a wide asphalt-paved avenue, past the two great statues at the western gate of the temenos of Phtha, and past the sacred lake of Phtha. Here, in a park on the borders of the lake, was a space inclosed by a towering fence of thick bronze bars, with soldiers standing guard and a crowd of sightseers jostling.

When we had wormed our way up to the bars, I saw that inside the inclosure stood the funeral car of the divine Alexander himself. A breath-taking sight it was. The coffin rested on an enormous four-wheeled carriage of the Persian type, with gilded spokes and iron tires, and hubs in the form of lions' heads, each head holding a golden spear in its teeth. Stretched out from the front axle were four huge jointed poles, each having four quadruple yokes, for the vehicle was made to be drawn by sixty-four mules.

Around the sides of the wagon ran a colonnade upholding a roof of golden scales inlaid with precious stones, with a cornice from which projected golden heads of goat-stags. From the cornice hung four long painted panels showing Alexander and his bodyguards, his elephants, his cavalry, and his ships. At each corner of the roof stood a golden statue of Victory, and there were bells, golden wreaths, and other ornaments too numerous to list.

Between the columns of the colonnade I could see the huge golden sarcophagus of Alexander, on which lay a gold-embroidered purple robe and the armor and weapons of the great king. Over all floated a vasty purple banner with an olive wreath embroidered in golden thread . . .

When we had looked our fill, we continued northward to the temple of the goddess Neïth, where Manethôs made further inquiries. These, however, added nothing to what we had already heard. We crossed a canal and climbed the slopes to the west of the city, to the temple of Anoubis, the dog-headed judge of the dead. This temple stands on the edge of the desert, where a stride takes one from green field to golden-yellow sandy waste.

Thence we trudged, under the scorching Egyptian sun, west along a road lined with brooding sphinxes, where buff-brown pyramids, great and small, rise from inclosures on either hand, and graveyards spread far into the shimmering distance . . .

Footsore and weary, we came to the temple of Osiris. Here the clamor of bustling Memphis is heard no more. There is nothing to see but blue sky, golden sand, and this vast complex of sacred buildings; no sound but the murmur of hymns from the temple and the gentle hiss of blowing sand. Inside the temenos stood a great ithyphallic statue of Osiris, draped in a flame-colored robe and symbolizing the generative powers of the sun, the moon, and the Nile . . .[26]

In —569, in the reign of King Apriês,[27] an official named Amasis[28] usurped the throne. He married into the royal family to legitimize his rule and is thus counted as a member of the Twenty-sixth Dynasty.

During Amasis' long, peaceful reign, portentous events shook the world. Cyrus the Great swallowed up the Median Empire, the kingdom of Lydia, and the Neo-Babylonian Empire in his own ever-growing Persian Empire. In —529, Cyrus fell in a campaign against the northern nomads and was succeeded by his son Cambyses.[29] Three years later, old Amasis died, leaving his son Psamtek[30] III to face the all-conquering might of Persia.

Soon (—525) Cambyses found a pretext for invading Egypt. Herodotos tells us Cambyses demanded that Amasis send him his daughter for a concubine. Affronted by the demand but not daring to defy it, Amasis sent instead a daughter of the late King Apriês. She, however, soon disclosed the deceit to Cambyses, who swore vengeance.[31] The story could be true, or have at least a basis in truth. But then, Herodotos' priestly Egyptian sources were not always scrupulous or accurate.

Anyway, Cambyses soon broke the Egyptian army. He sent a Greek ship to Memphis to demand its surrender. When the ship tied up, a mob rushed aboard and tore the Persian herald and the Greek crew to pieces. So, when he took the city, Cambyses held a mass execution of noble Egyptians.

The Egyptians from whom Herodotos got his accounts made Cambyses a cruel, capricious, and violent despot who, after various follies and outrages—stabbing the sacred Apis bull; burning King Apriês' mummy; sending an army to the Oasis of Sîwa in the West, which perished in a sandstorm; sending another army against the Kushites, which perished of starvation; and murdering kinsmen and sup-porters—went finally mad.

We cannot tell how much truth there is in these stories. The only other account of Cambyses, by Ktesias of Knidos,[32] says nought of these eccentricities. In the first place, though, it was written from Persian sources, which would put the best face on things. In the second, all we have of it is an abridgment in the compilation of the Christian Patriarch Photius. The two sources agree that Cambyses caused a brother, whom he suspected of plotting a coup, to be murdered. They also agree that Cambyses died of an accidentally self-inflicted wound in the thigh.

Otherwise, the two biographies differ in many details, and there is

60. Memphis during the Saïte period. (Drawing by Roy G. Krenkel.)

no present way to be sure which, if either, is truthful in a given case. This often happens in the lives of celebrated ancients when all the information that we have about them comes from one or two sources, passionately prejudiced either for or against the man in question. So we shall probably never know for sure whether in fact Sokrates was as good, or Nero as bad, as he was made out to be.

We can, however, be sure that some of Herodotos' tales are false. Heredotos himself seems to have been thoroughly honest and conscientious, but he could not check all his sources. Despite the disaster that is supposed to have befallen Cambyses' Ethiopian expedition, it is known from other sources that Persian power was in fact extended over northern Kush.

Furthermore, the stories of Cambyses and Croesus, the ex-king of Lydia, are purely fictional. Herodotos repeats an appealing tale of how Cyrus ordered Croesus burned alive when he captured Croesus' capital of Sardeis; how Cyrus took pity on Croesus and reprieved him; and how Croesus became Cyrus' trusted friend and adviser. In fact, an inscription of Cyrus records that Croesus perished in the fall of Sardeis; he may have immolated himself on his own pyre, as defeated kings sometimes did. In any case he was not alive in Cambyses' reign to give that testy monarch good advice.

Whether Cambyses was a cruel madman or just one more ancient autocrat, perhaps a little rougher and tougher than most, he died in —522. After a round of plots, murders, and civil wars, he was succeeded by his cousin Darius,[33] who was succeeded by his son Xerxes,[34] and so on for 200 years. This was a longer span than any earlier empire had achieved.

The Egyptians were quiet under the wise and capable rule of Darius, who completed Necho's Red Sea canal. But they rose at the beginning of Xerxes' reign, in —485. Xerxes sent his brother Achaemenes,[35] who in three years put down the rebellion. This, however, tied up the main Persian forces and postponed Xerxes' invasion of Greece. Xerxes burned to avenge the Persian defeat at Marathon; but the delay enabled the Athenians to build the navy that broke Xerxes' sea power at Salamis and caused the invasion to fail.

At the beginning of the reign of Xerxes' successor Artaxerxes I, the Egyptians rose again under Inarôs,[36] a dynast of Libyan origin. The Athenians, then at the height of their imperial power, sent an expeditionary force, while the Egyptians captured Memphis and besieged the Persian garrison in the White Castle. But Artaxerxes gathered a huge army, which beat the Egyptians and captured the survivors of the Greeks after a siege of a year and a half. The Athenians lost over 200 ships and thousands of men in their worst disaster up to their Sicilian expedition.

61. Cairo, the modern successor to Memphis.

Through the next two reigns, Egypt was quiet. During the disturbances that followed the death of Darius II in —404, the Egyptians again revolted and this time managed to keep their independence, with the help of a large mercenary Greek army, for sixty years. Three short-lived Egyptian dynasties—the last truly native rulers of Egypt for over 2,000 years—followed one another.

In —358, another forceful ruler came to the throne of the Persian Empire. This was Artaxerxes III Ochus, who seven years later organized another invasion of Egypt. Both sides used many Greeks. Repulsed in his first attempt, Artaxerxes came back in —340 and, after a hard battle, once more reduced Khem, with great harshness, to subjection.

In —338, an Egyptian eunuch named Bagoas poisoned Artaxerxes Ochus and put Artaxerxes' son on the throne. When that young man did not suit him, Bagoas poisoned him, too, and substituted a cousin, Darius III Codomannus. After a while, Bagoas tired of Darius and prepared to murder him; but Darius beat the eunuch to the draw and made him drink the poison.

While Artaxerxes Ochus was a cruel, murderous despot, he was at least able and vigorous. Alexander of Macedon would have found

Artaxerxes a much tougher opponent than he did Darius III, an amiable, well-meaning, but timid and indecisive mediocrity. Although, as a young man, Darius III had once slain an enemy chieftain in single combat, he proved hopeless as a general. In both his great battles with Alexander, he panicked while the fight still hung in the balance and fled. Thereupon his army, as armies generally did, dissolved in rout.

In —332, while Darius was still in the field, Alexander entered Egypt. This was only nine years after the last really Egyptian pharaoh[37] had fled to Kush from the seemingly invincible Persians.

The Egyptians did not even try to resist Alexander. They had carried on sporadic resistance against Artaxerxes Ochus, but repeated defeats had worn out their fighting spirit. They welcomed Alexander to Memphis and eagerly took him to see the sights. They soon found that, despite the differences between Greek and Egyptian culture, they and he got on very well. Alexander was handsome, charming, and (when given his own way) tactful. He was, moreover, truly impressed by the wealth and antiquity of Egypt.

When he had seen Memphis, Alexander sailed down the Nile, founded Alexandria-by-Egypt, and made a pilgrimage to the Temple of Amon-Ra in the Oasis of Sîwa. There the priests, who had doubtless been tipped off, hailed Alexander as the son of the supreme god, Amon-Ra-Zeus. The young conqueror found this title useful in controlling the millions of Asian and African subjects whom he brought under his sway.

Alexander died in —323 without leaving a successor qualified to rule, and his generals carved up his empire and fought over the pieces. One general, Ptolemaios the son of Lagos, seized Egypt and ruled it from Alexandria. Of all the realms of the Diadochi or Successors, as these generals are called, the Ptolemaic kingdom proved the most durable, surviving for nearly three centuries.

Alexander had seen Memphis at its peak. During the Persian rule in Egypt, Memphis had been the main administrative center. With the growth of Alexandria, however, Memphis declined—not suddenly, but little by little. If no longer the political capital, it still possessed an excellent commercial location, and its monuments had been attracting a lively tourist trade ever since Saïte times.

Ancient tourism must have been on a small scale compared with modern, since travel was so much slower and so much more beset by hazards and hardships, and since the number who could afford to wander the world sight-seeing was but a tiny fraction of what it is today. But the accounts of Herodotos and other classical writers who visited Egypt indicate that tourism was a going thing and fairly well organized. Some Greek visitor paused to scratch, on one of the toes of the Sphinx, several lines from an otherwise unknown Greek poem:

... they are perished also,
Those walls of Thebes which the Muses built;
But the wall that belongs to me has no fear of war,
It knows not either the ravages of war or the sobbing ...

So things continued through the Ptolemaic and Roman periods. At the beginning of the Christian Era, Strabon the geographer found that the mud-brick palaces had all fallen into ruins but that the city was otherwise populous. In late —IV, the Christian emperor Theodosius I ordered a general destruction of the temples and statues of Memphis, along with other relics of paganism throughout the eastern Roman Empire. There was some destruction, but the sheer size of the task prevented its completion.

The real downfall of Memphis came with the Arab conquest of +641. The conqueror, 'Amr ibn-al-'Âṣ, set up his capital[38] across the Nile and ten miles north of Memphis. Later medieval Muslim rulers founded a city still farther north and called it al-Qâhira or Cairo. The Memphites gradually moved to the new city, so that we might say that the soul of Memphis was reincarnated in Cairo as that of Babylon was in Seleuceia, Ctesiphon, and Baghdad.

Old Memphis was left to decay, and builders mined its ruins for stone and brick wherewith to build houses and bridges in Cairo. As late as 1200, the ruins of Memphis could still excite wonder. During the next few centuries, however, the structures aboveground almost entirely disappeared. The plain was left to the plodding peasant and the yapping jackal, with the step pyramid of King Joṣer brooding over the sandy waste.

VIII

VIOLET-CROWNED ATHENS

> . . . BEHOLD
> WHERE AT THE ÆGEAN SHORE A CITY STANDS
> BUILT NOBLY, PURE THE AIR, AND LIGHT THE SOIL;
> ATHENS, THE EYE OF GREECE, MOTHER OF ARTS
> AND ELOQUENCE, NATIVE TO FAMOUS WITS
> OR HOSPITABLE, IN HER SWEET RECESS,
> CITY OR SUBURBAN, STUDIOUS WALKS AND SHADES;
> SEE THERE THE OLIVE GROVES OF ACADEME,
> PLATO'S RETIREMENT, WHERE THE ATTIC BIRD
> TRILLS HER THICK-WARBLED NOTES THE SUMMER LONG . . .[1]
>
> *Milton*

62. Athens: View looking eastward across the ancient Agora. Beyond the Agora is the Stoa of Attalos (a modern restoration) and beyond that Mount Lykabettos.

THE SUN had not yet risen, but there was enough light in the east to show the jagged profile of Mount Hymettos against the paling sky. The dimmer stars winked out. The dark bulk of the Akropolis began to take shape: the huge, ship-shaped crag itself, 1,000 feet long and two-fifths as wide, surrounded by 100-foot cliffs, with a rim of massive fortification walls; the path lined with statues, stelae, and other monuments, which zigzagged up the west end; the cluster of buildings—the Propylaia and the little Temple of Victorious Athena—at the top of this path; the scattering of statues, altars, and shrines about the top of the crag; and in the midst of the plateau, the 200-foot-long bulk of the Parthenon.[2]

East of the Parthenon, where the monuments thinned out, much of the space was occupied by several hundred tents. At the eastern end of the crag, in an open space, a group of men sat or squatted around a small fire, warming their hands against the winter's chill.

These men did not look Athenian. They wore gnomish caps, which rose into points above their heads and were prolonged down over their ears into a pair of tails, which they sometimes tied under their chins. Their long hair escaped from under these caps and hung down their backs, while full beards brushed their chests. They wore short belted jackets and embroidered trousers tucked into the tops of calf-high boots. Stinking powerfully of dried sweat and leather, they looked like a group of actors gotten up to play medieval Russian peasants in some Slavic opera.

Another man approached the group around the fire. "Where's Skylas?"

"Still asleep, I suppose," said a seated man. They spoke Scythian, a tongue akin to Persian. "Why?"

"Because you and he seine the Agora this morning."

"Again?" said a squatting Scythian. "I thought they had their Assembly yesterday."

"They did," said the standing man, "but so many wanted to speak that, instead of dissolving the Assembly, the president adjourned it until this morning. Old Longpate has a speech, and he didn't want to cut it short."

"What's all the fuss about, sergeant?" asked another. A man detached himself from the group, went to a tent, and roused one of the occupants. Skylas appeared, rubbing his eyes and pulling on his cap. He stopped to urinate against the parapet and then joined the group around the fire, now wolfing rolls of coarse barley bread washed down with sour wine.

"The chief told me," said the sergeant, "that the Spartans have made a last offer. If the Athenians don't take it, there will be war."

"War is a good time for slaves to run away," murmured a Scythian.

"Don't talk rubbish! It's hundreds of leagues to Scythia, through half of Hellas and then through wild, unknown country. You'd have to steal your way, and they'd catch you and kill you. As I was saying: The Spartans want the Athenians to raise the siege of some place up north— Potidaia, I think the name is. I got it from the chief, who got it from the Board of Eleven. They also want the Athenians to evacuate Aigina and to let the Megarians trade in Athenian ports."

"These Greek politics are too complicated for me," yawned another. "Back home, everything was simple. If the next tribe had something your tribe wanted, you went out and took it. If they tried to stop you, you took their scalps."

"Yes, and look where that simple system landed you," sneered another.

"Oh, I don't know. I had rather be free, of course, but I get paid regularly, the work is easy, and the winters don't freeze your balls off."

The group grew as more Scythians crawled out of their tents. Others, coming off night patrol, threaded their way among the monuments towards the encampment. Around the entrance to the Parthenon, at the east end, priests puttered with the preparations for the dawn sacrifice and prayers. The sergeant gave the day's orders:

"Ariantas, pick twenty men and report to the Pnyx, to keep order at the Assembly. Bowstrings and full quivers."

A couple of Scythians groaned. "Oh, sergeant, what's the sense of lugging those heavy things around all day? We never get a chance to shoot anybody."

"Orders. The Spartans and their guards are here, and the Eleven don't want to risk a fracas. Idanthyrsos, you and Ariapeithes are to guard the jail. Skylas, you and Saulios shall seine the Agora."

He issued more orders until all the men of his command not on night duty, sick, or on leave had been assigned. Several other fires had been kindled, and the other sergeants were giving orders to their companies.

The light waxed, and sounds of activity from the streets below increased. Skylas and Saulios walked leisurely westward towards the Propylaia. The first had a coiled length of cord slung over one shoulder, while the second bore a pail full of powdered red chalk. Each carried, in his other hand, a stiff Scythian bowstave, unstrung. These bows served the function of a policeman's truncheon.

In the growing light, Skylas proved a young man, broad-shouldered and stocky, with wide cheekbones, a snub nose, a blond beard, and gray-green eyes. His companion was taller, leaner, darker, and older, with a sour expression. He nodded curtly to a member of the night patrol who called out a greeting.

"Lucky bastards," he growled. "On night duty, if a man wants to sneak off to his woman for a quick one, nobody's the wiser. As it is . . . Have you a regular woman yet, Skylas?"

"Not yet."

"You don't go in for these dirty Greek boy-loving games, I hope?"

"Gods, no! I have my eye on a Phrygian girl, a slave of Medon the potter . . ."

The flaming eye of the sun, half veiled in light clouds, peeked over the notched blade of Mount Hymettos. The first beams caressed the higher projections of the Akropolis: the entablature of the Parthenon, brightly painted in red, blue, and gold; the bronzen point of the spear of Pheidias' colossal statue of Athena, the special patron goddess of Athens, near the Propylaia. The Scythians passed a roped-off area where workmen were clearing the ground around a cluster of shrines for the projected Erechtheion. They strolled past a group of statues, painted in lifelike colors, on which a group of sleepy workmen were already at work. A life-sized Athena was already in place, and the workers, with ropes and beams and grunts, were setting up a companion statue of the satyr Marsyas. An elderly man was directing operations. Whereas the workmen wore only tunics in the form of knee-length singlets, the elderly man was bundled up in a himation—a huge, blanketlike rectangle of woolen cloth pinned and draped about his person. To this man Skylas spoke:

"Rejoice, Master Myron!"

"Stay well, my good Skylas!" replied the sculptor, with a condescending nod and a slight flip of his hand.

"He knows your name," said Saulios.

"Yes, I've talked to him about his sculpture. If the gods had been willing, I might have been a sculptor myself."

They passed a huge ornamental bronze chariot, with an inscription explaining that it had been made of the spoils taken from the Boiotians and the Euboians. They passed the 30-foot colossus of Athena and traversed the Propylaia. Then they began to descend the winding path from the Akropolis. Ahead on the horizon could be seen the houses of the harbor town of Peiraieus[3] and a stretch of the sea. Unlike Athens, Peiraieus had streets laid out on an orderly grid plan by the architect Hippodamos, whom Perikles had brought to Athens. Saulios grumbled:

"It's stupid, making us climb that polluted crag twice a day. They should have left our camp in the Agora."

"That was before my time," said Skylas.

"They moved us out of there to make room for the orators and the public meetings. Then they let the place fill up so with hucksters and their booths that the windbags abandoned the Agora anyway."

Several streets came together at the foot of the path, to form a small square. People hurried to and fro: housewives of the poorer classes and slave girls from the houses of the rich with water jars on their shoulders, stopping to fill their vessels at a nearby fountain; Hellenes—some bareheaded urbanites swathed in himatia, others farmers from the countryside in wide-brimmed felt hats, towing asses laden with produce. There were swarthy, curly-bearded Phoenicians in loose robes, with rings in their ears; shaven Egyptians in dirty white linens; and a few Negroes.

The Scythians turned right and followed a crooked street northward around the foot of the adjacent hill, called the Areios Pagos. The street was a mere 15 feet wide and unpaved. Boxlike houses of mud brick, mostly one-story, lined it. These houses—gray, buff, and sometimes whitewashed—each had a single door at ground level. The one-story houses otherwise presented blank, windowless walls to the street; those of two stories sometimes had a small, barred window high up on the second floor. The Scythians' boots squilched through mud, garbage, and ordure. Saulios wrinkled his nose.

"Just one big shit-house, that's all beautiful Athens is," he growled. "Give me the nice, clean steppe."

"The chief ought to put more men on night duty, to stop these people from dumping their slops in the street," said Skylas. "They're supposed to haul them to the Barathron."

Saulios shrugged. "The boys pull them in every night, but they can't cover every block all the time. The minute our backs are turned—splush! Let's go; there's the trumpet."

From the southwest wafted the silvery notes of the trumpet, calling the citizens to the Assembly. The whole Akropolis was now bathed in golden dawnlight, although the street in which the Scythians walked was still in shadow. The crowds thickened, so that Skylas and Saulios had to shoulder their way through.

The street opened out into the Agora. The market place and civic center was already crowded with hawkers: farmers selling their produce and peddlers proffering sundries. As Skylas and Saulios entered the open space, an Athenian herald mounted a pedestal and shouted:

"The Fourth Assembly of this sixth prytany of this year during which Pythodoros is archon is now reconvened following its adjournment of yesterday. All citizens shall report forthwith to the Pnyx on pain of a fine. The Fourth Assembly . . ."

In the Agora, another sergeant, in command of a handful of Scythians, went about urging non-citizens—slaves, foreigners, and women—to get out of the way. When he saw Skylas and Saulios, he called:

63. Akropolis of Athens from the southwest, with Mount Lykabettos in the background. (Courtesy of Ellen Kohler.)

"There you are! Come on; don't take all day!"

The pair wound their way to the north end of the Agora, while the non-citizens, the flower girls, and the breadwomen scurried into the side streets.

"Give them a little more time," growled the sergeant.

Grinning, Skylas and Saulios set down their pail, unwound their cord, and began dipping it into the pail, so that its entire length was soon covered with red chalk. "Seining the Agora" was a favorite duty of the Scythian archers, since it gave them a chance to see their masters, the Athenian citizens, scampering before them.

The position of the archers was ambiguous. On the one hand, they were slaves, bought and paid for. Skylas had fallen off his horse during a cattle raid and had been captured and sold to a dealer in Pantikapaion. They were chattels of the Athenians. If the Assembly wished to vote to send them to the silver mines of Mount Laureion to be worked to death, or even to have them massacred, the Assembly could do so.

On the other hand, the Scythians were policemen with full authority. One could arrest even the godlike Perikles if another citizen duly swore out a complaint against him. If a riot arose, the Scythians might whack the disturbers with their bowstaves to their hearts' content.

Skylas and Saulios stretched their cord across the north end of the Agora. The herald hopped down from his plinth.

64. Temple of Olympian Zeus, completed by the emperor Hadrian; the Akropolis in the background.

"Here comes!" shouted the sergeant.

Skylas and Saulios began to jog-trot down the length of the Agora, holding the cord taut between them so that it swept the area. Now and then they paused while another Scythian lifted it over a booth, a monument, or other obstacle, or to detour around one of the plane trees with which the square had been planted by Kimon.

The citizens had begun to flow out into the streets that led to the Pnyx. As the Scythians approached, the laggards speeded up until all were running: the Greeks slapping along in their sandals and low shoes, the Scythians clumping after them in their horseman's boots. Shouts, yells, and hoots of laughter arose. The mob of Athenians—urbanites and rustics mingled—streamed out of the Agora. A fat, elderly citizen, wheezing after his fellows, was caught by the cord and marked. Amid the derisive yells of his compatriots, he shambled after them, looking ruefully at the vermilion streaks on his cloak.

At the Pnyx—a partly natural half-bowl against the western city wall—a flag flapped languidly from a tall staff. The Athenians poured into the inclosure, past officials who checked their names off lists. Skylas and Saulios grinned at the fat citizen, who was taking small change out of his mouth to pay the fine incurred by the red marks on his cloak.

The Athenians jostled, crowded, chattered, bustled, argued, gesticulated, and gradually spread themselves around the theater, to sit down on the earth and the scanty grass. Scythians strolled about, settling arguments, parting disputants, and urging the citizens in broken Greek to spread out to the vacant parts of the bowl.

An hour after the initial trumpet blast, several thousand citizens were emplaced. The flag was hauled down. On the small stage, a priest prayed and cut the throat of a shoat. He carried the dripping piglet in a circuit around the Pnyx and back to his starting point. A herald shouted:

"All citizens, come within the sacred circle!"

The Scythians sauntered out to the periphery and, leaning on their bowstaves, took places outside the circle traced by the priest. Down in front, wooden benches were occupied by notables, including a small group of men in dirty cloaks, with shaven upper lips over full beards: the Spartan ambassadors. Nearly all the crowd was bearded, save for a few long-haired young exquisites who had taken to the Egyptian fashion of shaving. It was supposed that they did this to hold their middle-aged homosexual lovers.

After more prayers and routine announcements, the president of the Assembly mounted the plinth and cried:

"Who wishes to speak?"

All eyes turned to a man sitting in the front row. This man arose, adjusted his cloak, and strode to the plinth. The president placed a wreath of myrtle on the man's head, and the man mounted the plinth. This was Perikles the son of Xanthippos, *Stratêgos Dekatos Autos* or commander in chief of Athens.

Perikles was a gray-bearded, long-headed man of good height, handsome but showing the strain of recent events. He looked older than his sixty years. Within the past year he had not only been kept on the alert by the Spartan crisis but also had had to defend his friends—the sculptor Pheidias, the scientist Anaxagoras, and his mistress Aspasia—against charges brought by his political enemies. It was whispered that Perikles was losing control of the *demos;* that his foes would soon bring him down, ending three decades of his rule. Some said he wished war with Sparta to rally the people behind him. He spoke, in a clear voice with a sharp, staccato delivery:

> Athenians! I say, as I have always said, that we must never yield to the Peloponnesians, although I know that men are persuaded to go to war in one temper of mind, and act when the time comes in another, and that their resolutions change with the changes of fortune. But I see that I must give you the same, or nearly the same, advice which I gave before, and I call upon those whom my words may convince to maintain our united determination, even if we should not

escape disaster; or else, if our sagacity be justified by success, to claim no share of the credit. The movement of events is often as wayward and incomprehensible as the course of human thought; and this is why we ascribe to chance whatever belies our calculation.

For some time past the designs of the Lacedaemonians have been clear enough, and they are still clearer now. The treaty says that when differences arise, the two parties shall refer them to arbitration, and in the meantime both are to retain what they have. But for arbitration they never ask; and when it is offered by us, they refuse it. They want to redress their grievances by arms and not by argument; and now they come to us, using the language, no longer of exposition, but of command . . .[4]

In the end, Perikles convinced the Athenians that they must not yield to the Spartans on any point and that, if war came, the Athenians would surely win. And so began the end of the Golden Age of Athens.

As with most ancient cities, the history of Athens (in Greek, *hai Athênai*, "the Athenas") begins in a fog of myth and legend. The Athenians thought that Attika had been unified by the hero Theseus—who, however, is probably no more historical than his contemporary Herakles. The stories of Theseus tell how he was the son of King Aigeus of Athens and the daughter of the king of Troizen, where he was reared. When he grew up, he took Aigeus' sword and sandals to Athens, slaying robbers and ogres on the way. By these tokens he prevailed upon the king to acknowledge him. His stepmother Medea—the Colchian princess who had come to Greece with Jason—tried to poison him but failed.

Later, Theseus went to Crete, slew the Minotaur, and eloped with King Minos' daughter Ariadnê, whom he soon abandoned. Thinking that Theseus had perished in his quest, Aigeus killed himself. Theseus succeeded him and united Attika. He found time to war against the Amazons and kidnap their queen Antiopê, to accompany the Argonauts to Colchis (never mind the scrambled chronology), to take part in other heroic enterprises, and to beget offspring on his many women.

Subsequently, King Kodros of Athens gave his life in a fight with the Dorians (one of the main branches of the Greek peoples) because an oracle had foretold that only thus could the invaders be repulsed. Kodros was so good, they said, that the Athenians decided to have no more kings and chose an *archon* (regent) of limited powers instead.

Whether Kodros is based upon a real man or not, the fog of myth finally thins about —VII. Attika was already fully united. This had probably been done by force rather than, as in the legends of Theseus, by persuasion, because the voluntary union of neighboring states by peaceful means is extremely rare. It is rare because, in such a union, the head man of one of the uniting states—normally the weaker of the two—stands to lose his job, and so do his supporters stand to lose theirs. They therefore resist the union, calling upon their subjects to preserve their "liberty" and "independence." Contrariwise, a local leader in a larger nation, who feels that he is unlikely ever to attain supreme power in the nation, often starts a secessionist movement to form a new state with himself at the head. He exhorts his followers to strike for "independence" and "liberty" while the national leaders, whose power would be lessened by secession, combat it by calling for "loyalty" and "unity."

When authentic Athenian history begins, Attika was an aristocratic, oligarchic republic. The king had been reduced to a minor elected magistrate. The most influential body was the *Boulê* or Council of the Areopagus, so called because it met on the Areios Pagos. This was a council of elders, composed of the heads of the richest landowning families. This squirearchy monopolized all the important public offices.

From the Boulê, the three chief magistrates were elected annually. These were the king, who managed the state religion and judged law cases of certain kinds; the *polemarchos*, who commanded the army and judged certain other cases; and the archon, who held most of the remaining judicial powers. There were six other magistrates, who together with the previous three made up the Nine Archons. The ancient Athenians had no notion of a clear-cut separation of the legislative, executive, and judicial functions of government.

The people were organized into families, clans, and tribes. During —VII, as that revolutionary invention, money, came into use and fortunes were made in foreign trade, the *eupatridai* ("those of good fathers," i.e. nobles) were forced to admit to their class a lot of successful non-landowning bourgeoisie. The people were divided into classes according to wealth, with the richest and smallest class keeping its grip on the government.

Class conflict arose between the aristocracy and the lower orders, as the former tightened their hold not only on the wealth of the republic but also, by means of debt slavery, on the persons of the poor. Civil war was averted by a series of reforms. First, in —621, Drakon was appointed to reduce the laws to writing, so that a nobleman could no longer accuse a commoner at his whim and extemporize a law to cover the case.

Thirty years after Drakon's code, class conflict persisted. Then Solon, a successful merchant and a distinguished poet and intellectual, was elected archon with instructions to reduce the basic constitution to writing, also. Until then, the constitution had been unwritten, like that of the United Kingdom. Hence, when a dispute arose as to whether some act was constitutional, the disputants appealed to contradictory "traditions" to support their cases, and the question was likely to be decided by force and fraud.

Solon made enough changes to enrage the rich, if not enough to satisfy the poor. He canceled debts, abolished debt slavery, and reduced the power of the Boulê. He kept the division of the population into classes by wealth, but he extended political rights downward, opening some offices to the lower grades. The poorest class, which had had virtually no rights, was recognized as citizens and given limited political rights. The result was not what we, in this egalitarian age, should call a democracy, but it was much more democratic than it had been. We might say that Solon invented, if not democracy, at least constitutional republican government, without which democracy is impossible.

Little by little, *dêmokratia* (from *dêmos*, "people," + *kratein*, "to rule") made headway. When the division between rich and poor again became intolerable, a successful general named Peisistratos made himself dictator (*tyrannos* in Greek) with the support of the poor, to whom he distributed land taken from the rich. Having already conquered the island of Salamis, he occupied lands at the northern end of the Aegean Sea, on both sides of the Hellespont (the Dardanelles), and thus founded the Athenian Empire.

Being an able, affable, pious, and energetic man—he built waterworks and fostered the early development of the drama—Peisistratos kept his illegal rule on and off for over thirty years. When he died, his two sons ruled until one was murdered by the youths Harmodios and Aristogeiton. Later, the Athenians recalled the assassins as heroic tyrannicides and put up statues to them; but the actual occasion for the murder was a sordid homosexual love-triangle. While a permissive attitude towards sexual deviation has long characterized many Mediterranean peoples, the Greeks carried this tendency further than most others—albeit, to take a balanced view, one can also find plenty of disapproving and derisive remarks about the practice in Greek literature.[5]

The surviving brother ruled harshly until an exiled family of aristocrats persuaded the Spartans to send an army to expel the tyrannos (−510). After further disturbances, a gifted democratic leader named Kleisthenes effected further reforms.

A source of disturbance had been the strife among the noble families and their kinsmen and hangers-on. These clans carried on feuds in the style of Montague and Capulet. Kleisthenes ended this by reorganizing the people not on the primitive basis of kinship but on that of residence. He divided the city into wards (*dêmoi*) and precincts (*trit-*

65. Approach to the Akropolis of Athens from the west.

tyes), and formed ten new tribes of the inhabitants of arbitrary combinations of precincts. A new Council of Five Hundred, chosen by lot from the members of the new tribes, was the main political authority, and committees from this council carried on the day-to-day business of government.

Although the new Athenian constitution would seem to us, in the light of hindsight, clumsy and illogical, it worked well enough for a century.

Hardened by incessant warfare among their city-states, some European Greeks sent help to the Greek cities of Asia Minor when the latter revolted against Persian rule. After crushing this revolt, the Persian king Darius—justly called "the Great"—looked sternly across the Aegean at those he considered troublemakers. He had already, in —512, conquered Thrace and reduced Macedonia to a tributary state.

In —490, Darius sent an expedition by sea against the Athenians, whom he deemed the worst troublemakers of all. The Persians landed at Marathon, 18 miles northeast of Athens across the tapering Attic peninsula. Under General Kallimachos, the Athenians marched to meet them with their hearts in their mouths. For the Persian force, though small, still outnumbered the Athenians; the Persians were the world's most renowned warriors; and the promised help from Sparta had not come.

Here luck and technology came to the aid of the Athenians. The

66. Stairway leading up to the Propylaia of the Akropolis of Athens.

Persians depended on foot archers and cavalry. The archers, shooting from behind a palisade of wicker shields, softened up the foe; then the horsemen swarmed out and cut the enemy to pieces. But, as a result of some logistical difficulty like that which sent Teddy Roosevelt's Rough Riders to Cuba without their mounts, the Persians' horses had failed to reach the scene. So the world's most dashing cavalry had to stumble about afoot.

Moreover, Greek bronzesmiths had developed a new suit of armor for the Greek heavy infantryman or *hoplites*. A bronzen helm with projections to guard his nose, cheeks, and neck protected his head. A bronze cuirass, molded to fit his manly form, inclosed his torso. A kilt of leather straps with bronze buttons warded his loins, while bronzen greaves protected his legs. His shield was a circular structure of wood and leather, a yard across, sometimes with a facing of thin bronze. The Greek soldier's main offensive weapon was a short stabbing spear. He used his short, broad chopping sword only when his spear was lost or broken.

The Persians had no such panoply, although soon afterwards they began to wear shirts of scale mail. At this time, most of Darius' soldiers probably went into battle in their uniform hats, coats, and trousers, with a spear and a buckler.

Moreover, the Greeks had developed infantry drill beyond other peoples, save perhaps the Assyrians at the height of their power. Instead of rushing forward in a disorderly crowd, with each captain leading his own little knot of fighters, the Greeks had learned to march in ranks and files to the tune of flutes and to dress their lines, so that a company presented a bristling hedge of spears and shields. They may even have marched in step. So equipped and organized, they could withstand the attacks of cavalry. The Greek horsemen—usually of the aristocratic class, since they had to furnish their own horses—could not wear heavy armor because their horses were too small to bear the weight, and they could not charge home because they lacked stirrups and so were liable to fall off at any sudden shock. So their main duties were scouting, javelin-throwing, and hunting down fugitives after the fight had been won.

When the Athenian line advanced, the Persian archers loosed their withering blast. The Athenians plodded ahead, arrows bouncing from their bronze defenses. Then they charged. Once at close quarters, they had their unarmored foes at a grievous disadvantage. In the center, the Persians drove back the lobster-shelled Hellenes by weight of numbers and hard fighting. But the Athenian wings, where Kallimachos had placed most of his strength, closed in. The fight became a massacre, and the Persians fled to their ships, leaving over 6,000 on the field. The Persian commanders brought their ships around the peninsula to Phaleron, in sight of Athens, but changed their minds about landing when they found the Athenians already drawn up to meet them and learned that the Spartans were hastening up from the Isthmus of Corinth to help.

To the Persians, this was a minor border skirmish. To the Greeks, on the other hand, it was an event of great moment, for it gave them courage to face the greater host that Xerxes led into Greece twelve years later.

Xerxes the son of Darius was a man of ability but still a lesser man than his sire. In —480, he determined to end the squabble with these belligerent Westerners once and for all. He would extend his sway over European Greece, imposing upon these turbulent rogues the blessings of Persian peace and justice.

So Xerxes led a huge army across the Hellespont on a floating bridge. This included three of the six divisions of the Persian army, each of which ran to about 50,000 to 60,000 men. With them came several times that number of non-combatants. Later, Greek historians credited Xerxes with an army of 1 or 2 million, but this should not be taken seriously. The real Grand Army was impressive enough, especially since in ancient times any force of over 50,000 men was in a precarious position from sheer numbers. It was endangered by the difficulty of keeping enough food flowing in from the surrounding countryside to feed the men. If anything went wrong, the soldiers soon began to starve; then they deserted or mutinied.

A Greek suicide force briefly checked the Persians at Thermopylai. This merely annoyed the Persians, but it furnished the Greeks with a heroic legend to cherish. The Athenians fled to Salamis, leaving their empty town for the Persians to burn. Half the city-states of European Greece had already gone over to the Persians, and it looked as if nothing could prevent the addition of the whole peninsula to the Persian Empire. This might not have been the utter disaster for Western civilization that it is sometimes called. The Persians were a civilized folk, and their empire, if an exploiting despotism, was run in a more enlightened manner than earlier empires. But the conquest would certainly have drastically changed later history.

The Persian fleet (that is, a fleet from the Phoenician and Asiatic Greek cities under Persian rule) thought it had trapped the Greek fleet in the Bay of Eleusis, west of Peiraieus, between the island of Salamis and the mainland. When the Persian fleet advanced in column through the eastern passage into the bay, the Greeks surrounded the head of the column and smashed it, destroying a third of the Persian force. In a rage, Xerxes accused some of his Phoenician captains of cowardice and had their heads chopped off, whereupon the rest of the Phoenician contingent deserted.

Although he still had powerful land and sea forces in Greece, Xerxes decided to return to Asia with one of his three divisions. Herodotos' tale that Xerxes was frightened is probably mere patriotic propaganda. It is likely that Xerxes heard reports of impending revolts in other parts of his empire—the Ionian Greeks and the Babylonians were restless about this time. Furthermore, the difficulty of feeding so large an army had now, probably, become acute.

Xerxes made good his retreat, leaving two of the three divisions in Greece. Next year, after delays and petty bickerings, a large Greek army, under King Pausanias of Sparta, was raised to fight the Persians. This army engaged one of the Persian divisions near Plataia in a sprawling, confused, and bloody battle. The Persian general, Mardonius, was killed while leading a cavalry charge, and the Greeks defeated the Persian force and slaughtered the fugitives.

A few days later, an Athenian naval expedition destroyed a Persian fleet beached on Cape Mykalê, in Asia Minor, and a Persian army encamped nearby. The remaining Persian division was strung out along the route from Athens to the Hellespont. Hearing of the double defeats of Plataia and Mykalê, its general Artabanus had no choice but to take

67. Temple of Athena Nikê on the Akropolis of Athens.

his force back to Asia. The food supply had broken down at last, so many of his soldiers starved to death during the retreat.

After the Persian retreat, the Athenians, covered with glory, set about rebuilding their ruined town. For a while Themistokles, the outstanding Athenian leader, had great influence. Under his urging, the Athenians raised a new and larger wall around their city. They built up their navy and constructed harbors and a fortified naval base on the peninsula of Peiraieus. They formed a confederacy with the other maritime Greek cities of the Aegean to furnish ships and men to prosecute the war with Persia, which dragged on desultorily for another thirty years. City-states too small to contribute ships paid money into a treasury kept on the island of Delos. Hence the confederacy was called the Delian League.

Although Athens and Peiraieus were now fortified, they were still four miles apart. Therefore Athens could easily be cut off from the sea. So the Athenians adopted a measure already tried in neighboring Megara: to join the main city with its port by a pair of walls, the Long

68. Parthenon, seen through the columns of the Propylaia of the Akropolis of Athens. (Mrs. de Camp in the foreground.)

Walls.[6] Although this system might seem impractical because of the length of wall to be defended, it saw Athens through the Peloponnesian War. It worked because, at this time, the advanced siege machinery of the Assyrians, such as wheeled belfries with battering rams in their lower stories, was not yet used in Greece.

The Athenians also undertook to restore the temples on the Akropolis ("high city"). This crag had once served as a citadel but had been changed into a temple center as the city grew. The Persians had destroyed the old Temple of Athena—the Hekatompedon or "Hundred-Footer"—and it is uncertain to what extent it was rebuilt. In any case, the Athenians decided to build a new and grander temple nearby, which became known as the Parthenon.

While these things took place, Themistokles fell from power. He was accused of taking bribes. Perhaps he had, since the practice was usual among Greek statesmen. The Athenians ostracized him—that is, they voted that he should be exiled from the country for ten years. After he left the city, he was accused of treason and fled to the Persian court, where Xerxes had just been assassinated. Although many Persians who had lost kinsmen in the Greek invasion wanted Themistokles killed, he persuaded the new king, Artaxerxes, to grant him a year in which to learn Persian speech and ways so as to make the best defense. When the time came, he acquitted himself so well that Artaxerxes gave him a minor governorship, in which he lived out his days.

For a time a conservative, pro-Spartan general named Kimon led Athens; but then he, too, was ostracized (—461). Into his shoes stepped a rising young politician of aristocratic background but democratic sympathies, Perikles the son of Xanthippos, who earned the name of one of history's greatest statesmen. In his charm, courage, humanity, many-sidedness, high-mindedness tempered by low political cunning, and sagacity flawed by extravagance and grandiosity, he reminds one of Henri IV of France and of Franklin D. Roosevelt. Although his private personality was somewhat reserved and austere, he had Lenin's gift of presenting his ideas in such simple, clear, logical, and compelling form that he did not need to resort to the usual tricks of the demagogue to keep his following. For nearly thirty years he was the leading man of Athens, elected and reëlected, usually to the office of *Stratêgos Dekatos Autos.*

Perikles determined to make his beloved Athens the most beautiful city on earth, as well as the world's capital of the arts and sciences. To this end he embarked on a program of ruthless imperialism, which at that time was not considered wrong. The Athenians had already begun to convert the Delian League into an Athenian Empire. The city of Karystos was conquered and compelled to join the League. When Naxos tried to secede, the League's fleet blockaded her until she gave up the idea.

The "right" of secession is an old and insoluble problem. When a federation is formed, the question is usually ignored. If a right of secession were formally recognized, the federation would be too weak to be worth while. If it were expressly forbidden, many federating states would refuse to join at all. When the question comes up later, it is usually settled by force, as in the American Civil War.

Early in Perikles' rule, the Athenians sent an expeditionary force to Egypt. There Inarôs had revolted against the Persians. For a time he ruled the whole country, save for the White Castle of Memphis, where a Persian garrison held out. But Artaxerxes sent an army and fleet to Egypt, which captured Inarôs and his Greek allies. The common soldiers were allowed to straggle back home. Inarôs and the Athenian generals, although promised their lives, were executed on the insistence of the fierce old queen-mother Amestris, one of a number of singularly bloodthirsty queens with which Achaemenid Persia was afflicted.

The loss of men and ships in Egypt gave Perikles an excuse to move the Delian Treasury from Delos to Athens. There, he said, it would be safer from the Persians. The Athenians also persuaded or coerced most of the other members of the League, one by one, to pay an annual sum to Athens instead of furnishing men and ships. Then Perikles began to spend the funds of the Delian Treasury on a program of building, for the beautification of Athens.

The other members of the League protested, and even some Athenians thought that this was going a bit far. But Perikles retorted that so long as Athens protected the other members of the League, it was none of their business what was done with the money. Since the League navy was now mostly Athenian, what Athens said went. Some other territories, outside the League, were brought under Athenian rule, while members of the League who revolted or tried to secede were attacked and reduced to subservience. The Athenians deprived even the more docile members of the League of some of their self-rule by insisting that law cases of certain kinds be tried in Athenian courts.

Thus the Delian League became the Athenian Empire. For a decade, around −450, Athens reduced several neighboring mainland states to subjection; but they soon broke away, since Athens lacked the manpower to keep them under control. Thereafter, Perikles let the land empire go and concentrated on sea power. He cynically justified his imperialism to the Athenians:

> Do not think you are fighting for the simple issue of letting this or that state become free or remain subject to you. You have an empire to lose. You must realize that Athens has a mighty name in the world because she has never yielded to misfortunes and has to-day the greatest power that exists. To be hated has always been the lot of those who have aspired to rule over others. In the face of that hatred you cannot give up your power—even if some sluggards and cowards are all for being noble at this crisis. Your empire is a tyranny by now, perhaps, as many think, wrongfully acquired, but certainly dangerous to let go.[7]

While thus extending Athenian sway abroad, Perikles further democratized the constitution at home. Election by lot instead of by ballot was extended, and for the first time men were paid for public service. The point of such pay was that without it, only the richest could afford to serve in public offices. The rest could not take the time away from their work; hence the democratic state machinery took on an aristocratic bias in practice.

Service on the courts was also paid for the first time. The Athenians had a curious court system, although some cases remained in the jurisdiction of the archons. Most cases were heard before panels of *dikastai*—judges and jurymen combined—chosen by lot from the citizens. These courts ranged from 201 to 2,501 dicasts, the purpose of the odd numbers being to prevent tie votes. Hearings before so large a judicial body encouraged the parties to use flagrantly irrelevant and emotional appeals, as that a defendant should be let off because he had fought in some battle.

Choosing men for public office by lot may seem bizarre. But the Greeks believed that, in such a drawing, the gods would see to it that the lot fell upon a worthy choice. Even in Perikles' time, when skepticism about the gods' interest in men had arisen, it was still supposed that—as Andrew Jackson and his followers believed long afterwards—anybody of reasonably sound mind was competent to run any public job. The Athenians had a better excuse for such a belief than Jackson, since in their time questions of public policy were much less technical than those that bedevil a modern legislator.

Periklean Athens came as close as anything in history to what is sometimes called "direct democracy" or "participatory democracy." It was a government by amateurs. True, the voters were not the whole adult population. Women had no political voice; but then, they never had until late +XIX. A third of the population consisted of slaves with no political rights. Another fraction comprised the metics or resident aliens, who paid taxes and were subject to the laws but had no representation and no means of becoming citizens. Still, power was distributed more widely than anywhere else in the ancient world.

This "participatory democracy" worked fairly well for a while. If its weaknesses caused its eventual downfall, the same can be said for government of other kinds. An obvious weakness was that the system needed a Perikles to make it work well, and such men are hard to come by.

Another weakness was an old and hitherto insoluble problem: It is all very well to praise "rule by the people"; but what if the people commit acts that in an individual would be dishonesty, treachery, robbery, or murder? What reason is there to think that people collectively are any less liable to crimes and follies than individuals? In fact, "the people" can be just as wrongheaded as any individual, and all governments in general are inherently faithless, perfidious, and ungrateful. No matter what promises a government makes, a later government feels free to break them on the pretext of *"Salus populi suprema lex esto."*[8]

As an example, late in the Peloponnesian War, the Athenian fleet won a hard-fought naval battle at Arginousai, but a storm prevented the rescue of the crews of twenty-five Athenian ships destroyed in the fight. The kin of the lost crewmen raised an agitation. Demagogues stirred the Assembly to a passion for revenge and got it to condemn the eight generals who had commanded the fleet. When some—including

Sokrates, serving as a minor magistrate—questioned the legality of the procedure, "the majority kept crying out that it was monstrous if the people were to be hindered by any stray individual from doing what seemed to them right."9

So the Athenians killed the six of the eight generals, including Perikles' son, who were in their power. Later they repented and indicted the demagogues, who fled; but that did not bring back the dead generals. Thereafter, Athenian generalship was egregiously stupid and soon led to final defeat. The deaths of the six must have discouraged prudent men from seeking such posts. A purpose of the American Bill of Rights and of the slow and difficult procedures in many lands for amending the constitution is to prevent such blunders, resulting from momentary aberrations of the demos.

The other side of ancient Greek democracy was the jealous exclusiveness of city-states, and Athens in particular, in the matter of citizenship. Perikles early proposed a law restricting citizenship to people both of whose parents had been Athenians of the citizen class, and forbidding mixed marriages. This proved awkward later, when Perikles wished to marry his long-time mistress Aspasia—a brilliant woman who wrote his speeches—but could not because she was a native of Miletos, across the Aegean Sea. It took a special act of the Assembly to naturalize a foreigner, and this was seldom done.

This exclusiveness had a religious basis. The Greeks of a polis believed that the special gods of their city might be worshiped only by the descendants of the founders, and that these gods would be offended if outsiders were admitted to their rites. This belief furnished a powerful argument for those who—even if they did not take the gods very seriously—opposed a union with another polis.

This parochial prejudice led the Athenians to change the Delian League into an exploiting empire, wherein the resentment of the subject cities caused a built-in instability. While the democratic polis had advantages in releasing talents and arousing interest in public affairs, it broke down when applied to an area larger than a single city and its environs. Citizens living more than a few miles from the city could not come to the city daily to take part in public affairs, and the ancients never really grasped the idea of representative (as opposed to direct) democracy. When the state grew beyond a certain point, either the enlarged state broke up, or democracy gave way to autocratic rule. The process was repeated a few centuries later on a more spectacular scale in Rome.

Whatever the morality of Perikles' use of the Delian Treasury, the resulting buildings and art works aroused the admiration of many generations. At the end of Perikles' tenure, the visitor to the Akropolis

69. Erechtheion on the Akropolis of Athens.

climbed the zigzag path up the west end of the hill and passed through
the Propylaia. One wing of the Propylaia housed the municipal collection of paintings, and the marble ceiling beams were strengthened
by wrought-iron bars—a Greek constructional method centuries ahead
of its time.

Framed in the aperture of the Propylaia stood the Parthenon, built
by the architects Iktinos and Kallikrates in the austere Doric style.
These architects used curious optical illusions. Many lines that one
would expect to be straight are not. The columns have a slight bulge
and lean slightly inwards. The steps surrounding the temple bulge
slightly upwards in the middle. The columns at the corners are a little
thicker than the others lest, having only sky behind them, they appear
thinner.

Modern critics differ as to the true purpose of these irregularities.
To me the most plausible explanation is that they were meant, by
exaggerating the natural perspective, to make the temple look even
grander than it was.

For the Parthenon's statues, Perikles hired Pheidias, the leading
sculptor of the age. Pheidias had already made the 30-foot bronze

colossus of Athena Polias (or Athena Promachos) which stood about 100
feet from the Propylaia. For the main hall of the Parthenon, Pheidias executed a huge gold-and-ivory statue of the goddess. For the pediments
at the ends of the roof, he made two groups of statues showing scenes
from the myths of Athena. He also furnished reliefs for the frieze around
the main wall and for the metopes around the entablature (the structure
between the tops of the columns and the roof).

Later, Pheidias was attacked by Perikles' political enemies, who
accused him of stealing gold for the statue of Athena and of impiously
carving his own face on one of the warriors in the reliefs. According to
Plutarch (whose account seems the most plausible) the sculptor was
put in prison, where a sickness soon carried him off.

For almost 1,000 years, the Parthenon shed its glory on Athens.
Then, like many other temples, it was converted into a Christian church.
This involved removing statues, cutting doorways through the walls,
and bricking up the spaces between the columns to form new walls.
The gold-and-ivory Athena disappeared, so that today we can but guess
its appearance.

Under the Turks, the Parthenon became a mosque; but it was still
in fair repair in 1687. Then the Turks, at war with the Republic of
Venice, stored gunpowder in the temple. A German gunner with a
besieging Venetian army dropped a mortar shell through the roof,
igniting the stored gunpowder and blowing out the whole central
part of the temple.

After the city fell, the art-loving Venetian general, Francesco
Morosini, tried to remove the chariot of Athena from the West Pedi-
ment. Unused to such a task, the workman dropped the sculpture and
broke it. When the Earl of Elgin was British ambassador to Turkey in
1801, he found the Athenians of that less artistic age feeding the remaining sculptures into limekilns. Getting permission from the Turkish
government, which cared nought for such things, Elgin removed most
of the remaining sculptures and shipped them to England. When the
ship transporting the marbles ran on a rock off Kythera and sank,
Elgin hired divers to bring up the sculptures and got them at last to
their destination. There he sold them to the British Museum for £36,000
—little more than half of what he had spent in collecting them. Thirty
years later, when Greece became independent, the Greeks demanded
the sculptures back, but to this day the Elgin marbles continue to dwell
in London.

In +XX, with the help of American money, the Greeks began to
put the ruins of the Parthenon back together. Reassembly and restoration have continued slowly on the Akropolis ever since. The traveler
who wants to see an intact Greek temple, however, does better to look

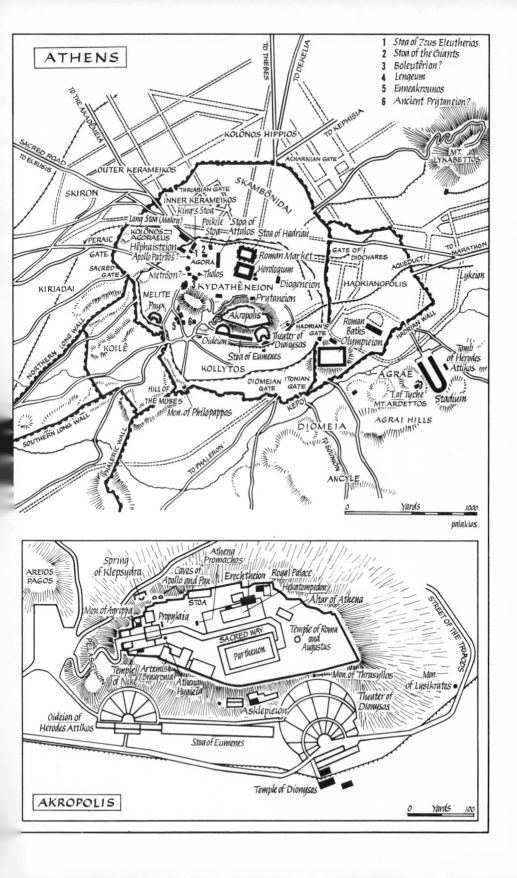

at the Temple of Hephaistos (the so-called "Theseum") a third of a mile northwest of the Akropolis. This temple, like several others, was preserved by conversion to a church.

I cannot describe all the classical monuments of Athens, such as the Theater of Dionysos and the small semicircular Oideion or music hall southeast of the Akropolis. Whole books have been devoted to such structures. Books have also been written about daily life in Periklean Athens. This life is known in rich detail because so much writing of —V and —IV was later admired for its literary qualities and therefore preserved. This is not so for the rest of Greece, nor for Athens in other periods, let alone for the rest of the ancient world—at least, until we reach the last decades of the Roman Republic.

During the Golden Age of Perikles' dominance, Athens grew and prospered, not only on the wealth taken from the subject cities of the empire but also on the silver mines of Mount Laureion, at the end of the Attic peninsula, and on a brisk export trade in painted pottery and olive oil. When the population became too large to be fed by the wheat fields of Attika, grain was imported from, among other places, the Scythian farms along the northern shore of the Black Sea.

As I have explained, the population of any ancient city is uncertain. Estimates of the size of Periklean Athens run from 155,000 to 350,000, and most of the time it probably stood between 250,000 to 300,000. This made it one of the world's greatest cities, along with Babylon and Memphis. You will recall that ancient cities were limited in size by the logistics of transporting food. At the time of the Persian Wars, the Athenian population was probably less but not much less. So, before sentimentalizing over the defeat of "mighty Persia" by "poor little Athens," let us remember that Athens was a big, populous, powerfully-armed place, with a martial, high-spirited people. It would have been a tough nut for any foe to crack.

The repute of Perikles' time as a golden age rests not only on prosperity and artistic achievement but also on the intellectual ferment that took place at this time. For instance, most of the existing genres of literature are of classical Greek invention, and most of these developed in Athens at this time, or soon before or after. We can see this merely by considering the names of Greek origin: poetry, epic, prosody, drama, tragedy, comedy, history, story, monograph, thesis, theme, myth, hymn, and so on.

Drama advanced swiftly. Before Peisistratos it had been little more than one performer singing a tale in verse to the tune of his lyre, with a chorus to accompany him. The productive lives of the great tragedians Aischylos, Sophokles, and Euripides overlapped during the Periklean age; the first of these died as Perikles was rising to power. The ribald comedies of Aristophanes, which closed the century, show the extraordinary freedom of speech that obtained in Athens. At the height of the Peloponnesian War, he brought out *Lysistrata*, about an imaginary Atheno-Spartan war, which poured scalding ridicule on the current war and those who wished to prosecute it to the end.

Aristophanes was a conservative; he had the interest of the squirearchy at heart and denounced the new ideas fermenting in Athens. Nowadays we think of conservatives as imperialists and vice versa, but in Athens it was the reverse. The rich were opposed to adventures abroad, while the poor—especially the sailors and rowers of Peiraieus—were all for expanding the empire, because they saw personal gain in such a policy.

In *The Clouds*, Aristophanes made a butt of his contemporary, the philosopher Sokrates, whom he treated with his usual bawdy humor. He made a joke, for instance, of a lizard that shat on Sokrates' head, causing him "the loss of a sublime thought."[10] Aristophanes would be quite at home in the modern theater, many of whose playwrights seem more eager to startle their audiences by the actors' uninhibited speech and conduct than to entertain them by well-wrought dramas.

Aristophanes libelously portrayed Sokrates as a mad scientist, of the sort that figured in many science-fiction stories of a generation ago. Aristophanes, however, was gunning for everything newfangled and praising the good old days. So far as we can tell, Sokrates was nothing like Aristophanes' caricature. On the other hand, we learn from Sokrates' pupil Xenophon that Sokrates was not quite so saintly as he appears in the dialogues of his other pupil, Plato.[11] He could drink everybody else under the table and dance the rowdy *kordax* with the best.

In fact, while Sokrates first directed men's attention to the importance of exact definitions, he was no scientist, mad or otherwise. If anything, he was anti-scientific, priding himself on "refusing to take any interest in such matters and maintaining that the problems of natural phenomena were either too difficult for the human understanding to fathom or else were of no importance whatever to human life."[12]

Scientific speculation had begun in the previous century in Asiatic Greece and in Sicily. Men like Thales, Pythagoras, and Empedokles formulated theories about the shape of the earth, the nature of matter, and the origin of life. With few facts to go on and little notion of experiment, they mostly guessed wrong; but they made so many guesses that they were bound to be right sometimes. At least, they sought rational answers to the problems of nature instead of resorting to dreams, oracles, and other supernatural sources. They were, as far as is known, the world's first class of secular intellectuals, who tried to learn

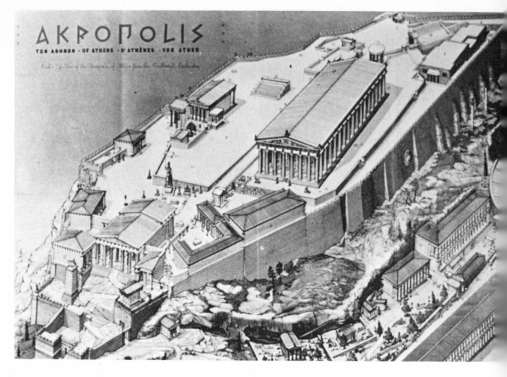

70. Perspective view of the Akropolis of Athens, restored, as seen from the southwest. The main building is the Parthenon; to its left, the Erechtheion; in the lower left, the Propylaia. (Courtesy of Ellen Kohler.)

things for the pleasure of knowing rather than for wealth, power, or the glory of themselves and their gods.

A later Ionian philosopher, Anaxagoras of Klazomenai, moved to Athens and became a tutor to the young Perikles. He taught that the sun was "a mass of red-hot metal . . . larger than the Peloponnesos," and "that there were dwellings on the moon, and moreover hills and ravines."[13] For these teachings, towards the end of Perikles' career, Perikles' enemies indicted Anaxagoras for impiety. Perikles saved his life, but old Anaxagoras had to pay a staggering fine and leave Athens.

Although Perikles patronized all intellectuals, scientific and otherwise, his Golden Age was a time of anti-scientific reaction in Athens. While there were some scientific philosophers, such as the astronomer Meton and the atomic physicist Demokritos, the *sophistai* or "wise men" (we should call them "professors") were more numerous. These sophists speculated less on science than on politics, morals, grammar, and rhetoric. They lived by schoolteaching, tutoring young gentlemen, and lecturing.

Sokrates, who lived frugally on the rents from some small properties he owned, chided the sophists because they lectured for vulgar money. This, he said, would debase and coarsen their philosophy. Told of this, the philosopher Protagoras remarked that he knew of no reason why philosophers did not have as much right to eat as other people.

The growth of the Athenian Empire aroused alarm elsewhere, especially in Sparta (or Lacedaemon, Lakedaimon, Laconia) at the southern end of the Peloponnesos. The city-states of Greece diverged widely in their cultures. The Spartans went in for austere militarism, the Corinthians for trade and luxury, the Thebans for rustic stolidity, and the Athenians for intellect. (Of course, individuals varied as they always have, but these cultural patterns were the norms, to which "well-adjusted" persons tried to conform.)

A greater contrast than that between the cultures of Sparta and Athens would be hard to find. Where the Athenians were garrulous, the Spartans were taciturn. Where the Athenians were commercially enterprising, the Spartans distrusted trade and used iron money, which discouraged users by its weight. Where the Athenians shut their women up in almost Muslim seclusion, the Spartans gave theirs wide liberty. Where Athens welcomed foreigners, Sparta periodically expelled them. Where the Athenians took pride in versatility, the Spartans devoted themselves with grim concentration to keeping their military supremacy and caste position.

Long before, the Spartans' ancestors had conquered their neighbors and reduced them to serfdom of a peculiarly grinding sort. (Between the ruling Spartiates and the serfs or *heilôtai* was an intermediate class, the *perioikoi*.) To keep the Helots down, the Spartiates used naked terror. A young Spartiate was supposed, as part of his training, to murder a Helot. A Helot who showed brains or character was killed to discourage the rest. Helotage lasted to around —200, when a hard-fisted communist dictator, Nabis, ended it with a massacre of the ruling caste and a redistribution of lands.

As for the Athenians, we have a couple of graphic pictures of them, one from their side and one from that of their enemies. In —431, when the Peloponnesian War had begun, Perikles pronounced a funeral oration over the first Athenians to fall. He said (or Thucydides credited him with saying):

> Our form of government does not enter into rivalry with the institutions of others. We do not copy our neighbours, but are an example to them. It is true that we are called a democracy, for the administration is in the hands of the many and not of the few. But while the law secures equal justice to

all alike in their private disputes, the claim of excellence is also
recognised; and when a citizen is in any way distinguished,
he is preferred to the public service, not as a matter of privilege, but as the reward of merit. Neither is poverty a bar,
but a man may benefit his country whatever be the obscurity
of his condition. There is no exclusiveness in our public life,
and in our private intercourse we are not suspicious of one
another, nor angry with our neighbour if he does what he likes;
we do not put on sour looks at him which, though harmless,
are not pleasant . . .

And we have not forgotten to provide for our weary
spirits many relaxations from toil; we have regular games and
sacrifices throughout the year; at home the style of our life is
refined; and the delight which we daily feel in all these things
helps to banish melancholy. Because of the greatness of our
city the fruits of the whole earth flow in upon us; so that we
enjoy the goods of other countries as freely as our own.

Then, again, our military training is in many respects
superior to that of our adversaries. Our city is thrown open
to the world, and we never expel a foreigner or prevent him
from seeing or learning anything of which the secret if revealed to an enemy might profit him. We rely not upon management or trickery, but upon our own hearts and hands. And
in the matter of education, whereas they from early youth
are always undergoing laborious exercises which are to make
them brave, we live at ease, and yet are equally ready to face
the perils which they face . . .

For we are lovers of the beautiful, yet with economy, and
we cultivate the mind without loss of manliness. Wealth we
employ, not for talk and ostentation, but when there is a real
use for it. To avow poverty with us is no disgrace; the true
disgrace is in doing nothing to avoid it. An Athenian citizen
does not neglect the state because he takes care of his own
household; and even those of us who are engaged in business
have a very fair idea of politics. We alone regard a man who
takes no interest in public affairs, not as a harmless, but as a
useless character; and if few of us are originators, we are all
sound judges of a policy. The great impediment to action is,
in our opinion, not discussion, but the want of that knowledge
which is gained by discussion preparatory to action. For we
have a peculiar power of thinking before we act and of acting
too, whereas other men are courageous from ignorance but
hesitate upon reflection . . .

To sum up: I say that Athens is the school of Hellas,

71. View of Athens from the Akropolis, looking southwest; the Theater of Dionysos in the foreground. (Courtesy of Ellen Kohler.)

and that the individual Athenian in his own person seems to have the power of adapting himself to the most varied forms of action with the utmost versatility and grace . . .[14]

Shortly before, at a conference among representatives of Sparta and her allies, a Corinthian delegate gave the Spartans his opinion of the Athenians. While less flattering than that attributed to Perikles, this picture is not inconsistent with it:

> And you have never considered what manner of men are these Athenians with whom you will have to fight, and how utterly unlike yourselves. They are revolutionary, equally quick in the conception and in the execution of every new plan; while you are conservative—careful only to keep what you have, originating nothing, and not acting even when action is most necessary. They are bold beyond their strength; they run risks which prudence would condemn; and in the midst of misfortune they are full of hope. Whereas it is your nature, though strong, to act feebly; when your plans are most prudent, to distrust them; and when calamities come upon you, to think that you will never be delivered from them. They

are impetuous, and you are dilatory; they are always abroad, and you are always at home. For they hope to gain something by leaving their homes; but you are afraid that any new enterprise may imperil what you have already. When conquerors, they pursue their victory to the utmost; when defeated, they fall back the least. Their bodies they devote to their country as though they belonged to other men; their true self is their mind, which is most truly their own when employed in her service. When they do not carry out an intention which they have formed, they seem to have sustained a personal bereavement; when an enterprise succeeds, they have gained a mere instalment of what is to come; but if they fail, they at once conceive new hopes and so fill up the void. With them to hope is to have, for they lose not a moment in the execution of an idea. This is the life-long task, full of danger and toil, which they are always imposing upon themselves. None enjoy their good things less, because they are always seeking for more. To do their duty is their only holiday, and they deem the quiet of inaction to be as disagreeable as the most tiresome

72. Theater of Dionysos, with medieval fortification walls surrounding the Akropolis in the background.

business. If a man should say of them, that they were born neither to have peace themselves nor to allow peace to other men, he would simply speak the truth.[15]

Sparta and Athens were dragged into war by their belligerent allies rather than by any implacable hostility between them. A fierce feud had sprung up between Corinth and her colony Corcyra (or Kerkyra). Since Corinth was an ally of Sparta, the Corcyraeans allied themselves with Athens. As the war approached, there were exchanges of embassies between Athens and Sparta and many proposals for a peaceful settlement. There was even an abortive disarmament conference; the Spartans, whose own city was unwalled, proposed that all the other Greek city walls be demolished but found no takers. As Edward Gibbon said in another context: "the war was preceded, according to the practice of civilised nations, by the most solemn protestations that each party was sincerely desirous of peace."[16] The trouble was that—like many contending states of more recent times—each wanted peace at a price the other was unwilling to pay.

Actually, it was not one war but two. First came the Archidamian War of —431 to —421. Yearly the Spartans ravaged Attika, while the Athenians, safe behind their Long Walls, thumbed their noses at them. Meanwhile, the Athenian navy ranged the sea, raiding the coasts of Sparta and her allies and seizing islands. It was a conflict between a lion and a whale, neither able to knock the other out.

In the second year of the war, a plague struck Athens. This is thought to have been measles (or perhaps smallpox?), more deadly then than now because it was a new disease to which men had developed no resistance. Perikles, whose power was declining, died of the plague the next year and so never lived to see what a ghastly mistake he had made by letting Athens drift into the war. Away went Athenian prospects, for no second Perikles appeared.

Instead, the leading man became Kleon, a reckless demagogue who had been playing Huey Long to Perikles' Franklin Roosevelt. Whenever one of Athens' allies tried to break away, Kleon urged that the offenders be exterminated—the men killed and the women and children enslaved. Sometimes this was done. At length Kleon was elected general and won some victories. Then he was caught in a rash move, routed, and slain. Athens and Sparta signed a peace treaty, the Peace of Nikias, and things quieted for a few years.

Then another demagogue, the brilliant and charming scoundrel Alkibiades, arose. He "had almost all the qualities needed for greatness in a democracy except the supreme one—character."[17] Wanting a war in which he could gain profit and glory, he persuaded the Athenians to send an expedition against Syracuse, with which Segesta, a Sicilian city allied to Athens, was quarreling.

Sailing in —415, the expedition was impressive to look at but as woefully mismanaged as the British expedition to the Dardanelles in 1915. Alkibiades was one of the three generals in command, but no sooner was he on his way than his opponents got the Assembly to demand his recall on trumped-up charges of sacrilege. He fled to Sparta; the Spartans sent a capable general, Gylippos, to help the Syracusans; and the Athenians were utterly defeated. The survivors were enslaved, and only a few trickled back home years later.

While the war in Sicily raged, Sparta recommenced the local war— the Peloponnesian War proper. Athens was convulsed by revolutions, alternately oligarchic and democratic. The landlubber Spartans were at last persuaded to build a proper fleet. After several indecisive naval battles, the Spartans, under their general Lysandros, surprised and destroyed the Athenian fleet at Aigospotamoi in —405, much as the Athenians had done to the Persian fleet at Mykalê seventy-four years before. Athens was beaten at last.

It was a smaller war than many others that are less well known. But the Peloponnesian War has long fascinated students because it was recorded by Thucydides, one of the greatest historians. Thucydides served as an Athenian general in the Archidamian War but was cashiered for failing to reach a beleaguered city in time to forestall its surrender. Exiled, he set himself to write an accurate, objective account of the war. Even to try for complete accuracy made him unique among writers of his time and for centuries thereafter. The one exception is the speeches that Thucydides put into the mouths of Perikles and other leaders. As he admitted, these were not stenographic transcripts of the real speeches; at best they gave the general sense of what was said.

Thucydides took a coolly pessimistic, Machiavellian view of men, and the motives he attributed to them can be seen to operate in times and places far removed from ancient Greece. His narrative, though unfinished, is a kind of microscope, under which a fairly typical sample of *Homo sapiens* at strife can be observed as it really is and not as preachers, philosophers, and idealists are wont to pretend that it is:

> For not long afterwards the whole Hellenic world was in commotion; in every city the chiefs of the democracy and of the oligarchy were struggling, the one to bring in the Athenians, the other the Lacedaemonians. Now in time of peace, men would have no excuse for introducing either, and no desire to do so, but when they were at war and both sides could easily obtain allies to the hurt of their enemies and the ad-

vantage of themselves, the dissatisfied party were only too ready to invoke foreign aid . . .

When troubles had once begun in the cities, those who followed carried the revolutionary spirit further and further, and determined to outdo the report of all who had preceded them by the ingenuity of their enterprises and the atrocity of their revenges. The meaning of words had no longer the same relation to things, but was changed by them as they thought proper. Reckless daring was held to be loyal courage; prudent delay was the excuse of a coward; moderation was the disguise of unmanly weakness; to know everything was to do nothing. Frantic energy was the true quality of a man. A conspirator who wanted to be safe was a recreant in disguise. The lover of violence was always trusted, and his opponent suspected . . . Any agreements sworn to by either party, when they could do nothing else, were binding as long as both were powerless. But he who on a favourable opportunity first took courage and struck at his enemy when he saw him off guard, had greater pleasure in a perfidious than he would have taken in an open act of revenge; he congratulated himself that he had taken the safer course, and also that he had overreached his enemy and gained the prize of superior ability. In general the dishonest more easily gain credit for cleverness than the simple for goodness; men take pride in the one, but are ashamed of the other.

The cause of all these evils was the love of power, originating in avarice and ambition, and the party-spirit which is engendered by them when men are fairly embarked in a contest. For the leaders on either side used specious names, the one party professing to uphold the constitutional equality of the many, the other the wisdom of an aristocracy, while they made the public interests, to which in name they were devoted, in reality their prize. Striving in every way to overcome each other, they committed the most monstrous crimes; yet even these were surpassed by the magnitude of their revenges which they pursued to the very utmost, neither party observing any definite limits either of justice or public expediency, but both alike making the caprice of the moment their law . . .

Thus revolution gave birth to every form of wickedness in Hellas. The simplicity which is so large an element in a noble nature was laughed to scorn and disappeared. An attitude of perfidious antagonism everywhere prevailed; for there was no word binding enough, nor oath terrible enough to reconcile enemies. Each man was strong only in the conviction that

nothing was secure; he must look to his own safety, and
could not afford to trust others. Inferior intellects generally
succeeded best. For, aware of their own deficiencies, and fearing the capacity of their opponents, for whom they were no
match in powers of speech, and whose subtle wits were likely
to anticipate them in contriving evil, they struck boldly and
at once. But the cleverer sort, presuming in their arrogance
that they would be aware in time, and disdaining to act when
they could think, were taken off their guard and easily destroyed.[18]

The Greeks had two words for "city": *asty*, meaning the inanimate
part—the streets, houses, walls, and so forth—and *polis*, meaning the
people and their institutions. After Aigospotamoi, the asty of Athens
survived almost undamaged for centuries. New public buildings, monuments, and sculptures were added. But the story of the polis is one of
gradual decline from —405 on.

While, however, the Peloponnesian War much damaged Greece, it
is an exaggeration to speak, as is often done, of the war's having
"ruined" Greece. Greece soon recovered from the effects of the war,
and its long subsequent decline can be traced to other causes—economic, demographic, and political—that would have operated without
any Peloponnesian War. Perhaps the most powerful cause of all was
the very polis form of organization, which, while it released human
talent in extraordinary profusion, at the same time made it impossible
for the *poleis* to unite firmly and thus to withstand the attacks of
foreign military powers. A Greek of —IV could always have retorted:
"Well, we beat the mighty Persians, didn't we?" But forces even
mightier than Achaemenid Persia were forming.

The victorious Spartans made the Athenians tear down their walls
—which, however, were soon rebuilt. Then an oligarchic cabal, the
Thirty Tyrants, seized power and ruled by terror until the democrats
raised an army and ousted them. One of the first tasks of the restored
democracy was to execute the aged Sokrates on vague charges of
impiety and corrupting youth. The real grudge against him was that he
had been a friend of the rascally Alkibiades and of Kritias, the leader
of the terrible Thirty. Besides, many viewed him as a subversive
nuisance because of his eternal questioning of eternal verities. And they
wanted to punish somebody, no matter whom, for the loss of the war.
If he had begged for mercy, they might have let him off; but the
stubborn old fellow defied them to do their worst, so they did.

During —IV, although Athens quickly recovered from the war,
she played a reduced rôle in Greek affairs. For a time the Spartans
were supreme, ruling the other Greek states through *harmostai* or

Cleon suborning the destruction of Mytilene — Athens — B.C. 427

73. Athens: The demagogue Kleon urges the destruction of Mytilenê,
—427. (Drawing by Roy G. Krenkel.)

governors. But the harmosts proved highly vulnerable to corruption (never having been exposed to it in their rigidly regimented homeland), and the Spartan hegemony was ended by the Thebans at the battle of Leuktra (−371).

During the century, Athens fought a few small wars: with Thebes against Sparta, with Sparta against Thebes, and a naval war against Prince Mausolos of Caria in Asia Minor. Athens joined with Thebes to resist the growing power of Macedonia, but was trounced by King Philip and his son Alexander at Chaironeia in −338. Thereafter, while Alexander overthrew the Persian Empire and spread a thin veneer of Hellenism from Egypt to India, Athens was forced to confine herself to peaceful pursuits.

During this century, while Athenian interest in politics and foreign affairs waned, the arts and sciences flourished in Athens as vigorously as ever. Praxiteles led the way to the more realistic sculpture of the Hellenistic Age; statues began to look like their subjects instead of the expressionless, godlike idealizations created by Pheidias and his colleagues. Menandros developed the New Comedy—the humorous play based upon an incongruous situation, as when a pair of identical twins, parted in infancy, are unknowingly confused with each other. The philosophies of Cynicism, Stoicism, and Epicureanism arose. A few radical thinkers even questioned the morality of slavery, although the institution was nowhere abolished until 1,500 years later, when some medieval Italian city-states took this drastic step.

During the first half of the century, Sokrates' pupil Plato ran his one-man school—the world's first university, in a sense—in the suburban park and gymnasium of Akadêmeia. Plato's pupil, Aristoteles of Stageira (better known as Aristotle) tutored young Alexander (later called "the Great"). Then he returned to Athens and set up a rival school in the other park, the Lykeion. Hence the terms "academy" and "lyceum." Aristotle, one of the greatest minds of all time, did more than any other man to found the scientific method. His successor at the head of his school was the pioneer botanist Theophrastos. After that, though, the center of scientific work shifted to Alexandria.

During the following centuries, Athens came under the sway of one conqueror after another, first Macedonian and then Roman. Most of them, out of respect for the city's glorious past, left it undamaged and allowed it a measure of self-government. Unable to resist by arms, the Athenians tried to tame their overlords by fulsome flattery. The one exception came in −87. Mithradates the Great of Pontus persuaded the Athenians to take his side in his war with Rome, and the Roman general Sulla sacked the city.

Greece declined during the Hellenistic and Roman periods, partly

74. Temple of Hephaistos (miscalled the "Theseum") in Athens.

as a result of unfavorable economic trends and partly from depopulation resulting from emigration and from the widespread practice of female infanticide. Aside from Sulla's looting, however, Athens continued a quietly prosperous existence as a seat of learning. Various benefactors added new public buildings. In —I, Andronikos of Kyrrha built an elaborate timekeeping structure: the Horologium or Tower of the Winds, which still stands a few blocks north of the Akropolis. It is a small, eight-sided building with a sculpture on each side representing one of the winds. Originally a gnomon (the shadow-casting part of a sundial) projected from each side, with a set of markings beneath it for telling time. There was also a water clock inside, and on top stood a weather vane in the form of a bronze triton.

About +130, the Roman emperor Hadrian completed the Temple of Olympian Zeus in Athens. This structure had been started as far back as the tyrannos Peisistratos (—VI). It was abandoned and started again a couple of times, each time on a more grandiose plan but each time stopped when the money ran out. As finally finished by Hadrian, it was the largest temple in Greece and one of the largest in the classical world, surrounded by 104 Corinthian columns 56.6 feet high. Sixteen of these columns still exist. Fifteen of them stand, a third of a mile southeast of the Akropolis; the sixteenth was blown over by a gale in 1852 and lies with its huge drums leaning one upon the next like a row of fallen dominoes. As late as +XV, twenty-one columns were standing; but in 1760 the Turks are known to have burned one for mortar to build a mosque, and doubtless the others met similar fates.

Through the Roman period, people still came to Athens to get an advanced, liberal education, but Christianity ended this source of income and prestige. The Christian Roman emperor Theodosius I restricted the freedom of the philosophical schools, and in +529 Justinian closed them altogether. Seven of the professors fled to Persia, which they had heard was under a Platonic philosopher-king. Alas for illusions! "They were astonished by the natural discovery that Persia resembled the other countries of the globe; that Chosroes, who affected the name of philosopher, was vain, cruel, and ambitious; that bigotry, and a spirit of intolerance, prevailed among the Magi; that the nobles were haughty, the courtiers servile, and the magistrates unjust; that the guilty sometimes escaped and that the innocent were often oppressed. The disappointment of the philosophers provoked them to overlook the real virtues of the Persians . . ."[19] and they soon returned to the Empire, Shah Khusrau having generously persuaded Justinian to exempt the naïve savants from the general persecution of pagans.

Thereafter, Athens declined to a provincial Byzantine town of little distinction. When the Crusaders seized Constantinople and carved up the Byzantine Empire into feudal domains, Athens came under a series of French, Spanish, and Italian adventurers, who ruled as "dukes of Athens" as in Shakespeare's *A Midsummer Night's Dream.* In 1458, the Osmanli sultan Mehmet II, in rounding off his conquest of Greece, had Duke Franco strangled and annexed Attika. Under Turkish rule the city became hardly more than a squalid village, cowering at the base of the Akropolis. Its monuments suffered grievously during the next three centuries, as the Turks and the invading Venetians pulled them down to use the stone in fortifications.

When the Greeks cast off Turkish rule in 1832, they chose Athens as their capital. For reasons of their own, the European powers decided that Greece should be a monarchy and foisted upon the new nation a certain Prince Otto of Bavaria, "slightly demented but quite royal—he gave way to delusions of his divine right, and was ejected in 1862."[20] Ever since, Greece has veered erratically among absolute monarchy, limited monarchy, republic, and military dictatorship. Meanwhile, Athens has become one of the greatest Mediterranean port cities, with half a million people (two million counting the suburbs) and a subway.

One curious angle of modern Greek history concerns the country's language. When independence was gained in 1832, Greek intellectuals gathered to decide what should be their official tongue. At that time the Hellenophone world spoke a multitude of local dialects, differing widely among themselves and resembling ancient Greek about as much as modern English resembles that of Chaucer.

The savants decided that Greek had reached its peak of perfection in the writings of Plato's contemporary Xenophon. They therefore ordained that the Greek of Xenophon, slightly modernized, should be the official speech of the land—the written form of the language, that is. They did not try to restore the ancient pronunciation, which is at best conjectural.

In accordance with linguistic laws, the common speech of Athens became the popular standard for the whole nation. Hence modern Greece speaks two main dialects: the *katharevousa* or "pure," which is the synthetic, archaic dialect devised in the 1830s, and the *dimotiki* or "popular," which is the ordinary speech of the educated Athenian. For laws, debates in Parliament (when Greece has a Parliament), and serious literature, one uses the *katharevousa;* for light literature, journalism, and everyday speech, *dimotiki.* Politics enters in, also. Greece is the only land where one can tell the politics of a newspaper from its grammar. If it uses the dative case, it is conservative!

But despite the decline and the ignominies that Athens suffered in later centuries, the story of Periklean Athens remains—as Thucydides hoped his history would be—"an everlasting possession."[21]

IX

SYRACUSE AND
ARETHOUSA'S FOUNTAIN

THERE IS AN ISLE, ORTYGIA, WHICH LIES ON THE VAPOROUS OCEAN
OVER AGAINST TRINAKRIA, WHERE THE MOUTH OF ALPHEIOS
BUBBLES AND MINGLES ITS FLOOD WITH BROAD ARETHOUSA'S FOUNTAIN.[1]

Pausanias

75. Fortress of Euryalos at Syracuse. (Courtesy of Ellen Kohler.)

I N —70 the honest Roman senator, Marcus Tullius Cicero, was prosecuting Gaius Verres before the Senate. Verres was one of the most rascally of the Senate's scoundrels. He had served as quaestor (treasurer and assistant governor) under the praetor (governor) Cornelius Dolabella in Cilicia. When Dolabella was prosecuted for his extortions, Verres turned state's evidence against his chief. Then, with the funds he had grafted during his quaestorship, he bribed his way to the praetorship of Sicily. He descended upon the unhappy Sicilians like a plague, torturing and killing people and stealing everything not firmly nailed down.

In describing Verres' activities, Cicero said:

> You have often heard that Syracuse was the largest of all Greek cities, and the most beautiful of all cities. And it is so indeed. For it is both strong by its natural situations and striking to behold, from whatever side it is approached, whether by land or sea. It has two ports, as it were, enclosed within the buildings of the city itself, so as to combine with it from every point of view, which have different and separate entrances, but are united and conjoined together at the opposite extremity. The junction of these separates from the mainland the part of the town which is called the Island, but this is reunited to the continent by a bridge across the narrow strait which divides them. So great is the city that it may be said to consist of four cities, all of them of very large size; one of which is that which I have already mentioned, the Island, which is surrounded by the two ports, while it projects towards the mouth of the entrance of each of them. In it is the palace of King Hieron, which is now the customary residence of our praetors. It contains, also, several sacred edifices, but two in particular, which far surpass the others, one a temple of Diana, the other of Minerva [strictly speaking the Greek goddesses Artemis and Athena, with whom the Romans identified their own deities], which before the arrival of Verres was richly adorned. At the extremity of this island is a fountain of fresh water, which bears the name of Arethusa, of incredible magnitude, and full of fish: this would be wholly overflowed and covered by the waves were it not separated from the sea by a strongly-built barrier of stone. The second city at Syracuse is that which is called Achradina, which contains a forum

of very large size, beautiful porticoes, a spacious Curia, and a magnificent temple of Jupiter [Zeus] Olympius; not to speak of the other parts of the city, which are occupied by private buildings, being divided by one broad street through its whole length, and many cross streets. The third city is that which is called Tychia, because it contained a very ancient temple of Fortune [Tychê]; in this is a very spacious gymnasium, as well as many sacred edifices, and it is the quarter of the town which is the most thickly inhabited. The fourth city is that which, because it was the last built, is named Neapolis; at the top of which is a theatre of vast size; besides this it contains two splendid temples, one of Ceres, the other of Libra, and a statue of Apollo, which is known by the name of Temenites, of great beauty and very large size, which Verres would not have hesitated to carry off if he had been able to remove it.[2]

Cicero made such an overwhelming case and produced such a cloud of witnesses and depositions that the Senate felt obliged for once to put justice ahead of class loyalty and condemn Verres, at least to a slap on the wrist. Taking most of his ill-gotten gains, Verres went into exile at Massilia. There he lived comfortably until killed on the orders of an even bigger thief, Marcus Antonius the triumvir, who coveted the multitude of art objects that Verres had stolen from the Sicilians.

According to legend, Syracuse (Greek, Syrakousai; modern Italian, Siracusa) was founded in −734 by Archias of Corinth. Archias had accidentally slain his boy friend in a fight with a rival for the youth's affection, wherefore Corinth was visited by a plague. When Archias consulted the oracle of Delphi, the oracle replied with the three hexameter lines at the head of this chapter. Ortygia means "Quail Island"; Trinakria or "Three-Pointed" is a name for Sicily, referring to its triangular shape.

As for the Alpheios, that was a river in western Greece. It was supposed to duck under the Adriatic and reëmerge on Ortygia, mixing its waters with the fresh-water spring of Arethousa. They said that the river god Alpheios had pursued the nymph Arethousa, who, to escape the divine importunities, changed herself (or was changed by Artemis) into the Sicilian spring. Such, however, was Alpheios' love that he made his river burrow under the sea, to be united at last in his watery form with his beloved.

Assuming that the founding of Syracuse took place as stated, Archias landed on Ortygia, which ever since has been the nucleus

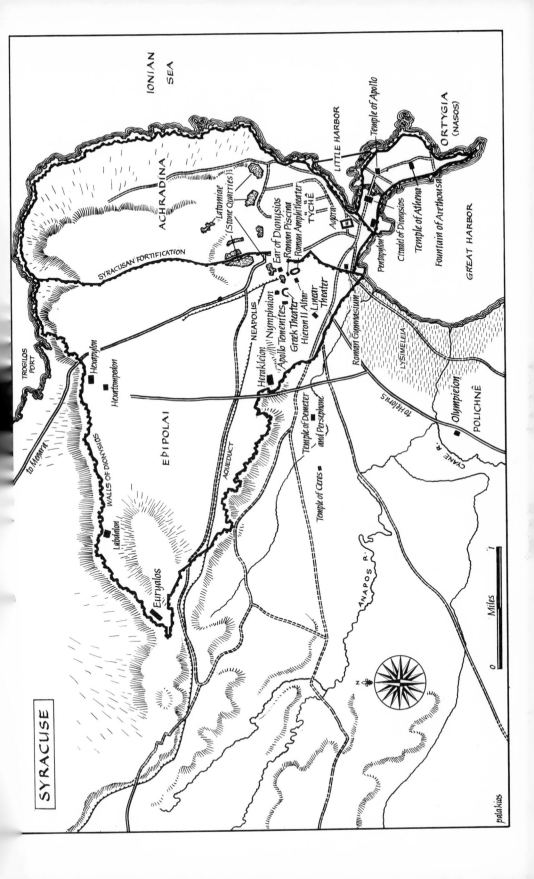

SYRACUSE

IONIAN SEA

ACHRADINA

Latomiae

Stone Quarries

SYRACUSAN FORTIFICATION

Ear of Dionysios
Roman Piscina
Roman Amphitheater

TYCHÊ

Agora

LITTLE HARBOR

Temple of Apollo

ORTYGIA
(NASOS)

Pentapylon
Citadel of Dionysios
Temple of Athena
Fountain of Arethousa

GREAT HARBOR

NEAPOLIS

Herakleion
Nymphaion
Apollo Temenites
Greek Theater
Hieron II Altar
Linear Theater

Roman Gymnasium

LYSIMELEIA

to Megara

TROGILOS PORT

Hexapylon

Hexatompelon

EPIPOLAI

WALLS OF DIONYSIOS

Labdalon

Euryalos

AQUEDUCT

Temple of Demeter
and Persephone

Temple of Ceres

to HLORIS

Olympieion

POLICHNÊ

ANAPOS R.

CYANE R.

N

Miles

0   1

palakios

of the city. I have told you of the advantages of an offshore island for an isolated settlement. Ortygia had the additional advantage of an abundant supply of fresh water, from the spring or Fountain of Arethousa. This was a natural artesian well, whereby water from the Sicilian mainland was conveyed under the sea and thence to the surface of the island, as legend credited the river Alpheios with doing. The legend was thus merely a fantastic exaggeration of a real geological phenomenon.

The island lies off the southeastern coast of Sicily, where several peninsulas jut out from an otherwise harborless coast. Two of these, Achradina and Plemmyrion,³ inclose a spacious bay, the Great Harbor. The isle of Ortygia, a mile long and a third of a mile wide, extends south from the southeastern extremity of Achradina and partly blocks the entrance to the bay.

Across the narrow strait that sunders Ortygia from the mainland lies a low, flat area. As a classical traveler proceeded around the bay to the left, the lowland became a marsh, through which the Anapos River wound its sluggish way. This marsh was called Syrakô, whence the name of Syracuse.

North of the valley of the Anapos rose a triangular, steep-sided plateau, extending from the seaward end of Achradina four and a half miles inland. This plateau was called Epipolai. As Syracuse grew, the city spread to the lowland next to Ortygia. Thence it crept north to the eastern part of the Epipolai, where the plateau thrust out into the peninsula of Achradina, and west along the foot of the bluffs that bounded the plateau.

The first Greek settlers in Sicily found a moderately mountainous land, whose mountains culminated in the two-mile-high volcanic peak of Etna near the east coast, but which elsewhere seldom exceeded a mile above sea level. The slopes were long, sweeping, and of moderate steepness, covered with grass and scrub. There were woods in the valleys, probably more extensive than now. In Sicily, as elsewhere around the Mediterranean, 3,000 years of improvident cutting, together with the ravages of the seedling-eating domestic goat, have deforested vast areas and reduced once pleasant woodlands to steppe or semi-desert. Sicily also contained broad valleys and flat plains, which made good wheat-growing land for the bread-loving Greeks.

Like other Greek arrivals in Sicily, the Syracusan colonists had to drive away the previous inhabitants, whose light armament and primitive tribal organization could not resist the armored, well-drilled newcomers. The natives were the Sikeloi or Siculi, a people of Italian origin, who had been driven out of Italy by stronger neighbors. They had displaced a still earlier Sicilian population, the Sicani, thought to have been of Iberian kinship. The Siculi had pushed the Sicani to the western end of Sicily, where they still dwelt.

Phoenicians had settled on the western end of Sicily. They founded trading towns like Panormus (our Palermo) and Motya, the latter on an offshore island at the western tip. The Phoenicians had pushed the Sicani back from the coast, just as the Greeks did to the Siculi in the east. Down to the Roman conquest, the Siculi and Sicani still lived in the mountainous interior, sometimes fighting the coastal *poleis* and sometimes half-resentfully absorbing their culture, as the Israelites had done with the Philistines. In —V, a Siculan chieftain, Ducetius, united the Siculi against the Greeks; but, after the Syracusans defeated him, his following broke up and he could never accomplish much thereafter.

For two centuries, the Greeks and Phoenicians of Sicily coexisted peacefully, since their territories were far enough apart not to overlap. As population increased and more cities were founded, conflict arose. Now, southwest of Sicily the Mediterranean is less than 100 miles wide. Beyond lies the projecting Tunisian corner of North Africa. Here were other Phoenician cities, including the mightiest of all: Carthage. To Carthage the Phoenician cities of Sicily cried for help.

According to Herodotos, Carthaginian intervention began when the tyrannos of Himera was driven out of his city by another adventurer. The exile persuaded his friend, the Carthaginian general Hamilcar, to bring an army to reinstate him. Herodotos says that this was "an army of 300,000 men, Phoenicians, Libyans, Iberians, Ligurians, Helisycians, Sardinians, and Corsicans."[4] This certainly sounds more like a force to conquer Sicily than one to put a local dictator back on his throne. Perhaps the Greeks, as they did with Xerxes' army, exaggerated the size of the foe by counting in the non-combatants and then doubling the total once or twice for luck.

Several Greek Siceliot cities banded together and raised an army, which defeated the heterogeneous Carthaginian host with great slaughter at Himera. Hamilcar perished with the rest. Gelon, tyrannos of Syracuse, commanded the Greeks. When the Greeks of Greece presently sent a delegation to ask Gelon for help against Xerxes and his Persians, he reproached them with having been unwilling to help the Siceliots against Hamilcar. He would, however, furnish ships and men if given command of the whole Greek force. But the Spartans insisted on commanding the allied army, and the Athenians the navy. Gelon remarked: "You have, it seems, no lack of commanders; but you are likely to lack men to receive their orders,"[5] or as we should put it, "Too many chiefs and not enough Indians."

So Gelon sent the ambassadors away disappointed. He then dispatched an associate named Kadmos with a tribute to pay to Xerxes if the Persians won. When the Persians were beaten, Kadmos returned to

Syracuse and gave Gelon back his money. Herodotos was amazed that any man could have been so honest when he could so easily have absconded with the treasure.

Intermittent wars, prosecuted with great ferocity and cruelty, continued for centuries between the Greeks and Phoenicians of Sicily. Each made strenuous efforts to throw the other out of the island altogether, but neither could ever muster quite enough force.

The Siceliot Greek cities evolved politically much as did the cities of mainland Greece. The remains of the earliest history of Sicily reveal city-states run by oligarchies of *geômoroi*[6] or landowners, who kept a monopoly of power by claiming religious privileges and manipulating the unwritten laws and constitution. In time the demos arose and expelled these aristocracies. Thereafter, rule seesawed between democracy and dictatorship.

On the whole, democracy did less well in Sicily than in mainland Greece. The Sicilian tyrannoi remind one of Renaissance princes: ambitious, gifted, versatile, ruthless, and wholly unscrupulous. They embody the cynical point of view that Thucydides put in the mouths of the Athenians. When the people of Melos complained of Athenian injustice and oppression, the Athenians are said to have replied: "Our opinion of the gods and our knowledge of men lead us to conclude that it is a general and necessary law of nature to rule wherever we can."[7]

76. Temple of Apollo on Ortygia, Syracuse. (Courtesy of Ellen Kohler.)

The gods of whom the Athenians spoke were, of course, the old Olympian pantheon. These were a jolly lot of deities but not morally very uplifting, since they were always seducing each other's wives and clouting each other over the head in brawls like a gang of drunken barbarians.

In Syracuse, the revolution against the geômoroi took place in —485. The exiled squires called for help upon Gelon—the same Gelon as the one mentioned above, but at this time tyrannos of Gela. Gelon brought his army to Syracuse and took the town. Then, however, instead of putting the landowners back in power, he thought it would be more fun to rule the city himself, since it was larger and richer than Gela. So he ruled successfully for six or seven years. To enlarge Syracuse, he kidnapped the people of neighboring towns and forced them to move to Syracuse. When two towns—Megara and Euboia (not the places of those names in Greece)—resisted, he starved them into surrender. Then he took the rich, who, having led the war, expected to be killed, brought them to Syracuse, and settled them as citizens. The common people, whom he considered less desirable, he sold into slavery.

A few years after his victory over the Carthaginians, Gelon died of dropsy, esteemed by many Syracusans. His brother Hieron I succeeded him, ruled harshly, and entertained leading littérateurs, including Aischylos the playwright and Pindaros the poet. After he died, a third brother tried to continue the tyranny but was soon expelled.

When democracy was restored, the city was riven by a typically Greek conflict. The mercenaries who had served Gelon and his brothers wanted full citizenship, but the rest of the citizens insisted on excluding them from public office. In the end, the mercenaries marched north to Messana—our Messina—where they settled.

This Syracusan democracy lasted over fifty years. The main event of this period was the great Athenian siege of —415 to —413. The Athenian armada arrived under two of the original three generals, Nikias and Lamachos. Nikias, the senior, was a rich, elderly, infirm, devout, superstitious man. Although he had been a successful soldier in his youth, he was now timid and indecisive; moreover, he had opposed the Sicilian venture in the first place.

The Athenians disembarked at Rhegion, in the toe of the Italian boot. They spent most of a year moving sluggishly about Sicily, making demonstrations and drumming up allies, before besieging Syracuse itself.

When they finally settled down to a siege, they began to build a wall across the plateau of Epipolai, facing and more or less parallel to the city wall. The Syracusans began a counterwall, extending out from their city at right angles to the Athenian wall. The Athenians drove the builders back into the city and tore down this wall; the Syracusans began another. For months, the building and tearing down of walls continued, with skirmishes and night attacks. In one of these battles, the competent Lamachos was slain, leaving the Athenians under the torpid Nikias.

Soon afterwards, a brilliant Spartan general, Gylippos, arrived with Sicilian reinforcements to help the Syracusans. Gylippos vigorously prosecuted the building of walls and forts to hem in the Athenians. Despite the arrival of reinforcements, the Athenians soon found themselves the besieged instead of the besiegers, although neither side was ever able completely to cut the other off from the outside world.

Failing to break out of the encirclement, the Athenians decided to retreat; but then came an eclipse of the moon. The soothsayers said it was a divine warning to wait another month. While the pious Nikias waited, the Syracusans twice defeated the Athenian fleet in the Great Harbor. At last the Athenians fled, trying to get into the Siculan hills; but the Syracusans blocked the roads and passes, slaughtered hundreds, and rounded up thousands. Nikias and his fellow-general Demosthenes, who had led the reinforcements to Syracuse, were killed.

Seven thousand surviving Athenians became state slaves, kept in the limestone quarries. These *latomiae* had been dug into the bluffs along the southern side of the Epipolai plateau for stone to build the city. After half a year of this, the survivors were sold.

These quarries are a major tourist sight of Syracuse today. A spectacular one, called the Ear of Dionysios, sends a curving tunnel back some distance underground. According to legend, its acoustic qualities are such that, to forestall plots, the tyrannos Dionysios I imprisoned political enemies there and listened from outside to their whispers. But this is only a dragomanic fable, dating from +XV.

Although the Athenian defeat was a triumph for Syracusan democracy, that regime did not long survive its victory. Another demagogue arose. Born into a bourgeois family of modest means, Dionysios got a job as a clerk in a public office and joined the faction of Hermokrates, who had led the Syracusans against the Athenians. The Syracusans decided that Hermokrates was getting too powerful and voted him into exile. When Hermokrates tried to get back by force, he was killed in a riot and Dionysios was wounded and left for dead.

When things quieted down, Dionysios—who had married Hermokrates' daughter—emerged as a popular leader. He persuaded the citizens to dismiss the Board of Generals and appoint a new board, including himself.

Then he played a trick that was also attributed to other tyrannoi. First he faked an attack upon himself. Then he demanded that the demos vote him a bodyguard to protect him, the champion of the masses, from murder by the reactionaries. Once he had a battalion of well-armed bully boys, it was easy to seize public buildings, proclaim himself boss, and kill any opponents. His favorite method of execution was by drowning, which was neater and more sanitary than some. The demos seems never to have learned its lesson from these *Putsche*. This should not surprise us, since—to paraphrase Hegel—"We learn from history that men do not learn from history."[8]

Once in power, Dionysios fought indecisive wars with the Phoenicians of Sicily and of Carthage. First, he was defeated in trying to relieve a Carthaginian siege of Gela. In the retreat, the aristocratic cavalry got back to Syracuse first and vented its displeasure on its general by engaging in a mass rape of Dionysios' wife. She died or killed herself, Dionysios, hurrying after with his mercenaries, surprised the mutineers and took vengeance.

Dionysios then spent several years in strengthening his position. He fortified Ortygia, built public buildings there, and allowed only his supporters and mercenaries to live there. He built harbor works and erected a powerful fortress, the Euryalos, at the western end of the Epipolai.

Although a dashing leader in war, Dionysios became very suspicious in private life, wearing an iron vest under his clothes and refusing to let a barber near him with an edged tool. An uprising of citizens was broken with the help of his mercenaries, but then he treated his opponents leniently. He was liberal in granting citizenship to foreigners and former slaves.

In dealing with other Siceliot cities, Dionysios, like other Sicilian tyrannoi, ruthlessly uprooted the inhabitants and moved them, willy-nilly, to Syracuse or elsewhere. Syracuse grew until it was indeed "the greatest of Greek cities." It has been called "the New York of the Greek world." Its population must have been over 250,000, and one estimate puts it at 400,000.[9] This would make it, perhaps, the largest city in the world at that time.

Although the Greeks were monogamous, Dionysios refused to be bound by convention. After the death of his first wife, he married two well-born girls at the same time and had children by each.

In —399, Dionysios planned a campaign against the Phoenician cities of western Sicily. To make sure that he had the advantage,

> . . . he gathered skilled workmen, commandeering them from the cities under his control and attracting them by high wages from Italy and Greece as well as Carthaginian territory . . . he divided them into groups in accordance with their skills, and appointed over them the most conspicuous citizens, offering great bounties to any who created a supply of arms.[10]

This was the first ordnance department. It was also the earliest-known instance of a government's hiring men to invent. Those who worry about the "military-industrial complex" may be interested to learn that it began with Dionysios the Elder.

One task of Dionysios' teams was to develop warships of a larger size than any then in use. The standard warship of the time was the triere (*trièrès*, "three-er") or trireme. In the triere, the oars of the three banks, although worked from different levels, were (by an ingenious staggered arrangement of the rowers) nearly all of the same length. Dionysios' "purpose was to make weapons in great numbers and every kind of missile, and also tetreres [ships with four banks of oars] and penteres [with five banks], . . . being the first to think of the construction of such ships."[11]

We have no details of these ships, although we can guess that the obvious first step would be to build enlarged trieres, with oars in four or five banks instead of three. But difficulties would arise, since the oars of the upper banks would have to be longer than those of the lower, and it would be hard to keep such a bristling mass of oars in time. Hence ships of the new types spread slowly at first. Then, we can infer, some genius thought to build a ship with a single bank of very large oars and put four or five men to pulling on each oar.

In medieval and Renaissance times, ships were tried out with oars of various lengths and numbers of rowers in different combinations. It was found that, for sizes above the triere, a single bank of large oars, each pulled by four or more rowers, was the most efficient. In Hellenistic times, "tenners," "sixteeners," and so forth were built, but the names refer to the number of rowers to an oar—or, in some cases, perhaps, the number of rowers on one upper and one lower oar of a two-banker. A recent theory by Dr. Lionel Casson plausibly explains the Ptolemaic twentiers, thirtiers, and fortiers as gigantic catamarans, each having two hulls united by a common deck, and two banks of oars on each side of each hull. The hulls would have to be far enough apart to keep the oars on the inner sides from clashing.

Another of Dionysios' teams invented the catapult. The first catapult was essentially a large crossbow mounted on a pedestal. It shot a dart like a huge arrow, up to 6 feet long.

Two years later, Dionysios took his new weapons to the siege of Motya. When a Carthaginian commander, Himilkon, brought a fleet from Africa to help the Motyans, he burst into the harbor and found the Syracusan ships drawn up on the beach.

> Himilkon attacked the first ships, but was held back by
> the multitude of missiles; for Dionysios had manned the ships
> with a great number of archers and slingers, and the Syracusans

77. Syracuse in the time of Dionysios the Great. (Drawing by Roy G. Krenkel.)

slew many of the enemy by using from the land the catapults which shot sharp-pointed missiles. Indeed this weapon caused great dismay because it was a new invention at the time. As a result, Himilkon was unable to achieve his design and sailed away to Libya . . .[12]

So began the story of artillery. Using his catapults to clear the walls of Motya and attacking with battering rams and movable belfries of the Assyro-Phoenician type, Dionysios forced an entrance into the city. Although the Motyans fought with bitter heroism, the Greeks beat down their resistance and began to massacre them. Dionysios stopped

the massacre, not from compassion but from thrift, for he wanted the
Motyans alive to sell, in order to pay for the war. But he satisfied the
blood lust of his men by crucifying the Greek mercenaries who had
fought for the Motyans.

As with tetreres and penteres, it took time for knowledge of catapults to spread around the Mediterranean. A few decades after the siege
of Motya, somebody took a 6-foot catapult dart to Sparta as a curio.
When King Archidamos III saw it, he cried:

"O Herakles! The valor of man is extinguished!"[13]

This was the first recorded protest against the mechanization of
war, and such protests have gone on unheeded ever since. By the
—340s, when Alexander's star was rising, catapults were well known.
There were small catapults for shooting darts at people. A one-man
portable catapult evolved into the crossbow. There were also large catapults for throwing balls of stone or brick, weighing 10 to 180 pounds, at
structures like ships and siege towers. Today, near the Ear of Dionysios,
one can see a pile of stone catapult balls a foot in diameter, weighing
one talent (60 to 70 pounds) apiece.

The swift advances of the art of poliorcetics or siegecraft during
—IV brought about changes in the construction of cities. Cities that
had been adequately protected by walls of brick or of mixed stone,
brick, and wood now built walls of solid stone to withstand the new
siege engines. The Assyrians had pioneered, the Phoenicians had spread
around the Mediterranean, and the Greeks further improved these engines. Besides heavy catapults, which could batter a wall from a distance,
the engines included the "tortoise," a shed on wheels to protect the
engineers while they filled up the ditch and undermined the wall; the
"ram tortoise," a similar shed with a battering ram hung by chains
inside; and the belfry or wheeled siege tower, often combined with a
battering ram or with catapults shooting through shuttered loopholes.

To protect a city, not only was the wall made stronger, but also
several lines of auxiliary defense were constructed in front of the wall.
These included simple ditches and moats, camouflaged pits into which
the wheels of the advancing engines would sink, and lines of "antlers."
These last were tree branches with the sub-branches sharpened to points,
planted in the earth to form a defense like a modern barbed-wire
entanglement.

Dionysios did not long enjoy his conquest of Motya, for the Carthaginians launched a major expedition against him. Their army landed
in western Sicily in —396, marched along the northern coast, and razed
Messana. Dionysios was driven back into Syracuse, where he sustained a
siege almost as severe as that by the Athenians. But a plague broke out
among the Carthaginians, who were camped around the swamp of

Syrakô, and Dionysios defeated them in a sortie. Then, in return for a huge bribe, he let the Carthaginians proper flee, deserting their mercenaries and Sicilian allies. He was suspected of having let Himilkon, the Punic commander, escape because he did not wish to beat the Carthaginians too badly, needing them as a menace to consolidate his own rule of Syracuse.

Dionysios' reign continued for another thirty years, to —367. He fought a few more minor campaigns against the Carthaginians. He also fought the other Siceliot and Italiot Greeks, adding their cities one by one to his empire. At his death he ruled more land and more subjects than any Greek before Alexander. He led a naval campaign against Etruscan pirates on the Tyrrhenian Sea, extended his influence by trade and alliances into the Adriatic, and sent a shipment of wheat to a minor but growing Italian city-state named Rome when that polis suffered a famine.

He also built public works and patronized sports and literature. He cherished literary ambitions and apparently had some talent, for after many tries he finally won a prize at Athens with a play called *Hector's Ransom*. He gave a feast to celebrate and died a few days later. His detractors said he had perished from having drunk too much at the party, but that may have been envious gossip. He was in his mid-sixties, and in the state of medical science he could, at that age, have been carried off by any of many ills.

Dionysios was succeeded by his son of the same name. But Dionysios the Younger was a mere playboy—weak, idle, and dissolute —whose overbearing father had never let him near the machinery of government. After a decade of ineffectual rule, Dionysios the Younger was ousted by Dion, a brother-in-law of his father and a man of stern, austere character. After a harsh rule of three years, Dion was assassinated. Following a quick succession of would-be tyrannoi, Dionysios the Younger returned to Syracuse. Factional strife continued until the city was partly depopulated by murder and flight, and grass grew in the agora. Then some Syracusans sent agents to Corinth, the mother city, to ask for an arbitrator. The Corinthians sent Timolean. This admirable man expelled Dionysios the Younger, who ended his days as a schoolteacher in Corinth, and restored the democracy.

The lives of the two Dionysioi are connected with that of Plato. The ancient manuscripts of Plato's works contained compositions of three kinds. First, there were Plato's authentic dialogues—little plays in which he represented his old teacher Sokrates as talking with his friends about such subjects as semantics, morals, and politics. These are not stenographic transcriptions of real conversations, but imaginative reconstructions, which may in a general way give the gist of Sokrates' actual opinions.

78. Catapult balls near the quarry of S. Venera, Syracuse. The prickly-pear cactus *Opuntia*, like the papyrus, is an exotic plant; it is native to the Americas.

Then there were several spurious dialogues, which others had written and sought to dignify by putting Plato's name on them. (We call such works "pseudepigrapha.") And lastly there were thirteen letters allegedly by Plato.

Scholarly opinion has varied widely about these letters, since it is notorious that ancient libraries paid for letters attributed to famous men and that, therefore, a multitude of such letters were forged by people out to make a fast drachma. The editor of the Loeb Classics edition of Plato (R. G. Bury) thinks that four letters are surely spurious, that two—Nos. VII and VIII—are authentic, and that the remainder are questionable.

Now, it is precisely on Nos. VII and VIII that the tales of Plato's visit to Sicily are based. According to these letters, Plato went to Sicily in −387, when he was a little over forty, and became a friend and teacher of Dion, about half his age. Later writers embroidered this visit with an account of Plato's making the acquaintance of Dionysios the Elder. Incensed at Plato's plain speaking, the tyrannos caused him to be sold into slavery, whence Plato's friends rescued him. While this is not impossible, the letters say nothing about it.

Twenty years later, when the older tyrannos died, Dion persuaded the younger one to summon Plato from Athens. Dion hoped that Plato would make a philosopher-king out of his scapegrace nephew. Plato tried to realize his theories by preaching to Dionysios on the glories of constitutional government and the duty of sovrans to act virtuously. But the lectures had no visible effect, and Plato returned to Athens. A few years later, Dionysios persuaded Plato to come west again. Plato's sermons, however, had no more effect this time. At last the tyrannos lost patience, put Plato under house arrest, and might have had him killed had not Plato's friend Archytas, the scientist-statesman of Taras, sent a galley to rescue him.

Most modern scholars seem to believe that Letters VII and VIII are authentic and that Plato really did make the three journeys to Syracuse. But some doubt that even these letters are genuine. They say that the letters contain illogicalities and that Plato probably never left Greece at all. Ancient biographers were wont to credit their subjects with imaginary journeys to interesting places. Those who wrote about Plato several centuries after his time sent him to Cyrene, Egypt, Palestine, Babylonia, and Persia—places we can be pretty sure he never went. His Sicilian voyages *may* belong in the same fictional category, but this is one of those historical enigmas that may never be solved.[14]

Timoleon's democracy lasted about twenty years, before succumbing to the demagogy of Agathokles. The singular career of Agathokles, the *ne plus ultra* of the political adventurer, has been so neatly summarized by Bertrand Russell that I shall take the liberty of quoting:

> Agathocles was a man of humble origin, the son of a potter. Owing to his beauty he became the favorite of a rich Syracusan named Demas, who left him all his money, and whose widow he married. Having distinguished himself in war, he was thought to be aspiring to the tyranny; he was accordingly exiled, and orders were given that he should be murdered on his journey. But he, having foreseen this, changed clothes with a poor man, who was murdered in error by the hired assassins. He then raised an army in the interior of Sicily, which so terrified the Syracusans that they made a treaty with him: he was readmitted, and swore in the temple of Ceres that he would do nothing to the prejudice of the democracy.
>
> The government of Syracuse at this time seems to have been a mixture of democracy and oligarchy. There was a council of six hundred, consisting of the richest men. Agathocles espoused the cause of the poor against these oligarchs. In the course of a conference with forty of them, he roused the soldiers and had all

the forty murdered, saying there was a plot against him. He then led the army into the city, telling them to plunder all the six hundred; they did so, and massacred citizens who came out of their houses to see what was happening; in the end, large numbers were murdered for booty . . .

Those of Agathocles' party spent the daytime slaughtering the men, and at nightfall turned their attention to the women.

After two days' massacre, Agathocles brought forth the prisoners and killed all but his friend Dinocrates. He then called the assembly, accused the oligarchs, and said he would purge the city of all friends of monarchy, and himself live a private life. So he stripped off his uniform and dressed in mufti. But those who had robbed under his leadership wanted him in power, and he was voted sole general. "Many of the poorer sort, or those that were in debt, were much pleased with this revolution," for Agathocles promised remission of debts and sharing out lands to the poor. Then he was mild for a time.

In war, Agathocles was resourceful and brave, but rash. There came a moment when it seemed as if the Carthaginian must be completely victorious; they were besieging Syracuse, and their navy occupied the harbor. But Agathocles, with a large army, sailed to Africa, where he burnt his ships to prevent them from falling into the hands of the Carthaginians. For fear of revolt in his absence, he took children as hostages; and after a time his brother, who was representing him in Syracuse, exiled eight thousand political opponents, whom the Carthaginians befriended. In Africa he was at first amazingly successful; he captured Tunis, and besieged Carthage, where the government became alarmed, and set to work to propitiate Moloch [Ba'al Hammon]. It was found that aristocrats whose children ought to have been sacrificed to the god had been in the habit of purchasing poor children as substitutes; the practice was now sternly repressed, since Moloch was known to be more gratified by the sacrifice of aristocratic children. After this reform the fortunes of the Carthaginians began to mend.

Agathocles, feeling the need of reinforcements, sent envoys to Cyrene, which was at that time held, under Ptolemy, by Ophelas, one of Alexander's captains. The envoys were instructed to say that, with the help of Ophelas, Carthage could be destroyed; that Agathocles wished only to be secure in Sicily, and had no African ambitions; and that all their joint conquests in Africa should be the share of Ophelas. Tempted by these offers, Ophelas marched across the desert with his army, and after great hardship effected a junction with Agathocles. Agathocles thereupon murdered him, and pointed out to his army that their only hope of safety was to take service under the murderer of their late commander.

He then besieged Utica, where, arriving unexpectedly, he captured three hundred prisoners in the fields; these he bound to the front of his siege engines, so that the Uticans, to defend themselves, had to kill their own people. Although successful in this enterprise, his position was difficult, the more so as he had reason to fear that his son Archagathus was stirring up disaffection in the army. So he fled secretly back to Sicily, and the army, in fury at his desertion, murdered both Archagathus and his other son. This so enraged him that he killed every man, woman, and child in Syracuse that was related to any soldier in the mutinous army.

His power in Sicily, for a time, survived all these vicissitudes. He took Segesta, killed all the poorer males in that city, and tortured the rich till they revealed where their wealth was concealed. The young women and children he sold as slaves to the Brutii on the mainland.

His home life, I regret to say, was not altogether happy. His wife had an affair with his son, and one of his two grandsons murdered the other, and then induced a servant of the old tyrant to poison grandpapa's toothpick. The last act of Agathocles, when he saw he must die, was to summon the senate and demand vengeance on his grandson. But his gums, owing to the poison, became so sore that he could not speak. The citizens rose, he was hurried onto his funeral pyre before he was dead, his goods were confiscated, and we are told that democracy was restored.[15]

Russell tells Agathokles' story to show the workings of a regime of "naked power"—that is, the form that government takes when people are not restrained by reverence, however irrational, for a royal dynasty, a religious doctrine, or a quasi-sacred constitution. Then politics becomes an uninhibited, cutthroat scramble for unlimited power and privilege. Anything goes if it works. Agathokles' methods worked well enough to keep him in power for nearly half a century, to the age of seventy-two.

It is easy to fall in love with some ancient time and place and to idealize or sentimentalize it. Nowhere is this easier than with classical Greece. But one should remember that every culture, if it has attractive features, includes others that, by our notions, are repulsive or horrifying. Thus Rome gave the world a logical, self-consistent system of law; but Rome also gave the world the gladiatorial arena. China gave the civil service, with promotion by competitive examination; but China cruelly deformed the feet of its upper-class women and sliced off heads with a casual extravagance that makes Nero look like a sissy.

In the case of ancient Greece, Russell cites some of the parallel murders and perfidies of the Renaissance prince Cesare Borgia, noting that these, being standard political procedure, aroused no general outrage or indignation. He says:

> In Renaissance Italy, as in ancient Greece, a very high level of civilization was combined with a very low level of morals: both ages exhibit the greatest heights of genius and the greatest depths of scoundrelism, and in both the scoundrels and the men of genius were by no means antagonistic to each other. Leonardo erected fortifications for Caesar Borgia; some of the pupils of Socrates were among the worst of the thirty tyrants; Plato's disciples were mixed up in shameful doings in Syracuse, and Aristotle married a tyrant's niece. In both ages, after art, literature, and murder had flourished side by side for about a hundred and fifty years, all were extinguished by less civilized but more cohesive nations from the West and North. In both cases the loss of political independence involved not only cultural decay, but loss of commercial supremacy and castastrophic impoverishment.[16]

People who wonder how Ayn Rand's philosophy of "Objectivism," which honors self-interest as the supreme virtue, would work in practice, need not guess. They can study the lives and times of men like Dionysios the Elder, Agathokles, and Cesare Borgia.

For a decade after the death of Agathokles, Syracuse muddled along. Then, threatened by another Carthaginian invasion, the Syracusans urged King Pyrrhos of Epeiros, one of Alexander's Successors, to come and help them. Pyrrhos, who had married several wives including a daughter of Agathokles, was fighting the Romans in Italy. A dashing leader and the possessor of a troop of Indian war elephants, he had been lured across the Adriatic as an ally by the Tarentines. Pyrrhos made a truce with Rome and cleared the Carthaginians out of nearly all of Sicily. But he failed to capture their stronghold of Lilybaion in the west, fell out with his Siceliot allies, and returned to Italy to resume his war with Rome.

After Pyrrhos had left, one of his officers, the Syracusan Hieron, was elected general by the Syracusans. He proved so successful that a few years later he was acclaimed as King Hieron II, although he never made much of the royal dignity. When the First Punic War broke out in −264, Hieron at first sided with the Carthaginians. When the war

79. Ear of Dionysios at Syracuse.

did not go well, he made a separate peace with Rome, of which he remained a staunch ally for all of his many days: He died in —215 in his nineties.

During the reign of Hieron II, Syracuse harbored one of the greatest minds of all: Archimedes, the leading engineer of the Hellenistic Age. Archimedes studied in Alexandria, where he came to know several leading scientists. Then he returned to Syracuse, where he spent the rest of his life. Although he was not rich, the fact that he was a kinsman of King Hieron assured him leisure to think and experiment.

Archimedes made many signal mathematical discoveries, such as the ratio of the surface of a right circular cylinder to that of a sphere inscribed in it, and the most accurate calculation up to that time of the ratio of the circumference of a circle to its diameter (π). He founded the science of hydrostatics and discovered "Archimedes' law": that a body immersed in water loses weight equal to the weight of the fluid displaced. This discovery came about thus:

> Hiero was greatly exalted in the regal power at Syracuse, and after his victories he determined to set up in a certain temple a crown vowed to the immortal gods. He let out the execution as

80. Greek theater at Syracuse.

far as the craftsmen's wages were concerned, and weighed the gold out to the contractor to an equal amount. At the appointed time the man presented the work finely wrought for the king's acceptance, and appeared to have furnished the weight of the crown to scale. However, information was laid that gold had been withdrawn, and that the same amount of silver had been added in the making of the crown. Hiero was indignant that he had been made light of, and failing to find a method by which he might detect the theft, asked Archimedes to undertake the investigation. While Archimedes was considering the matter, he happened to go to the baths. When he went down into the bathing pool he observed that the amount of water which flowed outside the pool was equal to the amount of his body that was immersed. Since this fact indicated the method of explaining the case, he did not linger, but moved with delight he leapt out of the pool, and going home naked, cried aloud that he had found exactly what he was seeking. For as he ran he shouted in Greek: "*Heurêka, heurêka!*"

Then, following his discovery, he is said to have taken two masses of the same weight as the crown, one of gold and the other of silver. When he had done this, he filled a large vessel to the brim with water, into which he dropped the mass of silver. The amount of this when let down into the water corresponded to the overflow of water. So he removed the metal and filled in by measure the amount by which the water was diminished, so that it was level with the brim as before. In this way he discovered what weight of silver corresponded to a given measure of water.

After this experiment he then dropped a mass of gold in like manner into the full vessel and removed it. Again he added water by measure, and discovered that there was not so much water; and this corresponded to the lessened quantity of the same weight of gold compared with the same weight of silver. He then let down the crown itself into the vase after filling the vase with water, and found that more water flowed into the space left by the crown than into the space left by a mass of gold of the same weight. And so from the fact that there was more water in the case of the crown than in the mass of gold, he calculated and detected the mixture of the silver with the gold, and the fraud of the contractor.[17]

Archimedes also discovered the law of the lever and the theory of mechanical advantage. He boasted to his cousin Hieron: "Give me a place to stand on and with a lever I will move the whole world!"[18]

The king challenged him to prove it. Archimedes did so by launching one of the largest ships in the world, then building in the Syracusan shipyards. He turned a windlass connected to the ship by a series of compound pulleys. He may, in fact, have invented the compound pulley block and the water-raising pump still called the Archimedean screw.

Archimedes furthermore built an instrument for demonstrating the movements of the heavenly bodies: a "planetarium" in the original sense of the word, as it was used before the Zeiss optical planetarium was invented to bring the wonders of the heavens to the masses at the cost of cricks in their necks. The older device is also called an "orrery" after the Fourth Earl of Orrery (c. 1700), who had one made for himself. As nearly as we can tell, Archimedes' orrery must have been a machine in which, by turning a wheel, pointers, balls, or disks representing the sun, the moon, and the planets were made to revolve around a bronze ball representing the earth. Later engineers are known to have made such devices. In 1900, the remains of one resembling a table clock a little over a foot high, with twenty-odd bronze gearwheels and many dials, was brought up by divers from a shipwreck of about —65 near the island of Antikythera.

After Hieron II died in —215, Syracuse suffered a quick succession of would-be tyrannoi. The Second Punic or Hannibalic War was raging, and these successors changed sides from Rome to Carthage. As a result, in —213 Syracuse found itself besieged by the Romans, with Appius Claudius Pulcher heading the Roman army and Marcus Claudius Marcellus commanding the fleet.

Before his death, Hieron had enlisted Archimedes as his general of ordnance. As a result, the Romans encountered the world's most advanced artillery. Pulcher attacked from the land side with scaling ladders and sheds on wheels to protect sappers. Soon his forces reeled back from the storm of arrows, sling bullets, crossbow bolts, catapult darts, and catapult balls that tore through their ranks.

Marcellus, attacking from the seaward side, had built four engines, each based upon a pair of galleys fastened together. On each platform over a pair of ships he erected a mast and a hoist. By means of this hoist, a "harp" or *sambuca* was brought into use. This was a large ladder or staircase with sides and a roof to shield those using it. At its upper end was a gangway, on which four soldiers, protected by wicker shielding, fought off those who tried to stop the operation. The attackers maneuvered the sambuca into place so that the gangway lay atop the defenders' wall, and the soldiers could swarm into the defenses. But when the scaling engines approached, a series of 600-pound stones and leaden weights, dropped by cranes from the wall, smashed them to kindling.[19]

Another Archimedean trick was to lower a grapnel from a crane, catch the bow of a small Roman ship, and hoist until the ship was vertical and the crew tumbled into the sea. Then the rope was let run, dropping the ship and leaving it awash and useless. A story also grew up in later centuries that Archimedes:

> . . . devised an hexagonal mirror, and at an appropriate distance from it set small quadrangular mirrors of the same type, which could be adjusted by metal plates and small hinges. This contrivance he set to catch the full rays of the sun at noon, both summer and winter, and eventually, by the reflection of the sun's rays in this, a fearsome fiery heat was kindled in the barges, and from the distance of an arrow's flight he reduced them to ashes.[20]

It is a colorful picture, but not likely. People who have experimented with sun-powered steam engines have found that it takes 200 to 300 square feet of mirror to generate steam for a little one-horsepower engine. Archimedes would have had to make an even larger array of mirrors, and I doubt if he could have done this with the technics of the time. Besides, he would have had to make the target ship hold still for some time for his burning glasses to take effect.

The siege lasted over two years. The Romans pierced the defenses around the Epipolai, overran the plateau west of Achradina, and captured the fortress of Euryalos, at the western end of the Epipolai. Attempts by the Carthaginians to break the siege were beaten off. Eventually, Marcellus captured Syracuse by a surprise attack, helped by treachery, on a weakly-defended tower while the citizens were celebrating a religious festival. He ordered his soldiers not to molest free Syracusans; but he could not forbid them to loot, because a general of ancient times who tried that after a hard-fought siege would have been killed by his own men.

During the sack, a legionary approached the 75-year-old Archimedes, who was drawing geometrical designs in the sand. Preoccupied with his mathematics, Archimedes cried: "Keep off, you!" and the angry soldier killed him. At least, that is the commonest story. There are others, any or none of which might be true. Marcellus mourned Archimedes but took the latter's orrery to Rome, where it could still be seen a century later. A few years later Marcellus, too, was slain in a skirmish with Hannibal's soldiers.

Under Roman rule, Syracuse declined to another Roman provincial capital. In late —II, Sicily saw two great slave revolts, thirty years apart, like the much better-known uprising of Italian slaves under Spartacus a few decades later. The rebels numbered as many as 200,000 fighters and defeated several Roman armies before being overcome.

Such wealth as remained in Sicily was then ravished away by Verres and his kind. During the civil wars, Sextus Pompeius, the son of Pompeius ("Pompey") the Great, took possession of Sicily in his war against Antonius and Octavianus and sacked Syracuse. By the time the Roman Empire had settled down under the Principate, Syracuse had shrunk from "the largest of all Greek cities" to a small town. The Roman garrison occupied Ortygia, and the Syracusans inhabited the adjacent low part of Achradina. The rest of the city, abandoned, was falling into ruins. Augustus sent colonists there in —21 to flesh out its population, but the city remained of modest size and undistinguished through the Roman period.

In late +III, Syracuse was sacked by Frankish pirates, who killed most of the inhabitants. With the breakup of the West Roman Empire in late +V, Syracuse fell under the rule of the Goths, was recovered for the East Roman Empire by Belisarius in +535, and was conquered by the Arabs in +878 after one of the most murderous sieges of all.

The Arab conquest of Sicily began in +827 and was not com-

81. Roman theater at Syracuse.

pleted until +965. Arab rule contributed little to the land save the importation of the papyrus plant, which grows to this day around the Fountain of Arethousa. Syracuse is the only place in Europe warm enough for this plant. The Arabs made Palermo their capital; hence Arab influence is plainer in western Sicily than in Syracuse.

After an unsuccessful Byzantine invasion of Sicily around 1040, the Normans in 1060 began a thirty-year conquest of the island and of southern Italy. This Norman conquest was actually greater, in terms of land and people, than the simultaneous one in England. At the beginning of the two centuries of Norman rule, the languages of Sicily were Greek, Arabic, and Norman French. During the next few centuries, all these gave place to an Italian dialect as a result of Italian immigration into Sicily. Although Greek disappeared from Sicily, it still survives in a few isolated villages in Calabria and Apulia, the toe and the heel respectively of the Italian boot.

Later, Sicily was shuffled about among French and Spanish overlords until finally united by Garibaldi with the new Kingdom of Italy in 1860–61. Then Syracuse housed a mere 14,000—fewer than the ancient Greek theater held. They all dwelt in Ortygia. Since then, Syracuse has grown until it now harbors more than 60,000. Ortygia is still the main business district, although hotels and residences have spread about the lower parts of Achradina and up on the plateau.

Ortygia is now guarded by a medieval-Renaissance castle, the Castello Maniace. This is named for an able Byzantine general, George Maniaces,[21] who led the eleventh-century attempt to reconquer Sicily from the Arabs and who fortified the area. The inner parts of the castle, built around 1239, originated with Emperor Frederick II, the brilliant German-Norman king of Sicily, Germany, and Jerusalem. The outworks, with embrasures for cannon, date from Emperor Charles V in +XVI, and the whole structure has been repeatedly modified and modernized.

The ancient Syracusans built a huge Doric temple of Athena, mentioned by Cicero, on the highest part of Ortygia. In +VII, this temple, which may go back to Gelon, was—like the Parthenon—converted into a church. It was designated a cathedral, underwent many changes, and received a baroque façade in +XVII. Now all that is left of the original temple in this hybrid structure consists of two dozen Doric columns, half embedded in the walls, and sections of the original cella wall between the arches later cut through it.

Of the temples of Apollo, on Ortygia near the bridge to the mainland, and of Olympian Zeus, two miles southwest of town across the Anapos, only a few columns remain. The second Hieron's 24,000-seat theater, on the edge of town to the northwest, is in fair condition, as is the Roman amphitheater nearby. In the same area, Hieron II built an enormous altar for sacrifices, but the medieval Spaniards demolished it for building stone.

There are minor sights: the quarries; the many tombs cut into the limestone slopes edging the Epipolai (whose dedicatory inscriptions have long since been chiseled out for museums and other collections); the various Christian churches, crypts, and catacombs.

Under the tufted stems of the feathery papyrus, Arethousa's fountain still swirls as fresh water from the mainland rises from its natural artesian well. But the water of the fountain is no longer fresh. An earthquake (perhaps that of 1693, which leveled most of the town) cracked the rock ledge sundering the spring from the sea and let in salt water. So Arethousa's waters are mingled, not with those of Alpheios as the legend had it, but with those of Poseidon.

X

CARTHAGE AND THE FAITHLESS HERO

RESIGNEDLY BENEATH THE SKY
THE MELANCHOLY WATERS LIE.
SO BLEND THE TURRETS AND SHADOWS THERE
THAT ALL SEEM PENDULOUS IN AIR,
WHILE FROM A PROUD TOWER IN THE TOWN
DEATH LOOKS GIGANTICALLY DOWN.[1]

Poe

82. Carthage, looking south from the Megara across the Byrsa, with remains of Roman fortifications in the foreground; beyond, the Gulf of Tunis and Cape Bon.

In —241, the First Punic War ended in defeat for the Carthaginians, who were forced to yield all claims on Sicily to the Romans. To fight this war, Carthage had hired a large army of mercenaries. Like their Phoenician forebears, the Carthaginians were daring explorers but not very warlike. Although they resisted fiercely when their cities were attacked, they were mainly businessmen, not brawlers. Since they were never numerous enough to raise large armies from their own masses, they hired others out of their abundant wealth to do their fighting.

At this time, Carthage was an oligarchic republic, in which a merchant aristocracy manned the Senate (Greek: *Gerousia*, also called the Hundred Magistrates) and controlled most matters of public policy. Like the Roman Republic with its consuls, Carthage had two chief executive officers, elected yearly. The Romans called these *suffetes*, and the Carthaginian name must have been much like the Hebrew *shôphêṭim*, which the Bible translates as "judges." There was an Assembly of citizens, but it does not seem to have had much power. The state had once suffered from class conflict; but a system of poor relief, by which the rich gave public banquets to the other citizens, had allayed this strife.

In these respects, Carthage was like many other Mediterranean city-states. As with them, the city-state form ran into trouble as soon as it was extended much beyond the neighborhood of the city. Although several other Phoenician cities in Tunisia were older than Carthage, the latter had become the largest and richest. Like the Athenians, the Carthaginians soon learned to use their power to reduce their sister cities to submission and to extort tribute from them.

The treaty with Rome did not bring Carthage peace for long. At the end of the First Punic War, Carthage had in Sicily a large army of mercenaries, including "Iberians and Celts, men from Liguria and the Balearic Islands, and a considerable number of half-bred Greeks, mostly deserters and slaves, while the main body consisted of Libyans."[2] The Carthaginian general Hamilcar Barca resigned his command to Gisco, the commandant at Lilybaion. The army was to be shipped back to Carthage and paid off. Foreseeing trouble if too many soldiers were gathered near Carthage at once, Gisco prudently sent them across in small detachments, expecting that each detachment would be paid off and dismissed to its native land before the next arrived.

Carthage, however, was feeling poor as a result of the war. The government let the soldiers accumulate in the city, foolishly hoping that, when all had arrived, it could somehow persuade them to accept a downward adjustment. Polybios dryly tells the tale:

But when this resulted in the commission of many acts of
lawlessness by night and day, they began to feel uneasy at their
numbers and their growing licentiousness; and required the
officers, until such time as arrangements for discharging their
pay should have been made, and the rest of the army should
have arrived, to withdraw with all their men to a certain town
called Sicca, receiving each a piece of gold for their immediate
necessities. As far as quitting the city was concerned they were
ready enough to obey; but they desired to leave their heavy baggage there as before, on the ground that they would soon have
to return to the city for their wages. But the Carthaginian government were in terror lest, considering the length of their absence and their natural desire for the society of their wives and
children, they would either not quit the city at all; or, if they
did, would be sure to be enticed by these feelings to return, and
that thus there would be no decrease of outrages in the city.
Accordingly they forced them to take their baggage with them:
but it was sorely against the will of the men, and roused strong
feelings of animosity among them. These mercenaries being
forced to retire to Sicca, lived there as they chose without any
restraint upon their lawlessness. For they had obtained two
things the most demoralising for hired forces, and which in a
word are in themselves the all-sufficient source and origin of
mutinies,—relaxation of discipline and want of employment. For
lack of something better to do, some of them began calculating,
always to their own advantage, the amount of pay owing to
them; and thus making out the total to be many times more than
was really due, they gave out that this was the amount that they
ought to demand from the Carthaginians. Moreover they all
began to call to mind the promises made to them by the generals
in their harangues, delivered on various occasions of special
danger, and to entertain high hopes and great expectation of the
amount of compensation which awaited them. The natural result
followed.[3]

Early in —241, Carthage sent Hanno, the general of the forces in
Africa, to deal with the mercenaries. As instructed, he asked them to take
a cut in their pay. At this, the multitude became wildly excited. Since no
one officer spoke enough languages to communicate with all of this polyglot army, the excitement rose unchecked. "Armies in such a state are not
content with mere human wickedness; they end by assuming the ferocity of wild beasts and the vindictiveness of insanity."[4]

The Carthaginians saw their folly when it was too late. It
was a grave mistake to have collected so large a number of mer-

cenaries into one place without any warlike force of their own
citizens to fall back upon: but it was a still graver mistake to
have delivered up to them their children and wives, with their
heavy baggage to boot; which they might have retained as hostages, and thus have had greater security for concerting their
own measures, and more power of ensuring obedience to their
orders. However, being thoroughly alarmed at the action of the
men in regard to their encampment, they went every length in
their eagerness to pacify their anger. They sent them supplies of
provisions in rich abundance, to be purchased exactly on their
own terms, and at their own price. Members of the Senate were
dispatched, one after the other, to treat with them; and they
were promised that whatever they demanded should be con-
ceded if it were within the bounds of possibility. Day by day the
ideas of the mercenaries rose higher. For their contempt became
supreme when they saw the dismay and excitement in Carthage;
their confidence in themselves was profound . . . And in short,
the ill-disposed and mutinous among them being numerous,
they always found out some new demand which made it impossible to come to terms.[5]

The mercenaries and the Carthaginian government finally agreed to
let the disputed points be arbitrated by General Gisco, whom the troops
trusted. Gisco sailed along the coast to the camp with the money
owing the soldiers, calmed them by soothing speeches, and paid them
off.

But there was a certain Campanian in the army, a runaway
Roman slave named Spendius, a man of extraordinary physical
strength and reckless courage in the field. Alarmed lest his master should recover possession of him, and he should be put to
death with torture, in accordance with the laws of Rome, this
man exerted himself to the utmost to break off the arrangement
with the Carthaginians. He was seconded by a Libyan called
Mathôs, who was not a slave but free, and had actually served
in the campaign. But he had been one of the most active agita-
tors in the late disturbances: and being in terror of punishment
for the past, he now gave in his adhesion to the party of
Spendius; and taking the Libyans aside, suggested to them that,
when the men of other races had received their pay, and taken
their departure to their several countries, the Carthaginians
would wreak upon them the full weight of the resentment which
they had, in common with themselves, incurred; and would
look upon their punishment as a means of striking terror into
all the inhabitants of Libya. It did not take long to rouse the

men by such arguments, nor were they at a loss for a pretext, however insignificant. Gesco postponed the payment of
the valuations of rations and horses [two of the disputed
points]. This was enough: the men at once hurried to make
a meeting; Spendius and Mathôs delivered violent invectives
against Gesco and the Carthaginians; their words were received
with every sign of approval; no one else could get a hearing; whoever did attempt to speak was promptly stoned to
death . . . A considerable number of privates as well as officers
were killed in this manner . . . The result was that soon no one
had the courage to offer them any counsel at all; and they accordingly appointed Mathôs and Spendius as their commanders.[6]

It all sounds somehow familiar—so much so, in fact, that one
cannot help wondering if the leaders of some contemporary disorders
have not been using Polybios as a tactical manual. General Gisco
"exerted himself with desperate courage and persistence" to keep the
situation under control.

> But on one occasion the Libyans, not having received their
> wages as soon as they considered that they ought to have been
> paid to them, approached Gesco himself with some insolence.
> With the idea of rebuking their precipitancy he refused to pro-
> duce their pay, and bade them "go and ask their general Mathôs
> for it." This so enraged them, that without a moment's delay
> they first made a raid upon the money that was kept in readiness,
> and then arrested Gesco and the Carthaginians with him. Mathôs
> and Spendius thought that the speediest way to secure an out-
> break of war was for the men to commit some outrage upon the
> sanctity of law and in violation of their engagement. They
> therefore co-operated with the mass of the men in their reckless
> outrages; plundered the baggage of the Carthaginians along
> with their money; manacled Gesco and his staff with every
> mark of insolent violence, and committed them into custody.[7]

A merciless war, wherein torturing prisoners to death became
standard practice, ensued. General Hanno set about organizing the
Carthaginians, arming and drilling them and hiring more mercenaries.
The Libyans, never reconciled to the serfdom imposed upon them,
revolted against their Carthaginian masters. Seventy thousand of them
joined the army of Spendius and Matho, which besieged the allied
cities of Utica and Hippo Zarytus.

Although Hanno did good work in arming Carthage, he proved
a sluggish commander in the field. Failing to relieve Utica, he was

replaced by Hamilcar Barca. Matho had occupied the peninsula joining Carthage to the mainland, but Hamilcar got an army past him by having them wade across the mouth of the nearby Macaras (or Bagrada) River on the harbor bar at low tide.

Hamilcar had the better of several battles with the mutineers. He made good use of a body of Numidian (that is, Algerian or Berber) cavalry led by Naravas, and of a troop of war elephants. Alexander the Great had brought elephants back from India, and for several generations his successors sought by fair means or foul to add them to their armies. The Seleucid kings, ruling Syria, Babylonia, and Iran, controlled the land route from India and so had the say as to who should get elephants. To evade this monopoly, the Ptolemaic kings of Egypt and the Carthaginians tamed elephants of the African species. The Ptolemies got theirs from the Sudan, and the Carthaginians, from the Atlas Mountains, where they dwelt until hunted to extinction in Roman Imperial times.

Still, the war went badly for Carthage. Sardinia revolted and called in the Romans, who kept the island thereafter. Hamilcar weakened the foe's resolve by treating prisoners leniently, enlisting some and letting the others go home. To counteract this and keep the antagonists in a suitable state of mutual hatred, Spendius and Matho persuaded their followers to kill Gisco and the other 700 Carthaginian prisoners. This they did by cutting off their hands and feet and throwing them into a ditch to die.

At length, Hamilcar trapped Spendius' army in a valley and destroyed it. Spendius and other leaders who fell into Hamilcar's hands were crucified. Matho won one more victory against the Carthaginians but was finally beaten, captured, and tortured to death.

Hamilcar married his daughter to the dashing Naravas. Then, taking his nine-year-old son Hannibal, he set out for Spain, of which he had persuaded the Carthaginians to make him colonial governor. Long after, when Hannibal was a fugitive in the East, he said that before setting out, his father had made him swear at the altar of the supreme god "that I would never be in friendship with the Romans."[8] Hannibal kept his oath.

In 1862, the French novelist Gustave Flaubert published a historical novel, Salammbô, which tells of the revolt of the mercenaries and which has had no small effect upon the general reading public's picture of Carthage, even though most of them may never have heard of Flaubert or his tale. This novel has been described by a recent authority as "a sinister masterpiece of imagination not to be compared with more pedestrian works of historical fiction far better briefed on the archaeological and religious background."[9]

Flaubert tells a whale of a story. Salammbô is Hamilcar's daughter, obsessed with the worship of Tanith, the moon goddess. She wants to be a priestess but is prevented by her father, who wishes her to make a politically useful marriage. During a riotous feast of the mercenaries in Hamilcar's gardens, when they have just arrived from Sicily, Matho falls in love with Salammbô. During the first siege of Carthage by the mercenaries, Matho and Spendius steal into the city and carry off the sacred veil of Tanith, the zaïmph.

Later, Salammbô goes alone to Matho's encampment to get the sacred object back. This she does by giving the soldier her all, albeit this consummation is described in much more delicately euphemistic language than is usual in contemporary fiction.

At the end, when the mercenaries have been broken and Matho has been flayed alive, Salammbô is unwillingly married to Naravas, whom Flaubert calls "Narr' Havas." Then she falls dead, "for having touched the mantle of Tanith"—a reason that might easily convince a Carthaginian but that seems a little thin in our skeptical age.

Flaubert's novel has flaws. The author took considerable liberties with history. Thus, to enable Matho to steal into the city, he provided Carthage with an aqueduct that was not built until Roman times, several centuries later. Since the Carthaginians were given to multiple use of a few given names, he simplified the cast to avoid confusing the reader with two characters named Hanno and two named Hannibal.

Moreover, except for the rascally Spendius, his characters are not outstanding. Salammbô is barely sketched in, albeit a section of modern Carthage is named for her. Matho is good-natured but childishly simple: much less shrewd, energetic, and eloquent than the real man. All the other leading characters are so unpleasant that it is hard for the reader to identify himself with any.

Still, if you want a story of violent, bloody, dramatic events, told in the grand manner, and a picture of an ancient world where everything is larger and more brilliantly colored than life, here is the story for you. Consider Flaubert's description of Carthage at eventide:

> The moon was rising just above the waves, and on the town which was still wrapped in darkness there glittered white and luminous specks—the pole of a chariot, a dangling rag of linen, the corner of a wall, or a golden necklace on the bosom of a god. The glass balls on the roofs of the temples beamed like great diamonds here and there. But ill-defined ruins, piles of black earth, and gardens formed deeper masses in the gloom, and below Malqua fisherman's nets stretched from one house to another like gigantic bats spreading their wings. The grinding of the hydraulic wheels which conveyed water to the highest stories of the palaces, was no longer heard; and the camels,

83. Carthage in the days of Hannibal. (Drawing by Roy G. Krenkel.)

lying ostrich fashion on their stomachs, rested peacefully in the middle of the terraces. The porters were asleep in the streets on the thresholds of the houses; the shadows of the colossuses stretched across the deserted squares; occasionally in the distance the smoke of a still burning sacrifice would escape through the bronze tiling, and the heavy breeze would waft the odours of aromatics blended with the scent of the sea and the exhalation from the sun-heated walls. The motionless waves shone around Carthage, for the moon was spreading her light upon the mountain-circled gulf and upon the lake of Tunis, where flamingoes formed long rose-coloured lines amid the banks of sand, while farther on beneath the catacombs the great salt lagoon shimmered like a piece of silver. The blue vault of heaven sank on the horizon in one direction into the dustiness of the plains, and in the other into the mists of the sea; and on the summit of the Acropolis, the pyramidal cypress-trees, fringing the temple of Eschmoun, swayed murmuring like the regular waves that beat slowly along the mole beneath the ramparts.[10]

Or again, his description of a temple at night:

The temple of Moloch was built at the foot of a steep defile in a sinister spot. From below nothing could be seen but lofty walls rising indefinitely like those of a monstrous tomb. The night was gloomy, a greyish fog seemed to weigh upon the sea, which beat against the cliff with a noise of death-rattles and sobs; and the shadows gradually vanished as though they had passed through the walls.

But as soon as the doorway was crossed one found oneself in a vast quadrangular court bordered by arcades. In the centre rose a mass of architecture with eight equal faces. It was surmounted by cupolas which thronged around a second story supporting a kind of rotunda, from which sprang a cone with a re-entrant curve and terminating in a ball on the summit.

Fires were burning in cylinders of filigree-work fitted upon poles, which men were carrying to and fro. These lights flickered in the gusts of wind and reddened the golden combs which fastened their plaited hair on the nape of the neck. They ran about calling to one another to receive the Ancients.

Here and there on the flagstones huge lions were couched like sphinxes, living symbols of the devouring sun. They were slumbering with half-closed eyelids. But roused by the footsteps and voices they rose slowly, came towards the Ancients, whom they recognized by their dress, and rubbed themselves against their thighs, arching their backs with sonorous yawns; the vapour of their breath passed across the light of the torches. The stir increased, doors closed, all the priests fled, and the Ancients disappeared beneath the columns which formed a deep vestibule round the temple.[11]

Although Flaubert was a conscientious researcher, almost nothing was known about ancient Carthage, at the time he wrote, save what ancient Greek and Roman writers had said about it. Since the main business of Greeks and Romans with Carthage was to fight her, their accounts were hardly unbiased. The few ruins to be seen on the site were nearly all of the Roman period. The Romans had so thoroughly destroyed the original city in −146 that nothing was left of it above-ground. They had cursed the site and forbidden anyone to dwell there again.

Nevertheless, the advantages of the location were too good to be wasted. After a couple of abortive Roman attempts to colonize the site, Augustus sent settlers there in −19. Reborn Carthage grew to a sizable city: the second or third city of the Empire, some said. In any case, the surviving masonry is of this city and not of Hannibal's.

Moreover, although Carthage had a considerable literature, hardly anything of it has survived. In −V, two Carthaginian admirals, Hanno and Himilco, sailed out through the Pillars of Hercules to explore the Atlantic coasts and to set up trading stations. Hanno turned south; Himilco, north. Hanno's report was inscribed on a tablet set up in the Temple of Ba'al Hammon in Carthage, and a translation of this report, in 600 words of Greek, has come down. It is disputed how far Hanno went, but he may have reached the mouth of the Senegal River.[12] Himilco's report, or fragments thereof, was incorporated in a poem by the late Roman poet Rufus Festus Avienus (+IV). The Roman Senate also caused a Carthaginian treatise on farming, by one Mago, to be rendered into Latin. Although the original work has not survived, about forty fragments exist in citations by Latin authors like the elder Plinius.

That is all that remains of Carthaginian literature. This literature may not have been anything marvelous, compared to the literatures of Greece and Rome. But still, there was a respectable mass of books, which Scipio gave to the Numidian kings at the time of the final destruction. The literature probably included many works that would be interesting to have; for instance, long theological or mythological poems, like the many of this kind that have come down in Greek and Latin. And if we had more of it, we should probably have both a more complete and a more favorable impression of the Carthaginians.

Nonetheless, archaeology has learned much about Carthage in the century since Flaubert wrote. Some of these discoveries make the concepts of *Salammbô* out of date.

For example, Moloch was not the name of a particular god. The word is a dialectical variant of the Canaanitish *melekh*, "lord," and was applied to the chief god of every Punic city. This god might be Eshmun, El, Dagon, or any of several others. In Carthage, the title belonged to Ba'al Hammon. The full form of the name was Melekh-Qarth or Melqarth, "lord of the city," whence the Greek Melikertes or Herakles.

The saddest casualty of this advance in knowledge is Flaubert's wonderfully colorful picture of the city. In place of his doomed metropolis of barbaric magnificence and sinister glitter, an authority says: "we have offered the tangible, if sordid, remains of a prosaic city of shopkeepers. Even the impression of a strange remote world, which is so powerfully evoked in the novel, evaporates rapidly in the presence of a legacy of remains, which, apart from a few provincial peculiarities, are only distinguishable from Greek and Roman remains by their extreme mediocrity."[13]

For instance, consider Flaubert's temple interior, as seen by Spendius and Matho when they are searching for the veil of Tanith:

> Then a dazzling light made them lower their eyes. Next they perceived all around them an infinite number of beasts, lean, panting, with bristling claws, and mingled together one above another in a mysterious and terrifying confusion. There were serpents with feet, and bulls with wings, fishes with human heads were devouring fruit, flowers were blooming in the jaws of crocodiles, and elephants with uplifted trunks were sailing proudly through the azure like eagles. Their incomplete or multiplied limbs were distended with terrible exertion. As they thrust out their tongues they looked as though they would fain give forth their souls; and every shape was to be found among them as if the germ-receptacle had been suddenly hatched and had burst, emptying itself upon the walls of the hall.
>
> Round the latter were twelve globes of blue crystal, supported by monsters resembling tigers. Their eyeballs were starting out of their heads like those of snails, with their dumpy loins bent they were turning round toward the background where the supreme Rabbet, the Omnifecund, the last invented, shone splendid in a chariot of ivory.
>
> She was covered with scales, feathers, flowers, and birds as high as the waist. For ear-rings she had silver cymbals, which flapped against her cheeks. Her large fixed eyes gazed upon you, and a luminous stone, set in an obscene symbol on her brow, lit up the whole hall by its reflection in red copper mirrors above the door.
>
> Matho took a step forward; but a flagstone yielded beneath his heels and immediately the spheres began to revolve and the monsters to roar; music rose melodious and pealing, like the harmony of the planets; the tumultuous soul of Tanith was poured streaming forth . . . Suddenly the monsters closed their jaws and the crystal globes revolved no longer . . .
>
> Then they penetrated into a small and completely cir-

cular room, so lofty that it was like the interior of a pillar. In the centre there was a big black stone, of semi-spherical shape like a tambourine; flames were burning upon it; an ebony cone, bearing a head and two arms, rose behind.

But beyond, it seemed as though there were a cloud wherein were twinkling stars; faces appeared in the depths of its folds—Eschmoun with the Kabiri, some of the monsters that had already been seen, the sacred beasts of the Babylonians, and others with which they were not acquainted. It passed beneath the idol's face like a mantle, and spread fully out was drawn up on the wall, to which it was fastened by the corners, appearing at once bluish as the night, yellow as the dawn, purple as the sun, multitudinous, diaphanous, sparkling, light. It was the mantle of the goddess, the holy Zaïmph which might not be seen.[14]

All that archaeology has found in the way of temples are meager little boxlike shrines. The earliest had walls of rough stone and clay; the later, walls of mud brick or of local stone—sandstone or limestone of poor quality, whose irregularities were hidden under coats of stucco. The sacred object inside might be a crude statue, a column, or a mere boulder.

During the earlier centuries, the temple-builders imitated Egyptian temple architecture, finishing off their buildings with the Egyptian cornice and ornamenting them with the winged disk. Later they added Greek colonnades and other motifs, so that the temples became a mixture of Greek and Egyptian styles. There is, alas, no trace of Flaubert's revolving crystal globes and roaring mechanical tigers.

According to the commonest tradition,[15] which may or may not be authentic, the princess Elissa of Tyre arrived at the site of Carthage in −814, sixty-one years before the traditional date of the founding of Rome. Neighboring Utica had been founded by Tyrian colonists over two centuries before, but Carthage soon outstripped its older sister.

For one thing, Carthage received waves of new settlers who fled the cities of Phoenicia before the attacks of Assyrians, Babylonians, Persians, and Macedonians. For another, the site was exceptionally strong. Carthage was built on the end of a peninsula three miles wide at its narrowest and about ten miles long, projecting eastward from the Tunisian mainland. The peninsula swelled at its end into a shape like a pick or hammer, partly inclosing two arms of the sea. The northern body of water is the Sabkhat ar-Riâna or Gulf of Utica; the southern, the Bahira or Lake of Tunis. The Lake of Tunis is connected with the

sea by a narrow channel between the end of the southern horn and
a similar tongue of land extending north from the mainland. North
of the main peninsula, the Gulf of Utica has become largely silted
up and is now a marsh.

The Libyan natives, it is said, greeted Elissa's colonists, being
eager to see a trading center set up in their midst:

> Having then bargained for a piece of ground, as much
> as could be covered by an ox-hide, where she might refresh
> her companions, wearied with their long voyage, until she could
> conveniently resume her progress, she directed the hide to be
> cut into the thinnest possible strips, and thus acquired a greater
> portion of ground than she had apparently demanded; whence
> the place had afterwards the name of Byrsa.[16]

True enough, *byrsa* is Greek for "hide." It is more likely, however,
that the name is a corruption of some Phoenician term with quite a
different meaning, and that the Greeks made up the story of the oxhide
to account for the name and to bolster their belief that the Phoenicians
were even more given to sharp practice than they themselves.

Smitten with Elissa, a local chieftain named Iarbas demanded her
hand in marriage and threatened war if denied. Elissa, however, had
other ideas. She

> . . . said (after calling for a long time with many tears and
> mournful lamentations on the name of her husband Acherbas),
> that "she would go whither the fate of her city called her"
> . . . having raised a funeral pile at the extremity of the city,
> she sacrificed many victims, as if she would appease the shade
> of her husband, and make her offerings to him before her
> marriage; and then, taking a sword, she ascended the pile, and,
> looking towards the people, said, that "she would go to her
> husband as they had desired her," and put an end to her life
> with the sword.[17]

It sounds too romantic to be true, but it may have some basis
in fact; the Carthaginians did practice such ritual suicides, and those
who thus killed themselves were admired. Like the people of East
Asia, the Carthaginians held life—their own and others'—cheap. They
often crucified unsuccessful generals.

A century after the final destruction of Carthage, Augustus'
favorite court poet, Publius Vergilius Maro (better known as "Virgil"),
composed an epic on the life of the Trojan hero Aeneas. Avid for
distinguished ancestry, the Romans claimed descent from Aeneas.

According to Virgil, Aeneas flees the fall of Troy with his father,
wife, and son; but the first two of these soon perish. After adventures

paralleling some of those of Odysseus, Aeneas and his surviving ships land near newly-founded Carthage, where the industrious Tyrians are busily raising walls. Aeneas meets Queen Elissa, whom for some uncertain reason Roman writers were wont to call "Dido."

He and she then engage in a *grande passion*. This might have gone on indefinitely, had not the gods sent a warning to Aeneas that his destiny was to sail on to Italy and found the Roman people, and he had better be going *celeriter*. A dutiful if colorless hero, Aeneas departs despite the furious scenes the queen makes over his perfidy. As he sails away, she kills herself. Looking back, Aeneas sees the smoke of her pyre. In the nineteenth century, Hector Berlioz made an opera, *Les Troyens à Carthage*, of Virgil's romance. Because of its intolerable length, it was unsuccessful despite some fine music.

Virgil's tale, unfortunately, entails an anachronism of over 300 years. The date most generally accepted in ancient times for the fall of Troy was —1184, whereas the date of —814 for the founding of Carthage is not only the best-attested in ancient writing but also the most plausible archaeologically. Actually, excavations at Troy have shown that it had not one fall but at least four, including destruction by earthquake, stretching from about —1300 to —1100.[18]

If we dismiss the Dido-Aeneas romance and question the story of Elissa and her importunate suitor Iarbas, we may still assume that a real Elissa probably did found the city in late —IX. The Tyrian settlers unimaginatively named the place Qarth Hadasht, "New City," whence the Greek Karchêdôn and Latin Carthago.

For nearly four centuries, Carthage flourished as a monarchial Phoenician city-state. Most of the time it was ruled by a dynasty called the Magonid, from its founder King Mago. The Carthaginians allied themselves with the Etruscans in Italy to resist the westward thrust of the Greeks, who had settled in southern Italy and eastern Sicily. Although they could never drive the Hellenes out of Sicily, the Carthaginians maintained a virtual monopoly of trade in the western Mediterranean. They simply rammed and destroyed any non-Punic ships they found poaching on what they deemed their preserves.

Carthage particularly valued her trade with mineral-rich southwestern Spain: notably with Gades (Cádiz), founded by Tyrians around —1100 and thus one of the oldest living cities in the world; and with the nearby semi-civilized region or city of Tartessos, around the mouth of the Baetis or Guadalquivir. Tartessos, which had begun to develop a native Iberian civilization of its own, mysteriously dropped out of sight about —500. It may have furnished Plato with ideas for his romance of the lost Atlantis. Asiatic Greeks' from Phokaia ran the Carthaginian blockade to Tartessos by using, instead of the normal tubby sailing merchant ships, light fifty-oared galleys. These, though ordinarily too costly for commerce, could run away when a Carthaginian trireme came crawling over the horizon in pursuit, like a big centipede chasing a little one.

In —V, as a result of disasters like the defeat at Himera in Sicily, came a change in the Carthaginian government. The merchant class ousted the kings and set up an oligarchic republic, which ruled Carthage until its final downfall. The new Senate imposed on the people a policy of austerity. Importation of foreign luxuries was forbidden. Temple prostitution may have been suppressed; at least, we do not hear of it in later accounts of Carthage. Tanith, the moon goddess, was exalted over Ba'al Hammon. Despite the frequent wars with the Greeks of Sicily, Greek influence crept in, including the worship of the goddesses Demeter and Persephonê.

In —IV, when Carthage was fighting the Siceliots, the city probably reached a population between 200,000 and 300,000. Perhaps half a million more dwelt in what Greeks called the *chora*, the territory included in the boundaries of the polis, which produced the foodstuffs on which the city subsisted. The city occupied the end of the peninsula. Within the walls, the southern part of the city was low and flat, while the northern part rose into a hilly plateau. The southeastern district around the harbor—the Byrsa—was the business district, full of apartment houses up to six stories high. The northern part, the plateau of Megara, was a residential area, with fields, gardens, mansions, and temples.

Massive walls surrounded the city, especially on the western side. Here a triple line of fortifications across the peninsula defended Carthage. The innermost and largest wall was 57 feet high and 28 feet thick. Casemates built into the inner face sheltered 300 elephants, 4,000 horses and their riders, and 20,000 foot soldiers.

From the shoreline of the Byrsa, a projection extended half a mile southward, consisting of a small island and a causeway joining it to the mainland. Quays were built along this artificial peninsula. West of the causeway were the two inner harbors, a rectangular merchant harbor about 1,200 to 1,600 feet long and perhaps half or a third as wide, and north of it the circular naval harbor, about 1,000 feet across. These harbors seem small in view of the large fleets that Carthage put to sea. But the ships were small, and at any one time many were either hauled out on land or were riding at anchor in the Lake of Tunis. These two harbors still form shallow lagoons in the midst of the modern city.

For one of my own novels, I have had occasion to draw a fictional picture of the city in the time of Dionysios the Elder (early —IV). If less gorgeous than Flaubert's, I hope it is more truthful, without being quite so drab as "prosaic city of shopkeepers" implies:

The hills of the Megara flattened out as the ship sailed
until it came abreast of the Byrsa. The Byrsa—the inner city
—was surrounded by its own wall, which joined the outer wall
along the waterfront to form a single enormous rampart,
strengthened at intervals by towers. Behind the double wall
could be seen the tops of houses five or even six stories high.
Beyond these, and separated by a short distance from the hills
of the Megara, stood the single fortified hill of the citadel.

Between the great wall and the sea ran a paved causeway,
with a parapet along its outer edge. Ships tied up along this
quay by rope looped around the crenelations of the parapet.
As Zopyros' [my hero's] ship proceeded, the causeway nar-
rowed into a long point, directed south, and ended in a huge
built-up stone pier. The captain tied up near the end of this
pier.

As Zopyros and his companions disembarked, a donkey
boy came running up, leading his beast. Knowing from the
steward's directions that Elazar's house was over a league from
the port, they hired the ass to carry their gear. When the
three duffel bags had been roped into place, the travelers set
out northwards towards the base of the pier and the great wall.

To the left of the pier was a gap in the wall, through
which Zopyros glimpsed the inner harbor. This harbor . . .
was crowded with merchant ships, some in the water and
some hauled out on skids around the margins. Beyond this
inner harbor but connected with it lay the cothon or naval
harbor, surrounded by a massive circular wall. A trireme,
issuing from the cothon, nosed its way through the merchantmen, like a shark in a pool of turtles, with shouted threats and
warnings to clear the way.

As the three reached the base of the pier, they approached
one of the gates in the main wall. Flanking this gate were a
pair of towers with a portcullis, like that on Ortygia, working
between them. Behind the portcullis was the main portal,
comprising a pair of wooden doors whose timbers were whole
tree trunks squared, held together by massive bronzen brackets.
The portcullis was raised and the gates stood open. Several
soldiers in corselets of gilded metal scales mounted guard at
the gate. One soldier questioned Zopyros and his companions
closely before letting them into the city.

Once within the gate, the travelers followed the animal
past the merchant harbor, across which they could see the
tophet or temenos of the temple of Tanith and Ba'al Hammon,
with its groves and shrines and stelae surrounding the home

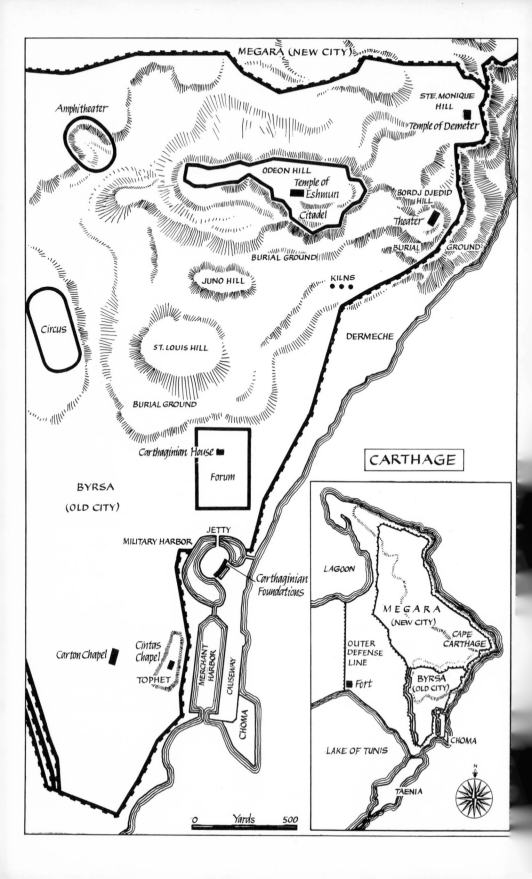

MEGARA (NEW CITY)

STE. MONIQUE HILL

Temple of Demeter

Amphitheater

ODEON HILL

Temple of Eshmun

Citadel

BORDJ DJEDID HILL

Theater

BURIAL GROUND

BURIAL GROUND

JUNO HILL

KILNS

DERMECHE

Circus

ST. LOUIS HILL

BURIAL GROUND

Carthaginian House

Forum

CARTHAGE

BYRSA

(OLD CITY)

JETTY

MILITARY HARBOR

Carthaginian Foundations

LAGOON

MEGARA

(NEW CITY)

CAPE CARTHAGE

OUTER DEFENSE LINE

BYRSA (OLD CITY)

Carton Chapel

Cintas Chapel

TOPHET

MERCHANT HARBOR

CAUSEWAY

CHOMA

Fort

CHOMA

LAKE OF TUNIS

TAENIA

0   Yards   500

N

of the divine pair. They trailed the ass around the curve of the wall of the naval harbor into the tangle of stone-paved streets beyond.

"Valetudo preserve us, but the houses are even taller here than in Motya!" said Segovax, looking apprehensively at the towering whitewashed façades on either side. The height of the buildings made dark canyons of the streets, into which an occasional scorching sunbeam struck slantwise. The dust made Zopyros cough; the rank city smells were overpowering.

The travelers jostled loose-robed Phoenicians, tattooed Libyans wearing ostrich-plume headdresses, and lean, swarthy Numidians capped with turbans of wildcat skins. There were Negroes from beyond the deserts: some of them huge, muscular men; other mere Pygmies, less than five feet tall.

They brushed past snake charmers, sorcerers, and beggars holding out fly-crusted sores and the stumps of withered limbs. They dodged around the litters, borne by gigantic blacks, of bejeweled oligarchs. They pushed past the flocks of goats and sheep that flowed like freshets along the narrow streets, with a skin-clad herdsman and his dog walking briskly behind each flock.

The streets were lined with shops, identified by wooden signs inscribed right to left with lines of Punic writing. Costly goods from near and far spilled out into the street. The shop-keepers stood in their doorways, importuning passers-by with seductive cries, low bows, and sweeping gestures. One man sold Etruscan candles; another, Persian umbrellas. An Egyptian tradesman featured two of his country's products: a salve for curing dandruff, made from genuine hippopotamus fat; and some large tame snakes, which Egyptian ladies of quality placed in their laps or around their necks to keep themselves cool in summer.

Everywhere—on street corners, in the entrance to shops, and in the midst of traffic—men pursued their eternal bargaining in the purring Punic tongue. If quieter than Greek hagglers, the Carthaginians were more energetic and business-like in their manner. Everybody seemed in a hurry. Nobody strolled about discussing philosophy or politics and illustrating his points with graceful gestures. Every Carthaginian seemed to have urgent business, to which he was hastening with an anxious, preoccupied air.[19]

The ordinary Carthaginian dwelt in a small house or apartment, rather bare of furnishings and ornament. The handsomest piece of furniture was likely to be a big cedar chest, in which the master of the house kept his valuables and on which he often slept to make sure that nobody stole them.

The Carthaginians displayed a marked indifference to the arts, with the possible exceptions of music, dancing, and cookery. Despite some obvious Greek influence, their plastic and graphic arts remained astonishingly crude. Their manufactures for export—textiles, pottery, jewelry, glassware, and carvings in shell, bone, and ivory—were mostly cheap, unesthetic, and produced in large quantities.

For active pursuits, Carthaginian men wore a singlet or light tunic and a kilt or a pair of shorts. For more sedentary occupations, they wore a long unbelted robe, often together with an apron, a jacket, a mantle, or some combination of these. On their heads some wore turbans; others, fezzes; still others, tall, conical felt hats. Beards were general, except among the shaven priesthood. Both sexes went in for earrings, nose rings, and other jewelry; they also jingled with charms and amulets.

The Carthaginians persisted in using the old Canaanitish language, even though this tongue was ousted by Aramaic in Phoenicia under the Persians. In Tunisia, Canaanitish persisted right down through the centuries of Roman rule. Some think that the present Semitic language of Malta is a remote descendant of the Carthaginian dialect of Canaanitish.

Greek and Roman writers professed no high opinion of the Carthaginians; but then, objectivity towards one's foes was even rarer in ancient times than now. Plutarch wrote: "The Carthaginians are a hard and gloomy people, submissive to their rulers and harsh to their subjects, running to extremes of cowardice in times of fear and of cruelty in times of anger; they keep obstinately to their decisions, are austere and care little for amusement or the graces of life."[20] Flaubert presented a similar picture (as usual, somewhat overdrawn) of a gathering of Carthaginian Senators (his "Ancients"):

> These men were generally thick-set, with curved noses like those of the Assyrian colossus . . . Those who had lived continually shut up in their counting-houses had pale faces; others showed in theirs the severity of the desert, and strange jewels sparkled on all the fingers of their hands, which were burnt by unknown suns. The navigators might be distinguished by their rolling gait, while the men of agriculture smelt of the winepress, dried herbs, and the sweat of mules. These old pirates had lands under tillage, these money-grabbers would fit out ships, these proprietors of cultivated lands supported slaves who followed trades. All were skilled in religious discipline, expert in strategy, pitiless and rich. They looked weary of prolonged cares. Their flaming eyes expressed dis-

trust, and their habits of travelling and lying, trafficking and commanding, gave an appearance of cunning and violence, a sort of discreet and convulsive brutality to their whole demeanor . . .[21]

To take a balanced view, we can describe the Carthaginians' culture pattern as follows, always remembering that individuals varied as much as they always have: They were clean, sober, and temperate. Monogamy was the rule, and neither eunuchs nor homosexuality were common enough to have left traces in the historical record. They had enormous commercial acumen and pursued their trading careers with great energy and determination. Although normally peaceful, they could fight as well as anyone when compelled to do so. They showed extraordinary daring and enterprise in exploring.

The "submissiveness" or "servility" for which the Greeks and Romans condemned them was merely the elaborate oriental politeness that has long been traditional in most of Asia. To a Carthaginian, the plain-spoken, informal manners of the Greeks and Romans doubtless seemed brusque and rude.

On the other hand, like some other ancient Semitic peoples, the Carthaginians were egregiously inartistic. Even during their last century, when they came under the influence of Greek religion and culture, all their art objects and little luxuries were imported from the Greek lands. They never learned to make their own.

They were devoted to their gloomy religion to the point of fanaticism. It took the Romans centuries to stamp out their custom of sacrificing their children to the gods. They were full of superstitious fears of evil spirits and bloodthirsty gods; they seem never to have attempted anything like the rationalistic philosophies of the Greeks.

The Carthaginians were hard-boiled and unsentimental in their dealings and held life cheaply. The Greeks and Romans called them cruel and treacherous, and so they were; but, on the evidence of their own historians, the Greeks and Romans were just as cruel and treacherous. It was a brutal age, and we may assume that in this respect, if not in some others, Flaubert has given a lifelike picture of it.

Whatever the Carthaginians' faults and virtues, Greeks and Romans must have found life in Carthage a great bore, since the city had neither sports, nor drama, nor art. Aside from the public banquets that the rich gave to the poor, the only public amusement was the religious spectacle. Here is my fictional version of such a procession:

> Then came the boom of drums, the clash of cymbals,
> the twang of harps, the clang of sistra, and the wail of flutes
> and pipes. The odor of incense filled the air. The first group
> of paraders appeared, from the temple of Bes.

In front marched a musical band. Then came groups of singers and dancers, the latter bounding and cavorting. Little girls threw flower petals at the crowd. The god himself, a painted and gilded statue on a litter borne by a dozen priests, followed. The priests wore thin, transparent robes over white loincloths. Bucket-shaped gauze caps covered their shaven heads.

The statue was that of a long-bearded, snub-nosed, dancing dwarf, naked but for a lion's skin thrown over one shoulder. Ostrich plumes waved from the corners of the litter. Other temple folk followed: priests swinging censers, which filled the avenue with blue clouds of sweet-smelling smoke; sacrificers, lamplighters, sacred barbers, lay brothers, temple slaves and serfs.

The crowd cheered the god of mirth and merriment. Another group of musicians followed, and after them the float of Eshmun, the healer. This was a statue of a long-bearded, long-robed god seated in a gilded wagon drawn by four mules. The god held out his arms to bless the people. Priests, walking beside the wagon, wore bandages, or had their arms in slings, or pretended to limp on crutches to show the ills of which their god cured his worshipers. After them came more ranks of minor temple personnel, for today even the meanest temple slave had his moment of glory.

More incense, more music. The next float was that of Hiyôn, the divine artificer, beating a piece of metal on his anvil. A real fire glowed in his forge. The priests who walked beside his wagon bore tools for working wood, stone, leather, and metal.

Next came Dagon, with his fish's tail. His priests carried his litter. Other priests, dressed in iridescent scales, went through the motions of fish, while yet others in blue-green cloaks swayed back and forth like waves. Pretty priestesses in green gauze sprinkled scented water on the crowd from golden aspergilla.

Then came Kusôr, the mariner and inventor. Priests pulled his wagon, which was a fishing boat on wheels. In the boat, the statue of Kusôr sat at a table and tinkered with a device of wheels and levers . . .

Next came the wagon of Resheph. A pair of black bulls drew it; a white ass, to be sacrificed at the end of the day, was led behind. The statue showed the god as standing on a bull and wearing a horned helmet. In one hand he held a battle-ax and in the other a three-pronged thunderbolt. The priests carried his emblems on poles: black thunderclouds of cloth, zigzag silver spears representing lightning, and silver vultures with outspread wings . . .

Now the wagon bearing the statue of Anath, the warrior goddess, swayed into view. The goddess rode a lion, with a shield on her right arm, a spear in her right hand, and an ax in her left hand. A necklace of severed human heads hung around her neck. Her priests carried shields and spears, which they clashed together in unison . . .

Next came El, seated in a chariot drawn by two red bulls. The symbols carried on poles included bulls' horns, rayed sun disks, and long blue streamers representing rivers.

Then came Ashtarth. The cheers became deafening . . . A living woman played the part of the goddess Ashtarth. She lounged on her wagon wearing a robe of many colors, draped to expose her body, while she threw kisses to the crowd. Her priests carried spiked silver balls, representing the planet Venus, and sexual symbols made of precious metals and adorned with jewels . . .

Then came the greatest god of all, Ba'al Hammon. The god sat on a throne on his wagon, his hands on the rams' heads that formed the arms of the throne. His beard hung to his waist, and horns curled up from his head. Some of his priests wore golden fillets, some feathered headdresses, and some tall pointed hats . . .

Last of all came Adon, god of the harvest, who on this occasion had the place of honor. Wild boars were led on chains before his litter, which took the form of a bier. The body of the dead god, painted white, lay supine with hundreds of stalks of wheat standing in holes in the upper surface of the effigy. A chorus dressed in sackcloth and ashes preceded the litter, singing a dirge for the dead god. Following the litter, a second chorus—bejeweled, wreathed, and garlanded—sang a hymn that rejoiced in his resurrection.[22]

Before the First Punic War, Rome and Carthage had entered into several treaties of friendship. It is practically a law of history, however, that two such neighboring powers, both vigorously expanding, will sooner or later come to blows.

In this case, a gang of mercenaries, finding themselves unemployed, seized Messana and embarked upon a career of piracy. When Carthage attacked the freebooters, the latter appealed to Rome; and Rome, jealous of Carthaginian wealth and strength, responded (−264). The land fighting was almost all in Sicily, except for an abortive invasion of the Carthaginian homeland by the Romans. The Romans, who had theretofore been landlubbers, tipped the scales in their own favor by building a fleet from scratch and becoming a naval power.

The war dragged on for twenty-four years, with victories and defeats, and the replacement of several Roman fleets destroyed by storms. The Romans won, annexed Sicily, and extorted an indemnity from Carthage.

Then came the revolt of the mercenaries. When Hamilcar Barca had suppressed this rebellion, he went on to Iberia to extend Carthaginian power. Soon he ruled all of southern Spain. He devoted his life to one overmastering passion: revenge upon Rome, and he brought up his son Hannibal to think likewise. When Hamilcar was killed in a disturbance, he was succeeded in the governorship by his son-in-law Hasdrubal and, when Hasdrubal was murdered, by Hannibal. A couple of coins give some idea of the appearance of the heroic father and son. The portraits give the impression of burly men with deep-set eyes under heavy eyebrow ridges, high-bridged noses, and massive jaws. Whereas Hamilcar wears a full, curly beard, Hannibal has adopted the clean-shaven Hellenistic fashion.

A quarrel arose between Hannibal and Rome over the town of Saguntum. Hannibal claimed the right to attack it, and the Romans, the right to defend it. The treaties assigning spheres of influence in Spain were not specific enough to settle the question. In −218, Hannibal astounded the Romans by marching his army, including thirty-six elephants,[23] along the Mediterranean shores of southern Gaul and over the Alps to Italy. Moreover, in his first three years in Italy he inflicted four crushing defeats on the Romans. The last of these was his annihilation of a 60,000-man Roman army at Cannae.

Hannibal remained in Italy fifteen years. It was the most brilliant raid in history but, in the long run, a futile one. For he could never muster enough force to attack the city of Rome, and the Romans wore him down by numbers and by guerrilla tactics, which kept him from scoring any more spectacular victories.

While the most brilliant tactician in history was marching about Italy, striving with some success to detach the southern Italian cities from Rome, a Roman expedition to Spain wrested that country from the Carthaginians. At last the Romans sent another expedition to Africa, and Hannibal had to return to defend his homeland. At Zama in −202 he tried the same enveloping maneuver that had brought him such sanguinary success at Cannae. But the Roman commander, Cornelius Scipio Africanus the Elder, was almost as brilliant a general as Hannibal. He countered Hannibal's moves and won the battle with the help of a regiment of Numidian cavalry.

Carthage gave up, losing her Spanish empire and her fleet. Hannibal fled to the East. A few years later, living in Ephesos, he met

Scipio, who had come thither on a governmental mission. Being personally friendly, they fell to talking about generalship. Hannibal said that he ranked Alexander as the number one man in that field, Pyrrhos second, and himself third.

"What would you have said if I had not defeated you?" he asked Scipio with a smile.

"In that case, Scipio, I should have put myself, not third, but first."[24]

Fearful of Hannibal's abilities, the Romans hounded him from city to city. For a time he served as adviser to the Seleucid king Antiochos III, sometimes called "the Great," in the latter's war with Rome. Antiochos had shown considerable ability in youth but had become self-indulgent and ineffectual in middle age. The Romans beat his armies and continued their pursuit of Hannibal until the great Carthaginian took poison.

Despite having lost her empire, Carthage, with the extraordinary resilience of her people, soon recovered from the ruinous war. She thus attracted the attention of a leading Roman Senator, Marcus Porcius Cato, when he came to Carthage as a commissioner to settle a dispute with the Numidians. This self-styled embodiment of the old Roman virtues was a grim, rancorous man who wrote that a slave should be working when not sleeping and that slaves too old for work should be sold. As censor, he expelled a man from the Senate for having kissed his own wife in the daytime in the sight of their daughter. Since he hated everything pleasant, Cato was roused to wrath and alarm by Carthaginian prosperity. Thereafter, he ended every Senatorial speech with the words: "*Delenda est Carthago!* [Carthage must be destroyed!]"

Half a century after Zama, Cato brought enough Romans around to his view. The Roman method was to stir up the Numidians to attack Carthage. When the Carthaginians defended themselves, the Romans pounced upon them, on the pretext that they had broken the treaty by making war without permission. The Carthaginians temporized, surrendered hostages, and gave up their arms. Then the Romans raised their demands, commanding the Carthaginians to leave their city and move ten miles inland—a death sentence to a nation of traders.

At this, the Carthaginian masses rose and lynched the commissioners who had agreed to these terms, together with any Italians they could catch. They set themselves to make new arms. The women cut off their hair for catapult skeins; day and night the forges glowed and the anvils clanged. They would at least take as many Romans with them as they could.

A ferocious siege followed. When the Romans finally forced their way in, it took six days of house-to-house fighting to master the city.

When the remnant—less than a quarter of the original population—surrendered, the Romans burned the city, plowed the ruins, and cursed them forever.

The Roman commander was Cornelius Scipio Africanus the Younger, an adopted grandson of the Elder. When he had ordered the burning of the city, he turned to his friend, the Greek historian Polybios, and said: "O Polybios, it is a grand thing but, I know not how, I feel a terror and dread, lest some one should some day give the same order about my own native city." When the fire was under way,

> At the sight of the city utterly perishing amidst the flames Scipio burst into tears, and stood long reflecting on the inevitable change that awaits cities, nations, and dynasties, one and all, as it does every one of us men. This, he thought, had befallen Ilium, once a powerful city, and the once mighty empires of the Assyrians, Medes, Persians, and that of Macedonia lately so splendid. And unintentionally or purposely he quoted,
> —the words perhaps escaping him unconsciously,—
> "The day shall come when holy Troy shall fall
> And Priam, lord of spears, and Priam's folk."
> And on my asking him boldly (for I had been his tutor) what he meant by these words, he did not name Rome distinctly, but was evidently feeling for her, for this sight of the mutability of human affairs.[25]

Refounded by Augustus, Roman Carthage throve for over four and a half centuries. Captured by Gaiseric[26] the Vandal in +439, it was retaken for the East Roman Empire by Belisarius in +533 but captured and destroyed by the Arabs in +647. Throughout the Middle Ages it was a mere village.

Nowadays Carthage is a suburb of Tunis, instead of vice versa as in ancient times. It looks rather like a run-down Miami Beach, with little sugar cubes of white stuccoed houses set amid cypresses. The men on the streets wear European suits with fezzes, either the regular kind or the low, rounded variety of fez favored in Tunisia. The women wear European dresses but, over these, the enveloping burka, a hooded coverall of thin material.

At the brow of the plateau of the Megara, the remains of a Roman fort overlook the Byrsa and the lagoons that remain from the ancient harbors. There is a small but good museum of local antiquities nearby. Cathage can be reached from Tunis by an electric interurban line, with wooden cars from which most of the white paint has long since peeled. They look as if they had been dug out of Hannibal's tomb and put back into service.

Still, the modern descendants of the men of Carthage and Utica are not doing at all badly. A Tunisian taxi driver, Charbti Tahar, told me: "We Tunisians are like the Swiss. We have no enemies. Everybody loves us, and they all come here to spend their money!"

I arrived at the end of an unseasonal winter drouth. The Tunisians had been worrying about their crops, but the day I landed it poured. On the way from the airport, I complained to my driver friend about being chased all over the Mediterranean by bad weather, which incidentally interfered with the photographs for this book. Beaming, he cried:

"*Ah, monsieur, il faut que Dieu vous aime!* [God must love you!]"

XI

ALEXANDRIA AND THE DARKHOUSE

POWERS, WHAT A CROWD! HOW SHALL WE GET ALONG?
WHY, THEY'RE LIKE ANTS! COUNTLESS! INNUMERABLE!
WELL, PTOLEMY, YOU'VE DONE FINE THINGS, THAT'S CERTAIN,
SINCE THE GODS TOOK YOUR FATHER. NO ONE NOWADAYS
DOES HARM TO TRAVELERS AS THEY USED TO,
AFTER THE EGYPTIAN FASHION, LYING IN WAIT—
MASTERS OF NOTHING BUT DETESTABLE TRICKS;
AND ALL ALIKE A SET OF CHEATS AND BRAWLERS.
GORGO, SWEET FRIEND, WHAT WILL BECOME OF US?
HERE ARE THE KING'S HORSE-GUARDS! PRAY, MY GOOD MAN,
DON'T TREAD UPON US SO . . .[1]

Theokritos

84. Alexandria: Archaeological excavations near the Serapeum. (Courtesy of Henry Angelo-Castrillon.)

I~N~ —IV, Alexander son of Philip, the third king of Macedonia of that name, subdued Greece. Then he led an army of Greeks and Macedonians to the conquest of the mighty Persian Empire. From the rocky shores of Ionia, his columns marched past bustling Phoenician seaports, where they captured Tyre after a bitter siege. They rumbled on to the shimmering sands of Egypt, and from Egypt to the ancient ziggurats of Mesopotamia. There they crushed the forces of the hapless Darius III. On they went, to the tiger-haunted jungles of Hyrkania, the lonely steppes of Central Asia, and over the Afghan crags to the Indus Valley, to vanquish the glittering rajas and their lumbering elephants.

By —323, Alexander had conquered a realm as great as that of the first Darius. He had encouraged the intermarriage of Macedonians with Persians and had laid grandiose plans for further conquests, explorations, and public works. Then, not yet thirty-three, he suddenly died, apparently of malaria, in Babylon. He left at least two widows and a pack of rapacious Macedonian generals to squabble over his inheritance.

These generals soon liquidated all the conqueror's kinsmen—mother, brother, wives, and child. Then they carved up the empire and set themselves up as kings. The ablest of these Diadochi or "Successors" was a huge man called Antigonos One-eye, who ruled Asia Minor for thirty years. Then the other Diadochi ganged up on him, and he fell at the battle of Ipsos (—301). Thereafter, the leading kingdoms of the Successors were Egypt, under Ptolemaios (or Ptolemaeus or Ptolemy) and his successors; Macedonia, ruled by the descendants of Antigonos One-eye; and the Seleucid kingdom—Syria, Mesopotamia, and Iran—under the line of the general Seleukos. Several kingdoms waxed and waned in Asia Minor.

Although most of Alexander's Macedonian officers soon discarded the Persian wives he had found for them, his hoped-for mixture of Hellenes with Orientals soon took place anyway. Alexander and the Successors founded scores of new cities in the conquered lands. They encouraged thousands of Greeks and Macedonians to settle in these cities side by side with Persians, Syrians, Egyptians, and other native peoples. Hellenes swarmed out of barren Greece to serve in the armies and bureaucracies of the Successors, forming a ruling class in the new kingdoms.

The interloping Greeks soon mingled with the native upper classes. Greek culture influenced the Orientals, while oriental ideas affected the

Greeks. The brilliant Graeco-Oriental civilization that resulted is called the Hellenistic.

The Hellenistic Age (roughly defined as the last three centuries before the Christian Era) was in some ways like our own century. It was a time of intellectual ferment, of travel and tourism, of scholarship and research, of popular outlines and lectures, of clubs and societies, of invention and promotion. It was a time on the one hand of a scramble for the wealth created by the advance of technology and the spread of commerce, and on the other of communistic revolutionary movements for the division of this wealth.

Another "modern" feature of the Hellenistic Age was a love of the grandiose. Hellenistic kings armed their soldiers with longer spears and massed them in bigger phalanxes than ever before; they built more sumptuous temples and palaces; they erected taller buildings and statues; they organized more splendid parades; they committed more dastardly crimes. Whatever inhibitions the émigré Greeks may have had against lying, theft, extortion, bribery, treachery, and murder they seem to have left behind them in Greece.

The Hellenistic Age, although progressive in many ways, was politically an era of amoral opportunism. The ensuing Age of Faith, which grew up under the Roman Empire and lasted for nearly a millennium and a half, paid more lip service to moral principles but was no more humane in practice. The murders and massacres of people like Agathokles and Physkon were no crueler than, say, the mass burning of Jews in Madrid in 1680, to celebrate the wedding of the half-witted King Carlos II and to amuse the gentry and clergy of Spain.

Alexander founded at least ten cities named Alexandria[2] after himself. The one that far outshone all the rest—*the* Alexandria—he founded in −331 on his visit to Egypt.

The coast of the Delta is not well provided with harbors, save at the mouths of the Nile, where sand bars and silting complicate the problem of safe anchorage. In the western part of this coast, however, a chain of limestone reefs and islands forms an arc sheltering over three miles of the coast behind it. In the *Odyssey*, King Menelaos of Sparta says:

An island there is in the loud-surging sea, which Pharos is called,
A sail of a day from Egypt. It has a good port, where ships
Put in to draw well water, before setting forth again.[3]

Alexander found the main island of the chain—the isle of Pharos, a mile and a half long—no "one day's sail" from the coast, but less than a mile from shore.[4] In the lee of this island lay the sleepy

Egyptian village of Rhakotis, which went back at least to —1300. Rhakotis stood on a long ribbon of sand and limestone, between one and two miles wide, which sundered the Mediterranean from a shallow lake, a dozen miles across. This lake, which the Greeks called Lake Mareotis (the modern Baḥr Maryût), was one of a chain of such lakes along the northern side of the Delta, heavily fringed with papyrus reeds and then swarming with brigands and hippopotami.

With him, Alexander had an architect named Deinokrates, who had tickled the conqueror's vanity by offering to carve Mount Athos into a statue, presumably of Alexander, holding a city in its left hand. Alexander had vetoed the plan but had kept the resourceful Deinokrates with him. Now he instructed Deinokrates to build a new city on the site of Rhakotis. The locale combined the advantages of a potentially good harbor with a delightful climate, where Egyptian heat was tempered by an almost constant sea breeze from the northwest.

When Deinokrates' assistants were laying out the walls and streets of the city with lines of chalk, the supply of chalk gave out. Since the king was coming to inspect, the architects hastily raided the store of barley meal that had been gathered for the workmen and continued marking lines. Then a swarm of birds descended on the site to gobble the barley. The portent disturbed Alexander until his soothsayers assured him that it was really a good omen, meaning that this Alexandria should feed not only itself but other nations as well.

Alexander went on to the Oasis of Sîwa, to be hailed as a god by the priests of Amon. Then he headed east for the final battle with Darius. He left as governor one Kleomenes, who soon displayed an egregious talent for corruption. For instance, Kleomenes let the merchants of Canopus bribe him not to move the market to Alexandria and then moved it anyway. He also cornered the grain market.

When Alexander died, one of his generals seized control of Egypt. This was the shrewd, farsighted, and amiable Ptolemaios son of Lagos, who had grown up with Alexander. Like most of the Ptolemies he was stocky and stout, with a bull neck, deep-set eyes under beetling brows, and a high-bridged beak of a nose. Having slain the grafting Kleomenes, he ruled a land that even then harbored several millions: the teeming peasantry of the Nile Valley and Delta, wild tribes of sand-dwelling nomads, and settlements of Greeks, Macedonians, and Jews. He extended his rule to Cyprus and Cyrene and beat off several attempted invasions by other Successors.

In —304, Ptolemaios declared himself king and added to his name the sobriquet Soter, "savior," by which he is sometimes known to distinguish him from the other Ptolemies. His full style is Ptolemaios I Soter. He chose Alexandria for his capital and vigorously pushed

Alexander's plans for making it a great city. When Alexander's body, in accordance with Alexander's expressed wish, was dispatched from Babylon in a huge, ornate wagon to be buried at the Oasis of Sîwa, Ptolemaios met it in Syria with a powerful escort and took charge of it. He kept it at Memphis for years while a colossal tomb, the Sema,[5] was building at Alexandria.

After a successful reign of nearly forty years, Soter abdicated in favor of his youngest legitimate son, Ptolemaios II Philadelphos ("Friend-of-sister"). Two years later, in −283, he died. About this time, Alexander's body was moved to Alexandria and entombed in the Sema.

Like most Successors, Soter had been more or less polygamous, with at least two wives and assorted mistresses and concubines. Having banished his first wife for plotting against him, Philadelphos adopted the old Egyptian and Macedonian royal custom of marrying his own sister. This custom lasted throughout the Ptolemaic dynasty. The pretext offered the "natives" was that the Ptolemaic blood was too divine to mingle with that of mortals.

The government was a bureaucratic absolutism, which held monopolies on oil, textiles, banking, and other forms of commerce. Crushing taxation, which fell heaviest on the peasantry, supported the glittering court and the gleaming army. The peasants often revolted, but never successfully. Alexandria and a few other cities with large Greek populations were organized like the Hellenic polis, with Assembly, Council, and elected magistrates; but we can be sure that the king kept a firm grip on municipal affairs. The diverse populations—Greeks, Egyptians, and Jews—retained their own systems of law and their own courts, with mixed courts for mixed cases.

At the center of this pageant, the king was an absolute autocrat. At the start, all the realms of the Successors were regimes of naked power, since the Successors had not been chosen by their subjects, nor did they have the anchorage of usage and custom that stabilizes long-standing dynasties.

The Ptolemies were parvenus, knew it, and looked it, being mostly fat. Lacking the divinity that doth hedge a king, they set about getting it. They had themselves worshiped as gods, paid lip service to ancient Egyptian customs and ceremonies, and surrounded themselves with a highly ornamental court. A Ptolemy's officials included his Usher, Chief Huntsman, Equerry, Chief Pantler, Chief Cupbearer, Physician-in-Chief and ordinary physicians, tutors and foster brothers, Servants of the Bedchamber, Royal Pages, and swarms of attendants. Courtiers were divided into Kinsmen and persons assimilated to that rank, First Friends and assimilated persons, Captains of Bodyguards, Friends, and Successors. Like other Hellenistic kings, the Ptolemies dared not delegate

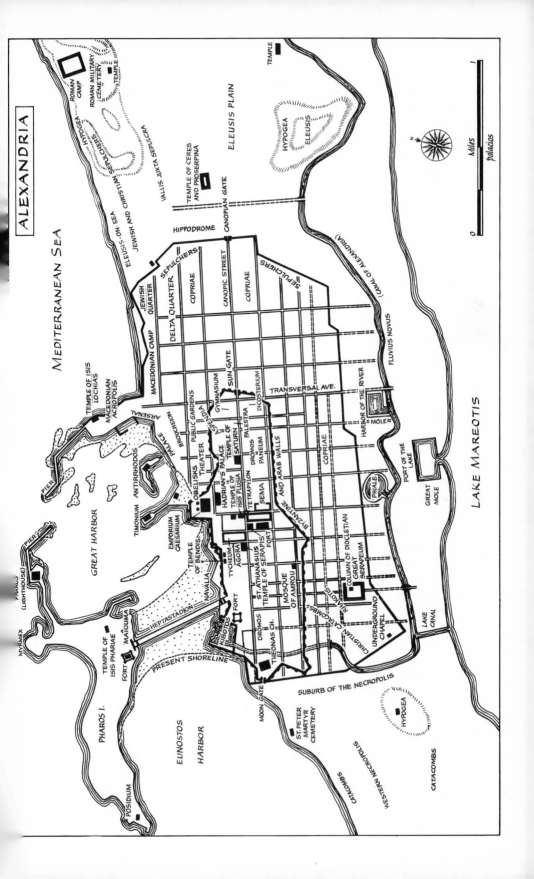

ALEXANDRIA

MEDITERRANEAN SEA

TEMPLE

ROMAN CAMP
ROMAN MILITARY CEMETERY
HYPOGEA
TEMPLE
VALLIS JUXTA SEPULCRA
JEWISH AND CHRISTIAN SEPULCHERS
ELEUSIS-ON-SEA

TEMPLE OF CERES AND PROSERPINA
ELEUSIS PLAIN
CANOPIAN GATE
HYPOGEA
ELEUSIS

HIPPODROME

SEPULCHERS
COPRIAE
CANOPIC STREET
JEWISH QUARTER
DELTA QUARTER
COPRIAE
SEPULCHERS
MACEDONIAN CAMP
(CANAL OF ALEXANDRIA)
FLUVIUS NOVUS

TEMPLE OF ISIS
LOCHIAS
MACEDONIAN ACROPOLIS
ARSENAL
TIMONIUM ANTIRRHODOS
PALACE
BROUCHEION
PUBLIC GARDENS
SPEMA
GYMNASIUM
SUN GATE
DICOSTERIUM
TRANSVERSAL AVE.
HARBOR OF THE RIVER
MOLE

THEATER
OBELISKS
HADRIAN'S PALACE
TEMPLE OF SATURN
TEMPLE OF ISIS PLUSIA
DROMOS PALESTRA
DROMOS PANEUM
COPRIAE
PORT OF THE LAKE

EMPORIUM
CAESARIUM
TEMPLE OF BENDIS
NAVALIA
TYCHEUM
TETRAPYLON
SEMA
BYZANTINE AND ARAB WALLS
PHIALE
GREAT MOLE

PHAROS (LIGHTHOUSE)
PIER
MYRMEX
PIER
GREAT HARBOR

TEMPLE OF ISIS PHARIAE
FORT MAIOUMA
HEPTASTADION
KIBOTOS
FORT
AGORA
ST. ATHANASIUS
TEMPLE OF SERAPIS
FORT
MOSQUE OF AMROU
COLUMN OF DIOCLETIAN
GREAT SERAPEUM
REMAINS
CATACOMBS
CHRISTIAN CHAPEL
UNDERGROUND
LAKE CANAL

PHAROS I.
POSIDIUM
PRESENT SHORELINE
DROMOS
THEONAS CH.
MOON GATE

EUNOSTOS HARBOR

SUBURB OF THE NECROPOLIS

ST. PETER MARTYR CEMETERY
HYPOGEA

CATACOMBS
WESTERN NECROPOLIS
CATACOMBS

LAKE MAREOTIS

N

Miles
Palacios

0   1

much power. Hence, trying to handle more details than any one man could, they were often worn out by middle age.

The creation of Alexandria entailed vast engineering works. A canal was dug to connect Alexandria with the Canopic branch of the Nile, so that river craft could sail directly between Alexandria and Memphis. The chain of islands to seaward of the city were joined to each other and to the mainland. A breakwater and causeway nearly a mile long, with two arched passages for small boats, was constructed from the island of Pharos to the shore. Called the Heptastadion or "Seven-Furlonger," it bisected the harbor. The eastern or Great Harbor contained the naval dockyards and an inner harbor for royal yachts; the western harbor was for fishing vessels and other small craft.

Alexandria was laid out on the typical Hellenistic grid plan, with its long axis east and west. Two main avenues, 46 feet wide and bordered by colonnades, crossed at right angles. The longer of the two main avenues, Kanobic or Canopic Street, ran from the Gate of the Sun at the eastern end of the walled city to the Gate of the Moon at the western end. The streets of Alexandria do not seem to have been paved, at least not until late in the city's history. For administration the city was divided into five "quarters" or wards, denoted by letters of the Greek alphabet.

At the eastern end of the arc of reefs and islands, a peninsula, Point Lochias, thrust out into the sea. The royal palaces, parks, and zoo occupied Point Lochias and the area around the base of this promontory. Not far away stood the Sema, the Museum, the Library, and other public buildings. The Museum and the Library are generally thought to have been southwest of the palaces.

Because Alexandria has been continuously occupied from Alexander's time to the present, few relics of Hellenistic times survive. And, because it is now a large, heavily built-up city, with about a million people, it cannot be thoroughly dug up by archaeologists to settle doubtful points. Many maps have been published, showing the city as the cartographer thought it was arranged in ancient times. But the wide differences among these maps show them to be largely based upon guesswork.

The Greeks called the city "Alexandria-near (or by)-Egypt,"[6] for the land upon which it stood was not considered part of Egypt proper. The population was mixed, and the various nationalities lived in their own sections: the Egyptians in Rhakotis to the southwest, the Jews in the Delta Quarter to the northeast, and the Greeks in the Broucheion between. The polyglot population had the repute of being lively, quick-witted, humorous, and irreverent, but lacking the more solid virtues. Though of little worth as soldiers, they were all too ready to riot.

The different communities, composed as they were of peoples of widely varying customs, manners, and morals, rioted against one another, and all together rioted against any king or emperor whom they disliked. Sometimes one of the fiercer tyrants, a Ptolemaios VII or a Caracalla, lost patience with this fickle and turbulent folk and ordered a massacre. But the Alexandrines never learned.

At the eastern tip of the enlarged Pharos, Soter's architect Sostratos erected a tower as a landmark for ships. This was the famous Lighthouse of Alexandria, one of the original Seven Wonders of the World. In time, the name of the island, Pharos, was applied to the Lighthouse, so that to this day the Greek word for "lighthouse" is *pharos,* and in the Romance languages it is *phare* or *faro.* A story tells that the king as usual wanted his name alone to appear on the Lighthouse. Sostratos craftily inscribed on the stone:

> SOSTRATOS SON OF DEXIPHANES OF KNIDOS
> ON BEHALF OF ALL MARINERS
> TO THE SAVIOR GODS

Then he covered this inscription with a layer of plaster, on which was chiseled the customary royal inscription. In time the plaster peeled off, removing the name of the king and exposing that of the architect.

Finished in Philadelphos' reign, the Lighthouse stood between 380 and 440 feet tall, compared with 480 feet for Khufu's Great Pyramid and 555.5 feet for the Washington Monument. It was built in three sections: the lowest square, the intermediate octagonal, and the highest cylindrical. Helical stairways led to the top, and the lowest section contained fifty rooms.

At a later date, the Pharos was certainly used as a lighthouse; that is, as a tower on whose summit a fire was kept burning at night to help navigation. There is some question, however, as to whether such a light was maintained in early Ptolemaic times, or whether the tower guided ships to harbor by daylight only. It would indeed have helped mariners thus, since it was visible long before the low, flat coast of the Delta rose out of the turquoise sea.

One small and inconclusive piece of evidence favors the idea that the tower was in fact a lighthouse from the first, not a darkhouse. A minor classical geographer, Dionysios of Byzantium (—II), wrote a description of the Bosporus region, of which the surviving fragment tells of a "Timean tower" standing on a hill beside the Golden Horn of Byzantium. Says Dionysios: "It has been built for the safety of the navigator, fires being kindled for their guidance."[7]

Dionysios does not identify the Timaios who presumably paid for

85. Column of Diocletian ("Pompey's Pillar") and a sphinx, near the site of the Serapeum in southwestern Alexandria.

the "Timean tower." But, of the seven known ancient worthies of this name, the likeliest is Timaios of Kyzikos, a contemporary of Aristotle and therefore of the generation before Soter. If this man was the author of the tower in question, then probably the use of beacons on navigational towers was already known when Soter and Sostratos began their project, and it is unlikely that they would overlook such an obvious method of doubling the usefulness of their skyscraper.

Our best descriptions of the Pharos, which stood for 1,500 years, come from two medieval Muslim travelers. The Spanish Moor Idrîsi,[8] who was in the eastern Mediterranean about 1115, wrote:

> We notice the famous lighthouse, which has not its like in the world for harmony of construction or for solidity; since, to say nothing of the fact that it is built of the excellent stone of the kind called *al-kadhdhân,* the courses of these stones

are united by molten lead, and the joints are so adherent that the whole is indissoluble, though the surge of the sea from the north incessantly beats against the structure. The distance between the lighthouse and the city is one mile by sea and three miles by land. Its height is 300 cubits of the *rashâshi* standard, each equal to three spans, making a height of 100 fathoms [646 to 755 feet], whereof 96 are to the lantern and four to the height of the lantern. From the ground to the middle gallery measures exactly 70 fathoms, and from the gallery to the top of the lighthouse, 26.

One climbs to the summit by a broad staircase built into the interior, which is as broad as those ordinarily erected in minarets. The first staircase ends about halfway up the lighthouse, and thence, on all four sides, the building narrows. Inside and under the staircase, chambers have been built. Starting from the gallery, the lighthouse rises, ever narrowing, to its top, until at last one cannot always turn as one climbs.

From this same gallery one begins to climb again, to reach the top, by a flight of steps narrower than the lower staircase. All parts of the lighthouse are pierced by windows to give light to persons ascending and to provide them with firm footing as they climb.

This building is singularly remarkable, as much on account of its height as its solidity; it is very useful in that it is kept lit night and day as a beacon for navigators throughout the whole sailing season; mariners know the fire and direct their courses accordingly, for it is visible a day's sail [100 miles] away. By night it looks like a brilliant star; by day one can perceive its smoke.[9]

When Yûsuf ibn-ash-Shaykh, another Spanish Moor, visited the tower in 1165, he found it no longer used as a lighthouse. Instead, a small mosque had been installed on top in place of the beacon. Faith had triumphed over utility. Being an experienced builder and architect, ibn-ash-Shaykh carefully measured the tower, and we rely on his figures today. (Idrîsi's seem to be somewhat exaggerated.[10]) We cannot, however, confidently translate ibn-ash-Shaykh's dimensions into modern units, because he gave his measurements in cubits and we do not know which of several possible cubits he meant.

In the century following ibn-ash-Shaykh's visit, an earthquake brought the Pharos crashing down. The ruins were still to be seen in +XV, but now they have disappeared, although scuba divers claim to have found some of the masonry on the sea bottom off the island. The ruins of a medieval fort, some of whose stones may come from the Pharos, stand on the site.

Ptolemaic Alexandria was not only a teeming political and commercial center but also the scientific and literary capital of the world. The city gained this eminence as a result of a genetic accident, which made the first three Macedonian kings not only able statesmen but also genuine intellectuals. Ptolemaios I Soter was a historian; Ptolemaios II Philadelphos dabbled in zoölogy; Ptolemaios III Evergetes ("Benefactor") was a mathematician.

Philadelphos was one of the two most brilliant of the entire line: sickly of body and luxurious in tastes, but immensely shrewd and versatile. He it was who remarked that the trouble with being a king was that one had to kill so many people who had not done anything really wrong, but whose existence was harmful to the state. He staged magnificent parades to amuse the effervescent Alexandrines. After the third Ptolemy, however, the line began to run down.

The man who enabled the Ptolemies to achieve their greatest single accomplishment was an exiled Athenian politician, Demetrios of Phaleron. This Demetrios had studied in the Peripatetic school in Athens, entered politics, and risen to prominence. Then Kassandros, a Successor who ruled Greece and Macedonia, made Demetrios governor of Athens. For ten years Demetrios ruled Athens as Kassandros' satrap, giving the city sound, moderate government.

During a war among the Successors, Demetrios Poliorketes, the brilliant but erratic son of Antigonos One-eye, landed in Greece and seized the port of Peiraieus (−307). Demetrios of Phaleron fled to Egypt. At Soter's court he soon worked himself into the position of the king's literary adviser. In this capacity he suggested that the king set up a universal library, to hold copies of all the books in the world.

A book in those days was a roll, sometimes of leather but oftener of paper, handwritten or dictated by the author and copied by scribes. The paper was made from thin ribbons cut from the papyrus reed, laid on a board in two layers at right angles, glued together, and dried in a press. The roll was a long strip of papyrus squares glued together, edge to edge, and wrapped around a wooden dowel at one end. The standard roll was twenty sheets, which gave a strip 15 to 20 feet long. Long works were usually divided into "books" according to the amount of text that could be conveniently written on rolls of standard size. One such "book" formed a cylinder about 6 inches in diameter and contained the equivalent, approximately, of ten to twenty thousand words of modern English text. A collection of such books was kept in pigeonholes, with their titles written on wooden tags that hung from their outer ends.

Papyrus paper was a glossy, crackly, golden-brown substance, brittle and fragile. The perishability of the material, the ease with which rolls were dropped and damaged, and the small number of copies usually made of a single book partly account for the fact that only a small fraction of the writings of classical times has survived. In the early Christian centuries, the more durable codex—the book in the modern sense, wherein separate sheets are bound by one edge between stiff covers—gradually ousted the roll.

The Ptolemies' buyers scoured the Mediterranean for valued books to add to their library. Travelers arriving in Egypt were made to give up their books. The books were copied, the originals placed in the Library, and the copies given the travelers.

Founded by Soter, the Library reached its definitive form under Philadelphos, who appointed Zenodotos of Ephesos as the first of a long line of chief librarians. At its height, the Library held nearly three-quarters of a million rolls. Many of these, however, must have been duplicates, for there were not enough authors in the ancient world to have produced so many titles.

While it endured, the Library made Alexandria the unquestioned intellectual capital of the world. In building the Library, the Ptolemies made a far greater contribution to civilization than all their parades and palaces.

Under the chief librarian were a number of scholars, paid from the royal treasury and given a good deal of freedom for writing and research. Sometimes they presumed too far on their freedom. When Sotades of Maroneia wrote a ribald verse about the marriage of Philadelphos to his sister, the poet was jailed. He escaped, but Philadelphos' admiral caught him, shut him up in a leaden jar, and dropped the jar into the sea.

Much of what is now classed as literary scholarship began in the Library. The professional "man of letters" appeared. Protagoras, Sokrates' friendly rival, had pioneered the study of grammar and distinguished the parts of speech; now an intensive study of the Greek tongue took place.

The common speech of the Hellenistic Mediterranean was the *koinê*, "common." This grew from the Attic dialect of Greek, with some admixture of foreign words and of usages from other dialects. During this age, certain tendencies, which distinguish modern from ancient Greek, began to appear. These included a tendency to "drop one's *h*'s"; to pronounce the vowels and diphthongs *ê*, *ei*, *oi*, *y*, and *yi* all like *i;* to pronounce *ai* like *e;* to sound *o* and *ô* alike; and to turn *b*, *d*, and *g* (except in certain positions) into the fricatives *v*, *dh* (as in "the"), and *gh* (like the French *r*).

Certain kinds of literature also first appeared in Ptolemaic Alexandria. One was the pastoral or bucolic idyll, practiced with notable success by Theokritos of Syracuse (—III). The Greeks of the Golden Age had cared little for the beauties of nature. Flower gardens they left to the Persians; if they planted anything, they preferred it to be something edible like onions or cabbages. But the Alexandrines, living on a monotonous and unscenic sand spit, discovered the beauties of nature and loved sentimental poems about shepherds piping in an imaginary Arcadia of groves and waterfalls, nymphs and satyrs. The real Arcadia (save for a small section in the west, along the Alpheios Valley) is a rugged, barren, inhospitable country, but few of the poets or their admirers had been there.

In his *Fifteenth Idyll,* Theokritos also presented a picture of a couple of Alexandrine matrons complaining about their husbands and then setting out for the festival of Adonis. Their comments (quoted at the head of this chapter) give a vivid picture of Alexandrian street crowds.

The novel in the modern sense—the long fictional prose narrative, with a more or less unified plot concerning a few characters—also appeared. Several Alexandrine novels of romance and adventure have survived, and in them we see the beginnings of modern novelistic techniques. For the first time, Greek writers made a feature of romantic love between man and woman. (Writers of the Golden Age, when they romanticized love at all, did so with homosexual love.) The longest of these is the *Aithiopika* of the Syrian writer Heliodoros (+III), which begins:

> Day had begun to smile and the sun was shining upon the hilltops when a band of armed pirates scaled the mountain which extends to the mouth of the Nile called the Heracleot, where it empties into the sea. They halted for a little to survey the waters which stretched before them. Out at sea, where they first directed their attention, not a sail was stirring to whet the pirates' appetite for plunder; but when they turned to look at the coastline nearby their eyes encountered a strange spectacle.
>
> A merchant ship lay moored by its hawsers, bare of crew but heavily loaded, as was easy to conjecture, for its weight pressed the ship down until the water reached its third loading line. The beach was strewn with fresh carnage; some of the victims were dead, of others the limbs were still quivering; obviously the battle had been recent. But it was not simply of a battle that the scene gave evidence, for intermingled with the carnage were the wretched remains of a feast whose conclusion had been so fatal. Tables were still loaded with victuals; some of

the tables had been seized by the combatants as weapons against a surprise attack and lay overturned; others men crouched under in vain hope of finding shelter. Overturned goblets slipped from hands that held them, some to drink from, others to hurl in place of stones. The suddenness of the mischief had improvised this novel use and taught men to make missiles of their cups. Here lay a man cloven by an ax; there one struck by a sea shell from the beach; another was crushed by a beam; another scorched by a brand. Diverse as were their wounds, the greater number had been inflicted by darts and arrows. On this single small spot fate exhibited a spectacle compacted of a myriad of forms; wine was imbrued with blood, war conjoined with banqueting, drinks were intermingled with death, toasts with slaughter. It was this spectacle that met the eyes of the pirates; and as if it were a contrived scene they stood and gazed upon it, puzzled to divine its meaning. There lay the vanquished, but victors were nowhere to be seen; an indubitable victory, but the spoils lay unplundered; a ship denuded of men, but otherwise untouched, as if secured by a numerous guard and peacefully riding at anchor. Though baffled by the situation, the pirates still had regard for gain and, appointing themselves victors, proceeded to their booty.[11]

The novel does not, alas, maintain quite so gripping a tone throughout; parts drag, and some to the modern reader seem silly. There are glaring anachronisms. Still, the work on the whole is an impressive effort with considerable entertainment value even today.

Still other new genres of literature were the utopia and the royalist political tract. Several romances were composed about an ideal commonwealth where everybody led a busy, happy, law-abiding life. Iamboulos (−III) wrote of a utopia in the Indian Ocean. In his youth, he said, he had been shipwrecked on one of seven wonderful islands, where people had flexible bones and forked tongues with which they could carry on two conversations at once. Their Sun State found complete communistic equality practical because they were all exactly alike, so that everybody took turns at all the jobs in the commonwealth.

As for politics, one can understand why the paid littérateurs of the Museum did not extol democracy. First, their paymaster the king might not have liked it. Secondly, democracy seemed to have failed; the known civilized world had fallen under the sway of adventurer-despots. So political writers confined themselves to little sermons addressed to various kings, urging them to act virtuously and altruistically.

Fires and depredations during the Roman period gradually destroyed the Library. As the books were stored in more than one building, no single fire consumed them all. When Julius Caesar occupied Alexandria in —48, Cleopatra urged him to help himself to the books, and he took away hundreds or thousands to ship to Rome. Then Alexandria revolted against Caesar and Cleopatra. In the fighting, either the books that Caesar had taken, or those in one of the Library buildings, or both, were burned. When Antonius formed his connection with Cleopatra, he stole and gave her the 200,000-roll library of Pergamon to replace the losses.

The Library probably suffered further damage when Aurelianus suppressed a revolt in Alexandria in +272; when Diocletian put down another revolt in +295; and again in +391 when Bishop Theophilus, a bloodthirsty fanatic, led a Christian mob to the destruction of the Temple of Serapis, where some of the books were kept. The remaining rolls were finished off by the Arabs of the Muslim general 'Amr ibn-al-'Âṣ when he captured the city in +646.

A story relates that 'Amr wrote his *khalîfah* ("successor," caliph), asking what to do with these books of the infidels. He received the reply that if they agreed with the holy Qur'ân they were superfluous, whereas if they disagreed with it they were pernicious, so it were well in any case to destroy them. Modern apologists for the Arabs have denied this story and put all the blame for the destruction on the Christians. Christian apologists, on the other hand, have striven to exculpate the godly Theophilus and put the blame back on the Muslims.

In fact, we shall never know just how many books perished at each devastation. Nor shall we know to what extent the destruction was due simply to the agents of time and neglect—mice and mold, thieves and termites—which were suffered to work their will unchecked when, with the rise of Christianity, governments lost interest in the preservation of mundane writings.

All we can say for sure is that theology—especially of the monotheistic kind—proved as deadly a foe of learning as war and barbarism. With the rise of Christianity and Islâm, the ancient custom of burning the books of one's foes, to torment them or simply to enjoy the fire, was aggravated by the fanatical animus of dogmatic theology. For over 1,000 years, the world was lit by the lurid glare of one bonfire after another as Christians burned pagan books, Muslims burned pagan, Zoroastrian, and Christian books, and Christians burned Muslim and heretical books. *Tantum religio potuit suadere malorum.*[12]

Connected with the Library was the Museum. The word "museum"[13] means "shrine of the Muses." The Peripatetic school in Athens had centered around such a shrine, which was also used by the school as a library, because in Athens a school had to have a religious basis to gain the protection of Athenian law.

The Museum of Alexandria was the nearest thing the ancient world

86. The Library of Alexandria in Ptolemaic times. (Drawing by Roy G. Krenkel.)

knew to a modern university. There was at least one building where specimens could be displayed, experiments performed, and lectures heard. In this building a number of scholars, paid from the royal treasury (and later by Roman governors), studied, wrote, and taught. A priest of the Muses, appointed by the king, headed the college.

More exact we cannot be, in the absence of detailed information. Sometimes the terms "Library" and "Museum" are used interchangeably, as if they were the same institution; but we do not know just how these centers of learning were administered.

Much brilliant scientific work was accomplished in the Museum during its first three centuries. Eukleides (Euclid) assembled all that was known about plane geometry and wrote a textbook on the subject that continued in use for 2,000 years. Eratosthenes the geographer calculated the size of the earth with amazing accuracy. Hipparchos compiled his great star catalogue and invented latitude and longitude. Aristarchos, who asserted that the sun instead of the earth was at the center of the solar system, may have worked at the Museum; Copernicus merely borrowed the idea 1,800 years later. Herophilos and Erasistratos launched the sciences of anatomy and physiology by dissecting corpses until unrest among the Egyptians, whose religious feelings were outraged by this practice, led the king to forbid dissection.

At the same time, advances took place in engineering. For raising heavy weights, builders no longer had to rely on long, sloping ramps; they raised stones by cranes and compound pulley blocks. They applied the power of human muscles by capstans and treadwheels, the latter like oversized squirrel cages in which men walked up the curving inner side to turn the wheel. They began to use water wheels for raising water into irrigation ditches and for grinding grain to flour.

In the reign of Philadelphos, a barber's son named Ktesibios became the Thomas Edison of Alexandria. He grew up in his father's trade but showed an early bent for gadgeteering. One day he wished to mount a mirror in his father's shop so that it could be pulled up and down, like a window sash, by a hidden mechanism. He installed a wooden channel under a ceiling beam with a pulley at each end. The cord from the mirror ran up, over one pulley, along the channel, over the other pulley, and down. At the other end of the cord was a leaden weight, sliding up and down in a tube.

When the mirror was pulled up, the counterweight trapped air below as it descended. This air, escaping from the tube, gave out a musical sound and furnished Ktesibios with the idea of a pneumatic musical instrument. So Ktesibios developed the first hydraulic pipe organ. To make it work, he also had to invent the musical keyboard, the metal spring, and the force pump.

Ktesibios also invented the water clock, in which a float bearing a pointer rose as a vessel was filled by a trickle of water. These clocks, worked by pulleys, strings, and the lately invented gearwheels, soon became very elaborate, with mechanisms to mark the hours by balls that fell with a clang into bowls, or mechanical birds that sang—the ancestors of the cuckoo clock.

Alexandrine geographers were kept busy by the mass of new geographical information that poured into Alexandria as a result of voyages and explorations. The most spectaclar feats of navigation were those of Eudoxos of Kyzikos, who arrived in Alexandria in late —II at the head of a delegation from his native city to a festival. The king was Ptolemaios VII Evergetes II (that is, the seventh Ptolemy, but the second Ptolemy the Benefactor).[14]

This king was an unpleasant person whose subjects called him Physkon, "sausage," in allusion to his enormous fatness. The inbreeding that had obtained in the dynasty had preserved in full vigor the tendency to obesity that appeared in the first Ptolemy. Physkon started his reign with several particularly heinous murders but later put into effect a number of sound legal reforms. He wrote a book on natural history and favored the native Egyptians against their Hellenic ruling caste.

The king's coast guard had found a castaway Indian on the shores of Africa near the entrance to the Red Sea. When the Indian had learned enough Greek to make himself understood, he explained that his ship had been blown across the Arabian Sea from India by a storm and wrecked on the African coast; he was the sole survivor. Wishing to get home, he offered to pilot any ship going that way, promising to show the Greeks how to sail directly from Africa to India without stopping at the ports of southern Arabia.

The king accordingly fitted out a ship loaded with gifts and trade goods and appointed Eudoxos captain. The Kyzikan succeeded not only on this voyage but also on another, on which he was sent by Physkon's widow-niece-stepdaughter Kleopatra. In the course of these voyages, he discovered the monsoon winds, which blow across the Arabian Sea from northeast to southwest for half the year and then the opposite way for the other half. The direct voyage from the Red Sea to India was thus a simple matter of timing.

Each time, however, that Eudoxos returned to Alexandria, his royal master accused him of stealing some of the profits and confiscated the entire proceeds. After being plucked twice, Eudoxos tired of this treatment and returned to Kyzikos, on the Sea of Marmara. To get to India without coming within reach of the grasping Ptolemies, he went to Gades in Spain and fitted out an expedition to circumnavigate Africa. He set out with one large ship and two longboats, equipped with all the latest devices including dancing girls. Alas! his big ship ran aground on a shoal off the West African coast.

The resourceful Eudoxos salvaged most of the ship's timbers and cargo. With the timbers he built a smaller ship, in which he returned. He drummed up backing for another voyage, this time using a merchantman for deep water and a galley for inshore exploration. He set out—and that is the last that is heard of him.[15]

Scientific progress in Alexandria slowed under the later Ptolemies and slowed even more under the Romans, albeit great minds still appeared. Of these, Heron (+I) was the ablest technical writer of antiquity and probably ranked close to Archimedes in the applied sciences. Seven of his works survive, with fragments of others.

Heron worked out the theory of mechanical advantage and described cranes and other construction machinery. He presented designs for catapults, a crossbow, a surveyor's transit, a pipe organ powered by a little windmill, a fire-fighting pump, and a primitive steam engine. This last consisted of a ball to whose interior the steam was admitted through trunnions, and which was made to spin by letting the steam escape through a pair of bent nozzles. He used siphons, air tubes, float valves, and check valves.

Some of Heron's inventions seem to have been made to enable the priesthoods of Alexandria to awe their worshipers. In one, the fire of a burnt offering caused air to expand in a tank, forcing water out into a bucket, whose descent opened temple doors. In another, opening a temple door made a trumpet toot. A combination of vessels and siphons apparently turned water into wine, as an older contemporary of Heron was alleged to have done at Cana in Galilee. The biblical anecdote may well be based upon tales of Heron's magical device. A combination of mirrors made specters appear and vanish. Heron also invented the original coin-in-the-slot device, combined with a holy-water dispenser. It was baldly labeled: "Sacrificial Vessel which flows only when Money is introduced."[16]

In +II, Alexandria gave birth to another genius: Claudius Ptole-maeus (no known relation to the royal Ptolemies), the geographer and astronomer. His astronomical work, known to later ages as the *Almagest*, advanced the work of Hipparchos in accurately locating and identifying the stars. His *Geography* used a quite modern system of latitude and longitude. Although his world map had some egregious errors, such as omitting the Gulf of Qabès and putting the Strait of Gibraltar 15° too far west, it was still the most accurate representation up to that time. More curious was his bending Africa around to the east to meet a pro-longation of southeastern Asia, thus inclosing the Indian Ocean and mak-ing it a landlocked sea. He may have been trying to square a common but erroneous belief of the time, that the Red Sea stood at a higher level than the Mediterranean, with Archimedes' discovery that intercon-nected bodies of water at rest would all have the same level.[17]

Ptolemaeus also wrote a treatise on astrology, the *Tetrabiblos*, which became the Old Testament of that pseudo-science. To the astrology of Babylonia he added many Greek ideas, such as that of the four funda-mental qualities: heat, cold, dryness, and wetness. Saturn, for example, was cold and dry. He classified the heavenly bodies as male or female, diurnal or nocturnal, good or evil. He introduced so many complications that, no matter what a man's horoscope said and no matter what befell the man afterwards, the astrologer could always find some factor in the dupe's nativity to explain his fate.

Ptolemaeus' excursion into astrology illustrates another feature of Alexandrine life: the ever-growing influence of the supernatural. To unify his diverse and quarreling subjects, Ptolemaios I Soter proclaimed a new cult: that of Serapis,[18] a god combining the features of Osiris, the Egyptian god of nature, fertility, and the underworld, and Apis, the divine bull. The Greeks variously identified Serapis with their own Zeus, or Asklepios (the healing god), or Plouton (the underworld god). Soter built a temple to Serapis, the famous Serapeum,[19] on a low hill in Rhakotis, and the worship of this synthetic god spread around the Mediterranean.[20]

Meanwhile, into Alexandria flowed the supernatural ideas of Egypt, Iran, Babylonia, Palestine, Syria, and Greece, to be worked over and synthesized into a family of marvelous new cults, which in time swept across the whole Mediterranean world. Resourceful wizards and sorcerers developed devices, or were furnished them by inventors like Heron, similar to those of modern Spiritualist mediums. Some had the client write his questions in invisible ink, which became legible when the sage secretly heated the paper. Book scrolls were pulled out to make speaking tubes to convey spirit voices across a darkened room. The coals of a fire were made to dance by placing a layer of powdered alum beneath them. These and many other awe-inspiring tricks were described by a sternly disapproving third-century Christian bishop, Hippolytus, who recorded an incantation for invoking demons:

> Infernal, earthy, and supernal Bombo, come!
> Saint of the streets, and brilliant one, that strays by night;
> Foe of radiance, but friend and mate of gloom;
> In howl of dogs rejoicing, and in crimson gore,
> Wading 'mid corpses through tombs of lifeless dust,
> Panting with blood; with fear convulsing men.
> Gorgo, and Mormo, and Luna, and of many shapes,
> Come, propitious, to our sacrificial rites![21]

In Alexandria's melting pot of science, philosophy, religion, and magic, Greek philosophy influenced both Judaism and Christianity. A leading religious thinker of +I was Philo Judaeus, an Alexandrine Jew who adapted Plato's philosophy to Judaism. He developed the Greek idea of the *logos*, or Word of God, as a creative principle emanating from God to make the cosmos. To Philo, the Word meant something like "divine wisdom." The *logos* doctrine appears in the opening verse of the Gospel according to St. John, whose author was probably a Christianized Jew living in Alexandria and inspired by Philo: "In the beginning was the Word, and the Word was with God, and the Word was God."

While still an obscure minor cult, Christianity was an active rival of a family of syncretic sects called "Gnostic," from the Greek *gnôsis*, "knowledge." These Gnostic sects combined ideas from Jewish, Christian, Greek, Babylonian, Egyptian, and Persian sources in varying proportions. About thirty such sects are known to have existed. Some were heavily magical and occult; some found mystical meanings in numbers and in the letters of the Greek alphabet. Some practiced vegetarianism

87. Alexandria in early +XIX. (From John Carne: *Syria, the Holy Land, Asia Minor, etc.*, Lon.: 1836)

and celibacy; others, sexual license. Some believed that the supreme God had produced a host of emanations or angels called Aeons. Some believed in a supreme God, too pure and perfect to have anything directly to do with this imperfect world; and a subordinate god, the Cosmocrator or Demiurge, who made and runs the earth. The Demiurge was regarded sometimes as wicked, like Satan; sometimes, like Koshchei in Cabell's *Jurgen*, he is merely stupid. Gnostics argued: If you don't think the creator of this world is an incompetent bungler, just look at this world!

Of the once-voluminous literature of the Gnostics, little survived the fourth-century book-burnings of the triumphant Christians. One work that escaped destruction was the *Pistis Sophia* ("faith-wisdom"), a group of five documents in Coptic, a late form of the Egyptian language. Judging from the wordy nonsense recorded therein, the loss of the rest of the Gnostic literature does not seem too profound a tragedy.

Other influential sects and cults were those of the Neo-Pythagoreans and the Neo-Platonists. Founded by the first-century ascetic Apollonios of Tyana, the Neo-Pythagorean sect claimed to preserve the secret wisdom of Pythagoras, the Ionian philosopher-mathematician of −VI. Apollonios was said to have traveled about his native Anatolia barefoot and then to have visited India, where he had miraculous adventures. Next, according to his fanciful biographer, he wandered about the Roman world exorcising ghosts, saving people from demons, and escaping from the very real prison of the emperor Domitianus. In his eighties or nineties, he vanished. We may presume that he died, albeit the twelfth-century alchemist Artephius claimed to be Apollonios, kept alive all those centuries by an elixir of life.

Subsequently, the similar mystical philosophy of the Neo-Platonists took the place of Neo-Pythagoreanism. Claiming to base their ideas on Plato, the Neo-Platonists indulged in number mysticism and believed the world to be full of spirits and other supernatural forces. The principal founder of Neo-Platonism was a saintly third-century Egyptian, Plotinus, whose wisdom is preserved in the *Enneads*. This is a vast collection of treatises aptly described as "philosophy's most difficult and disorderly works."[22]

The curious thing about Alexandrine science is that it accomplished so much—and then stopped. An extraterrestrial visitor, coming to Alexandria under one of the later Ptolemies, might have thought that the scientific revolution, which actually started in Western Europe a millennium and a half later, was about to burst into full bloom. After Claudius Ptolemaeus and Heron, however, we have only the names of a few more good mathematicians—Diophantos, Pappos, Theon—but no more scientific giants like Hipparchos or Archimedes.

Historians have put forward almost as many reasons for this halt in science, under Rome, as they have for the fall of the Empire. They blame the prevalence of slavery, the rigor of Roman rule, the anti-intellectual Roman tradition, and the rise of Christianity. But slavery declined under the Empire. The early emperors were on the whole no more tyrannical than the Ptolemies had been. Upper-class Romans of the Empire were strongly Hellenized. And Christianity had only local, minor importance during its first two and a half centuries.

Science, however, must compete for attention, belief, respect, interest, and financial support with politics, commerce, art, literature, religion, entertainment, sport, war, and all the other activities of men. If one of these interests greatly expands its appeal to the people, it does so at the expense of the others.

Now, the great intellectual movement of the classical world under Rome was toward supernaturalism: that is, religion, mysticism, and magic. None of these was new; all went back to primitive times. But, under Rome, those who exploited the human love of the marvelous, fear of the unknown, and craving to know the future made striking advances in methods, just as metalworkers learned at this time to make brass and glaziers to make glass windowpanes. They found that it added to their following and advanced their own power, glory, and wealth to flourish a body of sacred writings wherewith to confound the heathen; to promise lavish rewards and punishments after death, to right the wrongs of earthly life; to set up a tightly-knit, far-flung, conspiratorial organization; to expound a verbose and seemingly logical body of spiritual doctrine; to impose a code of morals and tabus—some reasonable and some arbitrary—on their followers; and, most of all, to incite a fanatical hatred of rival groups and a grim determination to win the world for one's own faith.

All these procedures were inventions, just as much as Heron's toy steam engine. With these new techniques, priests, prophets, and magicians could more effectively compete for public attention and support.

Hence the world witnessed a great "return to religion." The old Greek and Roman polytheisms, with no central organization, no theology but a mass of childish and inconsistent myths, and no particular doctrine of future life, crumbled before the tide. The worship of Kybelê, Mithra, Isis, Yahveh, Serapis, and Christ waxed mighty. The magical cults of the Neo-Pythagoreans, the Neo-Platonists, and the Gnostics throve. The pseudo-science of astrology flourished, and hedge-wizards like Simon Magus swarmed.

Of the mass religions, Christianity made the most effective use of the new principles. Having the tightest organization, the most bewildering logic, the most impressive sacred literature, and the most fanatical spirit of any, it captured the Imperial government while Christians were still a small minority in the Empire. Then, armed with the terrifying doctrines of exclusive salvation, eternal damnation, and the imminent end of the world, and backed by the Emperor's executioners, it soon swept its rivals from the board.

Ironically, it was precisely its tightness of organization that led various Roman emperors to persecute Christianity, for these emperors looked with hostile suspicion upon any highly-integrated organization not under their direct control. They suspected it *ipso facto* of subversive aims. Thus Trajan rejected the reasonable request of the younger Plinius, to let the city of Nicomedia form a professional police-and-fire brigade, like Rome's *vigiles*, for fear that they might "turn into a political club."[23]

The great growth of Christinaity, however, took place after classical science had already withered in the blast of a resurgent supernaturalism. It withered because fewer and fewer people paid it any heed. Who wanted to spend years in pursuit of some obscure natural law, or pay others to do so, when in one of the new cults one got drama, passion, mystery, a feeling of superiority, and a promise of eternal happiness after death? Supernaturalism could offer these things because nobody came back from the dead to confirm or deny the new eschatologies. Science could not, so science lost out.

Besides the local, temporary factors that helped to eclipse classical science, a certain revolt against reason, an aversion to science and logic, is a constant factor in human affairs and from time to time bursts out in the form of cults and movements. Witness the current interest in astrology and occultism among the radical young, to whom they serve as adult substitutes for Santa Claus. While such irrationalism is not very likely to take over the world, neither is it likely to go away in the foreseeable future.

For a picture of Alexandria under the seventh Ptolemy—the one called Physkon—permit me to quote from another of my novels:

> At the Bull Channel, a pilot boat, with the red-lion pennant of the Ptolemies whipping from its masthead, led us into the Great Harbor. To our right, on the isle of Pharos, rose Sostratos' colossal, gleaming lighthouse, towering up at least four plethra,[24] with a plume of smoke streaming from its top. On our left stood the fortifications and barracks at the end of Point Lochias, and then the temple of Isis.
>
> Once we were through the channel, the Great Harbor opened out on all sides. On the right was the mole called the Seven Furlonger, joining the Pharos to the city, with scores of merchantmen tied up along it on both sides. Beyond lay the Old Harbor, or Haven of Happy Return, devoted to commercial and fishing craft. On the left, as we entered the Great Harbor, were the naval docks, with squadrons of Ptolemaic fivers and larger ships. Their hulls were black, and each bore a gilded statue of Alexander on its stern. Beyond and above the warships, the gilded roof tiles of the royal palaces glittered and their marble columns gleamed.
>
> Near the palaces, a section of the harbor was marked off from the rest by a mole. In this harbor lay three of the largest vessels in the world. These ships had all been acquired about a hundred years before, in the time of the fourth Ptolemy—Ptolemaios Philopator, the degenerate with whom the dynasty began to go to seed.
>
> One of the ships was Philopator's pleasure barge. Another was a huge vessel built by Hieron of Syracuse. The tyrannos had meant to combine the virtues of a war galley, a merchantman, and a royal yacht in one hull; but the ship proved too slow for war, too costly for commerce, and too crowded for pleasure. So, in disgust, Hieron gave her to Philopator, who liked such nautical freaks.
>
> The third ship was the largest war galley of all time, a fortier over four plethra long. Four thousand rowers, pulling ten-man oars arranged in four banks, propelled her. She had proved too slow for any practical use, and the hire of so many rowers

would have strained the finances even of Egypt; so she had been tied up and neglected . . .

The pilot boat led us to a wharf to the right of the naval docks, near the temple of Poseidon on the teeming waterfront . . .

We were let in the main gate of the palace area by a pair of Celtic mercenaries: big men with long, brown mustaches, wearing checkered coats and trousers and armed with huge, oval shields and long swords. The palace compound was a vast complex of buildings in ornate modern style, with gilded capitals on the columns and brightly painted entablatures. The area bustled with people coming and going, since these edifices contained the offices of the Egyptian government as well as the living quarters of the rulers.

The party broke up, the guests of each of the three monarchs being taken to a different destination. Hippalos led us into one of the buildings and to a two-room apartment. In the living room, a marble-topped table bore a small water clock which, as we entered, gave forth a sharp *ping* to signal noon . . .

Our apartment in the royal palace had one delightful amenity. This was a tub or sink affixed to one wall. From the wall above it protruded a bronze pipe with a valve. This valve had a handle, so that, when one turned it one way, water flowed into the sink; when one turned it the other, the flow stopped. Thus one could wash one's hands and face without shouting for a servant to fetch a bowl and a ewer . . . With all these marvelous modern inventions, I foresee the day when we shall all be waited upon by mechanical servants, such as some of the myths tell of.[25]

Subsequently my narrator (Eudoxos of Kyzikos, the navigator) takes part in one of the parades with which the Ptolemaic and Seleucid kings were wont to amuse and appease their subjects:

Since I had to march in the middle of the parade, I never did get a view of the whole thing. We formed up at the Canopic Gate, where thousands of paraders milled in confusion and Hippalos galloped about on a horse, straightening them out and sending them off, group by group . . .

Xenokles and I marched at the head of our delegation, bearing poles between which hung a banner reading KYZIKOS. We trudged the whole length—thirty-five stadia—of Canopic Street, through the old Sun Gate and the main part of the city, breaking up at the Moon Gate at the west end of town. As soon as we had been dismissed, I hastened around the block to see those parts of the parade that were following us.

I was not sorry to miss the herds of Physkon's prize sheep and cattle, or the delegations from the other Hellenic cities. I did see the five elephants in their cloth-of-gold drapes and other animals from Physkon's menagerie: a two-horned African rhinoceros, a striped horse, several lions, leopards, and cheetahs, and antelopes of a dozen kinds.

There were also a number of freak objects carried in carts, which the Ptolemaic workshops had turned out to amuse the Alexandrines. These included a golden 135-foot Bacchic wand, a ninety-foot silver spear (made, I suspect, from a ship's mast), and a 180-foot golden phallus with a nine-foot golden star dangling from its end. The phallus, made of wicker work and covered with gilded cloth, enabled the reigning monarch to make a joke about having the biggest prick in the world. Needless to say, everybody went into gales of laughter on these occasions, although that joke had worn pretty thin from a century of repetition.[26]

Under Ptolemaic rule, upper-class Egyptians became superficially Hellenized, while the peasantry clung to their ancient ways. The country-folk still did much of their trading by barter, although the Ptolemies issued sound currency, including huge copper coins. The Greeks called the Egyptians *enchôrioi*, "natives," in exactly the same sense in which Europeans used the term during the great century of European colonialism, 1850–1950.

The position of Hellenistic women was generally better than it had been in Greece before Alexander, where society had been as male-dominated as among the Muslim Arabs. Fashionable women took to wearing transparent dresses made of a new material, Chinese silk, which had begun to reach the Mediterranean over the Silk Route through Central Asia. The Mediterranean peoples, however, still knew nothing about China. There had been a small silk industry in the Aegean islands, using the cocoons of the wild silkworm, but superior Chinese silk quickly put this industry out of business.

Camels, unknown in pharaonic Egypt, came into common use in Ptolemaic Egypt. They had probably been introduced from Arabia under the Persian Empire.

For soldiers, the reigning Ptolemy relied mainly on Greeks and Macedonians, on whom he had conferred titles to Egyptian farmland in return for military service. In practice this usually meant that the soldiers, called *klêrouchoi* or cleruchs, acted as landlords to Egyptian tenants. He also hired large forces of mercenaries, many of them

Celts; for during the Ptolemaic period the Celts swarmed out of Central Europe and overran great stretches of the Balkans, Italy, Gaul, and Iberia. There was also a native Egyptian militia, but the kings do not seem to have made much use of it. Perhaps they were afraid of what the "natives" might do if they got their hands on too many weapons.

Speaking of the Ptolemaic army brings up a case preserved in a papyrus (at last accounts in Germany), which tells how a young man named Apollonios set out to join this army. The case illustrates the complications that any large, bureaucratic organization develops and shows that some things change but little with the centuries.

Apollonios was a son of a Greek cleruch. In −158, he dutifully set out to join the troop of *epigonoi*, a reserve corps maintained for such sons, based on Memphis. His first step was to consult his brother Ptolemaios, a religious recluse at the Temple of Osiris. At the temple, Apollonios persuaded his brother to write a petition, to be presented to the king when the latter visited the temple on October 3.

The king arrived in due course. This was Ptolemaios VI Philometor ("Friend-of-mother"), a good-natured, indolent young man, the brother and predecessor of the bloated Physkon. The king entered the audience chamber with his scurrying clerks and settled himself to await petitions. These were not presented in person; the Ptolemies' divinity was too sacred for that. The petitions were thrown in through a small window.

Apollonios' petition whizzed in; a clerk picked it up and presented it. The king scanned the petition and wrote on it: "To be done, but report on how much it will come to." The petition, bearing the royal seal, was returned to Apollonios, whose responsibility it was to see that it went through channels.

Apollonios went to the office of Demetrios, the quartermaster general of the Ptolemaic army (*grammateus tôn dynameôn*), for the information requested by the king on how much the new *epigonos* would cost the state. Demetrios' permanent office was in Alexandria; but, as the king was visiting Memphis, his heads of department had followed him thither. Demetrios wrote on the petition a command to his clerk, Ariston, to procure the information. Apollonios bore the petition to Ariston. Ariston addressed a question to the local office (*eklogistêrion*) of the accountant general (*eklogistês*). Apollonios carried the petition, with its new addendum, to the head clerk (*grammateus*) of this office, Dioskourides. Dioskourides wrote the information required. Apollonios took the petition back to the office of Demetrios, to a clerk named Chairemon. When Chairemon had processed the petition again, Apollonios next bore the information with its addenda to one Apollodoros, attached to the court. On January 25, −157, Apollodoros

88. Contemporary downtown Alexandria, on Fuad I Avenue. On the left, buildings in Victorian-Oriental style; modern buildings on the right. (Courtesy of Henry Angelo-Castrillon.)

submitted it to the king. Nearly four months had elapsed between the two submissions to the king.

The king issued two commands (*prostagmata*) that Apollonios be enrolled in the troop desired. These were given to Apollonios, one to be taken to Quartermaster General Demetrios and the other to an official called the *dioikêtês*, which translates roughly as "minister of finance." The *dioikêtês* was Dioskourides, not to be confused with Dioskourides the clerk.

On February 7, Apollonios delivered one *prostagma* to Demetrios, who wrote his subordinate Sostratos, instructing him to carry out the king's command and attaching to his communication a statement by his clerks of the circumstances of the case.

On the twelfth, Demetrios wrote to Dioskourides the *dioikêtês*, attaching to his letter a copy of his communication to Sostratos and of the statement by his clerks. The purpose of this letter to the *dioikêtês* was seemingly to enable Apollonios to get from the office of the *dioikêtês* the papers (*symbola*) authorizing him to draw a soldier's pay.

On February 17, Apollonios set out to deliver this letter and three others from Demetrios concerning his enlistment. One was to Poseidonios, *stratêgos* or governor of the Memphite province. One was to Ammonios, paymaster-in-chief (*archipêretes*), and one to Kallistratos, perhaps a clerk in Sostratos' department. At the office of the *dioikêtês*, Apollonios delivered not only the letter from Demetrios but also the *prostagma* from the king to Dioskourides. He gave the *prostagma* to one of Dioskourides' secretaries, Ptolemaios the *hypomnêmatographos* or recording secretary. The letter from Demetrios he gave to another secretary, Epimenides the *epistolatographos* or corresponding secretary. Let Apollonios describe the ensuing steps:

"They were delivered to be read by the *dioikêtês*, and I received back the *prostagma* from Ptolemaios the *hypomnêmatographos*, and the letter from Epimenides. And I conveyed them to Isidoros, the *autoteles*, and from him I carried them to Philoxenos, and from him to Artemon, and from him to Lykos, and he made a rough draft, and I brought that to Sarapion, in the office of the *epistolatographos*, and from him to Eubios, and from him to Dorion, and he made a rough draft, and then back to Sarapion, and they were handed in to be read by the *dioikêtês*, and I received them back from Epimenides, and he wrote to Nikanor, and Nikanor wrote two letters—one to Dorion the *epimelêtês* [inspector] and one to Poseidonios, the *stratêgos* of the Memphite nome."[27]

Here the record ends. We do not know what further steps Appollonios had to go through before he was finally enrolled. It is believed that he was. Let us hope that he made a brave soldier. He was certainly a most determined one, or the endless procedures would have discouraged him far short of his goal. It is a little discouraging to think that, in the 2,100 years since the time of Apollonios, we have advanced so little towards the solution of the problems of the large-scale organization of men.

The most brilliant of the Ptolemies was the last and a woman: Cleopatra VII, or the Great. She was considered something of a wonder because she was the first of the dynasty to learn to speak Egyptian. Her father was Ptolemaios XI,[28] a lightweight king given to orgies and to playing the flute. The Romans did not mind the orgies but had the greatest contempt for a public man who played musical instruments, so they called him Auletes, "flute-player."

Having secured his throne by bribing Roman officials (probably including the great Pompeius) Ptolemaios Auletes died in —51. He left a will directing his elder daughter Cleopatra, then seventeen, to marry her next-younger brother Ptolemaios and to reign jointly with him. This was done, but presently the boy-king's partisans drove Cleopatra into exile in Syria.

During the Roman civil wars, Julius Caesar arrived in Alexandria in pursuit of his rival Pompeius. He arrived to find that Pompeius had already been murdered. Cleopatra had herself smuggled in to Caesar wrapped in a rug and soon persuaded him to take her part in the cutthroat struggle for the throne. Ptolemaios and his partisans began a brisk little war in and around Alexandria, in the course of which part of the Library was burned. Reinforcements tipped the scales in Caesar's favor; the boy-king disappeared and was commonly thought to have drowned.

Cleopatra bore Caesar a son, was married to a still younger brother, and followed Caesar back to Rome, where she lived for a year or two until Caesar was murdered in —44. Then she fled back to Egypt, where she prudently had her husband-brother killed. Later, in accordance with her hard-boiled principle of attaching herself to the strongest Roman in sight, she became the mistress of Marcus Antonius. She eventually married him and bore him two children, although he had a wife in Rome. She shared his downfall in his war with Octavianus. As a last resort, she tried her wiles on Octavianus but failed. Not wishing to be paraded in his triumph in Rome, she killed herself—it was later said by an asp, but this may be romantic embroidery.

Octavianus killed off the surviving Ptolemies and annexed Egypt. Thereafter, Roman emperors treated the country as their private property. They long forbade Roman Senators even to enter the land, lest one of them try by intrigue or subversion to take it away from the Emperor.

Under Rome, Alexandria shared the fortunes and misfortunes of the Empire. Save for occasional involvement in civil wars between rival claimants to the imperium, or local strife between Greeks and Jews, its existence was mainly peaceful and prosperous.

Like the rest of the Empire, Alexandria began to decline about +250 under a combination of barbarian invasions, civil wars, and army mutinies. In +270 the energetic Syrian queen, Zenobia, briefly added Alexandria to her short-lived Palmyrene Empire. The Romans recovered it but then faced the problem of Christian subversion. The emperors persecuted this communistic, pacifistic sect with increasing severity from the +280s on. The languid and spasmodic persecution was hard enough to fill the Christians with virtuous zeal but not hard enough to eliminate them. In the following century, Constantine legalized them and Theodosius I made Christianity the Roman state religion. Thereupon the Christians took their long-cherished revenge on the pagans.

Although in theory the Emperor ruled Alexandria through his Imperial prefect, the ruler in fact became the Christian Patriarch, who could call upon the swarms of unwashed monks to act as his bully boys. Filled with a virtuous hatred of learning, these monks lived in communities in the Egyptian desert. Persecution of the pagans culminated in the lynching of Hypatia, the daughter of the mathematician Theon, who herself lectured on mathematics and philosophy at the Museum. In +415, a Christian mob, incited by the Patriarch Cyril, snatched the lady from her chariot and cut her to pieces with oyster shells. Alexandrine thought was by this time pretty well suffused with Neo-Platonic nonsense; but what little scientific effort remained in Alexandria was now snuffed out.

Instead, Alexandrine life was enlivened for three centuries by theological schisms within the Christian fold. In +IV, a dispute raged between the Alexandrine priests Arius and Athanasius. Arius and his followers held that the Son was of a substance different from and inferior to that of the Father; Athanasius, that they were of the same substance. Constantine, to whom Christianity was mainly interesting as a tool for political leverage, called the Council of Nicaea (+325) to settle the question. The Council decided for Athanasius, but the conflict continued beyond the lifetimes of both belligerent clergymen. Eventually, the Athanasians won and cast the Arians into outer darkness, where they converted the conquering Goths to Arianism.

Then, in +V, another schism arose. The orthodox view was that the Son had two natures, one human and one divine. Against this, the Monophysites asserted that he had only one. The Coptic Church of modern Egypt still holds this view. Then the Monothelites claimed that the Son had but one will, not two; they are represented today by the Maronites of Lebanon. When bewildered emperors called councils to settle these questions, the leaders of the various factions brought gangs of monks with clubs under their robes and proved their points by setting upon their opponents and beating them senseless.

Demented as these arguments seem today, there was more to them than mere ghostly speculation. The disputes often masked struggles for power among emperors, generals, patriarchs, and other notables. With the breakup of the West Roman Empire in late +V, Alexandria found itself subject to Constantinople. Like their Western predecessors, the Eastern emperors thought it right to tax the rest of their domains to subsidize the people of their capital. Alexandria saw no good reason why it should be taxed to support Constantinople, when Alexandria was an older and more eminent city, quite as well qualified to be the capital of the Empire. When 'Amr's Arabs invaded Egypt in +641, Alexandria gave up with hardly a struggle. The semi-Hellenized Christian Egyptians deemed Byzantine garrisons and governors as much their enemies as they did the Arabs. Besides, long foreign rule had so thoroughly demilitarized them that the results have lasted to modern times.

Under Muslim rule, most of the Egyptian population eventually went over to Islâm, which at least did not waste time arguing over what substance God was made of. As Cairo, the new capital, waxed, Alexandria—now al-Iskandariyya—waned. By +XVIII it was a squalid little town of a few thousand, occupying only a fraction of the ancient site. As it had done at Tyre, current-borne sand had widened the Heptastadion causeway to a peninsula.

In the Napoleonic Wars, Alexandria saw French and British armies pass. In 1801, a British force attacked the French in Alexandria. Lake Mareotis had been drained nearly dry, and its bed was farmed, but for tactical reasons the British general cut the dyke and flooded the lake bed again.

Alexandria began to revive in 1805, when Egypt came under control of an Albanian adventurer, Mehmet 'Ali, who ruled as viceroy for the Sultan of Turkey. Mehmet 'Ali was a wily and unprincipled despot of the old oriental type but still a shrewd and able one. He built a new canal from Alexandria to the Nile, and the city grew back to something like its former importance.

In 1882, as a result of Anglo-French intervention in Egyptian affairs, an anti-foreign riot took place in Alexandria. Hence a conflict arose between Britain and Egypt in the persons of Admiral Sir Beauchamp Seymour and the Egyptian Minister of War, an earnest but rather simple-minded nationalist patriot, Aḥmad 'Arabi Pasha. Seymour bombarded the forts of Alexandria from eight ironclads, and British landing parties dispersed 'Arabi's forces. The British army stayed on in occupation; and, although Egypt continued to be under the nominal suzerainty of the Sultan of Turkey until the First World War, it remained in effective British control until after the Second.

Since then, Alexandria has grown apace but is still just one more big Mediterranean port city, all of which look much alike. There is not much that is really ancient for the tourist to see, save a column called "Pompey's Pillar" in the southwestern part of town, near the site of the Serapeum. This column has nothing to do with Pompeius Magnus; the Alexandrines erected it to honor the emperor Diocletian about +297. Nearby are several small stone sphinxes and the entrance to a set of complex underground burial vaults, probably dug about +II to serve some eminent family or some burial society.

Other sights of Alexandria, such as the mosques and the palace where the unlamented King Farouk used to read his collection of comic books and pornography, are more or less modern. Today, Alexandria is perhaps best known to Westerners as the locale of the "Alexandrian quartet" of novels by Lawrence Durrell. Some who have lived in Alexandria say of Durrell's milieu and its effete inhabitants: Yes, it was just like that. Others, who have known the city just as well, say: No, it was nothing like that. They merely prove that in any large city, there are so many social circles and subcultures that one can find almost anything.

Still, Alexandria is interesting as the place where the modern Age of Science almost started 2,000-odd years ago—and then aborted.

XII

ANURÂDHAPURA AND THE ROC'S EGG

BEHIND THE PAINTED DOORS AND EMBROIDERED CURTAINS
THERE USED TO BE MUSIC AND DANCING.
HUNTING OR FISHING PARTIES WERE HELD
IN EMERALD FORESTS OR BESIDE MARBLE POOLS.
THE MELODIES FROM VARIOUS STATES
AND WORKS OF ART AND RARE FISH AND HORSES
ARE ALL NOW DEAD AND BURIED.
THE YOUNG GIRLS FROM EAST AND SOUTH
SMOOTH AS SILK, FRAGRANT AS ORCHIDS,
WHITE AS JADE WITH THEIR LIPS RED,
NOW LIE BENEATH THE DREARY STONES AND BARREN EARTH.[1]

Pan Chao

89. Columns of former temples and palaces at Anurâdhapura.

SINDBAD the seaman (Shahrazad told her Sultan) had completed his first voyage. In the course of this journey, he was cast away when his ship stopped at an island, which turned out to be the back of a colossal fish. Vexed by the cooking fires kindled upon it, the denizen of the deep sounded, leaving Sindbad bobbing about in the ship's wash-tub.

Returning to Basra after divers gainful adventures, Sindbad soon sets out upon his second voyage. Again they stop at a lovely, fertile island. Going ashore with the rest, Sindbad eats, falls asleep, and awakens to find that his ship has sailed without him. After lamenting his own folly, Sindbad:

> . . . climbed a tall tree and looked in all directions, but saw nothing save sky and sea and trees and birds and isles and sands. However, after a while my eager glances fell upon some great white thing, afar off in the interior of the island; so I came down from the tree and made for that which I had seen; and behold, it was a huge white dome rising high in the air and of vast compass. I walked all around it, but found no door thereto, nor could I muster strength or nimbleness [to climb it] by reason of its exceeding smoothness and slipperyness. So I marked the spot where I stood and went round about the dome to measure its circumference which I found fifty good paces. And as I stood, casting about how to gain an entrance the day being near its fall and the sun being near the horizon, behold, the sun was suddenly hidden from me and the air became dull and dark. Methought a cloud had come over the sun, but it was the season of summer; so I marvelled at this and lifting my head looked steadfastly at the sky, when I saw that the cloud was none other than an enormous bird, of gigantic girth and inordinately wide of wing which, as it flew through the air, veiled the sun and hid it from the island. At this sight my wonder redoubled and I remembered a story I had heard aforetime of pilgrims and travellers, how in a certain island dwelled a huge bird, called the "Rukh" which feedeth its young on elephants; and I was certified that the dome which caught my sight was none other than a Rukh's egg. As I looked and wondered at the marvelous works of the Almighty, the bird alighted on the dome and brooded over it with its

wings covering it and its legs stretched out behind it on the
ground, and in this posture it fell asleep, glory be to Him who
sleepeth not! When I saw this, I arose and, unwinding my
turband from my head, doubled it and twisted it into a rope,
with which I girt my middle and bound my waist fast to the
legs of the Rukh, saying in myself, "Peradventure, this bird
may carry me to a land of cities and inhabitants, and that will
be better than abiding in this desert island." I passed the night
watching and fearing to sleep, lest the bird should fly away
with me unawares; and, as soon as the dawn broke and the
morn shone, the Rukh rose off its egg and spreading its wings
with a great cry flew up into the air dragging me with it;
nor ceased it to soar and to tower till I thought it had reached
the limit of the firmament; after which it descended, earth-
wards, little by little, till it lighted on the top of a high hill.
As soon as I found myself on the hard ground, I made haste
to unbind myself, quaking for fear of the bird, though it took
no heed of me nor even felt me; and, loosing my turband
from its feet, I made off with my best speed.[2]

The rukh (or roc, as earlier translators spelled it) carries off a
huge serpent in its talons, and Sinbad goes on to other adventures.
On his fifth voyage, Sindbad again encounters the rukh. They land on
another island. While Sindbad is still on the ship, the other merchants

90. Abhayagiri Dâgaba, Anurâdhapura.

discover the egg, which they break open with stones. They kill the chick rukh for its meat but flee when the adult rukhs appear. The birds pursue the ship and destroy it by dropping boulders upon it, and Sindbad alone survives to tell the tale.

The *Arabian Nights*, in which the story of Sindbad's voyages appears, is a collection of tales composed roughly between +900 and 1400, mostly in Egypt. When first translated into French by the orientalist Antoine Galland in early +XVIII, the *Nights* aroused much more enthusiasm among Western littérateurs than it ever had in Islâm, since cultured Muslims viewed it as low-brow "coffeehouse" literature. In +XIX, several English translations were made, the most celebrated being that by Captain Sir Richard F. Burton—soldier, explorer, adventurer, diplomat, swordsman, author, linguist, orientalist, and one of the most picturesque figures of his generation.

Many concepts of the *Nights* can be traced back to medieval, Roman, or classical Greek writers. Marco Polo, who dictated his memoir about 1297, had also heard of the rukh:

> The people of [Madagascar] report that at a certain season of the year, an extraordinary kind of bird, which they call a rukh [*chiamano quell' uccelli* ruc], makes its appearance from the southern region. In form it is said to resemble the eagle, but it is incomparably greater in size; being so large and strong as to seize an elephant with its talons, and to lift it into the air, from whence it lets it fall to the ground, in order that when dead it may prey upon the carcase. Persons who have seen this bird assert that when the wings are spread they measure sixteen paces in extent, from point to point; and that the feathers are eight paces in length, and thick in proportion . . . The grand Khan having heard this extraordinary relation, sent messengers to the island, on the pretext of demanding the release of one of his servants who had been detained there, but in reality to examine into the circumstances of the country, and the truth of the wonderful things told of it. When they returned to the presence of his majesty, they brought with them (as I have heard) a feather of the rukh, positively affirmed to have measured ninety spans, and the quill part to have been two palms in circumference.[3]

When, some years ago, the late Willy Ley and I wrote a book about geographical legends, *Lands Beyond*, we pointed out that the Sindbad stories were laid on the coasts and islands southeast of the Persian Gulf, especially the Malay Archipelago (which today we call Indonesia). The "feather" brought back to the Mongol emperor Kublai Khan was probably a frond of the *Raphia* palm of Madagascar, whose fronds reach unusual size and look like huge feathers when dried. Finally, rumors of gigantic birds in Madagascar had a sound basis in the form of the elephant bird, *Aepyornis ingens*. This creature dwelt in Madagascar and only became extinct about +XVII. It was a flightless emulike bird about as tall as an ostrich but much stouter. It weighed up to 1,000 pounds, making it the heaviest bird ever known to have lived. It laid a 2.5-gallon egg over a foot long.

We did not, however, think of another source for Sindbad's story of a "huge white dome . . . fifty good paces"[4] in circumference. For, on the way to Indonesia, the medieval Arab mariner passed the island of Ceylon, where a whole congeries of such domes littered the land. These are Buddhist shrines of the kind called a *stûpa* in India and a *dâgaba*[5] in Ceylon. (The *Great Chronicle* of Ceylon uses the Pâli terms *thûpa* and *cetiya*.[6])

A dâgaba houses the relic of a Buddhist saint. The main feature of the shrine is a large solid dome over the actual relic. There are also four symbolic gateways on the four sides, a railed walk around the base of the dome, and sometimes, in front of the main gateway, a pillar bearing the Wheel of Life. In India, the first such domes were made of brick, but under the emperor Ashoka[7] (—III) they began to be made of stone.

Some later stûpas had the dome squared off like the crown of a Victorian derby; some were stepped pyramids; but the standard form was the hemispherical dome. These domes were topped with stone finials. After Ceylon was converted to Buddhism, the dâgabas built there reached enormous size. In some the dome was over 350 feet in diameter and the whole monument over 250 feet high, so that in bulk they compared with middle-sized Egyptian pyramids.

Many dâgabas still stand in Ceylon. Some have been allowed to decay, so that the outer coating of stucco has flaked off and the dome has become covered with brush. Others have been restored or enlarged from time to time. One of the largest, the Ruvanväli Säya[8] at Anurâdhapura, has been there for over 2,000 years but—thanks to recent restorations—looks as good as new.

As we have seen, Greek navigators began sailing from the Red Sea to India around the end of —II, and Arabs had doubtless been trading with India before that. By the time the anonymous author of the *Periplus of the Erythraean Sea* composed his navigational guide, about +60, Western sailors had reached Ceylon:

> About the following region, the course trending toward the east, lying out to sea toward the west is the island Palaesimundu, called by the ancients Taprobane. The northern part is a day's journey distant, and the southern part trends gradually

91. Thûpârâma Dâgaba, Anurâdhapura.

toward the west, and almost touches the opposite shore of Azania. It produces pearls, transparent stones, muslins, and tortoise-shell.[9]

If the author of the *Periplus* thought that Taprobanê (Ceylon) extended almost to the East African coast ("Azania"), he was obviously misinformed. Still, he had the island more or less in the right place.

Arab maritime trade with the Farther East grew during Roman times and the Byzantine-Islamic period that followed, when the *Nights* were composed. Ceylon became a regular stop on these traders' voyages, and Ceylonese ambassadors appeared at the courts of the Roman emperors. Ceylon is the kind of place that people think of when they say "tropical paradise." As Sindbad described the rukh's island:

At last Destiny brought us to an island, fair and verdant, in trees abundant, with yellow-ripe fruit luxuriant, and flowers fragrant and birds warbling soft descant; and streams crystalline and radiant . . .[10]

In any case, some early Arab navigator who touched at Ceylon must have seen one or more dâgabas. Perhaps he asked about them and misunderstood the reply. This was a constant hazard of early explorers, who had no phrase books or Berlitz courses to help them to

92. Ruvanväli Dâgaba, Anurâdhapura.
(Courtesy of P. E. P. Deraniyagala.)

breach the linguistic barrier. Perhaps the person he questioned played a joke on him. Or perhaps he merely saw a dâgaba from a distance and his exuberant imagination did the rest. So he returned to Basra with a fine tale of the isle of colossal eggs and the birds that laid them. Once launched, such a story would keep circulating for centuries, long after the real Ceylon and its domes had become well-known to real Sindbads. In the same way, some early Greek mariner in the Mediterranean, coming upon the skull of an extinct elephant in a cave in Sicily, built up from that fossil a hair-raising tale of the one-eyed giant Polyphemos.

Ceylon is a pear-shaped island, 270 miles from north to south and 140 miles from east to west, lying east of the southern tip of India. Palk Strait, sundering the island from the continent, is 30 miles wide at its narrowest. A chain of islets and sandbanks links Ceylon with the mainland. Early Christian or Muslim visitors called this chain Adam's

Bridge, and the name has stuck. The Indians said the bridge had been built by an army of monkeys under command of the monkey-god Hanuman when Hanuman was helping the hero Râma to recover his wife Sîtâ, who had been abducted by the Ceylonese demon king Râvana.

Ceylon has low coastal regions, with a mountainous massif rising to over a mile and a half in the south-central part. Of the three highest mountains, the third is the 7,360-foot Mount Rohana, also called Sri Pada and Adam's Peak. The top exhibits a depression shaped like a human footprint 6 feet long, which sectarians identify, according to their creed, with a footprint of the god Shiva, or Buddha, or Adam.

The climate is warm and moist, with frequent rains alternating with brilliant sunshine. There is little seasonal change in temperature. From May to August, the southwest monsoon brings rain to the southwestern half of the island; from November to February, the northeast monsoon brings it to the northeastern half. The northeastern half is called the "dry zone," having a moderate annual 40 inches of rain; the southwestern "wet zone" gets a drenching 200.

Dense tropical forest covers most of the island where it has not been cleared away for agriculture. The main products are tea, rubber, coconuts, and gems—especially pearls and sapphires. The fauna includes the elephant, buffalo, deer (four species), leopard, sloth bear, and smaller animals like wildcats, monkeys, lemurs, and large fruit-eating bats. Most of the bigger beasts are now confined to game preserves in the southeast. The elephant, now reduced to fewer than 1,000 individuals, is a large but usually tuskless race of the Indian elephant. The motorist must keep a sharp eye for tame elephants on the roads, for they are still commonly used in forestry and construction work.

Around −500, the Aryans, who had conquered northern India during the preceding millennium, settled in Ceylon, brushing aside the Stone Age hunters, the Väddas, whom they found in possession. Of the several tribes that took part in this migration, the dominant one was the Siṃhala or Lion Tribe (from (siṃha, "lion"). Hence they called the island Siṃhala-dvîpa, "island (or continent) of the Lion Tribe," and hence the dominant people and their language are still called Sinhalese. The Arab traders made Siṃhala-dvîpa into Serendib. The Portuguese, arriving in +XVI, made it into Cilão and the Dutch into Zeylan, whence modern Ceylon. In ancient India, the island was commonly called Tambapanni or Tâmradvîpa, which the Greeks and Romans pronounced Taprobanê. The "Palaesimundu" of the Periplus looks like a combination of the Greek palaios, "old," with Simḥala. Present-day Ceylonese often prefer another old name for the island: Lankâ.[11]

The Sinhalese are a brown-skinned people of medium size, with

93. Moonstone at the foot of a flight of steps at the so-called "Queen's Palace," Anurâdhapura. (Courtesy of George F. Dales.)

94. Ceylonese moonstone, showing reliefs of animals, birds, and flowers—all Buddhist symbols. (Courtesy of the Commissioner of the Archaeological Department of Ceylon.)

features much like those of southern Europeans. They belong to the Hindi type or subrace of the white or Caucasoid race. As in India, however, there is also a mixture of another type related to the Australian aborigines, who are classed as a separate race of their own, the Australoid. Australoids are dark brown, with deep-set eyes under beetling eyebrow ridges, very wide bridgeless noses, large mouths, and abundant curly hair and beards. Although loosely called "blacks," the Australoids are quite distinct from the Negroid race. Australoid hunting bands probably wandered prehistoric India before the Hindis arrived.

The Sinhalese comprise two-thirds of the people of Ceylon. The next largest group is the Tamils—descendants of people who immigrated from South India. Some invaded Ceylon under South Indian kings before the Europeans came; many were brought in as farm workers in +XIX. British capitalists imported Tamils to work their tea planta⁺ tions, since the Sinhalese preferred to work their own farms rather than toil as day laborers on others'. The Tamils show their Australoid genes more strongly than most Indians, being small and very dark. They have the repute of being implacably hard-working and enterprising. They speak a language of the group called Dravidian, descended from the tongues spoken in India before the Aryan invasions and unrelated to the Indo-European family.

This practice of nineteenth-century imperial powers, of importing to colonies industrious workers from overcrowded countries like India and China, sowed the seeds of bitter conflicts in these colonies when the latter gained self-rule. It led, for instance, to the perennial feud between the Fiji Islanders and the descendants of Indians brought to Fiji and now more than equal in numbers to the Polynesian-Melanesian indigenes.

In Ceylon, smaller ethnoi comprise the "Moors" (Muslims of mainly Arab descent), Malays, descendants of European settlers, and a few primitive Väddas. Ceylon had fewer than 1 million people in 1821 and over 5 million in 1927, and now has nearly 10 million. The country has one of the world's fastest rates of population increase and is plainly headed for a demographic crisis soon. Although the island grows rice, the government is already importing rice to sell below cost.

The Sinhalese impress the visitor as an affable, self-respecting, level-headed people. The atmosphere is very different from that of India. Although Ceylon has seen its share of crimes and follies in high places and low, the people seem reasonably free of that fantastic lack of ordinary common sense that so enlivens travel in India.

Ceylon is fortunate in having a continuous ancient history. In +VI, a Buddhist *bhikkhu*[12] or monk, Mahânâma, assembled the then existing materials into a chronicle in Pâli verse. The Pâli language was a descendant of Sanskrit, the tongue of the Aryan invaders of India. Pâli is intermediate between Sanskrit and its many modern descendants (such as Hindi, Panjâbi, Gujarâti, Bengali, and Sinhalese), as Chaucer's English is intermediate between the Anglo-Saxon of *Beowulf* and modern English.

Mahânâma called his epic the *Mahâvamsa*[13] or *Great Chronicle*. He covered the period from the landing of the first Sinhalese king to the reign of King Mahâsena, +334 to +362. There are also other Sinhalese historical works, especially the *Dîpavamsa*, written in +IV—which, however, deals mainly with Indian events—and the *Chûlavamsa*,[14] a continuation of the *Mahâvamsa* by other hands down to +XVIII.

Ceylon is thus in much better shape as regards its past than India. In India, for centuries on end no written history has come down, and we can only surmise what happened from occasional coins or inscriptions, many of the latter on copper plates, recording land grants. There are several reasons for this. For one, after the Aryan conquest, writing did not again come into wide use for many centuries and then was used mainly for commercial records. For another, the usual writing material was a highly perishable paper made from palm fronds.

Most importantly, the Indians showed but little interest in history. Indian philosophy, with its doctrines of endless cycles and the unreality of the material world, led Indian interests away from mundane events. Therefore most of what we know of Indian history before the Muslim conquests is based upon the findings of archaeologists and the writings of foreigners, mostly Greeks and Chinese, who visited the land. The northwestern kingdom of Kashmîr alone has a chronicle to compare with the *Mahâvamsa*.

Mahânâma and his colleagues had the same limitations as medieval European monkish chroniclers. They believed in miracles and swallowed the most fantastic legends whole. They were much more interested in the affairs of their religion than in secular events. They judged kings according to how diligently they fostered the True Faith, no matter what else they did. Hence the *Mahâvamsa* is described as "not a history in the modern sense."[15]

Since there is little in the way of independent accounts of the events in the *Mahâvamsa* for cross-checking, there is room for wide disagreement as to how literally its various parts should be taken. The first five chapters deal with the life and death of the Buddha and the spread of his teachings. The sixth chapter tells how an Indian princess was raped by a lion and bore a son, Sîmhabâhu, with paws for hands and feet. Sîmhabâhu became king of Bengal and begat sixteen pairs of twins. The eldest of his thirty-two sons was a wild young man named Vijaya. Because of Vijaya's deeds of violence, Sîmhabâhu caused his son to be sent away on a ship with his 700 followers. They landed on Lankâ on the day of Buddha's death (as Mahânâma put it: "the day the Tathâ-

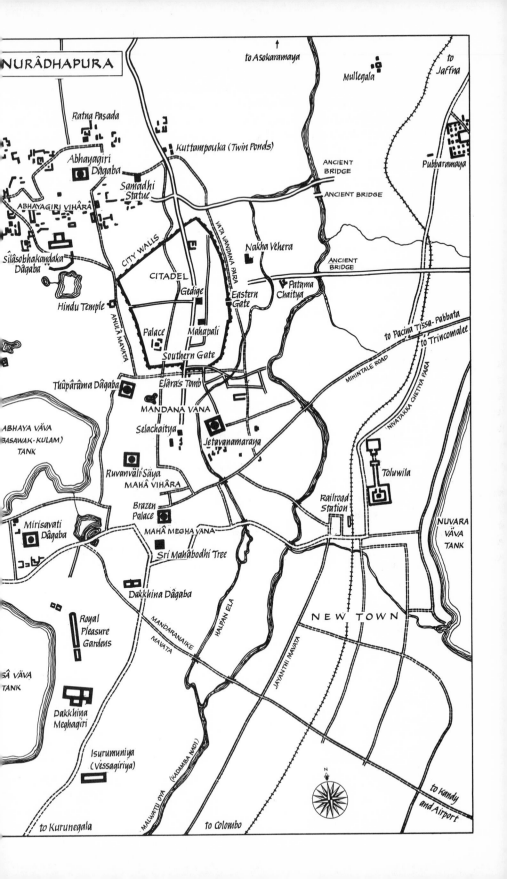

gata lay down between the two twinlike sâla-trees to pass into nir-vâna").[16] Various reckonings put this data at —544 to —483.

It is agreed that Prince Vijaya is probably legendary, not real, but opinion differs as to when the *Mahâvaṃsa* becomes serious history. The same is true of the other ancient chronicles, like the Old Testament and the records of the Greeks for the centuries following the Trojan War.

However that be, the Sinhalese did migrate from northern India to Ceylon around —500, although it is uncertain whether they came from the east coast, as in Mahânâma's tale, or from the west, or from both. Some married Vädda women. Most of their settlements were in the northwest, in the dry zone. They were sometimes under a single ruler and sometimes split among several kinglets.

During the first two centuries, some Sinhalese kings fixed their capital at Anurâdhapura, on the northwestern Malvatu River about 50 miles from its mouth. Mahânâma tells a story of this founding: how Prince Paṇḍukâbhaya[17] fought a host of wicked uncles. The prince was helped by a yakkhinî (a female supernatural being) who took the form of a white mare with red hooves.

> After speech with the yakkhinî, the prince, according to her cunning counsel, sent in advance a company of his soldiers taking with them kingly apparel and weapons as presents and the message: "Take all of this; I will make peace with you." But as they were lulled into security thinking: "We will take him prisoner if he comes," he mounted the yakkha-mare and went forth to battle at the head of a great host. The yakkhinî neighed full loudly and his army, inside and outside (the camp) raised a mighty battlecry. The prince's men killed all the soldiers of the enemy's army and the eight uncles with them, and they raised a pyramid of skulls. The commander escaped and fled (for safety) to a thicket; that (same thicket) is therefore called Senâpatigumbata. When the prince saw the pyramid of skulls, where the skulls of his uncles lay uppermost, he said: "'Tis like a heap of gourds"; and therefore they named (the place) Lâbugâmada.
>
> When he was thus left victor in battle, Paṇḍukâbhaya went thence to the dwelling-place of his great-uncle Anurâdha. The great-uncle handed over his palace to him and built himself a dwelling elsewhere; but he dwelt in his house. When he had inquired of a soothsayer who was versed in the knowledge of (fitting) sites, he founded the capital, even near that village. Since it had served as dwelling for two Anurâdhas, it was called Anurâdhapura, and also because it was founded under the con-

95. Reservoir at Anurâdhapura.

stellation Anurâdha. When he had caused the (state) parasol of his uncles to be brought and purified in a natural pond that is here, Pandukâbhaya kept it for himself and with the water of that same pond he solemnized his own consecration; and Suvannapâlî, his spouse, he consecrated queen . . .

Because his mother and he himself had been befriended by him, he did not slay the king Abhaya, his eldest uncle, but handed over the government to him for the night-time: he became the "Nagaraguttika" (Guardian of the City). From that time onward there were nagaraguttikas in the capital. His father-in-law also, Girikandasiva, he did not slay but handed over to this uncle the district of Girikanda. He had the pond deepened and abundantly filled with water, and since he had taken water therefrom, when victorious (for his consecration), they called it Jayavâpi.[18]

Actually, the capital seems at first to have been called Anurâdhagama. The modern form took hold only about +IV.

Around —2000, on the grassy plain that stretches from Poland to Turkestan, a wandering tribe of cattle-raising nomads tamed the horse, which then ran wild from the forests of Germany to the deserts of Mongolia. This feat had momentous results. The horse-tamers set out in their rattling chariots and easily conquered their neighbors. They set themselves up as a ruling class over the conquered, intermarried with them, and imposed their language and customs upon them. These mixed peoples set out in their turn and conquered more neighboring nations. Thus the horsemen spread their speech from Portugal to Assam; the Sinhalese occupation of Ceylon was one of the last ripples of this wave of migration.

The family of tongues derived from that of the original horsemen is called the Indo-European. The horsemen who conquered Iran and northern India called themselves *Ârya*, "noble ones." Therefore the original conquerors and their descendants are called sometimes Indo-Europeans and sometimes Aryans.

There is, however, no "Aryan race." Whatever the race of the first horsemen, it has long since disappeared by intermarriage and dilution.

96. Bathing pool at Anurâdhapura.

The words for certain plants and animals, common to widely-separated Indo-European languages, suggest that the original point of dispersion was south of the Baltic Sea—that is, on the plains of Poland.

When we read of ancient conquests, we must bear in mind that the conquerors were usually bands of fighting aristocrats and their henchmen, who formed only a small minority in the lands they over-mastered. When they settled down, they soon mixed with the conquered and lost any distinctive racial type by dilution in a few generations. Thus the Central Asian Turks conquered the land we now call Turkey and imposed their name and tongue upon it, but the invaders were so few that they have left only faint traces of their original Mongoloid racial type on that land. Hence, despite all the migrations and conquests of the last 5,000 years, the racial distribution in Europe and Asia has probably stayed much the same since the beginnings of recorded history. So the first Aryans were probably much like the modern Poles, predominantly of the Alpine type—stocky, broadheaded, and of medium to dark coloring. The original Noble Aryan may in fact have looked like the late Nikita Khrushchëv!

In the second millennium B.C., the Aryans overran northwestern India, conquering the darker but more civilized folk who already possessed the land. These barbarians extended their rule across the north of India and down the Ganges Valley to the Sea of Bengal, but in the south their conquests were halted by peoples whom they called the Dravida and who proved fiercer warriors than had those in the North. From this Sanskrit name *Dravida*, modern philologists have made the linguistic term "Dravidian," which they apply to languages like Tamil. It is usually assumed that the civilized North Indians whom the Aryans conquered were Dravidian-speakers, too, but this is not certain.

In the North, the Aryans imposed upon those they conquered or (more probably) took over from them a peculiar form of social organization. This system is marked by the division of society into castes. A member of a caste is confined to certain hereditary occupations and is forbidden to marry or even to eat with a person outside his caste.

The Aryans naturally gave themselves the highest ranks in the system. The priests developed a doctrine that, if a man was born into a low caste, it was a punishment for a sin in a prior incarnation. If, in this life, the sinner behaved himself by respecting and obeying those of the higher castes, he might be promoted in his next life. Some said that, if a man behaved badly enough, he would be reborn as an animal—say, a spider. This is perhaps the most diabolically clever method of making the downtrodden resigned to their lot that our ingenious species has yet devised.

From the religions of the Aryan invaders and their subjects evolved the religion of Brahmanism, which in turn developed into modern

Hinduism, with its bewildering multiplicity of gods, cults, tabus, and philosophies. By —VI, this religion had already attained a stunning complexity. Then a reformer arose in the northeast of India. This was Siddhârtha Gautama, the son of a chief of the Shâkyas.[19] The Shâkyas were a folk of the warrior caste, organized as a tribal republic, who dwelt in northern Kosala, a land corresponding more or less to modern Bihar.

After a youthful life of luxury, Siddhârtha, oppressed by a sense of what we today call "alienation," deserted his wife and newborn child to wander the land in search of wisdom. He tried austerities and self-mortifications but found them jejune. At last, sitting under a fig tree, he had what he believed to be a revelation of the ultimate truth. We need not believe with the devout that, at the moment of Siddhârtha's Enlightenment, "Rivers flowed back towards their sources; peaks and lofty mountains, where countless trees had grown for ages, rolled crumbling to the earth, . . . the sun enveloped itself in awful darkness, and a host of headless spirits filled the air."[20]

Thereafter, Siddhârtha's followers called him Buddha, "the Enlightened One." His doctrines spread over India, were adopted by the emperors of the Maurya Dynasty, and for a while ousted Brahmanism from its supernatural dominance. Then, while Buddhism spread far and wide over the rest of Asia, it dwindled and disappeared in India.

In its original form, Buddha's creed was less a religion than an ethical philosophy. Although Buddha accepted—with reservations—the Indian belief in reincarnation, he ignored the swarming legions of Indian gods and stressed right conduct and altruism.

Existence, he said, is misery: Birth is pain, life is pain, and death is pain. Nor is death the end of misery, because one is reborn into another body, to begin anew the wretched round of existence. The cause of misery is desire, which in the nature of things always extends beyond what can be satisfied and is therefore thwarted. The main forms of desire are the cravings for sensuous pleasure, for wealth, and for personal immortality. (There is a contradiction between Buddha's denial of the immortal soul and acceptance of reincarnation, but such inconsistencies, thinly hidden by a smoke screen of philosophical verbiage, occur in all theologies.) To escape misery, one must extinguish desire. This is done by following the eightfold path: right views, right intention, right speech, right action, right occupation, right effort, right alertness, and right concentration. By practicing these virtues, one at last achieves *nirvâna*.

Nirvâna is a slippery term. To some Indian moralists it means nonexistence; if one finds existence unbearable, one should logically prefer not to exist at all. To others it means a mystical union with the cosmos; to still others, merely a state of internal serenity, which enables one to face the vicissitudes of life without grief or passion. Buddhists, like

97. Anurâdhapura in the time of King Mahâsena (+IV). (Drawing by Roy G. Krenkel.)

98. The Bodhi Tree of Ceylon, near Anurâdhapura.

Hinduists, differ in their interpretation of the term. Parallels to Buddha's teachings can be found in Brahmanist literature of the same era, just as parallels to the teachings attributed to Jesus can be found in the Jewish writings of his and earlier times.

Later Buddhist theologians—especially in Tibet—fancied up the creed with a hierarchy of gods, demons, Buddhas, graduate Buddhas, and apprentice Buddhas. This "high church" Tibetan Buddhism is called the Mahâyâna; the simpler, non-theistic Buddhism of Ceylon, the Theravâda,[21] albeit the Mahâyâna has at times exerted influence in Ceylon also. Like Christianity, Buddhism developed a multitude of rival sects. Efforts by Indian kings to settle disputed points by calling councils were no more successful than the attempts of Byzantine emperors to do the same for Christianity.

After the incursions of Alexander and his Successors into northwestern India, an adventurer named Chandragupta Maurya[22] founded a powerful kingdom in the Northwest and conquered all of northern India. His grandson Ashoka conquered all of India save the extreme South. Then, converted to Buddhism, Ashoka forswore war. He made Buddhism his state religion and devoted the rest of his reign to good works like building hospitals. In fact, he took such an aversion to bloodshed that he ordained the death penalty for any subject who killed an animal, which seems like going beyond the bounds of logic. He did not free all the hundreds of tribes and kingdoms that he had conquered, but that would have been too much to ask. Besides, the subject peoples were probably better off under Ashoka's benign imperium than they would have been if left alone to fight out their countless local quarrels.

In Ashoka's time a Buddist missionary, Mahinda, set out with a party of followers to convert Lankâ to Buddhism. They brought with them a shoot of the Bo tree under which Buddha had received his Enlightenment. According to Mahânâma, Mahinda was a son of Ashoka, but some modern critics question this.

The journey was signalized by miracles. Mahinda and his party flew through the air to Lankâ and transported the shoot of the Bo tree (or Bodhi tree, as they call it in Ceylon) by levitation. At Anurâdhapura, Mahinda found the mighty and righteous ruler of Lankâ, Devânampiya Tissa (−247 to −207) on his throne. This king welcomed the missionaries and told them to go to it.

Mahinda planted the tree—at least, we may suppose that he did, although Mahânâma asserts that "with a hundred roots the great Bodhi-tree set itself there in the fragrant earth, converting the people to the faith."[23] The original Bo tree died soon after when, *selon* Mahânâma, Ashoka's wicked queen destroyed it because her husband venerated the tree more than he did her.[24] Mahinda's Bodhi tree, however, still stands just south of Anurâdhapura, with crutches holding up its ancient, decrepid limbs.

Most of the Sinhalese accepted Buddhism, although Brahmanism and Jainism (another reformed sect imported from India) persisted as minor sects. When the tantric cults, which went in for sacred orgies, arose around +V, tantric Buddhism flourished for a while in Ceylon.

Devânampiya Tissa also built the first dâgaba in Ceylon, the Thûpârâma Dâgaba, to house the right collarbone of Buddha. This dâgaba has been repeatedly robbed and restored ever since. At present it is in a state of elegant restoration, even if not so spectacular as when King Mahinda II (late +VIII) plated the dome with alternating bands of gold and silver sheeting.

After Devânampiya Tissa died, several short reigns followed. The main activity of these kings seems to have been the building of *vihâras* or Buddhist monasteries; but this impression may be due merely to the bias of the priestly historian.

Buddha had no use for caste. He said: "I do not call a man a brahmana [a member of the priestly and highest caste] because of his origin or of his mother. He is indeed arrogant, and he is wealthy: but the poor who is free from all attachments, him I call indeed a brahmana

. . . Him I call a brahmana who is free from anger, dutiful, virtuous, without appetites, who is subdued and has received his last body . . . Him I call a brahmana whose knowledge is deep, who possesses wisdom, who knows the right way and the wrong, and has attained the highest end . . ."[25] And so on through a long catalogue of Buddhist virtues.

The Sinhalese, however, had brought the caste system to Ceylon with them, and deeply-rooted social institutions are not easily overturned by a reformer, no matter how high-minded. Caste and Buddhism have coexisted in Ceylon down to the present day. The Ceylonese caste system is less cruelly invidious than that practiced in India, and in both nations the institution is slowly dissolving in the acid bath of modernity.

In early —II came the first of a series of invasions from Chola[26] (modern Madras State) in southern India. The invaders seized Anurâdhapura but were soon ousted by a native Sinhalese leader. Then another Tamil adventurer, Elâra, reconquered northern Lankâ and ruled from Anurâdhapura for a forty-four years.

Several petty kingdoms in southern Ceylon maintained their independence. About —140 or —130, a heroic son was born to King Kâkavanna of Rohana, in the extreme southeast. This prince was named Gâmani, "leader." His birth was accompanied by such favorable omens as the arrival at court of an elephant of the noble six-tusked race. He gathered a band of retainers, the feeblest of whom had the strength of six elephants, and began to harry the Tamils. When his father ordered him to stop, he defied the king and thus became known as Duṭṭhagâmani,[27] "angry Gâmani."

When King Kâkavanna died, Duṭṭhagâmani and his brother Tissa fought a civil war. After thousands had been slain, the brothers were reconciled, and Duṭṭhagâmani marched north to attack Elâra's kingdom. After defeating several of the Tamil king's underlings, he neared Anurâdhapura:

> When the king Elâra heard that king Duṭṭhagâmani was come to do battle he called together his ministers and said: "This king is himself a warrior and in truth many warriors (follow him). What think the ministers, what should we do?" King Elâra's warriors, led by Dîghajantu, resolved: "Tomorrow we will give battle." The king Duṭṭhagâmani also took counsel with his mother and by her counsel formed thirty-two bodies of troops. In these the king placed parasol-bearers and figures of a king; the monarch himself took his place in the innermost body of troops.
>
> When Elâra in full armor had mounted his elephant Mahâpabbata he came thither with chariots, soldiers and beasts

99. Wall painting at Mount Sigiriya.

for riders. When the battle began the mighty and terrible Dîghajantu seized his sword and shield for battle, and leaping eighteen cubits up into the air and cleaving the effigy of the king with his sword, he scattered the first body of troops. When the mighty (warrior) had in this manner scattered also the other bodies of troops, he charged at the body of troops with which king Gâmani stood. But when he began to attack the king, the mighty warrior Sûranimila insulted him, proclaiming his own name. Dîghajantu thought: "I will slay him," and leaped into the air full of rage. But Sûranimila held the shield toward him as he alighted (in leaping). But Dîghajantu thought: "I will cleave him in twain, together with the shield," and struck the shield with the sword. Then Sûranimila let go the shield. And as he clove only the shield thus released Dîghajantu fell there, and Sûranimila, springing up, slew the fallen (man) with his spear. Phussadeva blew his conch shell, the army of the Damilas [Tamils] was scattered; nay, Elâra turned to flee and they slew many Damilas. The water in the tank was dyed

100. Descent from Mount Sigiriya. The man in the foreground is Hector Ekanayake, Ceylonese motion-picture actor and former welterweight boxing champion of Ceylon.

red with the blood of the slain, therefore it was known by the name Kulantavâpi.

King Duṭṭhagâmani proclaimed with beat of drum: "None but myself shall slay Elâra." When he himself, armed, had mounted the armed elephant Kaṇḍula he pursued Elâra and came to the south gate (of Anurâdhapura).

Near the south gate of the city two kings fought; Elâra hurled his dart, Gâmani evaded it; he made his own elephant pierce (Elâra's) elephant with his tusks and he hurled his dart at Elâra; and this (latter) fell there, with his elephant.

When he had been victorious in battle and had united Lankâ under one rule he marched, with chariots, troops and beasts for riders, into the capital. In the city he caused the drum to be beaten, and when he had summoned the people from a *yojana* [5 miles] around he celebrated the funeral rites for king Elâra. On the spot where his body had fallen he burned it with the catafalque, and there did he build a monument and ordain worship. And even to this day the princes of Lankâ, when they draw near to this place, are wont to silence their music because of this worship.[28]

Dutthagâmani proved himself a favorite of the Buddhist priesthood by the wealth he lavished upon them. He built vast monasteries, one in the form of a nine-story ziggurat, in which the bhikkhus dwelt on higher levels in proportion to their degree of spiritual perfection. His main peacetime achievement, however, was a huge dâgaba: the Great Thûpa, now called the Ruvanväli Säya. It was to contain the bones of Buddha himself, brought by miraculous means to Ceylon. Gods and other supernatural beings helped the king to collect materials for the dâgaba.

To build the foundation, Dutthagâmani used advanced engineering techniques:

> . . . the lord of the land had the place for the thûpa dug out to a depth of seven cubits to make it firm in every way. Round stones that he commanded his soldiers to bring hither did he cause to be broken with hammers, and then did he, having knowledge of right and wrong ways, command that the crushed stone, to make the ground firmer, be stamped down by great elephants whose feet were bound with leather . . . The king commanded that the clay be spread over the layer of stones and that bricks be laid over the clay, over these a rough cement and over this cinnabar, and over this a network of iron, and over this sweet-scented marumba that was brought by the sâmaneras [Buddhist novices] from the Himalaya.[29]

We may doubt that Dutthagâmani topped off his foundation, as stated, with a layer of silver 7 inches thick. Even so, the king has a claim to be the inventor of reinforced concrete. Next day he put on a show for his people:

> The king supported, in order of their rank, by many ministers, richly clothed as befitted their office, surrounded by many dancers richly clothed like to celestial nymphs, (he himself) being clad in his state-raiment, attended by forty thousand men, while around him crashed the music (he being) glorious as the king of the gods; in the evening he who had knowledge of fit and unfit places went to the place of the Great Thûpa, delighting the people (with the sight).[30]

Bhikkhus came from all over India, to the number of a million and a half—but here we may justly suspect the pious Mahânâma of exaggerating. When the time came:

Eight vases of silver and eight (vases) of gold did he, with tireless zeal, place in the midst, and in a circle around these he placed a thousand and eight new vases, and likewise (around each of these) a hundred and eight garments. Eight splendid bricks did he lay, each one apart by itself. When he then had commanded an official chosen for this and adorned in every way to take one of them, he laid on the east side, which had been prepared with many ceremonies, the first foundation stone, upon the sweet-smelling clay.[31]

Then the highest officials laid stones and bricks in their turn. The enshrining of the relics called for equally sumptuous ceremonies, for which the gods played celestial music. But alas! as had been foretold, King Dutthagâmani fell sick before the dâgaba was finished and entered the Tusita-heaven. His brother succeeded him and ruled worthily for eighteen years.

The rest of the *Mahâvaṃsa* is largely a chronicle of plots, coups, murders, and civil wars among Anurâdhapura's royal families; for example, the tale of the amorous Queen Anulâ, who poisoned seven or eight husbands in succession as she tired of them and who also enjoyed the gallantry of her thirty-two royal guardsmen. In the reign of Bhâtiya I (+38 to +67) a Roman official, sailing the Red Sea to collect taxes, was blown out into the Indian Ocean by a gale and ended up at Ceylon. When he was presented at court, King Bhâtiya was struck by the fact that the denarii in the Roman's purse were all of the same weight, though issued under different emperors. Charmed by this evidence of Roman integrity, he sent an embassy to the court of the emperor Claudius.[32]

Then the Tamils attempted more invasions but were repelled. In +IV, King Mahâsena brought down upon himself the wrath of the chronicler by opposing the Buddhist priesthood. Deeming that they had become too rich and powerful, like a Sinhalese King Henry VIII, he confiscated their properties and tore down their vihâras. He also built the largest known dâgaba, the Jetavanaramaya, which stands brush-covered at Anurâdhapura.

Through these centuries, Anurâdhapura grew and grew. Some think it attained a population of over a million.[33] It was laid out on a grid plan, surrounded by a wall forming a square 15 miles around. Within the wall were seven or more dâgabas, large and small, and several temples and places, supported by slender stone pillars tied together with timber framing. In the palaces, a distinctive Ceylonese decorative feature was the moonstone, a threshold consisting of a semicircular slab of granite carved in low relief with bands of animals, birds, and flowers.

101. Remains of Prince Kassapa's brick-and-plaster lion at Mount Sigiriya. Left to right: Arthur C. Clarke, Alan E. Nourse, Hector Ekanayake, and K. D. P. Perera.

Then there were a multitude of houses of the common folk, made of wooden frames with removable reed mats for walls. Being cheap and practical, this type of construction is common in southern and southeastern Asia. The mats can be removed to let the breeze blow through in hot weather, and when they wear out they are easily replaced.

The people went about with long hair tied in a bun or a topknot. Men and women wore an ankle-length wrap-around skirt, leaving the upper body bare save in the rare cool spells, when they donned short-sleeved jackets. For active work, men stripped to a loincloth. Coins were oblong at first, but later round like those of most nations.

To grow the rice needed to support this vast population, the kings constructed huge artificial lakes or reservoirs, called "tanks," throughout the dry zone. Some of these had areas of more than 5,000 acres. Mahâsena, who confiscated the monasteries, built the noted Minneriya Tank, 45 miles southeast of Anurâdhapura. In modern times several

of these tanks, after long neglect, have been repaired and put back
into use.

Fifteen miles from the Minneriya Tank is a strange natural forma-
tion called Mount Sigiriya or Sigiriya Rock: a crag with 600-foot
vertical sides. The crag has a lurid story. King Dhâtusena, who reigned
from +460 to +478, married his daughter to his nephew, who commanded the army. The king's sister—the bride's mother-in-law and
aunt—quarreled with the girl, who was beaten by her husband. The
king blamed it all on his sister and had her burned alive. Then one
of Dhâtusena's sons, Kassapa,[34] joined forces with the general. They
captured Dhâtusena and walled him up alive to perish.

Kassapa took the throne but, fearing that his method of succession might not meet with general approval, retired from Anurâdhapura
to Sigiriya, which he converted into a fortress; Ceylon has several
such outcrops, which kings have put to this use from time to time.
At one end of the rock, Kassapa built a huge lion of brick and plaster,
of which only the forepaws remain. To get to the top of the rock,
one went through the lion and up a stair cut into the surface of
the cliff. The rock-cut steps, which have crumbled away, have been
replaced by a series of iron stairs and railings, but it is still an alarming
climb.

In one flank of the rock, above the pathway to the top and
below an overhang, is a set of famous mural paintings of women,
comparable to those at Ajanta in India. Whether the paintings are
of goddesses, or of Kassapa's wives, or of other persons, none knows.
(Unfortunately, one of these paintings was recently destroyed by a
gang of squatters who thus took revenge on the Archaeology Department for ordering them off the state property.)

For eight years, Kassapa remained safely in his eyrie, while a
royal city grew up around the base of the rock. Then his younger
brother Moggalâna[35] invaded the land. Perhaps Kassapa got bad advice
from his soothsayers; but in any case he came down from his rock,
gave battle, lost, and killed himself.

In +VII, Sinhalese politics took an ominous turn. Princes and generals, striking for the throne, went to South India to hire Tamil mercenaries. Soon the Tamil soldiery formed a Praetorian Guard, which made
puppets of the kings. When Tamil kings from Paṇḍya and Chola invaded
Ceylon, the mercenaries often went over to the invaders. The islanders,
usually divided into several quarreling kingdoms, could not resist effectively. Around 1000, the Chola king Râjarâja and his son Râjendra
I added Ceylon to their great if short-lived South Indian empire.

During these invasions, Anurâdhapura was destroyed. When Prâ-
krama Bâhu I, one of the greatest Sinhalese kings, threw out the Tamils

in 1153, he made his capital at Polonnaruva, east of Mount Sigiriya, where it would be less exposed to Tamil attacks. Deserted, Anurâdhapura was allowed to go back to jungle.

For several centuries, Ceylonese history is a tale of repeated invasions from India. Sometimes the Sinhalese invaded India in their turn; one king even sent an expedition against Burma.

In 1505, a Portuguese fleet, engaged in seizing the Arab trade routes in the Indian Ocean by *force majeure*, stopped at Galle on the southern coast of Ceylon. Soon there were Portuguese settlements along the coast. The Portuguese, against whose superior weapons the Sinhalese were helpless, fought and intrigued to bring the Ceylonese kingdoms under their control. Their objectives, like those of the Spaniards in the New World, were, first, to save the immortal souls of the heathen from Hell by converting them to the True Faith; and second, to relieve them of any property they might possess, this being deemed a fair exchange. So they demolished Buddhist and Hinduist temples. When they captured the capital of the mountain kingdom of Kandy, they took away Kandy's most sacred relic: an alleged Tooth of Buddha, brought to Ceylon in +IV. The Tooth was taken to Goa, where the Portuguese archbishop publicly burned it, pulverized it, and threw the remains into the sea.

Now, however, the Temple of the Tooth at Kandy has a Tooth, which they claim to be the original miraculously transported back to Ceylon. (Another story is that the Portuguese captured a substitute Tooth, the Buddhist priests having hidden the real one.) Before anybody accuses the Ceylonese of credulity, let him remember that in the churches of medieval Europe one could find such picturesque improbabilities as the tears of Jesus and the milk of Mary, not to mention enough fragments of the True Cross to build a ship, enough toenail parings of St. Peter to fill a bushel basket, seven or eight thighbones of the Virgin, two skeletons of St. Luke, and twelve Holy Foreskins.

After a century of predatory Iberian rule, the Dutch ousted the Portuguese. The Ceylonese welcomed the newcomers, hoping to use them against the hated Portuguese, but soon found that they had but traded one set of masters for another. Dutch rule, if heavy-handed, was less destructive than Portuguese. The Dutch promoted commerce; they persecuted the Catholics but let the other sects alone.

After two centuries, during the Napoleonic Wars, Great Britain took Ceylon from the Dutch. The British developed the island economically, brought in Tamils, and allowed the Ceylonese some self-rule. At long-abandoned Anurâdhapura, the jungle was cleared away and a couple of ancient dâgabas were restored. A small town grew up in the midst of the far-spread ruins. Today the dâgabas rise like roc's eggs amid little groves of stone pillars remaining from the palaces and monasteries. There are also several ancient tanks and swimming pools. Similar ruins may be seen at Polonnaruva.

In 1948, Ceylon got self-rule as a member of the British Commonwealth. Although the government has indulged in some erratic policies, Ceylon has perhaps been more successful than any other former colony of a European imperial power in practicing orderly, democratic self-government. King Duṭṭhagâmani would be pleased with his descendants.

XIII

ROME, THE CITY OF ALL TIME

HOW WONDERFUL IT IS! THE QUEEN OF FLOWERS,
THE MARBLE ROSE OF ROME! ITS PETALS TORN
BY WIND AND RAIN OF THRICE FIVE HUNDRED YEARS;
ITS MOSSY SHEATH HALF RENT AWAY, AND SOLD
TO ORNAMENT OUR PALACES AND CHURCHES,
OR TO BE TRODDEN UNDER FEET OF MAN
UPON THE TIBER'S BANK; YET WHAT REMAINS
STILL OPENING ITS FAIR BLOSSOM TO THE SUN,
AND TO THE CONSTELLATIONS THAT AT NIGHT
HANG POISED ABOVE IT LIKE A SWARM OF BEES.[1]

Longfellow

102. Remains of a Roman *castellum* or water-distribution point at Nîmes, France.

I<small>T WAS</small> the eighth of the Kalends of September, in the 870th *annô urbis conditae* (year of the founding of the city); or, as we should say, August 25, A.D. 117. An hour before sunrise, Flavius Adiatorix was on his way to work with a bundle of rods, cords, and other surveying implements over his shoulder. He had a little over half a mile to walk from the dark little fifth-story room, which he and his wife occupied on the Subura, to the Baths of Agrippa. He passed the towering fronts of apartment houses lining the broad Subura.

Traffic already was thick. The air was filled with the clop of hooves, the rumble of wheels, and the screech of axles as carts and wagons crowded the avenues on their way to the city gates. Since the law of the deified Julius allowed them in the city only at night, their drivers would be fined if caught on the streets after dawn.

At the crossing of the Vicus Longus, where carts feeding in from three directions tangled and muleteers shouted curses and threats, a soldier of the Urban Cohort, directing traffic, strove to straighten out the snarl. Adiatorix slipped around a wagon loaded with bricks, passed the Temple of Minerva, and entered the narrow Forum of Nerva. Turning right, he crossed the Forum of Augustus, cluttered with statues, bronzen chariots, and triumphal arches and flanked by the huge Temple of Mars the Avenger.

The fora were already aswarm with pedestrians: clients in togas on their way to the houses of their patrons, slave and free workmen, messengers on the run, trousered foreigners from the lands to the north and the east, Orientals in robes and turbans. The owners of the countless shops opening on the streets were folding back their shutters for the day's business.

Adiatorix entered the even larger Forum of Trajan. He passed through the forest of columns of the vast Basilica Ulpia or Ulpian Courthouse; he passed the scaffolding around Trajan's uncompleted column, and the two great public libraries flanking it. By getting his subcommissioner to vouch for him, Adiatorix had secured the right to borrow books. He needed this because, being a Gaul, he was not a full Roman citizen; he had inherited the rank of "citizen without franchise" from his grandfather, who had served in the Roman army.

Leaving the Forum of Trajan, Flavius Adiatorix zigzagged through a tangle of narrow, crooked, stinking alleys. Under a decree of Julius

Caesar, a century and a half before, they were supposed to have been paved and provided with sidewalks; but most had never received these amenities. Adiatorix worked his way around the Temple of Isis and emerged on the eastern side of the Baths of Agrippa. Here he found most of the rest of the crew awaiting him: Silius Probus the engineer; Fabius Agatho the clerk, with rolled-up plans under his arm; and the two municipal slaves, Ataulfus the German and Esdras the Jew, with a ladder. Titinius Celer, the overseer, was missing.

Adiatorix halted. "Where's himself?" He was a dark man of medium height and stocky build, with a round bullet-head. Although he had lived for years in Rome, he still spoke Latin with a strong Celtic accent.

Probus shrugged. "Sleeping it off, I guess. I got up with four heads myself." He referred to a minor festival of the day before, which had given them all a holiday. "Here he comes."

The small, gray-haired overseer appeared. The five aqueduct workers shot out their right arms in the Roman salute, crying: "Hail, boss!"

"Hail, boys," said Celer with a flip of his arm. The rising sun had begun to gild the ornaments on the temple roofs. "The commissioner wants us to run down a diversion in the Virgo, in a hurry. The bath people are screaming for more water. We'll start at the castellum."

As the crew trailed towards the distributing point, where water from the Aqua Virgo was piped away to the fountains, the Baths of Agrippa and Nero, and other authorized users, Adiatorix said: "Boss, you haven't shaved since I saw you last. Are you growing whiskers?"

"Why, you impudent scoundrel—" began Celer, then broke into a shamefaced grin. "No, you've got me there, Flavius. Something has happened."

"What?" said Adiatorix, echoed by the others.

"I wasn't supposed to tell; but the news is posted in the Old Forum this morning. We have a new emperor."

They all stopped. "You mean," said Adiatorix, "that the great Marcus Ulpius Traianus—the gods preserve him—is after dying?"

"I mean that."

"Who's the new man?" asked Probus.

"His kinsman, Publius Aelius Hadrianus."

"But, boss," said Adiatorix, "what has that to do with your whiskers, and them so dignified and all?"

"Hadrianus wears them," said Celer. "They say he has a scar on his chin. Now everyone in Rome will be wearing them."

"They say he likes the boys," said Agatho.

"That's his business. Let's get to work."

For the next few hours, the crew traced the course of the Aqua Virgo back from the castellum. At each stop, Probus and the two slaves

103. Aqueducts of Rome, restored. The Anio Novus and the Claudia
in the left foreground, combined in a single structure; the Marcia,
Tepula, and Iulia, also on one single arcade, on the right. (Painting
by Zeno Diemer; courtesy of the Deutsches Museum, Munich.)

climbed the ladder to the top of the arcade. The slaves pried up the
slabs of brick that roofed the water channel and held them on edge
while Probus leaned into the channel, measured the depth of the water
with a dip stick, and scrutinized the flow for an eddy or other sign of illegal diversion. Adiatorix measured distances, while Agatho unrolled
his plans to compare them with the structure.

The arcade shadowed streets and cut between building lots, so that
in places the whole crew had to climb to the top, draw the ladder after
them, and walk along the top between the walls of tenements. As he
heaved on the slabs, Esdras groaned:

"You idolaters will be the death of me yet! All this heaving and
prying will give me a rupture!"

"Oh, shut up and do your work!" growled Ataulfus in a thick
German accent.

The slaves slanged each other vigorously while the rest of the
crew grinned. The dislike between the two was well-known. The Jew
was a good-natured fat man, always amiable despite his laziness and
complaints. The German was tall, with graying blond hair, enormously
strong but morose and taciturn.

"A fine occupation for a respectable weaver," continued Esdras, sweating as he heaved up another slab, "and all because my foolish countrymen start a rebellion they can't win!"

"You'd complain in Elysium," said Probus. "If you drop that thing on my fingers, I'll stuff a piece of pork down your throat."

"Less chatter and more work!" snapped Celer.

As the crew moved along the aqueduct, the teeming crowds of Rome swirled past them. Wheeled traffic had almost disappeared, but the streets were more crowded than ever. There went a Senator in his litter, his toga draped to show the broad purple stripe on his tunic. He was surrounded by a score of clients and freedmen and an equal number of slaves. A century of the Praetorian Guard swung past, its *optio* barking: "*Un*', du', tre', quat', *un*', du' . . ."

By noon, the crew had inspected the Virgo for nearly a mile. The ground rose as they neared the north end of the city. When the ground level reached that of the water channel, the aqueduct changed from an arcade to a tunnel, skirting the slope of the Pincian Mount.

104. Fora of Rome from the west, restored. (Courtesy of Ellen Kohler.)

"Ha!" said Probus.

"Find something?" asked Celer.

"I think so. Let's have a light. Flavius, get that mirror out of my bag."

Adiatorix got out a steel mirror and reflected the sun past Probus' head into the tunnel. Poking with a rod soon disclosed that a hole had been bored in the channel and a leaden pipe inserted where the channel plunged into the hill. Prodding revealed that the pipe ran around the hill, just below the surface of the earth.

Titinius Celer stood back, stroking the silvery stubble on his chin. "Agatho, do your plans show any pipes at this point?"

"They do not, boss. See!"

"Who lives over that way?" Celer pointed northeast.

"It's the old gardens of Valerius Asiaticus," said Agatho. "It's been subdivided since his time, though."

"I think I see our answer," said Celer as a flash of steel caught his eye. *Heus,* vigil!"

A man wearing a light iron headpiece and a military tunic, with a short sword and a bludgeon suspended from his belt, scrambled up the slope. "Why hail, Celer!" he said, flipping his hand in the Greek manner.

"Hail, Eurus!" replied Celer. "By Hercules, I didn't know you at the distance." After small talk of personal fortunes and families, Celer asked: "Who lives around the curve of the hill, where this illegal pipe is headed?"

"Let me think. Several of the Valerii have houses there, but I can't tell you which is which. I haven't been on this beat long enough. Look, if I don't get back to the *excubitorium,* my sergeant'll hang me up by the balls. Nice seeing you."

"What's bothering you, boss?" asked Probus as they stared at the policeman's retreating back.

Celer sighed. "The Valerii still have plenty of pull, so I don't know if we can make a complaint stick. It will depend on the new Emperor's policy. Luckily, it doesn't concern us. I'll give my report to the sub-commissioner and let him sweat over it. Meanwhile, let's eat."

"We ought to rip this stinking pipe out," growled Ataulfus with his mouth full of bread, "and let the haughty gentlemen complain."

"One must be realistic," said Celer. "When Frontinus was water commissioner, we'd have done just that. Ah, there was a man for you! I remember when that fat literary man[2] who was commissioner of sewers and embankments—Flavius, you're our bookworm. What was his name?"

"Would you be meaning Gaius Plinius Secundus?" said Adiatorix.

"That's the name. Well, this Plinius had a no-good poet friend

105. Rome: Forum of Trajan. (Courtesy of Ellen Kohler.)

named Martialis, who wanted to tap the Marcia for his own use. He even wrote a poem to the Emperor about it. I can't remember how it goes . . ."

"I can," said Adiatorix. "I was reading it just the other day."

"You should have been a professor," said Esdras, "or better yet a Jewish professor, a *rabb*. But say the poem."

"Let me think." Adiatorix knotted his brow and moved his lips, then recited:

> I have, and by your grace I hope to keep,
> Caesar, my dwellings in and out of town,
> But the curved pole, bucket, and swinging sweep
> Hardly suffice to wet my garden down.
> My house complains that it is worse than dry
> Though the great Marcian flume is rushing near:
> Grant water to my household gods, and I
> Will think Jove's golden rain descended here![3]

The waterworkers applauded. Adiatorix bowed and said: "To be sure, didn't you know that we Celts were great poets when you Italians were living in reed huts, with pigs in the parlor? So what happened, boss?"

"Traianus passed the request on to Plinius, who took it up with Frontinus, who turned him down flat. The Emperor backed up Frontinus, too."

They ate in silence; then Ataulfus said: "Boss, how could I become a vigil, like your Greek friend that was here?"

"You'd have to get free first," said Celer. "The vigiles are recruited from freedmen."

"It looks more like a proper duty for a brave warrior than heaving bricks and stones around."

"Don't brag about being such a fearless fighter," said Agatho, "unless you want to end up in the arena."

"Oh, I suppose I shall never make it," replied the German.

Esdras said. "If your pay you'd save up instead of going on a drunken binge every month, you could buy yourself out."

"Look, you fat slug—" roared Ataulfus, but Celer and Probus squelched his outburst. When tempers had cooled, Probus said:

"The Jew is right, you know. And if you got into the vigiles, after three years you could transfer to the army and earn citizenship. But you'd have to convince the commissioner that it was for the good of Rome."

"Why don't you try?" said Esdras. "Just think: No longer with your sour visage we'd have to put up."

Ataulfus muttered a guttural curse, finished his lunch, and went off to sulk. Adiatorix asked:

"Where's Verus? I expected to see him instead of Agatho."

"He got pulled in on an accusation of being a Christian. I hope he has sense enough to deny it, whatever his beliefs."

"And how do you figure that, boss?" said Adiatorix.

"The orders are that if they deny their cult and do reverence to the Emperor and the Roman gods, they're to be let go. But a lot of those fanatics seem to want to get themselves killed."

Adiatorix turned to Esdras. "I'm after hearing about these Christians for some time, but I don't know about them. Aren't they some kind of Jew?"

Esdras waved his hands before his face. "Don't blame me for the folly of these people, my friend! A bad name they give us Jews by their antics. A hundred years ago, Judaea was overrun with prophets and wizards, each claiming a special message from God. As I understand, the fellow who started this Christian nonsense claimed to be a literal son of God, or at least his followers claimed it for him. Now, your Greek and Roman gods, they tell me, are always begetting bastards on mortal women. But we don't believe that the great God—whether you call him Yahveh, or Jupiter, or whatever—would do anything so undignified, when he can a world create by snapping his fingers."

"What about this God of yours?" began Adiatorix. "A philosopher says—" But Esdras held up a hand, saying:

"As to the nature of God, ask the philosophers and rabbis. I'm just a plain man trying to get along and keep out of trouble."

"I once knew a Christian," said Agatho. "He was a poor fishmonger on the Aventine. Quite a decent fellow, with very strict morals. He wouldn't fornicate or cheat the tax collector or anything."

"I daresay some are decent," said Celer, "but you ought to see them in mobs! Why, last month a gang burst into the services at the Temple of Isis, making their sign of the cross and yelling that they were putting the evil spirits to rout. We can't have that sort of thing."

Probus added: "My grandfather was here when the city burned in Nero's time. He told me the Christians thought the world was ending, and their prophet would come down and whisk them away to Heaven, while everybody else went to Tartarus. So, while all decent folk were trying to fight the fire and save their goods, the Christians went snake-dancing through the streets, singing: 'The end of the world, the end of the world, the end of the end of the end of the world!' and 'Jesus is coming! Jesus is coming! Jesus is coming, is coming, is coming!' No wonder Nero burned a batch of 'em!"

"Luckily," said Celer, "they are few, and I'm sure the Roman people will never swallow such crazy ideas." He yawned. "You know, boys, those trees look like the place for a nap. We'll trace the pipe later."

Soon the waterworkers were sprawled in the shade, snoring through the heat of the afternoon.

In +357, the emperor Constantius II entered Rome for the first time. A son of the first Constantine, he was the sole survivor of a brisk round of treachery, murder, and civil war that had followed the death of Constantine, who had divided the Empire among his three sons.

Rome was not what it had been. Constantine had founded his new eastern capital of Constantinople, and even in the West the emperors had been spending less and less time in Rome. They found Ravenna, surrounded by swamps near the head of the Adriatic, more defensible and strategically more advantageous. Many of the palaces were in ruins. Nonetheless, Constantius was stunned:

> So when he entered Rome, the home of empire and of every virtue, and when he had come to the Rostra, the most renowned forum of ancient dominion, he stood amazed, and on every side on which his eyes rested he was dazzled by the array of marvelous sights . . . Then, as he surveyed the sections of the city and its suburbs, lying within the summits

106. Rome: Market of Trajan in the Imperial fora. (Courtesy of Ellen Kohler.)

of the seven hills, along their slopes, or on level ground, he thought that whatever first met his gaze towered above the rest: the sanctuaries of the Tarpeian Jove so far surpassing as things divine excel those of earth; the baths built up in the manner of provinces; the huge bulk of the amphitheater, strengthened by its framework of Tiburtine stone, to whose top human eyesight barely ascends; the Pantheon like a rounded city-district, vaulted over in lofty beauty, and the exalted columns which rise with platforms to which one may mount, and bear the likenesses of former emperors; the Temple of the City, the Forum of Peace, the Theatre of Pompey, the Odeum, the Stadium, and in their midst the other adornments of the Eternal City. But when he came to the Forum of Trajan, a construction unique under the heavens, as we believe, and admirable even in the unanimous opinion of the gods, he stood fast in amazement, turning his attention to the gigantic complex about him, beggaring description and never again to be imitated by mortal men.[4]

The most that he could hope to duplicate, said Constantius, would be the bronze horse of Trajan's equestrian statue. An exiled Persian prince in the Emperor's suite slyly remarked: "First, Sire, you had better build a stable like the one before us—if you can."

Nearly all the foregoing buildings and plazas, save the colossal baths of Caracalla and Diocletian, had been completed by the death of Hadrian (+138). In Hadrian's time, the city was an irregular circle, about two and a half miles in diameter, on the east or left bank of the meandering Tiber. It lapped over the river to include the wedge-shaped peninsula on which rose the Janiculum Hill.

Rome was then an unwalled city. It had long since outgrown the wall built in —IV, according to legend by King Servius Tullius. This wall, linking the original seven hills, had been demolished or incorporated into later structures. Not until late +III, when barbarian inroads led Aurelianus to build a new and larger wall, would Rome again be fortified.

When a beholder of Hadrian's time climbed one of the taller buildings in the Campus Martius, in the northwest, he saw:

> . . . an indescribable confusion of enormous buildings, gilded roofs, stately domes, serried phalanxes of marble columns and far-stretching porticoes, some on level ground, others upon the summits or clinging to the slopes of several hills. Mixed with these are an incalculable number of red-tiled roofs obviously covering more humble private structures. Here and there, mostly on the outskirts, are also broad patches of greenery, public parks, and private gardens.
>
> After more study, however, the first confusion begins to adjust itself into a kind of order. It is possible, for example, to recognize directly in the foreground a small and comparatively abrupt hill crowned at either end by temples of peculiar magnificence. This is the *Capitol*, particularly the seat of the fane of *Jupiter Optimus Maximus* ("Jupiter Best and Greatest"), officially the chief temple of Rome. Beyond it at a certain distance rises a gray cylinder of enormous bulk. That, of course, is the *Flavian Amphitheater*, and in the hollow between it and the capitol but nigh concealed by many structures stretches the *Old Forum* of the Republic—the most famous spot in Rome. To the south of the Forum, and in no wise concealed, lifts another hill covered with a vast complex of buildings, which, even when seen in the distance, is of extraordinary splendor. This is the *Palatine*, the present residence of the Caesars and the seat of the government.
>
> Just to the south and right of the Palatine there runs a long hollow, the edges of which flash with settings of marble; it is the *Circus Maximus*, the chief race course. These are the

structures or localities that stand out clearly at first glance. Close at hand, in the Campus Martius itself, is a perfect laby- rinth of covered promenades, dome-capped public baths, the- aters, and circuses, as well as the remarkable *Pantheon* and other far-famed structures . . . behind the onlooker is winding the Tiber, spanned by at least eight bridges; and across the river, before the view wanders off into the hills of Etruria, are seen numerous suburban settlements and heights whereof the most conspicuous is that around *Mount Janiculum* crested with verdant gardens.[5]

Any detailed account of the public buildings and monuments of Imperial Rome would quickly fill several books. We may, however, note that the temples, except for the Pantheon, nearly all follow Greek design, using the Corinthian column with its stone foliage. They tend to be very large and ornate, with brightly painted entablatures and a lavish use of gilding. Thanks to improved methods of construction, columns are now monolithic instead of being built up of separate drums as formerly.

In other public buildings, such as basilicae (courthouses) and baths, something new has appeared: the large-scale use of the arch and vault. Arches uphold the above-ground parts of the aqueducts that radiate out from the city and the tiers of the Flavian Amphitheater, later called the Colosseum. The Romans got the arch from the Etruscans. Whether the Etruscans invented the arch on their own or borrowed it through some intermediary from the Mesopotamians, who used it for drains and graves, is not known. By combining the arch and vault (which is merely an arch prolonged along its central axis) in a variety of ways, the Romans erected large buildings with an uncluttered interior spacious- ness beyond anything the world had seen.

In earlier times, the unobstructed width of a chamber was limited by the length of the timbers that could be obtained to hold up a roof. In a country like Mesopotamia, where the only native timbers were palm trunks, a room could not be much more than 15 or 20 feet wide unless columns or piers were set up between the walls, as in the Hypo- style Hall at Karnak. With vaulting, however, unobstructed halls 80 or 90 feet wide became possible.

Furthermore, the roofs of vaulted halls did not have to be simple semi-cylindrical structures. In +I, the Romans learned that one vault could cross another at right angles, and the two vaults would still stand up. The inner surfaces of these vaults intersected along elliptical lines called groins. Such a structure is called a groined vault or a cross vault. Such a cross vault could roof a large square area and be supported wholly by piers at the corners. About —I, the Romans also began to

107. Rome: Forum Romanum. (Courtesy of Ellen Kohler.)

roof buildings by means of the dome and the cloister vault, which may be called a square dome.

Another Roman advance in building was the use of concrete. About —III, builders discovered that near Vesuvius and elsewhere in Italy were deposits of a sandy volcanic ash which, when added to lime mortar, made a cement that dried out to rocklike hardness. They called it *pulvis puteolanus* from Puteoli,[6] where it occurred in large beds. By mixing this cement with sand, they made a concrete as hard and durable as most natural rocks. The usual method of wall construction under the Empire was to make the bulk of the wall of concrete, spaced out with gravel, stones, and broken brick and tile, with a thin facing of brick or stone. Where prestige was important, as in temples and palaces, the facing was of slabs of marble. For putting up such marble-faced buildings, Augustus boasted, late in his reign: "I found Rome a city of brick; I leave her clothed in marble."[7]

The most spectacular Roman use of concrete was the Temple of All Gods—the Pantheon—begun in —27 by Marcus Vipsanius Agrippa, Augustus' right-hand man. It consists of two main parts: a rectangular portico and, behind this, a large rotunda, capped by a concrete dome

144 feet in diameter, with an 18-foot hole in the center. Not much if
any of the present building goes back to Agrippa, since it was damaged
by fire under Titus and again under Trajan, repaired or rebuilt under
Domitian and Hadrian, and subjected to various alterations—including
conversion to a Christian church—since then.

Dwelling houses were of two types. The private house or *domus*
was a courtyard house of the Mediterranean type. The domus of a
prosperous early Roman bourgeois had about a dozen rooms, ranged
around a partly-roofed court. There was a square hole in the roof to let
in the rain and a cistern beneath to catch it. The court was called the
atrium, from *ater*, "black," because the walls were blackened from the
smoke of cooking. Poor peasants continued to live in one-room huts.

When the Romans came under Greek influence, they added a
second court on the Greek model. This was called the *peristylum*,
from the Greek words meaning "surrounded by columns." Later, the
columns disappeared from some of the courts. The outer façade of
the house might be a blank wall facing the street, or a row of chambers
opening on the street and leased as shops. If there was a second story, it
was used mainly as sleeping quarters.

Inside, the house was embellished with mosaic floors and frescoed
walls, with a display of art objects from the East. The houses of the
rich were stuffed with copies of Greek paintings and sculptures; those
of some noble Romans boasted the originals, mostly carried off as loot
during the conquests of —III to —I. The furniture, in our sense of the
word, however, was rather sparse. A good Roman house was built in a
sturdier and more substantial way than most of the houses that one can
buy today. Roman builders had not learned all the short cuts used by
modern developers. The houses they turned out were quite as durable
and as handsomely decorated as a modern house—although, lacking running water, electricity, oil heat, upholstered chairs, substantial tables, and
closets, they would seem to us a lot less comfortable to live in.

Windows had long been closed by wooden shutters. In Hellenistic
times, builders experimented with translucent windowpane materials:
oiled cloth, sheepskin, mica, horn, and gypsum shaved down to a thin
pane. Some of these materials continued in use for many centuries; but,
in the more opulent houses, they were slowly ousted by glass, which at
last had become clear enough for the purpose. In the late Republic,
glass began to be used to let light into houses. The first panes were
little round skylights, the glass of which was too irregular and impure
for true transparency. But during +I, glass windowpanes of the modern type appeared.

The Romans also took strides in heating. They invented central
indirect heating; or rather, they reinvented it, for a similar system

had been known in Anatolia over a 1,000 years before. The redis-
coverer was a Roman businessman, Gaius Sergius Orata, who lived
near Naples. About —80, Orata, already successful at raising fish and
oysters for the market, thought he could do even better if he could
keep his sea creatures growing through the winter. So he built tanks
which, instead of being sunk in the earth, were propped up on little
brick posts. The smoke and hot air from a fire at one side of the tank
circulated through the space below.

Not yet satisfied, Orata applied his invention to human comfort. He
bought country houses, equipped them with *balnae pensiles* or "raised
bathrooms," heated by ducts under the floor, and resold them at a
profit. During the century and a half after Orata's invention, builders
learned to apply his system, called a *hypocaustum* (from the Greek for
"under" and "burning"), to whole buildings. In the early Empire,
Romans living in northern provinces built hypocaust houses to keep
the winter at bay. But central heating died out with the fall of the West
Roman Empire and was not revived until modern times.

In building their cities, the Romans did much what the Greeks had
done before them. In a new city, the town was well planned on a grid
scheme. An old city like Rome, which had started as a jumble of huts
in a tangle of alleys, kept on growing without any organization despite
the efforts of reforming sovrans to straighten it out. After the great
fire of +64, which destroyed most of the west-central part of Rome,
Nero supervised the rebuilding of the city. He tried with limited
success to impose a grid plan upon the burned-out section.

Under the Empire, land became so costly that few could any
longer afford to live in *domûs*.[8] Lack of transportation sharply checked
suburban sprawl. Except for a few rich men like Plinius the Younger,
who after a day in the city drove out to a country house 17 miles
away, everyone either lived where he worked or walked to work.
Dense crowding naturally followed, and apartment houses rose to five
or more stories by —I. Augustus limited the height of buildings to 70
feet, and Trajan reduced this to 60 for safety.

These big, modern-looking brick-and-concrete apartment houses,
filling whole blocks, were called *insulae* or "islands." Under the early
Empire, insulae became much commoner in Rome than private houses;
a survey about +300 listed 1,797 domûs and 46,602 insulae. Insulae
furnished accommodations of every grade, from dark little single rooms
several flights up to luxurious duplex apartments on the more desired
lower floors.

Writers of the time complain of jerry-built insulae, which are always either catching fire and frying their tenants or collapsing and
burying them.[9] But surviving remains of insulae, as at Ostia, indicate

108. Remains of a Roman *insula* or apartment house at Ostia, Italy.

well- and solidly-built structures. Perhaps that is why these particular buildings have lasted; all the flimsy ones fell down or were demolished in ancient times.

Another feature of Rome was its sewer system. The sewers of Rome began in the days of the Tarquins—the Etruscan kings expelled by a republican revolution in —VI. A ditch was dug to drain the swampy land between the seven hills, following the course of an existing stream. Successive generations improved this storm drain, covering it with a stone barrel vault. It became the great Cloaca Maxima, through which, before the water level rose in recent centuries, one could row a boat. It was connected with openings in the streets to drain off rain water.

By the time of the Empire, many public latrines had been built and connected with the sewer system. Used water from baths and industrial establishments was channeled to flush these appliances. A modern man would be struck by the complete lack of privacy and by the costly mosaics and marbles. So lavish was the decoration that, when a latrine was dug up at Puteoli about a century ago, the archaeologists at first mistook it for a temple.

Although this latrine system was an advance over primitive conditions, it was a long way from modern sanitation. Most insulae had latrines, usually on the ground floor and often connected with the sewer system. But myriads of Romans still lived either at an awkward distance from the latrines or on the upper floors of insulae not so equipped. These either carried their sewage to cesspools or, laws to the contrary notwithstanding, threw it out the window. So Rome, despite its splendid sewers, was pervaded by the bouquet of all pre-industrial cities.

The population of Imperial Rome is not closely known, and estimates vary from 200,000 to 2 million. The most reasonable figure, I think, is around 1 million—perhaps a little over. At that, it was a much larger city than any before. Ptolemaic Alexandria may have passed the half-million mark. But Roman technical improvements—paved roads and the big grain freighters that plied the Mediterranean between North Africa and Italy—made it possible to import food more cheaply from afar and hence to concentrate more people in one metropolis.

The tale of Aeneas' landing in Italy, and his descendant Romulus' founding of Rome in −753, is generally dismissed as legend. Archaeology tells us that, soon after −1000, several villages were formed on the tops of some of the hills of this region. Eventually, these merged into a single city.

The settlement had natural advantages. It was at the crossing of several trade routes. It was at the lowest point on a major river that could be conveniently bridged. The seven hills could be protected by modest fortifications. The ground between them was swampy and hence unsuitable for a besieger to camp in while assaulting the hilltop forts. These hills—originally seven, but two were added as the city grew— were much more precipitous then than now, when 3,000 years of city building and the accumulation of rubbish in the hollows have smoothed out the terrain.

According to tales of the Etruscan Dynasty, King Ancus Marcius bridged the Tiber about −600 with a bridge of piles or *pons sublicius*, built for religious reasons without metal. This was the bridge defended by brave Horatius in Macaulay's celebrated poem, which is based upon the more or less legendary accounts in Livius and Polybios.

With successive repairs, the Pons Sublicius survived down to the end of the Republic. Then a bridge of stone and wood took its place until a flood destroyed it in +69. Meanwhile, as cross-Tiber traffic grew, the Romans built other bridges. The Pons Aemilius began as a structure with stone piers and a wooden deck, like Nabopolassar's bridge at Babylon. Later, stone arches were installed and a stone paving took the place of the wooden deck. With repair and rebuilding, this bridge was kept in service until 1598.

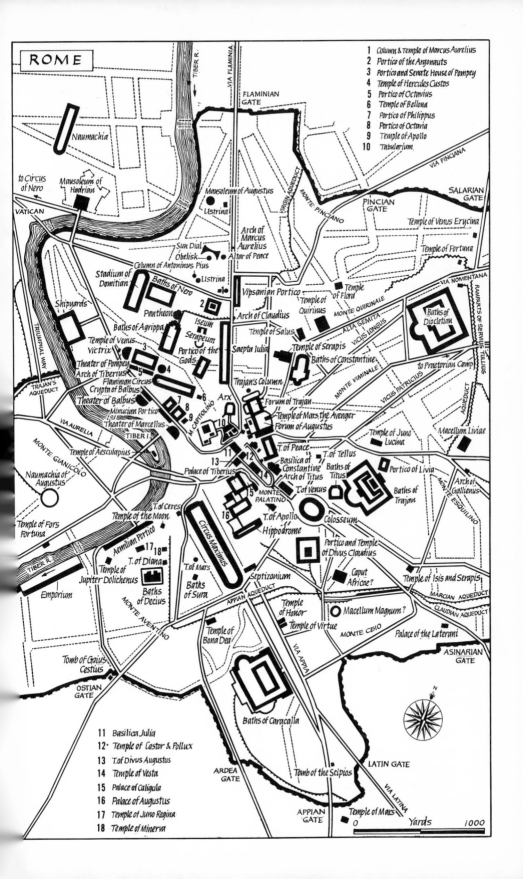

ROME

1 Column & Temple of Marcus Aurelius
2 Portico of the Argonauts
3 Portico and Senate House of Pompey
4 Temple of Hercules Custos
5 Portico of Octavius
6 Temple of Bellona
7 Portico of Philippus
8 Portico of Octavia
9 Temple of Apollo
10 Tabularium

11 Basilica Julia
12 Temple of Castor & Pollux
13 T. of Divus Augustus
14 Temple of Vesta
15 Palace of Caligula
16 Palace of Augustus
17 Temple of Juno Regina
18 Temple of Minerva

TIBER R.
VIA FLAMINIA
FLAMINIAN GATE
Naumachia
to Circus of Nero
Mausoleum of Hadrian
VATICAN
Mausoleum of Augustus
Ustrina
VIRGIN AQUEDUCT
MONTE PINCIANO
PINCIAN GATE
SALARIAN GATE
VIA PINCIANA
Temple of Venus Erycina
Arch of Marcus Aurelius
Sun Dial
Obelisk
Altar of Peace
Column of Antoninus Pius
Ustrina
Temple of Fortuna
Stadium of Domitian
Baths of Nero
Vipsanian Portico
Temple of Flora
Temple of Quirinale
VIA NOMENTANA
Shipyards
2
Arch of Claudius
Temple of Quirinus
MONTE QUIRINALE
ALTA SEMITA
Baths of Diocletian
RAMPARTS OF SERVIUS TULLIUS
Pantheon
Iseum
Baths of Agrippa
Serapeum
Temple of Salus
VICUS LONGUS
TRIUMPHAL WAY
Temple of Venus Victrix
3
Portico of the Gods
Saepta Julia
Temple of serapis
Baths of Constantine
to Praetorian Camp
Theater of Pompey
Arch of Tiberius
5
4
Trajan's Column
MONTE VIMINALE
VICUS PATRICIUS
TRAJAN'S AQUEDUCT
Flaminian Circus
Crypta of Balbus
Theater of Balbus
Arx
7 8 6
Forum of Trajan
AQUEDUCT
VIA AURELIA
Minucian Portico
Theater of Marcellus
M. CAPITOLINO
9
10
Temple of Mars the Avenger
Forum of Augustus
Temple of Juno Lucina
Macellum Liviae
TIBER I.
Temple of Aesculapius
T. of Peace
T. of Tellus
MONTE GIANICOLO
13
11
12
Basilica of Constantine
Arch of Titus
Baths of Titus
Portico of Livia
Arch of Gallienus
Naumachia of Augustus
Palace of Tiberius
14
T. of Venus
Baths of Trajan
MONTE ESQUILINO
Temple of Fors Fortuna
15
MONTE PALATINO
Colosseum
T. of Ceres
Temple of the Moon
16
T. of Apollo
Hippodrome
Circus Maximus
TIBER R.
Aemilian Portico
17 18
T. of Diana
T. of Mars
Portico and Temple of Divus Claudius
Temple of Isis and Serapis
Temple of Jupiter Dolichenus
Baths of Decius
Baths of Sura
Septizonium
Caput Africae?
MARCIAN AQUEDUCT
Emporium
MONTE AVENTINO
APPIAN AQUEDUCT
Temple of Honor
Macellum Magnum?
CLAUDIAN AQUEDUCT
Temple of Bona Dea
Temple of Virtue
MONTE CELIO
Palace of the Laterani
Tomb of Gaius Cestius
VIA APPIA
ASINARIAN GATE
OSTIAN GATE
N
ARDEA GATE
Baths of Caracalla
LATIN GATE
Tomb of the Scipios
VIA LATINA
APPIAN GATE
Temple of Mars
Yards
0   1000

The two short bridges joining the Isola Tiberina, the island in the Tiber, with the mainland—the Pons Cestius to the west and the Pons Fabricius to the east—are still in service, carrying swarms of Fiats and motor scooters during the rush hour. So are three other ancient bridges: the Pons Aelius, the Pons Mulvius, and the Pons Aurelius. These bridges can carry modern motor traffic because the Romans, not knowing the stresses in their bridges, built them much stronger than necessary to bear the loads of Roman times.

The five other bridges of Imperial Rome have all fallen. Nor are the surviving bridges in their original form. All have been repeatedly repaired; often one or more arches have been replaced. They were all built on one simple plan. Each consisted of one or more semicircular arches of stone, of a very solid, substantial design.

These bridges, however, met the same difficulty that Nabopolassar's bridge did. The thick piers seriously reduced the cross-sectional area of the river, like a dam with holes. Hence water rushed between the piers with augmented speed, and the swift flow scoured away the bottom until the undermined piers collapsed.

The bridges could be strengthened by building more massive piers, which further constricted the flow of water and increased the scour. Or the builders could use fewer and larger arches. But, since a semicircular arch is necessarily half as high as it is wide, such large arches raised the deck of the bridge above the ends, which had to be provided with stairs or steep ramps. The problem was solved by Renaissance architects, who discovered segmental and semi-elliptical arches. Such arches have a greater span between piers without a corresponding increase in height.[10]

When they expelled the Etruscan kings, the Romans set up a republic on the common Mediterranean model, with an assembly of warriors, a Senate of heads of rich families, and elected magistrates headed by two consuls. The descendants of the families that had originally settled the Seven Hills had appropriated all the land near Rome, so that later arrivals had to work as hired laborers or as tenant farmers for the landowners. Thus arose the two main classes of early Rome: the patricians and the plebians. The patricians owned the land and arrogated to themselves a monopoly of legal authority and of civil and religious offices. The plebians were everyone else, including those who for one reason or another had fallen out of the patrician class.

Soon a class struggle arose. Over several centuries, the plebians several times went on strike and marched out of town, leaving the patricians to do their own chores. In late Republican times, the differences between the two groups largely disappeared. Under the Empire, the only distinction left was that certain religious offices were confined to men of patrician *gentes* or clans. A new system of class divisions came into effect.

I might mention the distinctive Roman system of personal names. The three names of a Roman of the Republic and early Empire were his *praenomen* or personal name; his *nomen* or clan name; and his *cognomen* or family name. Hence Gaius Julius Caesar was Gaius of the Caesar family of the Julian *gens*. There were only eighteen *praenomina* to choose from, of which Marcus, Gaius, and Lucius were the commonest.

Women had no personal names, being called by the feminine form of the clan name: hence Caesar's daughter was automatically "Julia." (Historical novelists and movie-makers, often ignorant of this fact, give fictional ancient Roman women names like "Helena" or "Diana," which no Roman woman of those times ever bore.) If there were two or more daughters, the later ones were called by sobriquets like Livilla ("little Livia") or Secunda ("number two").

Another system of names was used for slaves, and freedmen added their former owners' clan names to their own. In Hadrian's time, men began to use more than three names—sometimes as many as six or seven—and with the coming of Christianity women began to receive personal names.

By the beginning of the First Punic War (−264) Roman rule included all of Italy to the south. Sicily was added in the First Punic War. Then the Empire grew until by the time of Augustus it had made the Mediterranean into a Roman lake.

These conquests were not carried out on any fixed or consistent plan. The Romans conquered their empire, as the British did theirs later, "in a fit of absent-mindedness." Along the frontiers there were always raiders from across the border and other troublemakers to give a Roman general or governor a pretext for war, and the Republic was so organized as to make such a man want war. If he won, he could celebrate a triumph, the nearest to deification that a citizen could attain.

Moreover, a Roman magistrate was expected to build public works for the free use and enjoyment of the Roman people. The grateful people, in their turn, would put up statues of their benefactor. Poets would compose panegyrics. This adulation would give the official the sense of glory, pride, and self-esteem that to a noble Roman was more than life itself. For money, the official used cash from the sale of public land, the spoils of foreign wars, or, when these sources failed, his own fortune. During the late Republic, some of the fierce foreign wars and the savage looting of the provinces by Roman officials were probably the result of their efforts to get funds, by the only ways they knew, for building the public works they felt obliged to furnish.

109. Rome: Ruins of the Palace of Domitian on the Palatine Hill.
(Courtesy of Ellen Kohler.)

Under the Empire, these motives became less compelling; for one
thing, triumphs were restricted to the Emperor. It was still, however,
thought necessary, in order to protect a peaceful Roman province, to
conquer the turbulent barbarian land across the border from it. Then the
barbarian land became Romanized and peaceful and in its turn needed
the protection of further conquests. Under the Empire, Romans evolved
the theory that the gods had given Rome a divine mission to reduce
the world to order, but this was retrospective rationalization.

As with the Assyrians, the Persians, and the Macedonians before
them, the Romans conquered a great empire less because of any peculiar
national virtues than because they had, at the time, a better army than
anybody with whom they fought. In −VI and −V, the Roman army
was much like those of the Greek city-states. It consisted of a number
of large, solid blocks of spearmen, divided into classes according to
how much the soldiers could afford in arms and armor. Those of the
richest class bore a panoply much like that of the Greek *hoplitai*.

Little by little, this army evolved into the form it attained in −I,
at the end of the Republic. Then the infantryman carried a pair of
javelins for throwing instead of a pike for thrusting. At close quarters
he fought with a 2-foot broadsword. Legions of 3,000 to 6,000 men
each were divided into maniples of 200 men (two centuries), which
could maneuver independently. The Republican legions consisted entirely of Roman citizens, armed as heavy infantry. Light infantry,
cavalry, and missile troops were always soldiers from allied or dependent

states, or from the provinces, and were called "auxiliaries." The Roman military successes were due less to the brilliance of generals than to an extremely high standard of drill and training of the legionaries.

As Roman rule expanded, Roman citizenship (of which there were several grades) was also extended to individuals, to groups, and to cities and other political units. All free Italian males became Roman citizens in −89. Recruiting of the legions spread with the expansion of Roman citizenship.

For the first two centuries of the Empire, an élite corps, the Praetorian Guard, was raised, first in Italy and then also in Romanized provinces like Spain. The men wore fancy uniforms, received two or three times the regular soldier's pay, and were stationed in or near Rome. They were supposed to be under the Emperor's absolute command, but sometimes things were the other way round. In +193, the Praetorians murdered the emperor Pertinax, who had tried to impose regular discipline upon them, and auctioned off the emperorship to the highest bidder. Soon afterwards, the grim Septimius Severus—a North African of Punic antecedents, whom the wits of Rome called "Hannibal's revenge"—abolished the corps. He substituted a guard made up of men picked from the border units, so that it became difficult for even the most martial-minded Italian youth to get into the army at all.

In +212, the emperor Caracalla, possibly thinking to collect more taxes thus, gave citizenship to all free males in the Empire. Thereafter, auxiliaries were barbarians from beyond the frontiers. Legionaries were recruited from border provinces in preference to those in the interior. This practice finally made the Empire into a kind of molluscan organism, with a hard shell surrounding a soft interior of provinces whose people had become demilitarized by long peace.

If the Roman army made the expansion of the Empire possible, the Roman policy of assimilation made this Empire more durable than its predecessors. Earlier Mediterranean city-states, believing that their gods would be affronted if outsiders were admitted to their worship, had been jealously exclusive in the matter of citizenship. But, although some Romans groused about the foreign influx:

Citizens, I can't stand a Greekized Rome. Yet what portion
Of the dregs of our town comes from Achaia only?
Into the Tiber pours the silt, the mud of Orontes,
Bringing its babble and brawl, its dissonant harps and its timbrels . . .[11]

the capital nevertheless welcomed both foreigners and their gods. The satirist Juvenal (Decimus Iunius Iuvenalis), who rails above against Greeks and Syrians, was himself a native of Aquinum, a south Italian city, which became Roman only in −298. It was a common Roman affectation to sneer at the Greeks even while imitating them. The fact that so many millions of Gauls, Spaniards, Illyrians, Greeks, Anatolians, Syrians, and North Africans were made into nominal Romans helped this vast, unwieldy organism to last as long as it did.

Towards the end of —II, Roman politicians discovered that the surest way to get elected was to promise the people anything and to count on the loot from a foreign conquest to pay for carrying out their promises. The formula that they worked out was later satirized by Juvenal as *panem et circenses,* "bread and the games."[12] The theory was that, as a conquering race, the Romans had a right to be supported on the labor of the conquered.

The "bread" began with the occasional importation, by the Republican government, of grain in times of famine and its resale to the people below cost. In —123, the reformer Gaius Gracchus pushed through a law for the regular sale of grain to citizens at half price. The law conflicted with some of Gracchus' other attempted reforms, but he needed the votes.

Once installed, the system proved politically impossible to abolish. In —58, at the instance of the demagogue P. Clodius Pulcher, the grain was made free. Every citizen residing in Rome was entitled to about 10 gallons a month of wheat grain, which under the later Empire was given out already milled and baked into bread. (The Romans were great bread-eaters; the army complained of upset stomachs when during shortages they were compelled to subsist on meat.)

We may suppose that the rich did not bother to collect their dole, but the vastly more numerous non-rich did. The recipients varied from 150,000 to 320,000, the number usually hovering around 200,000. When families are counted, this means that over half the city's population was on the dole. People with steady but modest jobs and professions found the dole a useful supplement.

In addition, Rome attracted a horde of citizens unable or unwilling to work. The dole did not provide other foods, clothing, or housing; but it furnished a basic diet, and an enterprising idler could make up the difference by begging, stealing, racketeering, borrowing, or toadying to the rich. Rome thus harbored a sizable proportion of people who without the dole either would have had to work or would not have been there at all.

Since, in the absence either of birth control or a swiftly advancing technology, a normal population always breeds up to the limits of the food supply, there is always a "starving margin."[13] In the Roman Empire, the provinces were taxed to feed the people of the capital. Thus starvation was in a sense exported from the city to the provinces, while people were drawn in the opposite direction to take advantage of this largesse.

For centuries Rome lived parasitically on taxes and tribute from the Empire, manufacturing only minor consumer goods for local consumption and exporting little if anything. Down to the fall of the Empire, no emperor dared to stop the dole for fear of an uprising. By attracting a large and dangerous non-working population, the dole insured its own perpetuation; although, with the extension of citizenship to the rest of the Empire, there was no longer any logical pretext for feeding one part of the citizenry at the expense of another. Conceivably there is a lesson here applicable to modern conditions.

As for "circuses": The rulers of the old watershed empires had staged religious processions of statues of gods, with which they doubtless hoped to pacify their subjects as well as to humor the powers above. Later, the Ptolemies and the Seleucids, with their huge parades featuring polar bears and other exotica, tried to reconcile their subjects to their rule and to divert any thoughts of revolt by staging shows for them. Roman politicians of the Republic and later the emperors carried this policy to the point of lunacy. Ninety-three days of the year were given over to spectacles; sixty-six other days were holidays of one kind or another.

Plays were given in semicircular theaters of the Greek type, but these appealed only to a limited upper-class audience. The masses preferred races and "games." Chariot races were staged in racecourses ("circuses" in the literal sense) a quarter of a mile or more long, with a long island, the *spina*, down the middle. The Circus Maximus, begun by Julius Caesar and completed by Trajan, seated over a quarter of a million.

The favorite mass entertainment, however, was the "games." The Romans had taken from the Etruscans the bloodthirsty idea of making slaves, prisoners, and criminals fight each other to the death. Becoming popular in —II, these games comprised fights between gladiators; the killing of animals; fights between animals; and the killing of people by animals and by other ingenious tortures. For instance, a play in which the hero was burned alive at the end would be produced with a victim really burned alive. The victims were condemned malefactors, prisoners of war, and sometimes, in the case of gladiatorial combats, volunteers.

The Roman games are almost *sui generis* in the history of mankind. Racing is a universal sport; rulers have staged countless public executions; other rulers have put on fights between animals from crickets to elephants. Medieval Europe and parts of India saw public duels to settle quarrels, lawsuits, or grudges. But Roman gladiatorialism stands by itself. "Every now and then the reader of Roman history, reading it in terms of debates and measures, politics and campaigns, capital and labor, comes upon something that gives him much the same shock he would feel if he went down to an unknown caller in his house and extended his hand to meet the misshapen hairy paw of *Homo Neanderthalensis* and looked up to see a chinless, bestial face."[14]

The scale and cost of these games was fantastic. Pompeius Magnus opened his theater with a show that included the killing of 500 lions and most of 18 elephants. When Titus opened the Colosseum in +80, 5,000 beasts were killed in one day; 11,000 were slain in a series of games given by Trajan in +107. In the last centuries of the Empire, when the Western emperors were at their wits' end for tax money to hire enough soldiers to keep out the barbarians, they continued to lavish wealth on the games.

The Roman excuse for gladiatorialism was that an imperial people had to be inured to the sight of bloodshed to teach them courage and contempt for death and to toughen them for the task of keeping the lesser breeds in order. The theory did not work. In +II and +III, when sadistic mobs were howling for more blood, the Italian people were becoming completely demilitarized, until as soldiers they were worth no more than rabbits.

Not everybody enjoyed the games equally. The kindly Cicero wrote: "But what pleasure can it be to a man of refinement when either a powerless man is torn by a very powerful beast, or else a magnificent beast is spitted on a hunting-spear?"[15] As a Hellenophile,

110. Rome: the Pantheon or Temple of All Gods.

Nero, despite his own weakness for murder, deplored gladiatorialism and tried to wean the Roman public away from it. When he gave games, he ordered that nobody be killed and even made hundreds of Roman gentlemen appear in the arena to see what it felt like. He also encouraged drama, concerts, and ballets as substitutes for the gory national spectator sport. But this cultural propaganda had no effect on the Romans, who went right back to blood and guts.

The two centuries following the defeat of Hannibal saw the swiftest extension of the Roman Empire. It also saw the Roman ruling class suffer from what Toynbee calls "the intoxication of victory." Feeling that they could get away with anything, they went on a binge of self-indulgence that lasted nearly three centuries:

> This [a reputation for temperance] is a high prize indeed and difficult to gain, but it was at this time easy to pursue at Rome owing to the vicious tendencies of most of the youths. For some of them had abandoned themselves to amours with boys and others to the society of courtesans, and many to musical entertainments and banquets, and the extravagance they involve, having in the course of the war with Perseus been speedily infected by the Greek laxity in these respects. So great in fact was the incontinence that had broken out among the young men in these matters, that many paid a talent for a male favorite and many three hundred drachmas for a jar of caviar. This aroused the indignation of Cato, who said once in a public speech that it was the surest sign of deterioration in the republic when pretty boys fetch more than fields, and jars of caviar more than ploughmen. It was just at the period we are treating of that this present tendency to extravagance declared itself, first of all because they thought that now after the fall of the Macedonian kingdom their universal dominion was undisputed, and next because after the riches of Macedonia had been transported to Rome there was a great display of wealth both in public and in private.[16]

Polybios, who wrote the above, picked the Third Macedonian War (−172 to −167) as the time of the breakdown of Roman conduct. Actually, the process began with the defeat of Hannibal in −202 and spread over at least a century. Not all Romans behaved thus, if only because most of them could not afford to. But the ensuing period of wild hedonism among the gentry produced such bizarre excesses as banquets at which the guests stuffed themselves to bursting and then went out and vomited so that they could return to their couches and continue gorging.

Politicians were as successful as other Romans in shedding their old-fashioned inhibitions. As a result, the nation was convulsed by civil wars, in which rival politicians butchered their opponents by tens of thousands and piled pyramids of heads in the Forum. Nobody heeded the Roman constitution any more; an ambitious man cared less for the rules of political advancement than for control of troops by which he could impose his will.

In the —40s, the most gifted of these politician-adventurers, Julius Caesar, crushed his opponents. Less than a year after he had attained supreme power, however, he was murdered (—44) by diehard republicans. After another round of civil war, Caesar's great-nephew succeeded to the murdered dictator's power. Originally named Gaius Octavius, this youth changed his name, as customary, to Gaius Julius Caesar Octavianus when his great-uncle adopted him.

In —27, having in turn liquidated his enemies, Octavianus took the name or title of Augustus, together with a number of Republican offices. Although in theory the Republican constitution remained in force, in fact the Republic had ended and the Empire had begun. The title of the early emperors was Princeps or "first citizen," so that the early Empire is properly called the Principate.

Augustus was a cold, crafty little man of enormous intelligence and ability, who in youth was as brutal and merciless as his opponents but who later learned to play to perfection the kindly rôle of father of his country. His forty-year reign was a time of peace and prosperity. He was succeeded by the gloomy and thrifty Tiberius, the mad Caligula, the timid and scholarly Claudius, and the gifted but eccentric Nero. Since these all belonged to the same family, they are called the Julio-Claudian emperors.

While some of the Julio-Claudians seem to have been pretty appalling characters, our main sources for the period are Suetonius and Tacitus, who, writing under Trajan, abominated the Julio-Claudian emperors. Their sympathies lay with the Senate, with which these *principes* were often in conflict; so they tended to magnify the emperors' faults and attenuate their virtues. The Julio-Claudians may not fully deserve the judgment: "An arch-dissembler was succeeded by a madman, and a fool by a monster"[17]; but, lacking evidence, we cannot tell how much better they were than their fearsome literary portraits.

When a general uprising drove Nero to suicide in +68, three would-be emperors quickly followed but came to violent ends. Then came the competent Vespasianus and his equally able son Titus. The latter's brother, Domitianus, who succeeded him, tried to run the Empire in off-with-his-head style until murdered in +96. Then the elderly Nerva reigned for two years and died, having appointed as his successor Marcus Ulpius Traianus—Trajan, as we call him. Trajan, an upper-class provincial of mixed Italian-Spanish descent, was one of the ablest principes. Under him, the Empire reached its greatest extent. Nerva, Trajan, and the three who followed (Hadrian, Antoninus Pius, and Marcus Aurelius) are sometimes called the Five Good Emperors. The period in which they reigned, +96 to +180, was the most prosperous time that Rome was ever to know; under Hadrian and Antoninus there were forty-three years of almost uninterrupted peace.

Trajan nominated as his successor his younger cousin Publius Aelius Hadrianus, who turned out to be the most brilliant of all Roman emperors. Hadrian was a writer, poet, wit, musician, artist, architect, critic, philanthropist, lawyer, diplomat, general, and sound executive. Thinking that the Empire was overextended, Hadrian gave up Trajan's conquests of Dacia (modern Rômania) and Babylonia.

By the time of Trajan and Hadrian, the Grand Orgy was nearly over. Under comparatively sober and circumspect emperors, the upper classes toned down their excesses and recovered something of their former dignity and sobriety. Of course, they did not all behave alike, either at the height of the Orgy or later. To read the satirists Martial (Marcus Valerius Martialis) and Juvenal, both of whom wrote under Trajan, one gets the impression that Romans spent all their time cadging, cheating, whining, bullying, fawning on superiors, kicking inferiors, and pursuing sexual gratification without regard to sex. These writers rail at the prevalence of homosexuality, albeit their satires hint that they were not strangers to perversions themselves.

On the other hand, the letters of their contemporary, the senator Gaius Plinius Secundus the Younger, give an entirely different impression. Both pictures were doubtless true according to which Romans one observed. Plinius (or Pliny, a nephew of the encyclopedist of the same name) was a genial, generous, kindly Roman gentleman of the best sort, a conscientious public official, and devoted to his third wife, the other two having died. He writes her: "You cannot believe how much I miss you. I love you so much, and we are not used to separations. So I lie awake most of the night thinking of you . . ."[18] When his literary friend Martial got fed up with Rome, Plinius gave him the money to take him back to his native Spain. He was a close friend of the historian Tacitus, whose writings he modestly admitted were profounder than his own.

The Romans varied as other folk do. At the height of the Grand Orgy, some families lived decorous, self-disciplined lives; when austerity again became fashionable, some persisted in their hedonism.

In the Rome of Trajan and Hadrian, the Emperor stood far above everyone else in power and wealth. Next to him ranked the 600 Senators, wearers of the broad purple stripe on the tunic. To be a Senator, one had to own a million sestertii in taxable property. (A sestertius was worth a fraction of a dollar—how big a fraction depends on the period and the method of computing it.) Nominally they were the heads of old landowning families and were still forbidden to engage in trade. Actually they were appointed to the Senate by the Emperor and augmented their fortunes as silent partners in businesses of all sorts. In theory the Senate still had much power; it governed about half the provinces and supposedly elected the Emperor. In practice, it had very little independence, since the Princeps commanded the army and the Senate had no armed force of its own.

After the Senate came the much larger order of knights. It had long been a practice in Mediterranean city-states to organize the cavalry of the polis from those citizens rich enough to own a horse and to call this class "horsemen" (*hippeis* or *equites*). The reformer Gracchus had established a similar class, entitled to wear a narrow purple stripe on their tunics; but now the equites were simply the business class. To be an *eques*, one needed 400,000 sestertii, whether one could ride a horse or not. Some equites had enough wealth to qualify for the Senate but preferred to remain knights in order to pursue their business careers.

The Senators and the knights—the noble Romans—were a mixture of the old patrician and plebian clans. Below them was the new class of *plebes*—the *humiliores* or ignoble Romans. In addition, there were provincials of limited citizenship; non-citizens or "aliens" not yet franked into the Roman system; freedmen or ex-slaves; and finally slaves. During the main period of Roman conquest, —II to +I, slavery reached vast proportions. In Italy, the number of slaves neared or perhaps exceeded that of free men. A rich household often included hundreds and sometimes even thousands of slaves. A proposal in the Senate to make the slaves wear distinctive dress was hastily squelched when somebody pointed out: "It would be dangerous to show the wretches how numerous they really were."[19]

Slavery in Rome, as elsewhere, varied according to the work to which the slave was put and the disposition of his master. It ranged from tolerable domestic service with a kindly master to an approximation of slave labor camps like that of Vorkuta of recent memory. Some slaves headed large businesses or governmental departments and had troops of slaves of their own. Littérateurs like Plinius the Younger and Lucius Annaeus Seneca, Nero's tutor and official, urged their readers to treat slaves kindly, but practically nobody questioned the institution itself.

If Roman slavery was often of the most brutal sort, on the other hand manumission was common, easy, and socially approved. Hence the multitude of freedmen in Rome of the Principate. A slave freed by a citizen master automatically became a citizen. This Rome was not at all

111. Rome: Tepidarium of the Baths of Caracalla, built in early +III.
(Drawing by Roy G. Krenkel.)

an egalitarian society; but, ironically, it was a lot more open than most
societies before or since. With intelligence, diligence, or luck, the freed-
man's son might become a knight and his son a Senator.

Romans of old upper-class families grumbled about vulgar parvenus
whose grandparents had been Syrian slaves. On the other hand, the

112. Bridge of Fabricius (−I) over the Tiber. (Courtesy of Ellen Kohler.)

social mobility that the Principate offered to able men was a factor that kept the Empire going even under eccentric or foolish emperors. We might say that the Egyptians invented the equality of women; the Persians, federal government; the Greeks, democracy; the Romans, the open society; and the Chinese, the civil service. We try to combine them all, not always with complete success.

A Roman citizen rose before dawn. Having slept in his loincloth or his tunic, he had little dressing to do. If his schedule called for strenuous activity, he donned one or more tunics. If it entailed any sort of formality, he put on his toga, which was forbidden to non-citizens but expected of citizens on any occasion of ceremony.

The toga was a huge, semicircular woolen cloak, draped over the left shoulder, under the right armpit, and over the left shoulder again; it might also have a flap to be drawn over the right shoulder in cold weather. Since this impractical garment was not supposed to be pinned or otherwise fastened in place, it imposed upon the wearer a slow, stately gait, because any sudden movement would dislodge it. If the citizen could afford it, he had several togas, in natural wool for every-day, dark for funerals, and whitened with chalk for formality.

His breakfast was a mere snack, probably a piece of bread dunked in wine. If it was a working day and he was a poor man, he hustled off to his job. If he was of the knightly or senatorial classes, the next act was to receive a crowd of shabby-genteel hangers-on, the clients whose patron he was. They filed in, were announced by the usher, exchanged greetings and kisses with the nobleman, and received a gift of money. (It had been food in earlier times.) If the patron meant to tour the fora and wanted a retinue to enhance his dignity, he might draft his clients for this purpose. If they were lucky, he would merely dismiss them with their handouts.

If the patron was a Senator in favor with the current Caesar, and the Emperor was in the Palatine, the Senator would leave his clients to the ministrations of his servants while he went forth to play client to the Emperor. Under Hadrian this did not often happen, for Hadrian was a compulsive traveler. Most of the time he was either roaming the marches of the Empire or was at his fantastic villa at Tibur (modern Tivoli), where he had built replicas of some of the most interesting monuments and sites that he had seen abroad.

Setting about a business day, a Roman knight—let us call him Quintus Cornelius Merenda—would have himself borne in his litter to the fora, getting down to greet persons of higher rank. The streets would be already crowded; as Juvenal complained:

Traffic gets in our way, in front, around and behind us.
Somebody gives me a shove with an elbow, or two-by-four scantling.
One clunks my head with a beam, another cracks down with a beer keg.
Mud is thick on my shins, I am trampled by somebody's feet.
Now what?—A soldier grinds his hobnails into my toes.[20]

In the Old Forum, our Cornelius Merenda—after greeting acquaintances who exchange kisses on the cheek with him—pushes his way to the row of bulletin boards. On these are posted the *Acta Diurna* or "daily doings." This is the government's daily report, which includes local scandal as well as weightier matters. Private notices are also put up. Slaves scribble copies of the *Acta* to take back to their masters or to publishers who make up further copies for subscribers. This is the nearest thing to a newspaper that the world would know until an enterprising German started one in 1609.

The day's business might be litigation, for which upper-class Romans had developed a passion. In that case, Merenda would repair to one of the basilicae. If he were acting as attorney, he might bring some of his clients as a claque. Law was a lucrative profession; although there were rules against demanding fees for advocacy, these were easily evaded.

The speeches were as long as Fidel Castro's. Plinius the Younger smugly tells how in a case he prosecuted: "My speech lasted for nearly five hours, for I was allowed four water-clocks in addition to my original twelve of full size."[21] Not everybody admired such loquacity. The acidulous Martial poetized:

You ask for seven water clocks
As time in which to plead.
The judge is none too pleased with this,
But sourly says, "Agreed!"
So you go on, and on, and on,
And heated by your task,
You pause for one long, lukewarm swig
Of water from your flask.
Cecil, for God's sake, kill two birds
With just one stone, or rock,
And end your thirst and speech alike—
Drink from the water clock![22]

Notwithstanding, Roman court procedure was much more rational than anything that had gone before. It is no accident that legal maxims— *impossibilium nulla obligatio est*, "the impossible is never required"; *de minimis non curat lex*, "the law takes no account of trifles"; *nemo dat quod non habet*, "no one can give what he does not have"; and so forth—are still quoted in their original Latin.

After a morning spent on his business, Merenda would eat a light lunch and like all the rest of Rome (then as now) go to sleep for an hour or two. If business were pressing, he would work some more; if not, he would head for the baths. He might go to one of the small private establishments or to one of the palatial public baths built by Agrippa, Nero, and other benefactors. Seneca, who once took lodgings over a bath, complained of the racket: the whack of the masseur's hand, the grunts of the gymnast as he swung his dumbbells, the splashing of the swimmer, the roars of the man who sang as he bathed, the yelps of the man having his armpits depilated, and the cries of sellers of sausage, cakes, and other goodies.

In the palatial public baths, around a central hall were ranged chambers for steam baths, hot baths, tepid baths, and cold baths; also exercise rooms, game courts, gardens, and even libraries. Under the Principate, men and women, not yet having succumbed to the Judaeo-Christian nudity tabu, bathed together save when some bluenose like Trajan or Marcus Aurelius forbade it.

After the bath, Merenda would head for dinner, served around 4 or 5 P.M. All day he had been fending off hints by acquaintances and clients that they would like to be invited. Even if he meant to entertain that evening, he had to keep count of his invitees, because the dining room of most Roman mansions accommodated exactly nine diners. Three large couches were set in a *U*-shape, and each held three diners sprawled diagonally along it. It is claimed that one can, with practice, eat comfortably in that position. The Emperor had an oversized dining room with three trios of such couches, so that his parties numbered twenty-seven.

Most such dinners were no orgies but much like those among business-class persons of our own day. Most of the talk was on business, children, servants, houses, aches and pains, and gossip about absent acquaintances. Unlike the Greeks, the Romans took their wives to dinner; the position of women under the Empire was relatively good.

When it came time to go, the guest would sway homeward in his litter, surrounded by slaves with lanterns and clubs. The ignoble Roman who had to go out at night, however, did not find the going so safe. Without street lighting he was liable at least to get lost or fall in a hole. Although, thanks to the police-and-fire brigade of 7,000 vigiles instituted by Augustus, Rome was safer than most ancient cities, Juvenal still complains of the hell-raising drunk spoiling for a fight, the knife-wielding robber from the Pomptine Marshes, and people who throw things out of windows.

Under Marcus Aurelius came the first trickle of those barbarian invasions that were to submerge the Western half of the Roman Empire. German tribesmen tried to cross the Danube to raid the Balkan provinces of the Empire. Marcus beat them back but died of the plague. Although deemed one of the best emperors, Marcus ended his career with the egregious folly of choosing as his successor his worthless son Commodus, who proved another Caligula.

The Empire had no rigid rule of succession. In theory the Senate picked the best-qualified man, but in practice the legions acclaimed somebody and the Senate went along. When they could, emperors tried to foreclose the legions' choice in advance, either by choosing one of their own sons or by adopting some promising young friend or kinsmen. A rigid succession may be stabler but puts more fools on the throne; a looser system, like the Roman, chooses fewer half-wits but fosters civil war among rival claimants.

After Commodus, everything went downhill. The barbarians became stronger and their invasions more frequent. Most emperors either were murdered or perished in civil wars. In the latter half of +III there were twenty-seven emperors and at least twice as many would-be usurpers.

Meanwhile, other changes took place. Slavery declined, because Roman armies were no longer overrunning foreign lands. Laws protecting slaves were tightened. On the other hand, net freedom did not increase, because the lot of the peasant worsened; his condition came nearer and nearer to medieval serfdom. Class distinctions increased and class barriers, which had been easily pierced under the Principate, hardened. The Emperor, who under the Principate had dressed and behaved much like other rich Romans, was surrounded by more and more pomp and ceremony.

In the +280s, the common Dalmatian soldier Diocletian (Gaius Aurelius Valerius Diocletianus) fought his way to the throne. The civil wars of the previous half-century had made a shambles of the Empire. Despite the strictness of Roman military discipline, soldiers of the Empire were a disorderly lot, much given to mutiny and to killing emperors who did not please them. In times of civil war they got out of hand and marched through the countryside, robbing, burning, and massacring like the barbarians against whom they were supposed to protect the people, while the generals and emperors who commanded them did not dare to try to stop their ravages for fear of being murdered.

Diocletian undertook drastic reforms. He divided the Empire in half, with an emperor called an "Augustus" and a vice-emperor called a "Caesar" in each half. (Septimius Severus' sons Caracalla and Geta had discussed a similar proposal, but Caracalla found it more expedient to murder his brother and take all.) Each Augustus was supposed to retire after twenty years, as Diocletian and his colleague actually did. But subsequent emperors ignored this limitation, much as the presidents of backward nations today are always forcing constitutional changes to permit them to succeed themselves forever.

Diocletian also restored discipline to the army. He reformed the coinage. He adopted the trappings of Persian royalty, with a stupefying parade of ceremonial formality, elaborate costumes, and prostrations. To stop inflation, he fixed prices and wages and bound every man (with few exceptions) to his fathers' trade. His reforms stabilized things enough to enable the Western half of the Empire to stagger along for nearly two centuries more.

113. Wall of Aurelianus (+III) on the south side of Rome. (Courtesy of Lionel Casson.)

Since the laws of economics had not yet been discovered, however, Diocletian could not understand that much of his restrictive economic legislation, however justified it seemed in an emergency, in the long run only made matters worse. He and his successors succeeded in combining the faults of socialism and of capitalism without the virtues of either.

In particular, the laws confining people to their ancestral occupations gave the Empire a system of universal serfdom like India's caste system. These laws probably affected the masses less than they would today because, in pre-industrial nations, most sons follow their fathers' calling anyway. Nevertheless, the ever-stricter ordinances of Diocletian's successors show that many wanted to quit their occupations because, under the Diocletianic system, they could no longer make a living at them. No ancient Roman could have imagined that the social mobility of the early Empire, which Diocletian suppressed, was one of the very factors that had made the Empire as successful as it had been.

Moreover, a caste system stops technological progress, as is shown by the long technical stagnation of ancient Egypt and of more recent India. What baker's son will fool around with an idea for a bicycle when he is doomed to make bread all his life? And when all occupations are hereditary, how could anyone even imagine a trade, like that of a maker of bicycles, if it did not already exist? The Romans, even if they had shown little interest in pure science, had been able and creative engineers; but now even their technology froze.

While Rome was standing still in science and engineering, the barbarians were not. They were learning the Roman arts of peace and war, the former by trading contacts and the latter by mercenary service in the armies of Rome, which became almost entirely barbarian. The arts of peace enabled their lands to support denser populations, while the arts of war made them as formidable, man for man, as the Romans. The tremendously long land frontiers of the Empire had posed no great danger when those beyond them had been only a thinly-spread population of primitives. But, when the barbarians waxed in numbers, knowledge, and power, these long frontiers became indefensible.

The two centuries following Diocletian are a long and dismal tale of ever-increasing barbarian invasions. The Christianization of the Empire, even if it raised moral standards (whch cannot now be proved one way or the other), helped not at all against the invaders. If anything, it contributed to the decline by fostering the growth of a large, parasitic clerical class. Talk about Roman "decadence" is meaningless. When the Romans were at their most "decadent"—that is, when they behaved in ways that we should most severely disapprove—they conquered the Mediterranean world. When their conduct improved, the barbarians overcame them.

At first these incursions were mere raids, destructive but not fatal.

In +406, however, the Vandals, the Suevi, and the Alani burst into Gaul and headed for Spain when the emperors of East and West were too busy fighting each other to defend the frontiers. A few years later the Franks, the Burgundians, and others came in, settled, and refused to leave. Although at first willing to acknowledge the Emperor's rule, they proved too many to absorb and too strong to oust; so it was only a matter of time before they took over the rule of the lands they occupied.

Rome was sacked by Alaric's Goths in +410, by Gaiseric's Vandals in +455, and anything worth stealing but overlooked by them was taken care of by Ricimer's barbarian "Roman" army in +472. In +476 Odovacar, one of the Empire's German generals, booted the boy-emperor Romulus Augustulus off his throne and declared himself king of Italy. A half-century later, the emperor Justinian's generals recovered Italy for the Empire by overthrowing the Gothic kingdom that briefly flourished there. But then the Lombards wrested most of the peninsula from Byzantium's grip, although the Eastern Empire kept enclaves in Italy for several centuries.

During the dark centuries that followed, the city of Rome declined to a mere town, ruled by a murderous group of "nobles" who were merely successful gangsters. The aqueducts were fitfully repaired for a while, but all of them finally failed in +X. The shrunken city could not support so elaborate a water system.

The rebuilding and beautifying of Rome began with the popes of the Renaissance. Nicholas V started restoration of the Aqua Virgo in 1453, and others followed, either repairing the old aqueducts or building new ones. They often tore down old structures for their masonry. The headstrong and energetic Sixtus V was especially ruthless. Deeming himself—like Egypt's Mehmet 'Ali—a modernist, he was not sentimental about monuments of antiquity and demolished for its stone the Septizonium, an ornamental façade Septimius Severus had built on the Palatine in +203.

Now, with over 1,700,000 people, Rome is probably larger than it ever was under the Empire. Subway construction is difficult because tunneling at once exposes remains of ancient buildings and art works, to which the archaeologists must be given access before they can be moved. But today the Corso Umberto Primo follows the route of the old Via Flaminia, which goes back to −200. And you can drive over the old Appian Way, built by the censor Appius Claudius Caecus around −300, and admire the survivors of the ancient mausolea that once lined it solidly for miles. The Italians have laid down a layer of asphalt over the Roman flagstones, but there are gaps in the asphalt where you can go bumping over the selfsame stones that once rang to the tread of the legions and the triumphs of the Caesars.

XIV

PÂTALIPUTRA AND THE MILLION GODS

THE DOORS WERE CEDAR
AND THE PANELS STRIPS OF GOLD
AND THE GIRLS WERE GOLDEN GIRLS
AND THE PANELS READ AND THE GIRLS CHANTED:
 WE ARE THE GREATEST CITY,
 THE GREATEST NATION:
 NOTHING LIKE US EVER WAS.
THE DOORS ARE TWISTED ON BROKEN HINGES.
SHEETS OF RAIN SWISH THROUGH ON THE WIND
 WHERE THE GOLDEN GIRLS RAN AND THE PANELS READ:
 WE ARE THE GREATEST CITY . . .[1]

Sandburg

114. Street scene in modern Patnâ.

WHEN Alexander's empire split up, the easternmost part fell to his general Seleukos. For a while, Seleukos was kept too busy by wars among the Successors to pay much heed to his Indian lands. During that time, the rajas whom Alexander had conquered reasserted their independence.

About —305, Seleukos led an army over the Khyber Pass to see how his Indian possessions were faring. He found that all of northern India had fallen under the sway of the low-born adventurer Chandragupta Maurya[2] (the Sandrokottos or Sandrokyptos of the Greeks). Seleukos found himself confronted by an emperor who mustered a huge army including 9,000 elephants. It is not known if they fought; probably Seleukos thought better of the idea. Presently, Seleukos was back in Iran with 500 of Chandragupta's elephants, given him in return for relinquishing his Indian claims and giving his daughter to Chandragupta in marriage. The elephants helped to destroy Seleukos' strongest rival, Antigonos One-eye, at Ipsos in —301.

Before this battle, about —302, Seleukos ordered an official named Megasthenes to go to Chandragupta's capital of Pâṭaliputra (Greek Pali[m]bothra; modern Patnâ, in Bihar State).[3] Megasthenes came down the Khyber Pass, crossed the Five Rivers that give the Panjâb its name, traversed the fertile corridor that joins the Indus and Ganges watersheds, and proceeded down the Ganges (Sanskrit gangâ, "goer").

The Greek found the lower Ganges country an immense flat brown plain, looking much as it does today. The modern air traveler sees the plain beneath him, dotted with hundreds of tiny mud-hut villages. These are joined by a web of crooked dirt roads, all of the same sad brown color. To the north, the colossal white rampart of the Himalayas rises over the murky haze above the flatlands. From the ground, the mountains are no longer seen. Here and there a tree or a grove breaks the plain, but there are few trees outside the larger towns. In Megasthenes' day there were probably many more trees; since the population did not then press so desperately hard upon the land's resources, there was more wild or waste land. In his time, villages had walls.

Megasthenes found the self-made emperor reigning in a fine palace with vast hypostyle halls in the Persian manner, but all of wood, lavishly gilded and painted. Wooden pillars upheld the roofs, and round these pillars twined golden vines whereon perched silver birds.

Eventually, Megasthenes returned to the West and wrote a book.

Although this book has perished, it is cited by many other classical writers. They say:

> The largest city in India, named Palimbothra, is in the land of the Prasians, where is the confluence of the river Erannoboas and the Ganges, which is the greatest of rivers . . . Megathenes says that on one side where it is longest this city extends ten miles in length, and that its breadth is one and three-quarters miles; that the city has been surrounded with a ditch in breadth 600 feet and in depth 45 feet; and that its wall has 570 towers and 64 gates.[4]

> It is said that Palibothra lies at the confluence of the Ganges and the other river, a city eighty stadia in length and fifteen in breadth, in the shape of a parallelogram, and surrounded by a wooden wall that is perforated so that arrows can be shot through the holes; and that in front of the wall lies a trench used both for defense and as a receptacle of the sewage that flows from the city; and that the tribe of people amongst whom the city is situated is called the Prasii and is far superior to the rest . . .[5]

Others give smaller excerpts. In Pâṭaliputra, the royal palace was surrounded by a walled park with ornamental lakes. Outside the park, the streets are said to have been laid out in orderly fashion, with "bazaars, theatres, and gambling-places; these and the race-tracks, inns, and meeting-places for guilds and sects, were crowded with people and animals. Houses were of two or three stories and, as they were constructed of wood, an elaborate system of fire precautions was enforced."[6]

To the best of my knowledge, the Indians were the first to adopt a rule of the road: they kept to the left, as they and the British do today. Then as now, beggars swarmed. Beggars doubtless did to their children what they still do: mutilate them, as by cutting off the fingers of one hand or breaking an ankle joint, so that the little cripples can beg more effectively when they grow up.

In the days of Alexander, India—such of it as was known—was divided into a multitude of states. (We have no information on the extreme south.) The prevailing forms of government were monarchy and the oligarchic tribal republic, in which most of the power resided in a senate of big landowners. The larger states were all monarchies. Largest was the kingdom of Magadha in the lower Ganges Valley, including Pâṭaliputra.

Then as now, men feared cruel and oppressive rulers; but even more they feared a time of anarchy. They called it "the way of the fishes," when the strong devoured the weak without hindrance. Their poets chanted:

Where the land is kingless the rich are unprotected,
And shepherds and peasants sleep with bolted doors.

A river without water, a forest without grass,
A herd of cattle without a herdsman, is the land without a king.[7]

The king claimed to own all the property in the kingdom and merely to lend the individual farms to their cultivators, but this was sometimes disputed. Although regarded as quasi-divine, the king ostensibly did not make new laws but merely issued injunctions to assure the enforcement of the unchanging body of existing traditional law. While in theory the king was absolute and his council of ministers and assemblies of the people were merely advisory, in practice a king who made himself too obnoxious might be deposed by the unanimous voice of the council or the people.

Even kings no worse than the general run of men did not often live to old age and die natural deaths. If they did not fall in battle, they were often murdered by usurping kinsmen, generals, or other rivals. Many kings ended their reigns by abdication or by committing ritual suicide.

If a king survived all other hazards, his life was still no bed of houris. He had to have all his food tasted by someone else to guard against poison. Some kings slept in a different bed each night to foil the knives of assassins. Although the king commanded the best that the kingdom had to offer in comforts and luxuries, he was, like most ancient monarchs, a religious functionary. Much of his time was spent in rituals to make the rain fall, the crops grow, and the gods sustain the people. The *Arthashâstra*[8] ("success manual"), an ancient handbook on how to be a king, filled the monarch's day with so packed a schedule of rites and duties as to leave the poor man only four and a half hours out of every twenty-four for sleeping. Needless to say, real kings did not observe so taxing a routine. Instead, they delegated the more tedious of their duties to priests and officials.

In Alexander's time, a dynasty called the Nandas ruled Magadha. Chandragupta Maurya overthrew the Nandas, made Magadha part of his empire, and chose Pâtaliputra, the Magadha capital, as his own. He had the help of an able, unscrupulous brâhman adviser. This adviser is called by several names, the best-known being Kautilya.[9] This is also the name given the author of the *Arthashâstra*, which therefore purports to set forth the principles on which Chandragupta Maurya ran his empire. There are difficulties to this simple view, but a moderate modern interpretation is that the work was originally written in Maurya times —just possibly by Kauṭilya himself—and that later hands inserted interpolations. This uncertainty about date and authorship is typical of Indian literature, since ancient Indian writers seldom bothered to mention dates or to identify their sources.

The *Arthashâstra* depicts the despotic rule of the king by means of a highly-organized, centralized, efficient police state, with a complex bureaucracy including a horde of spies and assassins. Kauṭilya, the Indian Machiavelli, makes no pretensions to altruism. Of his advice, he says: "The chief end is material advantage, for the other aims of life, both religion and pleasure, depend upon it." To solve the problem of the urban proletariat, he urges the king to round up surplus members of the low shûdra caste and resettle them on wastelands, where they should be allowed no distracting amusements whatever: "Actors, dancers, singers, musicians, raconteurs, bards are not to disturb the work. From the helplessness of the villages there come the concentration of men upon their fields, hence increase in taxes, labor supply, wealth, and grain."[10] At that, Kauṭilya was more scrupulous than some of his predecessors, whose books had advised princes and ministers on the best ways to murder the king and usurp the throne.

Along with his other benevolent policies of building hospitals and encouraging vegetarianism, Chandragupta Maurya's grandson, the pious Ashoka, relaxed the rigors of Maurya rule. Ashoka also lightened the ferocious penalties of the earlier legal codes. For example, the *Laws of Manu*, compiled by a fanatical brâhman, ordained that a shûdra who "arrogantly teaches brâhmans their duty" should be slain by pouring boiling oil into his mouth and ears. Other favorite Indian methods of execution were impalement and trampling by elephants.

To understand the Indian culture, one must grasp the fact that some of the ideals professed and to some degree practiced in twentieth-century America are just the opposite of the ideals of ancient India. Among the American assumptions is the concept that men are "equal." When it is objected that men in fact differ in character and ability, "equality" is interpreted to mean that they should be deemed equal before the law, receive the same pay for the same work, the same punishments for the same crimes, and so on. Another is the idea that a man should be allowed to rise as far in the social scale as his efforts and abilities permit.

The Indians believed just the contrary. They believed in fixed inequality, with a place for everybody and everybody in his place. They thought that the gods had organized mankind into a multitude of mutually

115. Remains of Ashoka's hypostyle hall of audience at Patnâ.

exclusive groups and assigned to each its duty. Nobody had to wonder about his career, because he was born into it. The dúty of the king was to protect his people from foreign foes and domestic disturbance; the duty of the *chandâla* or untouchable was to empty latrines, bury corpses, and perform other disagreeable tasks. To seek to change one's class was utterly wicked.

When everybody did his duty, said the brâhmans, then we should all be healthy, wealthy, and wise. Similar theories of rigid inequalitarianism are known from other times and places—for instance, in the Roman Empire after Diocletian—but nobody carried out the theory with such rigor as the Indians.

The original, divinely ordained groups of mankind were four: the brâhmans[11] or priests, the kshatriyas[12] or warriors, the vaishyas[13] or herdsmen, and the shûdras[14] or servants. Each class was called a *varna*, "color." Then there were the chandâlas,[15] the outcasts or pariahs or untouchables (they have borne many names) outside the system altogether. The *Laws of Manu* laid down that brâhmans and kshatriyas might oppress the vaishyas and kill the shûdras at will, without sin. As for the untouchables, they were treated in a manner that makes most forms of slavery look kindly and wholesome. Sometimes, like medieval lepers, they had to sound a wooden clapper on entering a town to warn upper-caste persons of their approach, since their mere proximity would pollute those they encountered.

The usual explanation for these distinctions is that the brâhmans, the kshatriyas, and the vaishyas were descendants of the conquering Âryas; the shûdras were descendants of the Dravidians they conquered; the chandâlas were derived from wild primitive tribes who had never been formally conquered and enrolled in the system. The brâhmans, kshatriyas, and vaishyas were "twice born," the second birth being the rite of *upanayana*, wherein the boy was invested with a sacred thread. Shûdras and chandâlas might not perform such a ceremony or hear the sacred scriptures. Although the system was originally set up to prevent intermixture of the light-skinned Âryas with the darker but more civilized folk they conquered, boys and girls will be boys and girls. Hence, today, in any one part of India, all the people are of about the same complexion regardless of caste.

By Mauryan times, the system had become more complicated. At first the kshatriyas were at the top of the scale, but the brâhmans promoted themselves to top place on the ground of their sanctity. They also claimed immunity from any punishment more severe than fining and exile. (In +XIX, the British roused the Indian masses to a frenzy of rage and horror by hanging brâhman murderers like any others.) Since there were too many brâhmans for all to be full-time priests, they devised theological excuses for following other occupations. The vaishyas had taken to commerce and industry on a large scale, and many shûdras had become peasant farmers. Kings were originally supposed to be kshatriyas, but in time members of other varnas—even shûdras—attained to royal rank.

Despite rigid tabus against intermarriage between colors, many such unions occurred, producing anomalous offspring. The advance of technology created more and more specialized occupations. Geographical, occupational, linguistic, and cultural differences promoted the breakup of the four colors into a host of smaller occupational divisions, each called a *jâti*. The census of 1901 listed 2,378 jâtis. Foreigners use "caste," a word of Portuguese origin, indiscriminately for *varna* and *jâti*.

If you think that is all, you do not know the Indian genius for complicating life. Each jâti was subdivided into clans or *gotras*. A man was forbidden to marry outside his jâti or inside his clan. He was also forbidden to marry a woman more closely related to him than fourth or sixth cousin. These tabus made the search for a suitable mate no small task. Marriage was of several kinds, all the more respectable sorts being indissoluble.

In each place, each jâti, organized into a guild, managed its own affairs, observed its own customs, and kept aloof from all the other jâtis. A man was polluted by eating with or being served food by a man of a lower jâti. Hence ordinary social contacts across caste barriers were kept to an absolute minimum. For a king to permit "confusion of colors" —inter-caste marriage—was one of the greatest villainies he could commit.

Indian society was thus divided into a host of little watertight compartments. This system proved extraordinarily resistant to pressures from outside. If Greeks or Huns conquered the country, the brâhmans announced that the newcomers were degenerate kshatriyas, who would be assimilated to that color when they had learned decent Indian manners. If a religious reformer founded an aggressive new sect, the brâhmans said in effect: "Welcome to the club" and enrolled the new sect as one more jâti. Encapsulated in their castes, the vast majority of Indians were little influenced by the ideas of new groups, since they had no free-and-easy social contact with their members. Slavery also existed, but on a small and unimportant scale.

While India was never completely static, the caste system made the country extraordinarily conservative. The system purchased order and stability at the cost of progress and adaptability. Indian technology remained almost stationary, save when foreign invaders introduced a new technique. Indian workmanship shows the qualities to be expected when the workman is born into his trade without hope of leaving it: high technical skill and finish with an almost complete lack of progress from age to age. Indian methods of warfare changed with glacial slowness; hence Indian history is a long tale of conquest by aggressive outsiders: Persians, Greeks, Scythians, Parthians, Huns, Turks, and Britons.

Next to caste, the most striking feature of Indian civilization is its supernaturalism. This is sometimes exaggerated, especially by those who wish to acquit India of charges of backwardness on the ground that she surpasses the West in morality or spirituality. Actually, Indians have probably obeyed the injunctions of their moralists about as well as Christians have followed the communistic, pacifistic teachings of their founder.

Nonetheless, there has been a strong Indian bias towards supernaturalism: religion, theology, mysticism, and magic. The gods of the Âryas were added to those of the pre-Âryas, as the Romans combined their pantheon with that of the Greeks. The universe was filled with gods, demigods, nature spirits, demons, ghosts, and other entities. Intellectuals speculated wordily whether these spirits were all manifestations of the same divine something, and about multiple souls, cosmic cycles, and planes of existence. Witches were dreaded, and people were often

116. Temple of Deogarh, restored, showing the structure from which the Hinduist *shikhara* evolved. (From Radhakumud Mookerji: *The Gupta Empire*, Bombay: 1947.)

legally executed or illegally lynched on charges of witchcraft. One who wished to organize a gang of robbers or murderers did so on a religious basis, making rituals of their crimes and assuring them that thus could they best achieve union with the divine.

A manifestation of Indian religiosity was its bent for mysticism: that is, belief that spiritual truth can be had by direct communion with the divine, by introspection, insight, intuition, or trance states, ignoring the material world. Truth was a matter of subjective conviction, not of objective observation. Being the opposite of the scientific method, this belief may partly account for India's scientific backwardness.

Another Indian characteristic is a belief that the material world is unreal—a mere illusion. This occurs in Buddhism and Jainism as well as in the orthodox traditions. Perhaps there is a connection between disbelief in the reality of the world and certain Indian attitudes and actions that seem to an outsider irrational and senseless. These include such outré usages as cow worship, or the belief that, if the shadow of a lower-caste person falls on the dinner of a high-caste one, the food is polluted and must be thrown away. If the world is an illusion, one would not expect it to obey a rigid system of cause and effect, any more than one would expect cause and effect to obtain in a dream.

Indian thought has been pessimistic towards the material world. Doubtless the thinkers found much to be pessimistic about. With such an outlook, reincarnation was viewed as a misfortune to be avoided.

A pious Indian was expected to go through four stages of life: first, a student, diligent and chaste; then a householder, begetting sons to carry on his line; then a holy hermit living in the forest; lastly, having broken all earthly ties, a homeless wanderer. Only a small minority ever followed this program to the end. Those who became hermits and wanderers, however, told of the ineffable joy of casting off mundane responsibilities. In so highly organized, regulated, and compartmentalized a society, escape from the smothering web of rules, tabus, and obligations might be worth the sacrifice of physical comforts. The well-adjusted Indian had to be an organization man par excellence, and not everybody is suited to the rôle. Parallels with present-day attempts of some "alienated" American youth to return to the simple life suggest themselves.

In −VI and −V, a reaction against the cruelties of caste, the pretensions of the brâhmans, and the multiplication of gods, rites, and religious rules incited Siddhârtha Gautama and his younger contemporary Vardhamâna dit Mahâvîra to found the reform movements of Buddhism and Jainism respectively. Jainism (which made a virtue of nudism as a form of austerity) shared many tenets with Buddhism. Both were agnostic about the gods. They held that gods might exist but, if they did, they lived in their own heavens and had nothing to do with earthlings. Jainism generally took a more extreme line than Buddhism. Thus, where Buddhism deplored the killing of living things, a pious Jaina carried a broom wherewith to sweep from his path any insects he might tread upon. As things turned out, the million gods of India were not to be routed by even such earnest and high-minded sects as these.

Indian philosophy has also produced a few materialists like Ajita, atomists like Kanâda, and skeptics like Jayarâshi. These may be likened, respectively, to Anaxagoras, Demokritos, and Pyrrhon in Greece. But their effect remained small.

Although India early acquired systems of writing, serious thoughts were not written down for many centuries thereafter. The sacred scriptures—the Vedas and the Upanishads—were passed on orally, with mnemonic exercises to help the student to memorize them verbatim. When writing came into general use in Mauryan times, it was long confined to commerce. Westerners have been so long oriented to writing that they have no suitable word for a body of traditional compositions, handed down orally but not written, since the very word "literature" means a corpus of preserved and collected *writings*.

Like Christianity, Brahmanism preached pacifism and militarism at the same time. A king was told that his duty was to expand his realm over all of India, so as to become a *chakravartin*[16] or universal emperor. A crown prince was advised at his consecration: "after thy coronation, wander round the world for conquest, and bring under thy sway the earth with its seven continents . . ."[17] Since there could not be two chakravartins at once, the rival kings could only fight it out.

The typical Indian army was huge but weakly organized, incorrigibly old-fashioned in weapons and tactics, moving with a minimum of speed and a maximum of noise and confusion. Rajas clung with childlike faith to the war elephant, a weapon about as dangerous to the user as to his foe.

After Ashoka's death, his descendants ruled for another half-century. Then a general named Pushyamitra Shunga[18] overthrew the last Mauryan king and set up the Shunga Dynasty. The empire had been losing ground and now it largely broke up, although Shungas continued to rule Magadha from Pâṭaliputra, striving against the powerful Andhra kingdom directly south of Magadha. India returned to its normal condition of a multitude of contending states, each practicing anarchy abroad and, at home, despotism tempered by assassination and inefficiency.

Meanwhile, portentous events took place outside of India. About the middle of —III, the satrap who ruled the northeastern part of the Seleucid Empire, Diodotos, declared himself king of an independent Bactria—that is, a land comprising most of modern Afghanistan and adjacent parts of Soviet Asia. Diodotos was succeeded by his son of the same name, but the second Diodotos was overthrown by the usurper Euthydemos. Around —190, Euthydemos began to extend his rule into North India. Succeeding him, his son Demetrios advanced down the Ganges, fought King Pushyamitra of Magadha, and threatened Pâṭaliputra. For the moment, under Demetrios' successor Menandros, a great Greek empire stretched from North India into Central Asia.

But Greek factionalism and ruthless self-assertion soon brought down this structure. While Demetrios was fighting in India, his general Eukratides made himself king of Bactria. Soon, revolts and usurpations had changed Demetrios' empire into a patchwork of small states, ruled by Greeks who became more Indianized with each generation.

Then more waves of invasion broke over North India. In the first half of —I came the Shakas,[19] an eastern branch of the folk whom the Greeks called the Scythians. These were nomads speaking languages related to Persian. The best guess as to their racial affinities is that they were predominantly Alpines, like their modern kinsmen the Russians.

Hard on the heels of the Shakas came the Pahlavas. These were kin of the semi-nomadic Parthians, who, starting from the lands east of the Caspian Sea, had wrested Iran from the Seleucids and set up the powerful Parthian Empire. Each invasion left a few enclaves ruled by survivors of the previous invaders and their descendants.

In the middle of +I came the Kushânas,[20] a branch of a nomadic horde—probably of the Mongoloid race—called Yüe-chi by the Chinese. This invasion extinguished the last-known of the Indo-Greek kingdoms, which had held out around Kabul. In early +II, the Kushâna king Kanishka[21] ruled an empire even larger than that of Menandros. Like Menandros, he patronized Buddhism.

After Kanishka, the Kushâna Empire fell apart. For over a century there is practically no information, save a few faint traces like the inscription of Rudradâman, a Shaka king of Ujjain around +150. King Rudradâman took justifiable pride in the fact that he had rebuilt and enlarged an irrigation dam without resorting either to forced labor or to special taxation. He also listed his victories, his treasures, and his poems.

About +320, another chakravartin arose. This was Chandra Gupta I, whose father and grandfather had been kinglets in what is now Bihar State and who seized and enlarged the remains of the Magadha Empire. We spell his name as two words to help to tell him apart from Chandragupta Maurya, and also because he and his dynasty used "Gupta" as a hereditary surname. In Sanskrit it makes no difference, since the writing of the ancient Indians, like that of the classical Greeks, ran words together without divisions.

For a century and a half, under Chandra Gupta and his successors—Samudra Gupta, Chandra Gupta II, Kumâra Gupta, Skanda Gupta, and Pûru Gupta—North India was united. The police state was less tightly organized than under the Mauryas. Modern Indians look back to the Gupta Empire as a golden age. There is probably wishful thinking in this; but still, from what scanty information we have, the country seems to have been better off than most of the time before or since.

In Gupta times, Pâtaliputra was but one of several great Indian cities, such as Kâshî[22] (modern Banâras). Pâtaliputra was still a long, narrow town stretching for ten miles along the south bank of the Ganges and extending one to two miles inland. It still had its massive wooden wall. Wooden walls were the rule in the Ganges country, despite their vulnerability to rot and fire, because, as in Mesopotamia, good stone was rare. One exception was Râjagriha, a onetime capital of Magadha, which had a wall of cyclopean stonework. The populations of these cities are not known, but we may guess that they were on the order of a quarter to half a million.

The wall of Pâṭaliputra was pierced by several massive gates, probably armed with spikes to keep war elephants from pushing them in. A main gate had a small door to let authorized persons in after hours. Outside the easternmost gate rose a pillar of stone, topped by a statue or a sculptured wheel, meaning that the city was under the king's protection.

We have no very detailed accounts of life in Gupta Pâṭaliputra. Our main sources are the writings of the Chinese Buddhist monks Fa-hsien, Yüan Chwang, and Yi-tsing, who set out in +399, +629, and +671 respectively to visit India. Coming to copy more authentic versions of Buddhist scriptures than were to be had in China, they made journeys of fantastic length, overcame amazing hardships, and returned at last with massive hauls of manuscripts, statues, and other pious acquisitions. They wrote up their journeys, giving many valuable sidelights on the state of India. Unfortunately, they devote more attention to petty details of Buddhist monasteries and to edifying stories of Buddhist miracles than they do to the mundane affairs.

For a picture of Gupta Pâṭaliputra, our best recourse is to a Tamil poem describing Madurai, a city near the southern tip of India, a little before Gupta times. Differences of time and place are slight enough so that the description applies about as well to the Gupta capital:

> The poet enters the city by its great gate, the posts of which are carved wih images of the goddess Lakṣmî, and which is grimy with ghee [melted butter], poured in oblation upon it to bring safety and prosperity to the city it guards. It is a day of festival, and the city is gay with flags, some, presented by the king to commemorate brave deeds, flying over the homes of captains, and others waving over the shops which sell the gladdening toddy. The streets are broad rivers of people, folk of every race, buying and selling in the market-place or singing to the music of wandering minstrels.
>
> A drum beats, and a royal procession passes down the street, with elephants leading to the sound of conchs. A refractory beast breaks his chain, and tosses like a ship in an angry sea until he is again brought to order. Chariots follow, with prancing horses and fierce footmen.
>
> Meanwhile, stall-keepers ply their trade, selling sweet cakes, garlands of flowers, scented powder and betel quids. Old women go from house to house, selling nosegays and trinkets to the womenfolk. Noblemen drive through the streets in their chariots, their gold-sheathed swords flashing, wearing brightly-dyed garments and wreaths of flowers. From balconies and

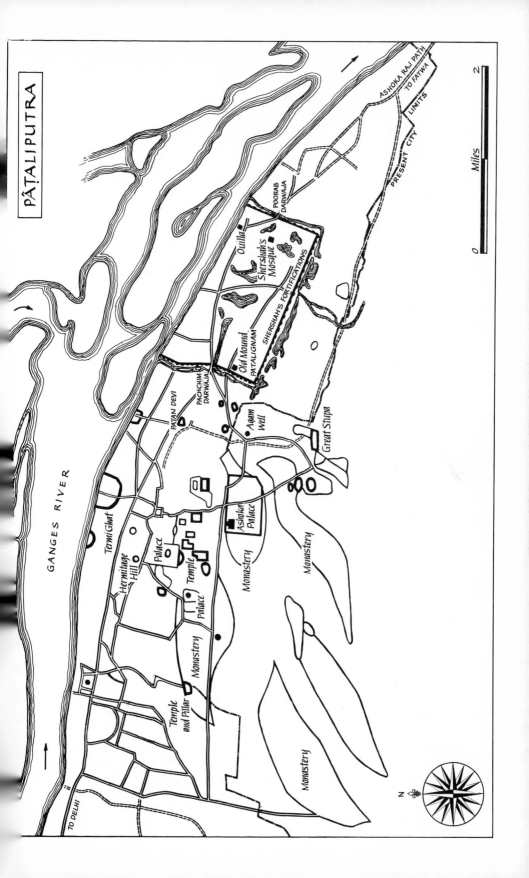

PÂTALIPUTRA

GANGES RIVER

TO DELHI

Hermitage Hill

Termi Ghat

Palace

Temple

Palace

Monastery

Temple and Pillar

Monastery

Palace

Patan Devi

Pachchim Darwaja

Agam Well

Ashoka Palace

Monastery

Monastery

Great Stupa

Monastery

Old Mound PATALIGNAM

Outila

Shershah's Mosque

Shershah's Fortifications

Poorab Darwaja

Ashoka Raj Path

TO FATWA

PRESENT CITY LIMITS

N

0   1   2
Miles

turrets the many jewels of the perfumed women who watch the festival flash in the sunlight.

The people flock to the temples to worship to the sound of music, laying their flowers before the images and honouring the holy sages. Craftsmen work in their shops—men making bangles of conch shell, goldsmiths, cloth-dealers, coppersmiths, flower-sellers, vendors of sandalwood, painters and weavers. Foodshops busily sell their wares—greens, jak-fruit, mangoes, sugar candy, cooked rice and chunks of cooked meat.

In the evening the city prostitutes entertain their patrons with dancing and singing to the sound of the lute, so that the streets are filled with music. Drunken villagers, up for the festival, reel in the roadways, while respectable women make evening visits to the temples with their children and friends, carrying lighted lamps as offerings. They dance in the temple courts, which are clamorous with their singing and chatter.

At last the city sleeps—all but the goblins and ghosts who haunt the dark, and the bold housebreakers, armed with rope ladders, swords and chisels, to break through the walls of mud houses. But the watchmen are also vigilant, and the city passes the night in peace.

Morning comes with the sound of brâhmans intoning their sacred verses. The wandering bards renew their singing, the shopkeepers busy themselves opening their booths. The toddy-sellers again ply their trade for thirsty morning travellers. The drunkards reel to their feet and once more shout in the streets. All over the city is heard the sound of opening doors. Women sweep the faded flowers of the festival from their courtyards. Thus the busy everyday life of the city is resumed.[23]

Inside the wall of Pâṭaliputra, the center of the city was the royal palace, with its parks and walls. Ashoka had introduced building in stone to India and erected a big hypostyle audience hall, modeled on those of the Persian kings at Persepolis. The root was upheld by 100 stone pillars, of which the stumps have been uncovered by modern excavations. Fa-hsien wrote: "The king's palace, with its various halls, all built by spirits who piled up stones, constructed walls and gates, carved designs, engraved and inlaid, after no human fashion, is still in existence."[24]

This does not clearly state whether the palace was still in use in Fa-hsien's time. An idea of the furnishings can be had from the *Kâmasûtra* ("sex manual")[25] of Vâtsyâyana, who *may* have written under the Guptas. When an inmate of the palace shows a visitor around, says Vâtsyâyana,

. . . she should show her the bower of the coral creeper, the
garden house with its floor inlaid with precious stones, the
bower of grapes, the building on the water, the secret passages
in the walls of the palace, the pictures, the sporting animals,
the machines, the birds, and the cages of the lions and tigers.[26]

The houses of ordinary folk continued to be of composite wood-
and-brick construction. Building was a complicated matter. One hired
a brâhman to choose the site. This he did by testing the earth to see
which caste ought to live there and examining the plants on the lot to
see if they would radiate auspicious soul-force on the new dwellers.
An astrologer was retained to calculate the lucky day to begin construction, and the brâhman performed the rituals necessary to a pious
ground-breaking.

Such houses varied from the meanest mud hut to the mansion of
a nobleman or a prosperous bourgeois. Vâtsyâyana tells the sort of house
a man of means should have:

This abode should be situated near some water, and divided
into different compartments for different purposes. It should be
surrounded by a garden, and also contain two rooms, an outer
and an inner one. The inner room should be occupied by the
females, while the outer room, balmy with rich perfumes,
should contain a bed, soft, agreeable to the sight, covered with
a clean white cloth, low in the middle part, having garlands and
bunches of flowers upon it, and canopy above it, and two pil-
lows, one at the top, another at the bottom. There should be also
a sort of couch besides, and at the head of this a sort of stool,
on which should be placed the fragrant ointments for the
night, as flowers, pots containing collyrium and other fragrant
substances, things used for perfuming the mouth, and the
bark of the common citron tree. Near the couch, on the ground,
there should be a pot for spitting, a box containing ornaments,
and also a lute hanging from a peg made of the tooth of an
elephant, a board for drawing, a pot containing perfume, some
books, and some garlands of the yellow amaranth flowers. Not
far from the couch, and on the ground there should be a round
seat, a toy cart, and a board for playing with dice; outside the
outer room there should be cages for birds, and a separate place
for spinning, carving and such like diversions. In the garden
there should be a whirling swing and a common swing, as also a
bower of creepers covered with flowers, in which a raised
parterre should be made for sitting.[27]

Such a house was usually whitewashed. The people who lived in it
comprised a joint family—that is, not only a man, his wife, and their

117. The Iron Pillar of
Meharaulî, with the
Qutub Minar behind it.

minor children, but also his grown sons and their wives and children;
his brothers and their families; otherwise unattached aunts, uncles, cous-
ins, nieces, and nephews; extra wives of any of the men; a host of
servants; perhaps a few student boarders; and so on until the house
might easily harbor fifty persons. When the crowd became too large,
the household would break up. Custom decreed that lone kinsmen must
be kept even if they were loafers or ne'er-do-wells who contributed
nought to the familial income.

Like the peoples of the ancient Mediterranean, the Indians of Gupta
times dressed mainly in pieces of cloth draped and pinned about the
person without tailoring. One such piece, worn around the waist, varied
in size from a mere loincloth to an ankle-length skirt, which in men
might or might not be tucked up between the legs like a modern
dhotî. The Shaka invasions had made trousers fashionable in the northwest. Another piece, worn above, formed a shawl; a large, thicker
piece might be added as a cloak in cool weather.

On their heads, men wore turbans; women, veils or tiaralike headdresses. Men shaved their faces but sometimes wore mustaches; they let
their beards grow for mourning or upon taking up an eremitic life.
Brâhmans shaved their heads except for a scalp lock. Most others let their

hair grow long and tied it in a bun or a topknot. Jewelry was worn with lavish abundance.

Women sometimes wore a short tailored jacket or bodice, and men a tunic or vest; but in general, when the weather was hot, women as well as men went bare above the waist. The idea that women should cover their most attractive assets did not become general until after the Muslim conquests, and the topless custom persisted in parts of India down to modern times. Aubrey Menen, the Indo-Irish writer, wrote of his grandmother, a member of the Nayyar caste of the extreme south, where Muslim rule was never firmly established:

> My grandmother, like Michelangelo, had *terribilità*. She had a driving will; she would not be balked and whatever she did was designed to strike the spectator with awe. She was also something of a stick. She rarely spoke to anyone who was not of her own social station and she received them formally: that is to say, with her breasts completely bare. Even in her time women were growing lax about this custom in Malabar. But my grandmother insisted on it. She thought that married women who wore blouses and pretty *saris* were Jezebels; in her view, a wife who dressed herself above the waist could only be aiming at adultery.[28]

Members of higher castes were mostly vegetarians (whose diet is more practical in India than in colder lands) and teetotalers. The higher their caste pretensions, the more austere their alimentary regimen. A local jâti that wished to raise itself in the social scale could do so by giving up some mundane pleasure like eating meat or drinking wine.

For amusement, Indians played lutes, harps, zithers, flutes, and other instruments. They painted, carved, modeled, and composed poems. They attended theaters, cockfights, and religious festivals. Although neither the climate nor the culture encouraged strenuous outdoor sports, there was some chariot racing and competitive archery.

Most of all they gambled, mainly with dice. The state got much of its revenue from gambling taxes. They also played board games. One, *chaturanga*,[29] was played on a board of sixty-four squares. Four persons played as pairs of partners. Each had eight pieces: a king, an elephant, a horseman, a ship, and four foot soldiers. Moves were governed by a throw of dice, although it is uncertain just how this worked; perhaps the dice determined the order of play. After the Arab conquests, the game spread over the Caliphate and, gradually evolving into modern chess, reached the Byzantine Empire by the time of the Crusades. Around 1100, the Byzantine emperor Alexius I played the game "with one of his relations," whence it can be seen that it had become a two-man game by then. The game spread to Europe in the Renaissance.

As always, men pursued women. Vâtsyâyana's *Kâmasûtra* gives detailed instructions for the capture and treatment of harlots, mistresses, and legitimate wives. This book was once deemed pornographic; its candid accounts of copulation, as translated by the terrible Captain Richard F. Burton, no doubt appeared dreadful to a generation that printed "By God!" as "By——!". Nowadays it seems tame enough. Vâtsyâyana's advice to a bridegroom on the gentle treatment of a scared young bride could hardly be improved upon by a modern marriage counselor. There is also much besides simple sex. The book tells how to conduct family matters, how to break off an illicit love affair, even how to manage a lovers' quarrel.

Vâtsyâyana had the usual fascination of the ancient Indian littérateur with pedantically classifying things and drawing up lists. Thus we learn the three objectives of life; the sixty-four subjects an accomplished woman should master; the nine kinds of sexual intercourse; the four kinds of love; the eight kinds of embrace; and so on, all of which makes for tedious reading. Some of the positions listed seem more acrobatic than enjoyable. The effect is to make the *Kâmasûtra* about as erotically stimulating as Adam Smith's *Wealth of Nations*.

The kind of woman that the ancient Indian womanizer admired is known from many paintings and sculptures. She had broad hips, well-padded buttocks, a slim waist, and huge globular breasts. These last would put to shame any of the movie actresses who in recent decades have based their success upon their mammary development. A salient example of this form is the famous *yakshî*[30] (demigoddess) of Dîdârganj, in the Patnâ Museum. Alas! we can be sure that real Indian women, by and large, did not present so voluptuous a façade to the beholder, any more than all women of European descent look like the Aphrodite of Melos.

Although Vâtsyâyana gives directions for the fellation of a man by a eunuch, he mildly disapproves of it. Homosexuality and eunuchism seem to have been uncommon in India before the Muslim conquests.

In Gupta times, the plastic and graphic arts throve. In sculpture, Indians never attained the skill of the Greeks in depicting details of muscles and organs. Their gods, saints, and heroes all have smooth, feminine-looking limbs; brawn never excited much admiration in India. Their painting, however, is more lively and lifelike than anything found in the Western world down to the Renaissance, even though the Indians never discovered perspective. The splendid cave paintings at Ajanta and Elephanta are unfortunately badly flaked. The copies one sees in books are often heavily restored and prettified, giving a false impression of the battered originals. Strictly speaking, these paintings should not be called "Gupta," since they were executed outside the Empire and since some were made before and some after Gupta times.

In Gupta times, a voluminous literature began to be written down. This was not in the vernaculars but in the complex and long-dead Sanskrit tongue, the ancestor of the many Indo-European languages of modern India and Ceylon. Upper-class Indians used Sanskrit as Latin was used in medieval Europe. A letter was written on a sheet of palm-leaf paper, which was folded between a pair of wooden covers. These were bound together by a string, which was secured by a seal of clay.

In crafts and manufactures, Indians made exquisite textiles and jewelry but only crude pottery. Their ceramics were cheap and in-artistic because most Indians, when they ate off wooden or pottery vessels, broke them afterwards as polluted.

India was one of the few ancient lands that could make good steel. Ingots of Indian steel were taken to Damascus, where Syrian smiths made them into the famous Damascene sword blades. In early +V, one ruler—probably Chandra Gupta II—erected a solid iron pillar 16 feet 8 inches high and 16 inches in diameter, inscribed:

> He, on whose arm fame was inscribed by the sword, when, in battle in the Vanga Countries [Bengal], he kneaded (and turned) back with (his) breast the enemies who, uniting to-gether, came against (him);—he, by whom having crossed in warfare the seven mouths of the (river) Sindhu [Indus], the Vahlikâs were conquered;—he, by the breezes of whose prow-ess the southern ocean is still perfumed;—he, the remnant of the great zeal of whose energy which utterly destroyed (his) enemies, like (the remnant of) the great glowing heat of a burnt-out fire in a great forest, even now leaves not the earth; though he, the king, as if wearied, has quitted this earth and gone to the other world, moving in bodily form to the land (of paradise) won by (the merit of his) actions, (but) remain-ing on (this) earth by (memory of his) fame;—by him, the king—who attained sole supreme sovereignty in the world, acquired by his own arm and (enjoyed) for a very long time; (and), having the name of Chandra, carried a beauty of coun-tenance like (the beauty of) the full moon; having in faith fixed his mind upon (the God) Vishnu, this lofty standard of the divine Vishnu was set upon a hill . . . (called) Vish-nupâd.[31]

Half a millennium later, the pillar was moved to the village of Meharaulî, nine miles south of Delhî. There are several contradictory stories of who moved it and whence.

In the 1190s, Qutb-ud-Dîn Aibak, the first Turkish sultan of Delhî, tore down the Hindu temple of Vishnu at Meharaulî and built a mosque in its place. As part of this mosque he began the world's largest minaret, the Qutub Minar, but died during its construction by falling off his polo pony. Polo was an old Turkish sport, which the British picked up later in India. As finished by later hands, the Qutub Minar reached a height of 233 2/3 feet, not counting a gazebo installed on top but later removed. A spiral stone stairway leads up the inside, and visitors may climb to the balcony of the first of the tower's five stages, 95 feet high.

I visited the Iron Pillar and the Qutub Minar with my guide in Delhî, Rajendra Singh. Mr. Singh, as is obvious from his surname (meaning "lion"), was a Sikh—a member of a sect of monotheistic, militant, anti-caste Hinduism founded in +XV by the Panjâbi reformer Nanak. In the oriental adventure fiction of half a century ago, Sikhs were always tall and ferocious; but my Singh was a small, clerkly person despite his fierce whiskers and turban.

As it was Republic Day (January 25, 1967), Delhî was jammed with visitors and it was hard to get close to any monument. Mr. Singh explained that Indians were not allowed to go up the Qutub Minar alone, because young persons disappointed in love had taken to climbing to the top of the first stage and jumping off. They would make an exception for me because, first, "Europeans" were not so sensitive as to commit suicide, and second, who cared if they did?

In the tower, people were jammed five abreast on the left side of the broad stairway, leaving the other side clear for those who had already been up to come down. Then a crowd of young Indian mods, with pointed shoes, tight pants, and long hair, rushed in behind me. *They* wouldn't wait in line for anybody. They crowded up the right side of the stair, encountering those bound downwards on that side. At once everybody was packed in an immovable jam, unable to advance or retreat. It needed only for somebody to lose his footing on the rounded surfaces of the worn stone steps, and there would be a mass of a hundred Indians rolling down the steps with me on the bottom. So, exclaiming loudly: *"Maim jâtâ hûm! Maim jâtâ hûm!* [I'm going]" and using knees and elbows, I forced my way down and out. That is why I have no pictures of Delhî from the Qutub Minar.

The nearby Iron Pillar is smooth and polished part of the way up. The cause of this polish is a local legend that if you can stand with your back to the Pillar and clasp your hands around it behind you, fame and fortune shall be yours. Hence it is constantly rubbed by the hands and coats of visitors trying out this Indian version of the Blarney Stone. Its ornate capital is thought to have once borne a statue of a *garuḍa* or man-bird, the steed of Vishnu. Another tradition says that

118. Pâṭaliputra in late Gupta times. (Drawing by Roy G. Krenkel.)

the Pillar continues down "into the body of a serpent asleep in the deeps of the world."[32]

The Iron Pillar poses two problems. One: How did Indian smiths of $+V$ ever make it? And two: Why has it not rusted away in a millennium and a half? The answer to the first is only a guess: that they welded together a pile of iron disks and smoothed them down by endless hammering and filing. The second question is easier. The pillar is of wrought iron, 99.72 per cent pure, and therefore rusts less readily than steel and cast iron, which contain more carbon. Furthermore, the climate of Delhî is too dry most of the year for rust to get a start.

Although most Indian rivers remained bridgeless, Fa-hsien asserted that the Indians made suspension bridges held up by iron chains. In most other respects, however, Indian technology remained static. The brâhmans aggravated this tendency by imposing a religious tabu on sea travel and relegating sailors and fishermen to the lowest castes. Indian maritime trade was on the whole timid and unenterprising, carried on in small ships. The tabu discouraged Indians from traveling about and learning what the rest of the world was doing.

Indian architecture did evolve during Maurya and Gupta times. Before the Mauryas, most religious structures were unpretentious little wooden shrines—hardly more than sheds over the cult objects. The Buddhists, however, developed religious structures of new kinds. One was the monastery, with scores of cells ranked about a compound or placed in tiers up a hillside. Another was the domed monument over the relic of a Buddhist saint, called a *stûpa* in India and a *dâgaba* in Ceylon, as described in Chapter XII. But no Indian stûpa reached the size of the larger ones of Ceylon.

The third distinctive Buddhist structure was the rock temple, dug into the side of a hill. Such temples might have an ornamental entrance, built up of wood or stone, but the main part was a series of artificial caves. In these chambers, the architects painstakingly imitated, in stone, the shapes employed in wooden buildings. Later, Hinduists (the successors of the Brahmanists) and Jainists dug cave temples in imitation of the Buddhist ones—not, however, anywhere near Pâṭaliputra, because the country around there is too flat.

Lacking hills into which to excavate their temples, the people of the lower Ganges Valley began to build freestanding stone temples, first of simple cubical shape and then with a tower over the shrine. The sixth-century ruined temple at Deogarh,[33] in Jhânsî, about 450 miles west of Pâṭaliputra, shows the beginnings of this development. (In $+XIX$ Jhânsî produced a famous warrior queen: the *rânî* Lakshmî Bai, who was slain leading her army against the British in the Mutiny of 1857–59.) In post-Gupta times, temple evolution culminated in the huge Hinduist temples of eastern India—especially in the state of Orissa—with their entranceways, halls of assembly, vestibules, and sanctuaries. The sanctuary or *shikhara*[34] is a stone tower looking like a gigantic salt shaker with a screw cap, over 100 feet tall; the Deogarh temple shows an earlier form of this structure.

Despite India's long technical and scientific torpor, some modern Indians assert that India had airplanes or nuclear power thousands of years ago. These ridiculous claims are based upon the references in ancient myths, legends, and epics to their heroes' magical powers and devices. One Indian told me:

"If you compare the modern types of airplane, you find that they correspond exactly to the flying chariots and such in the *Mahâbhârata* and the *Râmayâna*. That means that we had airplanes 10,000 years ago."

"Indeed?" said I. "Very interesting. But, you know, we 'Europeans' had electric washing machines at least 12,000 years ago."

"Oh, not really?"

"Yes. Take the lines in Homer's *Odyssey:*

"'Neath it the deep, black water is swallowed by mighty Charybdis;
Thrice in the day doth she swallow it down, and thrice she rejects it.[35]

"That's obviously a description of an electric washing machine. It must also be connected with Plato's Atlantis, because Homer's land of the Phaeacians resembles Atlantis, and Plato said Atlantis existed 9,000 years before his time . . ."[36]

At this point my interlocutor manifested a desire to change the subject, and no more was heard of the Vedic Air Force.

There is some reason for calling the Gupta period a golden age. During this time, trade and wealth increased and the arts advanced. There was, however, another side of the picture. The Gupta era saw the growth of several Indian beliefs and usages that, from any point of view other than that of an orthodox Hinduist, would be deemed regressive and malignant.

In the South, the old Brahmanism had developed into Hinduism. In Gupta times, the new Hinduism was carried northward by its devotees with missionary zeal and grew at the expense of Buddhism and Jainism. It was never one creed but, like Brahmanism, a whole congeries of cults. The strongest of these were the cults of Shiva[37] and Vishnu.[38] The Shaivite worshiped Shiva as the high God, holding the other gods to exist but merely as aspects or emanations of Shiva; the Vaishnavite regarded Vishnu in the same light.

Shiva (who goes back to the pre-Aryan civilization of the Indus Valley) was worshiped as a god of fertility, whose emblem was the

119. Avenue in Patnâ. The vehicles are pedicabs.

lingam or erect phallus. India is still dotted with these objects, which range from a mere stone post with a rounded top to a painstaking sculpture, realistically representing the tumid organ on a colossal scale. The record lingam was a hundred-footer put up by the Cambodian king Jaya-Varman IV in +X. Temples depicted the lingam and the *yoni*, its female analogue, on their seals.

Vishnu, on the other hand, was supposed to have undergone successive incarnations in earthly bodies. These included a fish, a tortoise, a pig, a dwarf, a brâhman, the hero Râma, and the divine cowherd Krishna. To neutralize the competition of the Buddhists, the Vaishnavites blandly enrolled Buddha as one more incarnation of Vishnu.

This eclectic, pluralistic spirit of Hinduism, quite different from the intransigent, intolerant monopolism of Christianity and Islâm, enabled the two sects to coexist without much open conflict. "Occasionally this difference in viewpoint has led to friction and some degree of persecution, but generally the two great divisions of Hinduism have rubbed along happily together, in the conviction that, on ultimate analysis, both are equally right. Hinduism is essentially tolerant, and would rather assimilate than rigidly exclude. So the wiser Vaiṣṇavites and Śaivites recognized very early that the gods whom they worshiped were different aspects of the same being. The Divine is a diamond with innumerable facets; two very large and bright facets are Viṣṇu and Śiva, while the others represent all the gods that were ever worshiped. Some facets seem larger, brighter, and better polished than others, but in fact the devotee, whatever his sect, worships the whole diamond, which is in reality perfect. The more devout Hindus, even when illiterate and ignorant, have always been fundamentally monotheist."[39]

In this respect, Hinduism is like other mass religions. All these religions differ within themselves according to the educational and economic levels on which they are practiced. On the higher levels they tend to be monotheistic, intellectual, and abstract, concerned with moral principles and shading off into philosophy. On the lower levels, they tend to be polytheistic, emotional, and concrete, concerned with the practical benefits to be had from rites and ceremonies and shading off into magic.

There were many other forms of Hinduism beside Shaivism and Vaishnavism; for instance, some Gupta emperors adhered to the cult of Bhagavatism (allied to Vaishnavism), which worshiped Krishna-Vâsudeva as the supreme God. As Hinduism rose in popularity, Buddhism declined and finally flickered out altogether.

The contrast between the fates of Buddhism and Jainism, which have much in common, has never—to my satisfaction at least—been adequately explained. Buddhism spread far and wide over eastern Asia but died out altogether in its homeland. Jainism, which failed to spread, has survived as a minor but lively sect down to the present.

All we can do is to present such facts as are known. Jainism adhered strictly to its agnosticism towards the gods, but Indian Buddhism compromised with Brahmanism. The compromise was the Mahâyâna. This theistic Buddhism was first presented at a Buddhist council called about +100 by the Kushâna king Kanishka. Followers of the new sect called it Mahâyâna, "Great Vehicle," and referred to the older, non-theistic Buddhism as the Hinâyâna or "Lesser Vehicle." Followers of the latter indignantly rejected the name "Hinâyâna" and called their sect the Theravâda. The Mahâyâna soon prevailed over its rival in India and reached its greatest elaboration in Tibet.

Mahâyânist pandering to the lust of the common Indian for a million divine beings to worship did not, however, save Indian Buddhism from extinction, even while it was spreading to Tibet, China, and Japan. Later Buddhist writers complained of Hinduist persecution. Doubtless there was some—more, probably, than modern Indians care to admit. But some Gupta kings, though Hinduists, made gifts to Buddhist monasteries. Although there were plenty of acrimonious public debates among the adherents of the various sects, there seems never to have been any such war of extermination as that waged a few centuries later between Catholics and Protestants in Europe.

With the rise of Hinduism went other changes. Some were towards a more restrictive, puritanical life; others, towards orgiastic hedonism. Religious fanaticism increasingly took the form of self-torture, as by reclining on beds of spikes, staring at the sun until blinded, or holding an arm overhead until it froze in that position and withered. Cow worship was intensified. Rules against the consumption of meat and strong drink became stricter and more inclusive.

Women, who had theretofore been fairly free even if male-dominated, were increasingly confined to their houses under the system of *parda* ("purdah"), about like that of the classical Greeks. Indian girls, who like most girls everywhere had wedded in adolescence, were married off by their parents at earlier and earlier ages. As in most of the world throughout its history, most marriages had been arranged by the parents—a system that, anthropologists tell us, works about as well on the average as our system of free choice. Now, however, to let a daughter reach her first menstruation unmarried was deemed wicked, since men believed that all women were naturally lustful and if not mated would fornicate as soon as they reached puberty. Marriages to child brides were normally not consummated until puberty; but, since the husband was often several times as old as his wife, she was likely soon to be widowed.

Not only had the more respectable Indian marriages long been indissoluble, but also Indians entertained curious ideas of widowhood. Although opinions differed—Vâtsyâyana said he "thinks that a widow may marry any person she likes, and that she thinks will suit her"[40]— most moralists of Gupta and later times forbade widows to remarry at all.

There was, furthermore, the old Indian custom of *satî* ("suttee"), rare before Gupta times, that a widow should mount her husband's funeral pyre and calmly let herself be burned alive. Under the Guptas, the brâhmans insisted more and more on what a modern Indian historian calls "this gruesome custom,"[41] until it was *de rigueur* among the upper castes. The custom survived to modern times and has not completely vanished even yet.

Widows who insisted on living were compelled to lead such wretched lives—sleeping on the ground, wearing rags, eating coarse food—that death would seem a welcome relief. On the other hand, the widow who immolated herself was told that she would thereby atone for all her husband's sins and spend 35 (or 55) million blissful years with him in heaven before returning to another earthly incarnation. In its cruelty to widows and untouchables, India, as a generator of pain and suffering, easily rivals Rome with its arenas and medieval Europe with its Inquisition.

At the same time, Indian society developed an obsession with the erotic, somewhat like that of contemporary America. A mass of sexy literature was written, and temple prostitution became common. The magical tantric sects appeared, worshiping *shakti*,[42] the "female creative principle," by ritual orgies. These sects put up temples like those at Konârak and Khajurâho, with their spectacularly erotic sculptures. There were both Hinduist and Buddhist tantric sects.

Two developments doomed the Guptan Golden Age. One was the change from a centralized monarchy to a looser form of government. This decentralized system may be called "feudal" in a broad sense, although India never developed the elaborate European system of feudal ranks, titles, and ceremonies of fealty. Perhaps the Indian system should be called "quasi-feudal." It arose when local governors, becoming increasingly powerful and independent of their emperor, succeeded in having their sons as a regular thing appointed their successors. Becoming thus the holders of hereditary vested interests, as opportunity offered they declared themselves rajas, independent or not of the Emperor.

The other development was the overrunning of northern India in late +V by a new wave of barbaric nomads, the *Hunas* or Huns, called Hephthalites by Byzantine historians. These were a branch of the same group of Mongoloid invaders of whom another horde, shortly before under Attila, had swept the German tribes before it and threatened the Roman Empire.

Having learned horsemanship and nomadism from their Caucasoid neighbors the Scythians, the Mongoloid peoples of the Gobi Desert region soon outdid their teachers. They were stocky, bowlegged, flatfaced, slant-eyed, mud-colored horsemen in baggy woolens and fur caps, shepherds by trade but raiders and conquerors by preference. Normally their many tribes lived in constant strife with one another. From time to time, an outstanding leader arose among them and welded the tribes into a mighty if short-lived nation. This nation was called by the name of the leader's tribe: Huns, Avars, Turks, Uighurs, Tatars, Mongols, or Uzbegs as the case might be.

For 1,000 years, whenever a series of bad seasons made the steppe unable to support even the thinly-spread population of nomads it normally harbored, and an able inter-tribal leader arose, the nomads swarmed out of their barren prairies into the civilized lands to the east, south, or west. When the Chinese Empire was weak, they flooded into China; when the Celestial Empire was strong, they galloped into India, Iran, or Europe. Possessed of the extreme hardihood, valor, and practicality demanded by the nomadic life, their first attacks were nearly always successful.

Their contempt for human life was extreme. Until Hitler and Stalin applied modern scientific efficiency to the extermination of their fellow-men, no group on earth could compare with the nomads of Central Asia for the magnitude of their massacres. In some places they undertook the complete extermination of the conquered, regarding sedentary folk as vermin to be destroyed so that the land could be returned to its proper use as pasture. Sometimes they continued this policy even when, like Timur the Tatar in +XIV, they had gained a smattering of civilization in the borderlands surrounding the steppe. The victims of Timur, who dotted Asia with pyramids of heads, numbered in the hundreds of thousands; those of his predecessor Jengiz Khan, in the millions.

Likewise, no group has struck deadlier blows at civilization. When the Mongol general Hulagu Khan took Baghdad in 1258, he killed 800,000 inhabitants, dumped the contents of the huge libraries into the Tigris, and burned the city. He also destroyed the complex irrigation system that for thousands of years had made Iraq one of the world's greatest granaries, letting the land go back to desert and swamp; the consequent famine reduced the population to a tattered remnant.

In 1400, Timur captured Baghdad again. Although the city had begun to recover, it was still but a fraction of its former size. Timur sent his 90,000 soldiers into the city with orders that each man should bring out one Baghdadi head for the pyramid he was building. The soldier's failure would mean that his own head would be used instead.

In India, towards the middle of +V, the Hunnish kings Khiṃkila and Toramâna conquered much of North India. They overwhelmed the Shaka and Kushâna states of the Northwest and destroyed the ancient University of Taxila,[43] a city whose king had allied himself with Alexander 700-odd years before. Kumâra Gupta did little against the invaders. His successor Skanda Gupta, who reigned in late +V, put up a fight and had some success. But then he was beaten by Toramâna and driven back down the Ganges, losing his western provinces and tributary kingdoms. Toramâna's son Mihiragula[44] extended his father's conquests, worshiped the sun, and persecuted Buddhism. He earned a reputation for fiendishness; according to the *Kashmîri Chronicle*, one of his favorite amusements was the costly one of rolling elephants over cliffs in order to enjoy their sufferings. His abominations stirred up his tributary princes to revolt. With the help of the remnant of the Gupta Empire they drove him back to Kashmîr, whose king he ousted.

Little was now left of the Gupta Empire. A second dynasty, also called Gupta but not related to the first one, ruled for a while in

120. The market in modern Patnâ.

Magadha. An able and cultivated king of another line, Harsha Vardhana,[45] built an ephemeral North Indian empire, of which the second Gupta kingdom was a feudatory. He made his capital at Sthâvîshvara instead of Pâṭaliputra. The Chinese Buddhist pilgrim Hsüan-tsang, who traveled in Harsha's empire, found Pâṭaliputra deserted. Harsha died in +647 without heirs, leaving a patchwork of quarreling petty kingdoms, which proved easy game for the Turks three centuries later.

The Turks, of the same stock as the Huns but converted to Islâm, mastered Afghanistan and in late +X began invading India. At first they raided to loot, to wreck the temples of the "idolaters," and to wipe out the last Buddhist monasteries in India; but mostly to loot. Brâhman moralists had urged the rajas to gather hoards of gold and jewels for emergencies, and these treasures drew the Turks like flies to honey.

Around 1200, some Turkish marauders, instead of retiring to Afghanistan with their booty, settled down as rulers. By early +XIV one of these freebooters, Muḥammed Tughluk, ruled an empire as large as Ashoka's. Dynasties rose and fell; Turkish adventurers and usurpers seized kingdom after kingdom. In early +XVI the thoughtful, hard-drinking, tubercular Babur of Kabul, of Turkish and Mongol ancestry, brought some stability by founding the Mogul or Mughal (Hindi for "Mongol") Empire. With ups and downs, this polity endured to the establishment of the British Raj. Pâṭaliputra, now called Patnâ, dwindled to a provincial town.

Today Patnâ, the capital of Bihar (and the model for "Chandrapore" in E. M. Forster's celebrated novel *A Passage to India*), still stretches along the south bank of the Ganges amid the vast, flat, sad, brown Gangetic plain. The Bankipore Club, which half a century ago allowed no Indians "even as guests," is now solidly Indian. Older Indian members, admitted in the 1930s, fret that "the wrong class of people have been getting into the club." One of them, M. K. Sinha, said: "After independence the floodgates were opened. I don't call it my club any longer."[46]

My colleague Dr. Nourse and I arrived in Patnâ the day they had riots and the police killed ten people. Luckily, we were in the museum at one end of town while the shooting was going on at the other. Later, in traveling to the site of Ashoka's palace, we passed a couple of the many buses that the mob had set afire, still crackling merrily. The riot was to protest the killing of three people in a previous riot. The students started it, and then all the local roughnecks and the refugees from Bihar's current famine joined in.

Patnâ is the kind of place that a tactful traveler calls "interesting" without saying whether he liked it. It was certainly interesting, but neither of us felt an overwhelming urge to return thither. After staying at the best hotel in Patnâ, I shall never again sneer at the Hiltons.

Of all the lands I have visited, India gives the most profound transcultural shock. Although the country includes many things of extraordinary interest, it also has features that take a lot of getting used to. One, for instance, is the fanatical Indian meticulousness about petty details, combined with an unworldly impracticality in matters of real importance.[47] Another is the Indian habit of staring solemnly at a foreigner for fifteen or thirty minutes at a stretch, as if the traveler were something in the zoo.

Now India is caught up in vast, convulsive changes. Although caste is said to be weakening, at least in the cities, Hinduist orthodoxy (in India basically a front to enable the twice-born castes to hang onto their power and property) is still strong. In cities one sees parades of yellow-capped cow worshipers, chanting: *"Gâo hamârâ mâtâ hai!* [The cow is our mother]."

But the inevitable dissolution of traditional Indian society in the acid of the industrial age continues. India makes a practical compact automobile, the Hindustan "Ambassador." It also—to my astonishment when I found out—makes a quite potable whiskey. As a result of industrialization, India has even begun to experience the "servant problem," in a land where for thousands of years servants have crawled out of the woodwork. A friend writes me:

> It has evidently changed since I last saw it over 30 years ago, but even so I can hardly believe the letter from an Indian friend who said that their great difficulty was getting good domestic staff, when I remember servants in swarms all over the place, sleeping on marble palace stairs and appearing as by magic when ones' hosts clapped their hands.[48]

Much more will change in the next century. Much that is picturesque will disappear; but much that will disappear is the sort of thing that the world can well do without.

XV

CONSTANTINOPLE
AND THE HOLY WISDOM

WHITE FOUNTS FALLING IN THE COURTS OF THE SUN,
AND THE SOLDAN OF BYZANTIUM IS LAUGHING AS THEY RUN;
THERE IS LAUGHTER LIKE THE FOUNTAINS IN THAT FACE OF ALL MEN
FEARED,
IT STIRS THE FOREST DARKNESS, THE DARKNESS OF HIS BEARD,
IT CURLS THE BLOOD-RED CRESCENT, THE CRESCENT OF HIS LIPS,
FOR THE INMOST SEA OF ALL THE EARTH IS SHAKEN WITH HIS SHIPS.[1]

Chesterton

121. İstanbul from the sea. Hagia Sophia on the right; the Sultan Ahmet Camii ("Blue Mosque") on the left. (Courtesy of Ellen Kohler.)

In the preface to the great code of Roman civil law that his committee of lawyers compiled, the emperor Justinian (Flavius Petrus Sabbatius Iustinianus) wrote: "Every government, whether democratic, oligarchic, or monarchist, has two duties, both of which must in some measure be performed if it is to remain in being. The community must be safeguarded against enemies from without, and its members must be protected against maltreatment from within. The former is achieved by arms, the latter by laws."[2] Shortly before, Justinian had had the adamantine truth of this statement impressed upon him by a hard lesson: the revolt of the racing factions.

It happened in +532 in Constantinople, five years after Justinian had succeeded his aged uncle Justin. A man of nondescript appearance and cold personality, Justinian nevertheless was conscientious, devout, shrewd in his judgment of people, and possessed of an awesome capacity for hard work.

During the last years of his uncle's reign, Justinian had married the former actress Theodora, who at that time was making a respectable living as a weaver. In her days as a comedienne she had augmented her income by harlotry, in which occupation she had been reared. Her career as an amorist, however, was perhaps less spectacular than that attributed to her by the historian Procopius.

This Procopius of Caesareia served as secretary to Justinian's general Belisarius and later became a high official. He wrote the authorized history of Justinian's wars, paying due deference to his imperial master. Apparently, though, he secretly detested Justinian, Belisarius, and their wives. A work later appeared under his name, with the title *Anekdota*, giving in rich and scandalous detail the "shameful deeds" of these persons. The work may be compared to the hatchet jobs done every four years on candidates for the Presidency of the United States.[3]

Since publications of the latter kind normally consist of a mixture of truths, half-truths, exaggerations, innuendos, and plain lies, we may guess that the *Anekdota* is made of similar elements. For want of evidence, however, we cannot tell just where the truth and the falsehood lie. If Justinian and the rest had been such monsters of dishonesty, depravity, stupidity, and cowardice as they are portrayed, the Roman Empire would hardly have survived Justinian's thirty-eight-year reign, let alone have expanded its territory.

In any case, Theodora—petite, pretty, and vivacious—not only captivated the stodgy emperor but proved a priceless helper and partner in the business of ruling. Justinian showed equally sound judgment in giving the army he sent against the Persians to an unknown young officer named Belisarius. That army was nothing like Caesar's.

Ever since the Goths had destroyed a Roman army at Adrianople in +379, cavalry had been the dominant arm. The likeliest cause for this shift is the fact that the stirrup was coming into general use, enabling the horseman to charge home without falling off from the shock of contact or being pushed back over his horse's rump when his lance struck a target. The stirrup has been credited to the Sarmatians of the Kuban, the Indians, and the Chinese; but whoever invented it revolutionized warfare.

Belisarius commanded a miscellany of armed retainers of local magnates, called "Buccellarians"; regular cavalry, recruited partly from Roman citizens and partly from the barbarians; barbarian mercenaries like Huns, Arabs, and Herulians; and local levies to form second-rate infantry. As a general, Belisarius was entitled to his own Buccellarians. He enlarged his private guard or *comitatus* to 1,500 and armed it with uniform equipment: a coat of scale mail, a lance, a long sword, and a powerful bow. Such a *kataphraktos* ("armored man") became the standard for the whole Byzantine army. Being the best-trained, best-equipped, and most versatile soldiers in the world, the *kataphraktoi* repeatedly saved the Eastern half of the Roman Empire when it was assailed by wave after wave of Huns, Bulgars, Arabs, Avars, Pechenegs, Kumans, Russians, Normans, and Turks.

When Belisarius had soundly beaten the Persians, Justinian recalled him to Constantinople, together with his fellow-officer Mundus, who commanded the German Heruli. Justinian then married Belisarius off to a close friend of Theodoras. This was a lady of colorful past named Antonina. When Justinian became suspicious of Belisarius because of the latter's military success and power, the two women usually managed to smooth things over.

Such suspicions were not unreasonable, for emperors faced a dilemma in dealing with generals. If the emperor strongly supported the general, the latter might beat the foe but then get inflated ideas and try to seize the throne. If the emperor kept the general in his place, the general might either lose his war or, resenting his shabby treatment, try to seize the throne. So the emperor was wrong no matter what he did.

Roman chariot racing had become the world's most highly professionalized, formalized sport before modern television wrestling. In the old Roman Empire, the racing fans were originally organized into the Red and the White factions, so called from the charioteers' costumes. Then the Greens and the Blues were added, and lastly the Purples and

122. İstanbul: Chrysokeras or Golden Horn.

the Golds. The Purples and the Golds dwindled and disappeared, and the Reds and the Whites merged with the Blues and the Greens respectively. In Justinian's time, only the Blues and the Greens remained. The Blue and Green factions took their rivalry as seriously as two modern urban juvenile fighting gangs disputing a piece of "turf." Procopius wrote:

> In every city the population has been divided for a long time past into the Blue and the Green factions; but within comparatively recent times it has come about that, for the sake of these names and the seats which the rival factions occupy in watching the games, they spend their money and abandon their bodies to the most cruel tortures, and even do not think it unworthy to die a most shameful death. And they fight against their opponents knowing not for what end they imperil themselves, but knowing well that, even if they overcome their enemy in the fight, the conclusion of the matter for them will be to be carried off straightway to prison, and finally, after suffering extreme torture, to be destroyed. So there grows up in them against their fellow men a hostility

which has no cause, and at no time does it cease or disappear, for it gives place neither to the ties of marriage nor of relationship, and the case is the same even though those who differ in any respect to these colours be brothers or any other kin. They care neither for things divine nor human in these struggles . . .[4]

Although the main animus of the factions was sporting partisanship, they became so powerful that they got official status. They formed divisions of a civic guard, with military duties. Their leaders had official seats at the races, the Greens on the Emperor's left and the Blues on his right.

With so much frenzied partisanship looking for causes, political and religious differences gravitated to the factions. In Justinian's time, the Blues favored the aristocracy and the Greens the proletariat. The Blues also favored the Orthodox Church, while the Greens tended towards the Monophysite heresy. Monophysitism in turn was partly a cloak for the separatist, nationalistic feelings of the Syrians and Egyptians, who resented Constantinople's heavy taxation and sought a pretext to break away from the Empire.

Like other "youth movements," the factionists affected distinctive dress designed to outrage their elders. In Justinian's time, the Huns were admired for their valor, feared for their ferocity, and scorned for

123. İstanbul: Aqueduct of Valens. (Courtesy of Ellen Kohler.)

their barbarism. So the factionists were pleased to look like Huns. They shaved the hair back from their foreheads and let it grow long and hang down behind. They wore Hunnish trousers and boots, and tunics with baggy sleeves. They spoke in growling voices in imitation of Huns and carried short swords under their cloaks to waylay and rob citizens. When not so occupied, the factions fought each other; under Anastasius the Greens massacred 3,000 Blues in one affray.

Chariot racing and its factionalism played an even larger rôle in Constantinople than it had in Rome. For one thing, racing did not have gladiatorial combats to compete with. When he founded Constantinople, Constantine I, as a Christian, had refused to allow public combats. Gladiatorialism was not so easy to stop in the West; it was not finally ended in Rome until nearly a century later.

The termination of gladiatorial combats did not, moreover, end public bloodshed. Combats of men with beasts continued, and the Christian Roman emperors amused the mob with the public torture of pagans, heretics, and suspected sorcerers, who were burned alive, fed to the lions, and otherwise picturesquely disposed of.

Chariot racing, however, remained the first love of the Constantinopolitans. A later emperor, Andonicus I Comnenus,[5] after a life of wild adventure spangled with betrayals, seductions, and murders, got the throne in 1182. He proved a competent ruler; but, in trying to save money to hold off the foreign foe, he stopped the races. Then it took only a pretext for his infuriated subjects to revolt, drag him to the Hippodrome, and slowly kill him with fiendish cruelty and ingenuity.

The Hippodrome was a huge racecourse just west of the complex of palaces at the end of the main peninsula on which Constantinople was built. It is said to have had a seating capacity of 100,000. Today its site is merely an elongated open space, with the Serpent Column (see below) at one end and an obelisk, originally built for Thothmes III of Egypt and erected in Constantinople by Theodosius I in +390, at the other.

Being Orthodox and a centralist, Justinian was notoriously a partisan of the Blues. Progressive though he was in some ways, the idea that the chief executive should be neutral in such rivalries was a bit too advanced for him. When he presided at the races on Sunday, January 11, the Greens began shouting complaints about persecution by Justinian's ministers and by the Blues. Justinian first ignored them, then answered through his *mandator*, a leather-lunged crier who roared: "Be patient and attentive, you insolent railers! Be quiet, you Jews, Samaritans, and Manichaeans!"[6]

The Greens replied, calling the Emperor an ass, a liar, and a murderer. The Blues rose threateningly in their seats; the Greens left the Hippodrome in a body.

As it happened, seven convicted rioters of both factions were being paraded through the city before being taken across the Golden Horn to execution. Four were beheaded and three hanged, but the ropes of the last two broke, and the factionists—one Green and one Blue—escaped. They found sanctuary in a church, where the monks protected them while the Urban Prefect threw a cordon of police around the church.

Some historians suspect that the subsequent outbreak was plotted by conspirators who wished to overthrow Justinian; perhaps a group of Senators, who viewed the taxes of Justinian's finance minister, John of Cappadocia, as extortionate, since Justinian's wars and grandiose building projects called for crushing taxation. If this be true, the plotters were never caught.

On Tuesday, the crowds assembled again for the final races. Meanwhile, the leaders of the Blues and the Greens had agreed upon a truce until they rescued the two factionists holed up in the church.

> The temper of the gathering was evident from the beginning; they began appealing to the imperial box for clemency for the two men in St. Lawrence, and as Justinian refused to make any reply, the shouting became more and more vehement. At the twenty-second race someone started to chant, "Long live the humane Blue-Greens!" The whole assembly reacted with such enthusiasm that by the time the last race was run the humane Blue-Greens poured out of the Hippodrome as a mob.
>
> Whoever was stage-managing the affair showed excellent tactical sense. Instead of marching to the Church of St. Lawrence, as might have been expected, the mob made for the central police station, the Praetorium. There they broke in the doors, released all the prisoners, killed the officials or beat them up and drove them into hiding, including the Prefect Eudaimon, then set fire to the place. With the police force scattered and deprived of its command, the mob poured down the main street, the Mesé, growing in numbers and fury. At the terminus they began smashing and burning in the great colonnaded forum known as the Augusteum; the big main entrance to the imperial palace was soon in flames, and so were the Senate House behind the Augusteum and Constantine's Church of St. Sophia.
>
> The fires burned most of the night. In the morning the mob began again, at the Baths of Zeuxippus, in the angle between the Hippodrome and the Augusteum . . .[7]

124. İstanbul: Site of the Byzantine Hippodrome, with obelisks brought from Egypt.

which was duly burned. The factionists were shouting *"Nika!* [conquer!]" whence the outbreak is known as the Nika Sedition. (*Nika* is Greek, which was the common speech of Constantinople even though the official language was still Latin.)

Justinian hesitated to use his two companies of Imperial guards, the Excubitors and the Domestici, for fear that, having friends and kinsmen among the rioters, they might be tempted to join the revolution. He sent Mundus with his Heruli and Belisarius with his comitatus for three more days of indecisive fighting in the streets. In the course of this, more of the city was burned, including the Hospital of St. Sampson for incurables, with its unfortunate inmates.

On Sunday morning, the mob learned that Hypatius and Pompeius, the nephews of a former candidate for the emperorship, had been sent home from the palace by Justinian. They hauled Hypatius to the Forum of Constantine and crowned him with the nearest thing available, a golden necklace or collar. Justinian appeared in the Hippodrome to temporize and reason with the insurgents but was howled down. When he had left, Hypatius was pushed into the Imperial box.

Back at the palace, Belisarius reported the military situation hope-

125. İstanbul: Serpent Column, originally from the temple of Apollo at Delphi. (Courtesy of Henry Angelo-Castrillon.)

less. John of Cappadocia advised Justinian to fly. The Emperor, no hero, almost agreed. Then Theodora spoke:

"My opinion is that this is not time for flight—not even if it is the easiest course. Everyone who has been born has to die; but it does not follow that everyone who has been made an emperor has to get off his throne. May the day never come when I do! If you want to make yourself safe, Emperor, nothing stops you. There is the sea over there, and boats on it and money to pay your way. But if you go, you may presently very much wish that you had not. As for me, I stand by the old saying, that the best winding sheet is a purple one."[8]

His feeble courage revived, Justinian sent the eunuch Narses—later a famous general—with money to bribe the leaders of the Blues to desert the Greens. Then Belisarius and Mundus took their troops around through smoldering ruins to the Hippodrome, burst in by two entrances, and methodically slaughtered the 30,000 insurgents gathered inside. Hypatius and Pompeius were executed on general principles and thrown into the sea, and so ended the Nika Sedition.

Where the waters of the Black Sea flow out, a blunt-ended peninsula, 50 miles long and half as wide, thrusts out from the European side to meet a similar projection from the Asiatic shore. Between the two runs the strait of the Thracian Bosporus, half a mile wide and 15 miles long. At the southwestern end of this strait, where the Bosporus opens out into the Sea of Marmara—the ancient Propontis—a winding arm of the sea projects four miles into the European peninsula, forming a splendid harbor and sundered from the Sea of Marmara by a triangular cape, about three miles on a side.

This arm of the sea looks like the estuary of a great river, although there are no great rivers nearby. A couple of small streams, only, empty into this body of water, which the ancient Greeks called the Chrysokeras or Golden Horn. (We think of a geographical "horn" as a tapering point of land, but the Greeks used the term for a body of water of a similar hornlike shape.)

Thither about −658, according to half-legendary later accounts, came a certain Byzas, leading a colonizing party from Megara. The oracle of Delphi had advised the colonists to settle "opposite the blind." This advice greatly puzzled them. Byzas, however, noticed that an earlier party of Megarans had settled across the strait and built the town of Chalkedon, ignoring the great natural harbor on the European side. The Chalkedonians, quoth Byzas, must have been blind . . . *oi*, that must have been what Apollo meant!

So they crossed the Bosporus to the fishing village of Lygos and founded Byzantion or Byzantium. For many centuries, Byzantium throve as a Greek maritime city. In −340, Philip of Macedon besieged it; but the moon gave away his attempted night attack, and the grateful Byzantines adopted the crescent moon as their symbol. Long afterwards, the Turks borrowed this crescent for their own use when they made the city part of their empire.

As we have seen, Diocletian experimented with dividing the Roman Empire in two; but in his time the Eastern half had no real capital. Constantine I (Flavius Valerius Aurelius Constantinus) was a son of one of Diocletian's successors. After defeating and killing off his rivals, he undertook to supply this lack. He chose Byzantium as the site for his New Rome or Konstantinopolis; it had about as many hills as the original Rome.

But Constantine had no intention of dividing the Empire with anybody. He kept it all to himself. In +324 in Asia Minor, he beat his last rival, his brother-in-law Licinius, whom he imprisoned and had killed. (By all evidence, Licinius would have done the same to him.)

Constantine then crossed the Bosporus and ordained his new city, to which he lured settlers by promising free bread and games as in Old Rome. Years were spent in gathering materials to build the city and art objects to adorn it. Constantine had Pheidias' colossal Athena fetched from Athens. From Delphi he brought a bronzen column in the form of three intertwined serpents, which had formed part of the sacred paraphernalia of the priestess of Apollo, the Pythoness. In —V, a number of Greek cities had put up the money for this column, which celebrated the rout of the Persians at Plataia in —479. The names of these cities are still inscribed on the base; but the heads of the snakes, which branched out from the top, have all been broken off over the centuries.

On May 11, +330, Constantine dedicated his New Rome, and the date was a public holiday as long as the Empire lasted. Much of the hasty building soon began to crack and crumble and had to be done over by Constantine's successors. Constantine built a wall across the base of the triangle; but the city soon outgrew it, and nothing remains of it today.

In +410, the Constantinopolitans heard the incredible news that Alaric's Goths had sacked Rome. The Praetorian Prefect of the East, Anthemius, who ruled the East Roman Empire for the boy-emperor Theodosius II, ordered a new wall built a mile and a half west of Constantine's. The Blues and the Greens were put in charge of the work, which was done by 16,000 volunteers besides the hired masons. The wall was 13 to 15 feet thick, 30 to 40 feet high, and 4 1/2 miles long, with ninety-six towers. Most of it, with later additions, still abides. Between Constantine and the first Theodosius, around +370, the emperor Valens furnished the city with a new aqueduct, of which a considerable stretch of the arcade still cuts through the city. Later, a huge chain was stretched across the mouth of the Golden Horn, with winches for pulling it up to keep out ill-wishers in ships.

Constantine settled down in his new capital and devoted himself to killing off members of his family whom he suspected of thinking ill of him. His other main accomplishment was to make Christianity the Roman state religion.

Christians then constituted only about one-tenth or one-fifth of the Empire's population, but they were rapidly growing in numbers and influence. An able, ambitious, and unscrupulous politician, Constantine does not seem to have taken their creed very seriously. He issued coins inscribed with the Mithraist dedication to the Invincible Sun, and he was not baptized until +337, shortly before his death. In backing the Christians, he simply bet on the right horse. Besides, he probably thought, it was just possible that the priests were right with their talk of eternal torture in Hell for all mankind save virtuous Christians.

Constantine divided the Empire among his three surviving sons. These, together with a couple of nephews whom Constantine had missed having killed, fought it out. All perished but the nephew Julian (Flavius Claudius Iulianus), a brooding intellectual who tried to reëstablish paganism. His cult, however, was a rarefied philosophical credo with little popular appeal. After he got himself killed in the perennial war with Persia, the Christians regained their power.

Whereas the pagans were at least tolerated under Constantine, Theodosius I, who reigned from +379 to +395, forcibly suppressed the pagan cults. He sent agents around the Empire to demolish pagan temples and to burn non-Christian books. But for him, our heritage from classical Greece would be a good deal richer.

Diocletian's idea of a permanent division of the Empire, each half to have its Augustus and its Caesar, revived. During the century after Theodosius I, history tells of the dismemberment of the West Roman Empire by the barbarians; of the rise and fall of Attila's ephemeral Hunnish empire; of German generals bossing powerless Western emperors who idled in Ravenna. In +476, Odovacar made an end of the West Roman Empire altogether, only to be defeated and treacherously slain soon after by Theodoric the Goth. The German kings who occupied most of Gaul, Spain, and North Africa sometimes acknowledged the suzerainty of the other emperor in Constantinople; but, within a few years, all effective Roman rule in these lands faded away.

Formerly, when Europeans assumed that Europe was the only civilized part of the world, this revolution was described as the downfall of civilization. The "Dark Ages" followed, and civilization did not revive until +XI. This is nonsense. Even at its greatest, the Roman Empire comprised only a fraction of the world's civilized lands, and the Chinese Empire under the T'ang Dynasty (+VII) was much larger and just as civilized. What really happened was that civilization withdrew from its westernmost outposts, where it had never been too securely established anyway, but continued much as usual in the East.

The shrunken East Roman Empire—the richer and more populous half of the Empire—proved a tougher nut for barbarian hordes to crack. In fact, it held out against constant assault for 1,000 years, alternately advancing and retreating. Yet, while civilization continued in the eastern Mediterranean lands and in Iraq, Iran, India, and China as if nothing had happened, the fall of the West Roman Empire was no trivial event. Over a vast area, Roman roads, aqueducts, and harbors fell into ruin, because there was no central government strong, rich, and enlightened enough to maintain them. Literacy, which had been fairly high under Rome, declined to the vanishing point. Science became superstition of the most idiotic sort, and engineering declined to rule-of-thumb craftsmanship.

Such was the state of affairs inherited by Justinian, who may with equal justice be called the last Roman emperor or the first Byzantine emperor. He never imagined himself to be anything but *the* Roman Emperor. His successors clung to this title to the bitter end, even though Greek replaced Latin as the official tongue around +600, and in +XI the Normans wrested from the Empire its last Italian possessions.

Little by little, the realm evolved from a classical Mediterranean empire into a medieval Christian Greek kingdom. We use the term "Byzantine" as a convenience to distinguish this later polity from the earlier and unmistakably Roman one, but the Byzantines themselves hardly ever employed the word in that sense. They called themselves *Romaioi* or *Romanoi* and their realm "Romania," right down to the end when the "Empire" was nothing but the city of Constantinople. This reminds one of the Kuomintang government on the island of Taiwan, calling itself the Republic of China. The Byzantines were insulted when the Crusaders referred to their sovran as the "king of the Greeks." They got even by calling the other pseudo-Roman emperor, the "Holy Roman Emperor" reigning over Germany and northern Italy, the "king of the Germans."[9]

As Roman Emperor, Justinian made it his first business to get back the Western provinces that had fallen to the barbarians. He sent Belisarius and later Narses, with armies that were small but trained and equipped on Belisarius' new system. These armies achieved astonishing success, recovering Italy, most of North Africa, and the southeastern coast of Spain.

In +548, when both Justinian and Belisarius were getting on, court intrigue and the ruler's natural suspicion of a too-successful general led Justinian to recall and retire Belisarius. Theodora died that same year and so was no longer able to smooth things over. Fifteen years later, the aging Belisarius was suspected of conspiracy and put under house arrest. Justinian, however, soon restored his honors. He died soon after; the tale that Justinian had him blinded is almost surely untrue.

Justinian's gains proved beyond the resources of the Empire to maintain, for his successors soon lost them to new barbarian incursions. Justinian is often blamed for having overstrained his realm in futile adventures, but Justinian could hardly have known this. A succession of Justinians and Belisariuses might have made these reconquests good, but things did not turn out that way.

Like Augustus and Hadrian, Justinian was a great builder. But, whereas the earlier emperors had built temples, baths, and circuses, Justinian's constructions ran more to churches and fortifications. He strengthened eastern Anatolia by a network of walls, forts, and blockhouses, and he erected several churches in Constantinople. For his churches he employed Anthemius of Tralles and Isidorus of Miletos, among the ablest architects of their time. Anthemius also built machines, including some sort of steam or hot-air engine, which shook his house

126. Wedding of Justinian and Theodora, at Constantinople, +524.
(Drawing by Roy G. Krenkel.)

when he ran it. To get rid of unwanted callers, Anthemius had only
to start his engine; the visitors, thinking that the earth was quaking,
fled.

One victim of the Nika Sedition was the Church of the Christians,
more popularly known as the Church of Hagia Sophia.[10] This name

127. Hagia Sophia, İstanbul. (Courtesy of Dündar Ozar.)

has been commonly Latinized as Santa Sophia, or even St. Sophia, giving the impression that it was named for some Saint Sophie. The original Greek, however, meant "holy wisdom" or "divine knowledge" and did not refer to any mortal being.

To replace the old church, Anthemius and Isidorus built an enormous new Hagia Sophia of stone and brick. The central part covered an area 120 feet square. At each corner of this square rose a huge 100-foot stone pier. These piers in turn supported four arches, each 60 feet high. The arches upheld a pendentive dome; that is, a dome cut away to make four pendentives joined at the corners. The pendentive, an architectural invention of Imperial Roman times, was a triangular section of a sphere, used to fill the solid angle between the corner of a chamber and the ceiling and thus to form a transition between walls making a square and a circular dome placed atop them. You can get an idea of the shape of a pendentive dome by setting a half-orange flat side down, making four vertical cuts around the edge so that the half-orange becomes square in plan and shows a semicircle of pulp on each side, and then slicing off the top level with the tops of these semicircles.

In Hagia Sophia, they mounted a single low dome on the pendentive dome. This was not a complete hemisphere but a smaller part of a sphere, so that its silhouette was flattened at the top. On the east and west sides of the square, half-domes supported by semicircular walls buttressed the structure and provided room for the chancel and nave. The inside of the church was partitioned by arcades mounted on rows of columns plundered from temples at Athens, Ephesos, and Ba'albakk. Additional buttressing and half-domes strengthened the structure from without. Most of the ornate decoration was inside, in the form of gilding, mosaics, and colored marbles; the outside was left functionally bare.

In +558, an earthquake damaged Hagia Sophia. When Isidorus the Younger, grandson of the first Isidorus, repaired the damage, he dismantled the original dome and built a new and taller one.

For many centuries, Hagia Sophia, the most sumptuous building in the world, dazzled visitors to Constantinople. In +987, the mighty Prince Vladimir of Russia decided to abandon the paganism of his forefathers, with its hearty human sacrifices, for one of the religions of the neighboring lands. So he sent envoys abroad to learn how the followers of the Roman, Greek, Muslim, and Jewish faiths managed their affairs.

The envoys reported that the Muslim Bulgars seemed a sad and dirty lot. The Roman Catholic churches of the Germans struck them as ugly. But, in Constantinople, the representatives of Orthodoxy welcomed them to Hagia Sophia and turned on the full splendor of the Greek ritual. The dazzled envoys told Vladimir: "We no longer knew whether we were in heaven or on earth."[11] Thanks to the charm of Hagia Sophia, the terrible Slav embraced the Greek Orthodox faith, sent his 800 concubines packing, and devoted the rest of his life to good works.

From Justinian I to Constantine XI Dragases, there were nearly 100 Byzantine emperors, including the Latin emperors installed by the Crusaders. (The exact number depends upon which of the borderline cases, such as would-be usurpers who lasted only a few days, are counted.)

For half a century after Justinian, his heirs held the throne, before the last of these, Maurice (Flavius Tiberius Mauricius), was ousted. On being told to spend a winter north of the Danube, the army mutinied, killed their higher officers, and chose an illiterate centurion, Phocas, their leader. When they marched to Constantinople, Maurice fled but was captured. Phocas had Maurice, his wife, and his nine children beheaded. After eight years of military disasters under Phocas, the military governor of Africa—an Armenian named Heraclius—arrived with a fleet, and off went Phocas' head.

128. Interior of Hagia Sophia. (Courtesy of Henry Angelo-Castrillon.)

Heraclius' reign (+610 to +640) was full of ups and downs. Barbarians attacked from all sides: Bulgars, Avars, and Slavs in the Balkans, Lombards in Italy, and Goths in Spain and North Africa. The Avars, a nation of the Hunnish group, besieged Constantinople. Failing to take it, they invited Heraclius to a farewell parley on the shores of the Propontis, then tried to surround and capture him. Heraclius escaped by riding hell-for-leather, but the Avars killed his escort and thousands of Constantinopolitans who had come out to enjoy the show. Then the Avars marched away, herding over a quarter of a million captives.

East of the Euphrates, the warlike Iranians had ruled their vast, thinly-peopled land of parching deserts and towering crags ever since the expulsion of the Macedonians in —II. For about three centuries, the land formed the Parthian Empire, so called because it began in the northern province of Parthia. It is also called the Arsacid Empire after its founder Arshaka.

In +III, a kinglet in the southwestern province of Fars—"Persia" in the narrowest sense—overthrew the Parthians and set up a Persian dynasty called the Sassanid after Sassan, an ancestor of the founder.

This dynasty proved more aggressive and nationalistic than that of the easygoing Parthians. Although Iran was far inferior to the Roman Empire in population and resources, the valor of its knightly class enabled Iranian rulers for seven centuries to meet Romans and Byzantines on equal terms. As a result, the Romans and the Byzantines kept half their army on the eastern frontier, next to the only adjacent state that compared with their own in culture and power.

The Persian king Khusrau II sent an army into Anatolia to avenge the murder of Maurice and, on Heraclius' accession, refused to call off the war. Heraclius conducted brilliant campaigns in Armenia, Mesopotamia, and finally Iran itself, which he invaded even while a combined Persian and Avar force was attacking Constantinople in his rear. But these Persians, lacking shipping, could not get across the Bosporus in the face of the Byzantine navy. The Avars, already on the Constantinopolitan side of the strait, were again beaten off.

Heraclius won his war, but the result was fatally to weaken both powers in the face of a new menace, Muḥammad's Arabs, who in the +630s swarmed out of their desert peninsula. They conquered Iran completely, and they took Egypt, Syria, and Mesopotamia from the Byzantines. The peoples of those Byzantine provinces resisted but feebly, having no love for the tax collectors from Constantinople. Now old and infirm, Heraclius stayed in Constantinople arguing theology with the priests and did little to resist the new tide. When this tide had spent itself for the moment, the Byzantine Empire was reduced to the dimensions it would keep for the next four centuries. It consisted of Asia Minor, the Balkans south of the Danube, the Aegean isles, and enclaves in Italy and Sicily.

The seventh was a century of disaster, with constant invasions, usurpations, assassinations, and civil wars. In the Balkans, the Bulgars became a powerful kingdom. These were a mixed people, with a Hunnish aristocracy ruling a Slavic peasantry. They got a smattering of culture from the Byzantines, causing their khans to look longingly at Constantinople and to wonder if they would not make better emperors than those who had the job.

From the South, in +674, came a huge Arab fleet, built on the orders of the caliph Mu'awiyyah to besiege Constantinople. They hung around for two years, sustaining great losses before they gave up and sailed away. They perished not only from sickness, starvation, and steel but also from "Greek fire."

The year before the siege, the architect Kallinikos fled ahead of the Arab invaders from Ba'albakk to Constantinople. There he revealed to Constantine IV an improved formula for a liquid incendiary with a petroleum base. Byzantine galleys were armed with a flame-throwing apparatus in the bow, consisting of a tank of this mixture, a pump, and a nozzle. The Arabs tried again in +716–18 with no more success. Of 800 Arab ships that then attacked the Queen of Cities, only five returned home. The Byzantines kept the composition of Greek Fire such a dark secret that it never became generally known. When asked about it, they blandly replied that an angel had given the formula to the first Constantine.

During the second Arab siege, the accession in +717 of Leo III, or Flavius Leo the Isaurian, stabilized things. The Isaurians were tough hillmen from southern Asia Minor, from whom the Excubitors had been recruited in Justinian's time. Leo and his immediate successors of the Isaurian Dynasty were cruel and tyrannical but also able and energetic. Much of their energy, however, was expended in a direction that to us would seem wasteful: the Iconoclast controversy. The Isaurians had caught from the Arabs the puritanical notion that the worship of images was wicked. So the Isaurian emperors attacked the use of ikons in the Orthodox Church. They incidentally campaigned against the power of the monks, which had grown to threatening proportions. The monks, who prided themselves on never bathing more than thrice a year, used the ikons to control the Byzantine women, who in turn tried to control their men. Multitudes of ikons were destroyed. While I do not find bug-eyed Byzantine saints attractive, any large destruction of works of art must be regretted.

The campaign against images was interrupted by the reign of the empress Irene (+780 to +802). The widow of Leo IV, she acted as regent during the minority of her son, the boy-emperor Constantine VI. She corresponded with Charlemagne, whom the Pope had crowned Holy Roman Emperor, about the possibility of their getting married, but this plan fell through.

When Constantine grew up, he tried to take his place as emperor. Having acquired a taste for ruling, Irene refused to let him; when he persisted, she lured him to her palace and had him blinded in his sleep. The Byzantines had found that one could make a rival harmless without the sin of homicide by a few simple mutilations. Blinding was the favored one, with castration and cutting out the tongue as alternatives. To us this sounds sadistic, but a Byzantine would doubtless justify it as more merciful than killing, which might send the slayer to Hell.

After Irene, the realm suffered further distress through most of +IX. From +829 to +842, the throne was occupied by Theophilus, who, though fairly able and upright, was called "the Unfortunate" after the Arabs repeatedly beat him. His reign is mainly remarkable for the splendor of his throne room. The Emperor sat on a throne which, during the presentation of foreign dignitaries, rose into the air by means of a hidden mechanism. Beside the throne were mechanical lions, which roared as did the mechanical tigers in Flaubert's Carthage, and a golden tree whereon twittered golden birds. W. B. Yeats had this in mind when he wrote:

> Once out of nature I shall never take
> My bodily form from any natural thing,
> But such a form as Grecian goldsmiths make
> Of hammered gold and gold enamelling
> To keep a drowsy Emperor awake;
> Or set upon a golden bough to sing
> To lords and ladies of Byzantium
> Of what is past, or passing, or to come.[12]

Theophilus was succeeded by his son Michael II, called "the Drunkard" from his orgies. During his reign (+842 to +867) the Orthodox Church broke with Rome in the Great Eastern Schism. There were various pretexts for this long-simmering quarrel: differences of dogma, liturgy, and discipline. But these were a mere smoke screen in a struggle for power. The real point at issue was not whether the Holy Ghost proceeded from the Father alone, as the Greeks asserted, or from the Father "and from the Son" (*filioque*), as the Latins insisted, but who gave orders to whom.

The Pope wished the Ecumenical Patriarch at Constantinople to obey him; the Patriarch, deeming the Pope a mere bishop, refused. On the other hand the Byzantine Emperor, who kept the Orthodox

129. İstanbul: Underground Byzantine cistern (Yerebatan Sarayı). (From J. M. Pardoe and W. H. Bartlett: *The Beauties of the Bosphorus*, Lon.: 1839.)

130. İstanbul: Wall of the Comnenian period. (Courtesy of Ellen Kohler.)

Church under his control, wished the Pope likewise to obey his commands; but the Pope, deeming himself as God's deputy above all mere mortal monarchs, would do nothing of the kind. Intermittent efforts were made during the next six centuries to patch up the quarrel, but without effect, since one side or the other would have had to yield real power.

Michael the Drunkard was murdered by his friend and co-ruler Basil,[13] a Macedonian horse-trainer of Armenian descent. So began the Macedonian Dynasty, which, with interruptions, ruled for nearly two centuries. This was the climax of Byzantine (as opposed to Roman) civilization.

During the usurpations from +919 to +976, Romanus II died suddenly, it was thought poisoned by his consort Theophano.[14] Needing a man to handle the army, Theophano married a general, Nicephorus Phocas.[15] Then she decided that, even if the man was a good soldier, she could not stand him. He was short, potbellied, and spindle-shanked, with a grizzled beard, a gruff manner, and an austere character. So she took as a lover another general, John Zimisces,[16] an Armenian. John was a small man, but a vest-pocket Hercules who astounded all by his deeds of dought on the battlefield and then had been disgraced as a result of a court intrigue.

One night, Theophano admitted John and his henchmen to the

water landing of the Boukoleon Palace, so called because a statue of a lion fighting with a bull had once stood there. They were hoisted up in a basket, one at a time, to the floor where Nicephorus slept. They killed him after a little torture, and Theophano waved his dripping head from a window to announce that Byzantium had a new emperor.

John I Zimisces proved a surprisingly good emperor. Deciding that an empress who had done in two husbands would have no qualms about a third, he packed Theophano off to a convent. After signal victories over the Russians in Bulgaria and the Arabs in Syria, he died with suspicious suddenness. The son of Romanus II succeeded him as Basil II.

Under this Basil (+976 to +1025) the Byzantine Empire reached the greatest size and power it would know from the death of Heraclius to the end of the Empire. Basil was a tough character of the type of Leo III and Nicephorus Phocas. One who knew him called him "austere and abrupt in manner, an irascible person who did not quickly change his mind, sober in daily habits and averse to all effeminacy."[17]

Basil was also cruel beyond the call of duty. He fought a thirty-year war with the Bulgars, which ended in total victory. In his last battle he took 15,000 prisoners. Out of every 100 of these he put out all but one eye, leaving the one-eyed man to lead the ninety-nine blind men home. When the Bulgarian khan Samuel saw the prisoners coming home, he fell senseless and shortly died. Basil annexed Bulgaria, which did not regain independence for two centuries.

The empire of Basil Bulgaroctonus ("Bulgar-slayer") was the richest, strongest, and most civilized state of its time. In China, the great T'ang Dynasty had ended, and Tatar tribes were taking over the northern provinces. In India, the Gupta Empire had broken up. In the Caliphate, Turkish adventurers were setting themselves up as independent sultans. In the West, the Holy Roman Emperors ruled a larger area in Germany and Italy, but their rule was weak and loose, and most of their domain was still fairly barbarous.

The Byzantine emperor was an extreme autocrat. He was head both of church and of state, a condition sometimes called "Caesaropapism." Byzantium continued the late Roman trend towards a highly centralized, bureaucratic, despotic government, minutely regulating the lives of its subjects. Russia was to inherit the Byzantine governmental tradition, with results of worldwide moment for our own times.

The Byzantine emperors lived, like the Persian kings, in godlike seclusion, surrounded by a huge apparatus of servants—many of them eunuchs—and agents. Administration, ceremony, and military leadership

131. Hagia Sophia seen from the Sultan Ahmet Camii (Mosque). (Courtesy of Dündar Ozar.)

used up practically all the Emperor's waking hours. When the emperors appeared in public, their appearance was made the occasion for ceremonies of stupefying formality, with a parade of precious metals and jewels, gorgeous costumes, pompous titles, and gestures of servility. St. John Chrysostom's description of Arcadius (late +IV) would apply to later Byzantine rulers:

> The Emperor wears on his head either a diadem, or a crown of gold, decorated with precious stones of inestimable value. These ornaments, and his purple garments, are reserved for his sacred person alone; and his robes of silk are embroidered with the figures of gold dragons. His throne is of massy gold. Whenever he appears in public, he is surrounded by his courtiers, his guards, and his attendants. Their spears, their shields, their cuirasses, the bridles and trappings of their horses, have either the substance, or the appearance, of gold;

and the large splendid boss in the midst of their shield is encircled with smaller bosses, which represent the shape of the human eye. The two mules that draw the chariot of the monarch are perfectly white, and shining all over with gold. The chariot itself, of pure and solid gold, attracts the admiration of the spectators, who contemplate the purple curtains, the snowy carpet, the size of the precious stones, and the resplendent motion of the carriage.[18]

The Byzantines thought that this ostentatious display of wealth would overawe the simple barbarians who came to pay their respects. In times of Byzantine military might it may have done so; but later, when the Empire declined, it merely whetted the visitors' predatory appetites. Being set in their ways, the Byzantines never learned.

The Orthodox Church sometimes resisted the Emperor's domination, but not very effectively. The Senate—now consisting of all present and former holders of high office and their descendants—had a few vestigial functions but seldom exercised real power, save sometimes when it had a chance to choose a new emperor. Having no regular law of succession, the Byzantine Empire was exposed to the risk of a civil war after the death of each emperor. From $+395$ to 1453, Byzantium saw sixty-five revolutions, together with a much larger number of unsuccessful revolts. Gibbon said: "Of the various forms of government which have prevailed in the world, an hereditary monarchy seems to present the fairest scope for ridicule,"[19] but quickly added that it is sometimes better to have one dim monarch upon whom everybody agrees than several gifted ones who must needs fight it out.

Gibbon devoted most of the second half of his vast *Decline and Fall of the Roman Empire* to the Byzantine Empire, although he did not admire it; he found its history "a tedious and uniform tale of weakness and misery."[20] His contempt was imitated by several generations of historians. In $+XX$ the pendulum swung the other way, and much was found to admire in Byzantium. Certainly, no feeble regime could have lasted so long under such tremendous pressure.

A moderate view would perhaps be that the Byzantine Empire performed functions valuable to civilization, by preserving part of the classical Greek literature and by rolling back wave after wave of barbarians, and that compared with most of the world at that time it offered a comparatively good life. Although Heraclius ended the free bread at Constantinople, there was, practically speaking, no starvation there. Charity was well organized, and an able-bodied unemployed man could always get a job on a public-works project. Education was esteemed, and the Empire never sank to the state of early medieval Europe, wherein bad King John of England never signed the Magna Carta because he could not write. (He stamped it with the royal seal instead.) Law was comparatively humane, and the bureaucracy seems to have been as honest as any other of that age.

On the other hand, the culture of the Byzantines would not seem attractive to most intelligent people today. The dominant trends of Byzantine society pointed in a direction opposite to those of our own civilization. It practiced an extreme, illiberal, undemocratic autocracy, closely regulating not only prices, wages, and interest rates but also occupations, dress, and beliefs. Although some of Diocletian's laws making occupations hereditary seem to have been eased off or forgotten, Byzantium kept its social classes rigidly stratified. It lacked interest in science and technology; the Arabs of the Caliphate, for a few centuries at least, were much more scientifically minded. It combined a late-Roman passion for empty rhetoric with a medieval religious fanaticism. And the recurrent themes of blinding and castration leave an unpleasant taste.

All the keen Greek intellect that had gone into art, science, and philosophy was now turned into the channel of subtle theological dispute. Next to chariot racing, this became the leading obsession of the Byzantine masses. As early as +IV, the bishop Gregorius of Nyssa complained that at Constantinople:

> People swarm everywhere, talking of incomprehensible matters, in hovels, streets and squares, marketplaces and crossroads. When I ask how many oboloi I have to pay, they answer with hairsplitting arguments about the born and the unborn. If I inquire the price of bread, I am told that the Father is greater than the Son. I call a servant to tell me whether my bath is ready; he rejoins that the Son was created out of nothing.[21]

Of the large literature that Byzantium produced, half was theological, and so shrewd and realistic an emperor as Alexius I spent time in public debate with the heretical priest Nilus over "the doctrine of the hypostatical union of the divine with the human word."[22] History also flourished, although today only professional scholars read the works of the excellent Byzantine historians.

To keep his ship of state afloat in a raging sea of barbarism, the Emperor relied upon his bureaucrats, his soldiers, and his churchmen. The civil service was highly organized, with titles of nobility attached to certain ranks in the bureaucracy, as they were later in Tsarist Russia.

Under the Macedonian Dynasty (from Basil I to Theodora, or from +867 to 1056) the mainstay of the army was still the mounted kataphraktos, used with great skill by adroit and crafty Byzantine generals to defeat many times their numbers of foes. Military textbooks explained the best tactics to employ against the warriors of each foreign nation. For example, the impetuous Franks, though individually fierce and fearless, were easily lured into ambush. On the other hand, one should never pursue the wily Turks across open country unless one could pin them against an obstacle like a cliff or a river. Mercenaries were still hired from abroad; under Basil II, a corps of ax-wielding Russian and Scandinavian infantry, the Varangian Guard, was set up.

Byzantine diplomacy was shrewd, subtile, and highly professionalized. The Byzantines were quite successful at playing off one dangerous neighbor against another: for instance, Russians against Pechenegs, or Hungarians against Bulgars. Byzantine diplomats were prepared for their task by studies of the strengths and weaknesses of the Empire's neighbors, and of the leading men of those nations. They learned who could be bribed and for how much. The information was gathered by a network of intelligence agents. These included many priests, who spied on one hand and acted as missionaries on the other, converting barbarians to the Orthodox Church and thus bringing them indirectly under the Emperor's sway.

The emperors used this information not only for the defense of the realm but also in pursuing the impractical goal of restoring the Empire of Trajan, or even the chimerical objective of uniting the entire world under their rule. The Byzantines failed to endear themselves abroad by insisting that their Empire was "by nature mistress of the other nations."[23]

Under the Macedonians, Constantinople—the Tsarigrad of the Russians, the Miklågard of the Northmen, and the Qustantiniyya of the Arabs—was the land of heart's desire for many peoples. It was one of the world's largest cities, with a population between half a million and a million; its only rival as a center of culture and civilization was Baghdad of the caliphs. Constantinople had spread across the Golden Horn to the suburb of Galata (modern Beyoğlu). Another suburb, Scutari or Chrysopolis (modern Üsküdar), arose across the Bosporus.

The eastern end of the city proper—the rounded point of the triangle—was occupied by palaces and other public buildings. Almost every emperor added something until:

> It was a complex agglomeration of every sort of building: reception halls, pavillions buried in greenery, palaces, barracks, baths and libraries, churches and prisons, long galleries and terraces commanding views far across the Bosphorus and the Sea of Marmara, stairs, towers, and gardens arranged without symmetry or general plan, but with the charm of the fantastic and with an unprecedented magnificence.[24]

From the palace area, the Mesê ("middle") or main street ran west and northwest, past the Hippodrome and the fora of various emperors. Then it turned southwest, while another avenue continued the original direction of the Mesê northwest. Aside from these main thoroughfares, whose exact location is somewhat conjectural, the normal street width was 12 feet. Scattered about the city were monumental columns, obelisks, churches, and monasteries. The huge walls of Theodosius II, now reinforced by a second line of walls in front of the first, surrounded all. Streets were lit at night; this innovation was first practiced in Antioch around +350.

> Between the squares of the Augusteum and the Taurus, the bazaar quarter ran the whole length of the great street of the Mese, its stalls being set up under porticoes. Here were workbenches where goldsmiths carried on their craft in the open; money-changers' tables, covered with coin; booths of provision merchants, who sold meat, salt fish, flour, cheese, vegetables, oil, butter, and honey; and those of the perfume sellers, who had their stands in the square before the palace. These bazaars, like the whole of Istanbul today, were Oriental in character. In the neighborhood of the Long Portico, between the Taurus and the Forum of Constantine, the sellers of silks and cottons had their allotted places . . . In the Taurus and the Strategion, sheep and pigs were sold; in the Amastrianon, horses; while the fish market was on the quays of the Golden Horn. In addition to all these, under close State supervision and control, closed guilds manufactured the luxury articles that were the glory and renown of Byzantium.
>
> So much buying and selling made no little bustle in the great city. The harbour, both along the Golden Horn and on the shores of the Propontis, swarmed from morning till night with a cosmopolitan crowd, as if the whole world had arranged to meet there. Hooknosed Asiatics with pointed beards and black hair falling to the shoulder; turbaned traders from Babylon, Syria, Egypt, or Persia; shaven, dirty Bulgars, wearing an iron chain round their waists by way of a belt; Russians with long, drooping moustaches, green-eyed, snub-nosed, and dressed all in furs; Khazars and Pechenegs; men from Spain and Lombardy; merchants from Pisa and Amalfi, Genoa and Venice, who had their own quarter—with its quays, warehouses, and churches—on the Golden Horn; all races, languages, and religions met and mingled here.[25]

In the main streets, the toga had gone the way of all fashions. The normal man's main garment was either a long robe or coat, or a knee-length, long-sleeved tunic, worn over breeches or over hose-tights—trousers and stockings combined—like those that had come into use in the West. The ceremonial robe or *skaramangion* was like that of a

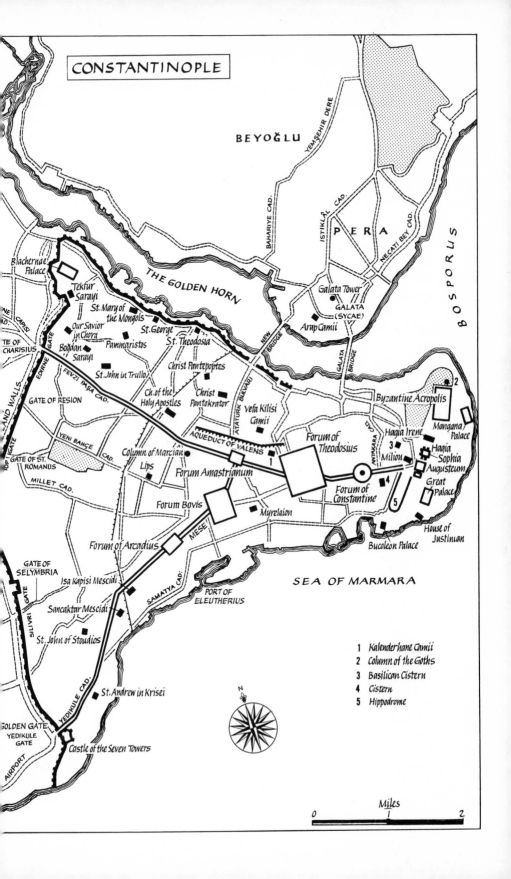

CONSTANTINOPLE

BEYOĞLU

PERA

BOSPORUS

THE GOLDEN HORN

Blachernae Palace

Tekfur Sarayı

St. Mary of the Mongols

Our Savior in Chora

St. George

St. Theodosia

Bogdan Sarayı

Pammaristos

St. John in Trullo

Christ Pantepoptes

Ch. of the Holy Apostles

Christ Pantokrator

Vefa Kilisi Camii

Column of Marcian

Lips

Forum Amastrianum

Forum Bovis

Myrelaion

Forum of Arcadius

Isa Kapisi Mescidi

Sancaktar Mescidi

St. John of Stoudios

St. Andrew in Krisei

GOLDEN GATE
YEDIKULE GATE

Castle of the Seven Towers

GATE OF SELYMBRIA

GATE OF ST. ROMANUS

GATE OF RESION

EDRNE GATE

LAND WALLS

TE OF CHARISIUS

NE CAPSI

TOPKAPI

SILIVRI GATE

YEDIKULE CAD.

SAMATYA CAD.

MESE

MILLET CAD.

FEVZI PAŞA CAD.

YENI BAHÇE

AQUEDUCT OF VALENS

ATATÜRK BULVARI

ANTMARA CAD.

Forum of Theodosius

Forum of Constantine

Byzantine Acropolis

Mangana Palace

Hagia Irene

Milion

Hagia Sophia

Augusteum

Great Palace

House of Justinian

Bucoleon Palace

SEA OF MARMARA

PORT OF ELEUTHERIUS

Galata Tower

GALATA (SYCAE)

Arup Camii

NEW BRIDGE

GALATA BRIDGE

ISTIKLÂL CAD.

BAHARIYE CAD.

NECATI BEY CAD.

YEMİŞEHIR DERE

1   Kalenderhane Camii
2   Column of the Goths
3   Basilican Cistern
4   Cistern
5   Hippodrome

N

Miles

0   1   2

AIRPORT

mandarin and had, in fact, been brought from China by the Huns. There were cloaks of various cuts, one variety being a poncholike square with a hole in the middle for the head. The clothes of the rich and noble were stiff with embroidery in golden thread. Occupations favored certain colors: thus physicians wore blue, and ascetics, red. As in most civilizations before modern times, costume was regulated, and dressing above one's station was a penal offense. After two bearded centuries, Constantine I had revived the fashion of shaving; but beards returned about +VIII and remained in vogue thereafter.

For the four centuries following the death of Basil II in 1025, the story of Byzantium is a dismal tale of long decline with an occasional rally. After an extraordinary reign of fifty-two years, Basil II was succeeded by his brother Constantine VIII, an elderly man who in theory had been co-ruler with Basil but who, being idle and self-indulgent, had left the ruling to his brother. The Macedonian Dynasty ended a quarter-century later with the joint rule of two eccentric old ladies, Constantine's daughters Zoê and Theodora, of whom the first fitted up her quarters in the palace as a chemical laboratory where she made perfumes. She had had three husbands, who served as co-rulers. The joint empresses cared for little but spending the riches of the Imperial treasury as fast as they could.

During this time, the general George Maniaces led the attempted reconquest of Sicily from the Arabs. Maniaces' subordinate was the most romantic figure of the century: Harald Sigurdson, the giant commander of the Varangian Guard and later King Harald Hardraade ("the Ruthless") of Norway and Denmark. After a lifetime of adventures that would seem incredible in fiction, Harald was slain invading England, three weeks before his opponent, Harold of Wessex, fell at Hastings in 1066.

When his campaign was defeated by the labyrinthine intrigues of the Byzantine court, Maniaces revolted. He had some of the qualities of Basil II, which the Empire needed; but in an early battle he received a fatal wound.

Several trends worked against the Empire. One was the growth of landlordism, which reduced more and more of the peasantry to serfdom. A similar trend appeared in Europe (where it gave rise to the feudal system properly so called) and in Iran. The expansion of big estates, despite the vigorous efforts of some emperors to check it, was probably connected with the new techniques of warfare, in which the armored horseman or knight was supreme; and these in turn resulted from the invention of the stirrup. As much as anything, the European feudal system and its oriental analogues were a form of government, worked out by trial and error, to enable nations to support a class of professional warriors who spent all their time practicing the complicated art of fighting on horseback—and, what is more, to support an especially large, voracious, and costly breed of war horses for these knights to ride.

The growth of landlordism, however, bore hard upon the peasantry, who were stimulated to migrate to the cities. Thus the main source of kataphraktoi shrank, while after a generation or two of city life the descendants of the peasants were demilitarized. Even Anna Comnena, the first Alexius' literary daughter and as patriotic a Byzantine as one could find, calls the people of Constantinople a "cowardly mob."[26] When the city finally fell to the Turks, out of a population of more than 30,000 (most of its people having fled before the final debacle) exactly 4,973 Constantinopolitans bore arms.

The other adverse development was the appearance of more and stronger foes. Norman adventurers attacked the Byzantine possessions in Italy and Sicily, striving to carve out kingdoms for themselves as a better-known Norman was doing in England. The Serbs became a powerful kingdom in the western Balkans. In the eastern Balkans appeared the Pechenegs or Patzinaks, Central Asian nomads of the Hunnish type. After them came their kinsmen the Kumans or Comani, who eventually merged with their fellow-nomads the Magyars to form the Hungarians.

The Kuman invasion had an odd by-product. When the Kumans occupied the Ukraine, they warred with the Russians, who called them Polovtsi (singular, Polovets). This conflict produced an epic poem, *The Lay of Igor's Host*, which is a landmark in early Russian literature. In the 1870s and 1880s, Russia's chemist-composer Alexander Borodin used the *Lay* as the basis for his colorful opera *Prince Igor*.

From the East came the most ominous incursion of all: the Turks. These were originally Mongoloid nomads like the Huns and the Kumans, living in Turkestan. Two Turkish tribes feuded. The Arabs, who had become their neighbors with the conquest of Iran, took the side of one; the Chinese, of the other. The forces of the Prophet defeated those of the T'ang emperor in a mighty battle at the Talas River (+751), drove the Chinese out of Turkestan, and converted the Turks to Islâm.

In the next century, the Turks began filtering, by tribes, families, and individuals into the Islamic world. Their legends said that they had been led out of the steppes by a gray wolf. The caliph al-Mu'taṣim hired a corps of Turks as mercenaries. They proved splendid fighters but a trial in other ways; for they got drunk, galloped full-tilt through the streets of Baghdad, and rode down the Baghdadis, who lynched them when they caught them alone. To end these disturbances, Mu'taṣim built a new capital at Samarra, with a conical minaret having a spiral path

132. Nineteenth-century İstanbul: Sinan's Mosque of Süleyman (Süleymaniye Camii). (From John F. Lewis: *Illustrations of Constantinople.*)

to the top, which still stands. But, by some engineering blunder, the canal that was supposed to bring water to Samarra failed to do so, and after a few years the capital was moved back to Baghdad.

After the great caliph Harûn al-Rashîd died in +809, the Caliphate fell upon evil days. Central authority dwindled to the vanishing point. For a while there were two rival caliphs, one in Baghdad and one in Cairo. Adventurers—Arabs, Persians, and Kurds—began seizing parts of the Caliphate and setting themselves up as dynasts, paying only lip service to the caliph. All over the Middle East, ephemeral kingdoms bloomed and vanished under short-lived dynasties, whose very names are all but forgotten: Samanids, Buwayhids, and others.

The Turks, hired in great numbers by these dynasts as mercenaries, soon outdid their employers at this game; the evanescent Muslim kingdoms gave way to Turkish sultanates. In 1055 a Turkish tribe, called Seljuks after a legendary ancestor, took command of Baghdad itself and reduced the caliph to a kind of Muslim pope, but with even less authority.

They were no longer Turks in a strict ethnic sense. As a result of their boundless appetite for the women of the conquered peoples, their original Mongoloid racial type almost disappeared by dilution in a few generations. Their great sultan Süleyman the Magnificent (+XVI) was an example of the Armenoid type, with the broad skull, heavy beard, and great hooked nose that has predominated in Anatolia ever since Hittite days.

The Turks excelled in the martial virtues. Even their foes the Crusaders found them brave, chivalrous, and sometimes even honest. But they had the defects of their virtues. They had little imagination and little interest in technical or scientific matters. These were a people who destroyed much but created little. They looked upon those they subdued much as they looked upon their sheep and camels. They built, or commanded their subjects to build, some fine mosques and palaces, but they invented little or nothing.

In 1059, there came to the Byzantine throne Constantine X Ducas,[27] of one of the great landowning families that more and more ran the Empire. Constantine's loves were oratory and litigation, to which he devoted his full time. He also had what would today be deemed advanced, liberal ideas. He was kindly and merciful. He promoted deserving lower-class persons to the Senate. He drastically reduced the budget for the army:

> For example, international differences, according to his ideas, had to be settled, not by recourse to arms, but by the sending of gifts and other tokens of friendship—for two reasons: in the first place, he would avoid having to spend the greater part of the imperial revenues on the army, and secondly his own manner of life would not be disturbed.[28]

Numbers, pay, rate of promotion, supplies, and upkeep of fortresses were all cut. In 1067, Constantine died. A younger man who had made a reputation as a soldier married Constantine's widow and ascended the throne as Romanus IV Diogenes.

The next year, the Turks of the Seljuk sultan Alp Arslan invaded the eastern provinces of the Empire. The reckless and pugnacious Romanus led out the Byzantine armies, weakened by Constantine's economies but still formidable. In two campaigns, Romanus had considerable success. Then in 1071, he met a superior force at Manzikert, Armenia, under Alp Arslan himself. Romanus deployed and, against the instructions of the textbooks, sent the whole army forward at a gallop. The light Turkish horse fled before them until the more heavily laden Byzantine horses tired. Meanwhile, the Turks showered the Byzantines with arrows from their long-range compound horn bows, killing many horses.

Then, apparently, Romanus realized his mistake and ordered a retreat. The Turks closed in; Romanus ordered his men to face about to repel them. But the reserve, which was in front in the retreat, was commanded by Andronicus Ducas, a kinsman of the late emperor and a secret enemy of Romanus. Saying that the day was lost and the Emperor might fight his own battle, Andronicus led his force back to camp. During the night, the Turks broke Romanus' line into segments and destroyed it piecemeal. Romanus was captured.

Alp Arslan treated Romanus kindly and sent him home with a bag of gold. He doubtless reasoned that the more emperors the merrier, since they would fight among themselves and leave him to do as he pleased. Romanus got to Constantinople to find his successor, Michael V Parapinaces, already installed. Romanus raised a rebellion but fell into his opponent's hands, was blinded, and shortly died.

Meanwhile, the Seljuks spread over Anatolia, until they occupied it all save a few scattered Byzantine possessions along the northern and western coasts. For a while they tried to exterminate the Anatolian peasantry, no doubt hoping to revert the land to steppe. They called their new dominion Rum, meaning "Rome," since that was what they understood the Byzantines to call their realm.

Thus, at one stroke, by the combination of Constantine's anti-militarism, Romanus' rashness, and Andronicus' treachery, the world's finest army was destroyed and the Empire was raped of half its territory. It was reduced to little more than Greece and Bulgaria. Anatolia had been the main recruiting ground for the kataphraktoi. Although Byzantium still raised a few units of such soldiers from Greece, its main reliance thenceforth was perforce on mercenaries: Bulgars, Latins, Northmen, Kumans, and Turks.

The loss of the Anatolian coastline, furthermore, deprived the Empire of sailors and ships. This in turn led to a decline in the Byzantine navy and merchant marine. Manzikert was thus one of the most important battles in history.

Before the winter of destruction set in, Byzantium enjoyed an Indian summer under another feudal family, the Comneni. Alexius I Comnenus[29] usurped the throne in 1081 and reigned for thirty-seven years. If brilliance, self-control, courage, a virtuous life, and sheer hard work could have saved the Empire, Alexius would have saved it. Most of the time he was leading his army against Normans, Pechenegs, Kumans, Turks, or Crusaders, and he often got to handstrokes with the foe himself. He was endlessly fertile in novel expedients, as the time he was defending Tzouroulos from the Pechenegs. He lured them under the wall and routed them by bombarding them with wagon wheels, which rolled down the slope outside the wall and scattered their cavalry. When he was old and suffering from asthma and gout, he dragged his devoted empress with him on campaigns so that she could massage his feet.

Early in his reign, Alexius had to cope with Robert Guiscard, a Norman adventurer who, having conquered southern Italy, began nibbling at Byzantine lands across the Adriatic. Alexius wore down Guiscard until Guiscard died, but then he had to face Robert's formidable son Bohemond.

Then came the First Crusade. After Manzikert, the Byzantine emperors had sent appeals to the West, hoping for some well-trained soldiery they could use in recovering Asia Minor. The last thing they wished was a horde of ignorant, undisciplined fanatics, inflamed with the hope of redeeming the Holy Sepulcher in Jerusalem and devastating the Christian lands they passed through as woefully as they did those of the paynims—a horde commanded, moreover, by Western lordlings whose piety thinly masked a burning lust to carve their own kingdoms out of whatever lands proved too weak to resist them.

Alexius handled the Crusaders with Byzantine shrewdness, subtlety, and patience. Between the Greeks and the Latins (that is, Westerners) it was a case of dislike at first sight. The Crusaders found the Byzantine Greeks pompous, sly, subtle, bitter, and cynical. The Greeks for their part found the "Franks" (so called because most of the Crusaders were Frenchmen) dirty, noisy, rude, and violent. Each party found that it liked the Saracens, the common foe, much better than it liked its nominal ally.

The Byzantines had never shown much ethnic prejudice. All the Mediterranean peoples had been mixing freely ever since Hellenistic times, so that racial differences among them had been reduced to negligible proportions. So long as a man spoke good Greek, adhered to the Orthodox Church, and used decent Byzantine manners, the Byzantines were prepared to welcome him as a fellow-citizen, regardless of whether his forebears had been Arabs or Armenians, Slavs or Swedes. But the newcomers spoke no Greek; they followed the heresy of the Bishop of Rome; and their manners were awful. The loud, rough Westerners made a shambles of the finical Byzantine courtly etiquette:

> Now the Frankish Counts are naturally shameless and violent, naturally greedy of money too, and immoderate in everything they wish, and possess a flow of language greater than any other human race; and they did not make their visits in any order, but each Count as he came brought in as many men as he liked with him; and one came after another, and

another in turn after him. And when they came in, they did not regulate their conversation by a waterglass, as the rule was for orators formerly, but for as long as each wished to talk to the Emperor, be he even a mere nobody, for so long as he was allowed to talk. Now, as this was their character, and their speech was very long-winded, and as they had no reverence for the Emperor, nor took heed of the lapse of time, nor suspected the indignation of the onlookers, not one of them gave place to those who came after them, but kept on unceasingly with their talk and requests . . . For even when evening came, the Emperor who had remained without food all through the day, rose from his throne to retire to his private bedroom; but not even then was he freed from the Franks' importunity. For one came after the other and not only those who had not been heard during the day, but the same came over again, always preferring one excuse after another for further talk, whilst he stood unmoved in the midst of the Franks, quietly bearing their endless chatter.[30]

Bohemond impudently showed up with the Crusaders. Fearing that Alexius would poison him, he gave the dinner that the Emperor sent him to his servants. When they showed no ill effects, he accepted Alexius' victuals.

Alexius persuaded the Frankish lords to do homage to him as their suzerain and to turn over to him the former Byzantine cities they recaptured. He gave them money and packed them off to Asia Minor, promising to follow with his army.

The Crusaders beat the Turks at Dorylaeum and marched on to Antioch in Syria. They captured Antioch but then found themselves besieged by the Turks. Alexius followed tardily; he had been held up by sieges along the way. Fugitives from Antioch met Alexius and his army deep in Asia Minor. They told him that all was lost and that a vast new army of Turks was coming. Alexius turned back, causing the Crusaders to damn him ever after as a treacherous recreant. Then the starving Crusaders in Antioch, heartened by the "finding" of the True Lance under the floor of a church, sallied out and defeated the besieging Turks.

Saying that Alexius had betrayed his allies, Bohemond seized Antioch. He and Alexius squabbled over the city for years. Once, when the Byzantines were on the offensive, Bohemond decided to go from Antioch back to Italy to collect more soldiers. But how to do so without being caught by the Greeks, who bestrode all the feasible routes?

Nothing daunted, Bohemond had his death announced. Then he had himself nailed up in a coffin furnished with air holes, with a dead

133. Nineteenth-century İstanbul: Fountain and Great Gate of the Seraglio. (From Robert Walsh: *The Turkish Empire Illustrated*, Lon.: 1842.)

chicken. The coffin was placed aboard a galley. At sea, Bohemond's men let him out; but when the ship stopped at Byzantine ports, Bohemond was back in his casket, while his henchmen looked sad. Since the chicken had now fully ripened, the Byzantine officials did not find it necessary to pry up the lid for a look at their crafty foeman.

At last, Alexius and Bohemond came to a feudal gentleman's agreement. But then Bohemond died, and Antioch passed into the hands of his equally tough nephew Tancred.

Alexius regained a good part of northern, western, and southern Anatolia. He also made blunders, albeit they would not have seemed so to him. He persecuted heretics and burned one at the stake. He gave money indiscriminately to Western visitors—an old Byzantine habit, which sharpened the appetites of the callers for more. He made hard decisions by drawing lots, trusting to God to see that he drew the right one. He gave the Venetians free-trade privileges in the Empire in return for their help against Guiscard. Then the Genoese and Pisans demanded the same rights and little by little got them. These privileges enabled

Italians to take the place of Greek merchants in the eastern Mediterranean and also deprived the Empire of needed revenue.

While the Crusaders were passing through the Byzantine Empire on their way eastward, an ethnic movement was taking place in the opposite direction. Some time before, an Indian tribe or caste of smiths and magicians had migrated westward through the lands of Islâm and entered the Empire. There they led a wandering and not overly-law-abiding life. In +XIV, they· spread over Europe. Europeans, baffled and alarmed by the sudden appearance of swarthy folk speaking an unknown tongue, called them various inappropriate names, such as Nubians, Tartars, or Egyptians, whence our word "Gypsies." They themselves, when asked, said they were *Romani*. This was simply the medieval and modern pronunciation of the Greek *Romanoi*, "Romans," the Gypsies having adopted the name by which the dwellers in their last host country called themselves.

The next catastrophe was the sack of Constantinople by the Latins. It was not unprovoked. Manuel I Comnenus, who reigned from 1143 to 1180, was a fearless, venturesome, reckless man of the type of Romanus Diogenes. Not satisfied with beating the Turks, the Normans, the Serbs, the Pechenegs, and the Hungarians in battle, he intrigued against the Holy Roman Empire to bring all Italy and the Papacy under his sway. The mutual prejudices between Greeks and Latins had already been aggravated by the Crusades, but now the Westerners were thoroughly alarmed and incensed. Manuel's ecumenical pretensions were dimmed when the Turks beat him at Myriocephalon in 1176 and deprived the Empire of most of Alexius' gains in Asia Minor.

Meanwhile, friction arose in Constantinople between the Italians, who had won special privileges, and the Greeks, whom they treated as mere "natives." After Manuel I Comnenus died in 1180, leaving the throne to the boy-emperor Alexius II, the wicked, gifted Andronicus Comnenus—the one who was lynched for stopping the races—spread a rumor that the Latins meant to attack the Greeks from their quarter. Egged on by Orthodox priests screaming for vengeance on the heretics, a frenzied mob of Byzantines attacked the quarter and killed all the Latins they caught, regardless of age or sex. This massacre gave Andronicus an excuse to seize the throne and murder the boy-emperor.

The Venetians, who had lost heavily in the sack, decided that only the destruction of the Empire would secure their eastern trade. This deed was engineered by the doge of Venice, Enrico Dandolo—eighty years old and blind but still a man of infinite craft and avarice. For a pretext, Dandolo had a rival claimant, another boy-emperor, to the Byzantine throne. For means, he had the warriors of the Fourth Crusade, passing through Italy on their way to Egypt. Since they depended upon Venetian ships to get across the Mediterranean, Dandolo prevailed upon them first to attack Constantinople, the loot from which would pay the costs of the enterprise with a healthy profit. This attack was to be their fee for chartering the ships. No longer protected by its former naval power, Constantinople fell in 1204.

For fifty-three days, the Crusaders enjoyed an orgy of looting, arson, vandalism, rape, and murder. A vast treasure of ancient works of art, including original statues by Pheidias and Lysippos, vanished. Bronzen statues of pagan deities were melted for coin and marble ones smashed. (A superstitious Byzantine mob had already destroyed Pheidias' colossal Athena, thinking she was beckoning the invaders.) Orthodox priests were burned alive to light the Crusaders' banquets, as Nero had done with Christians. This was perhaps the greatest single loss of classical literature; hundreds of works, which had survived till then, went up in flames at last.

The conquerors carved up the Empire into feudal domains. Members of leading Byzantine families, however, held out in parts of the Empire. They gradually forced the Latins out of most of their conquests and in 1261 recaptured Constantinople. Michael VIII Palaeologus took the throne; but now he ruled only a corner of Asia Minor, Thrace, and parts of Greece. The "Roman emperors" in Epeiros and in Trebizond remained independent.

This sad little remnant of the Empire lingered for nearly two centuries, being slowly nibbled away. The emperors became tributaries of the Osmanli sultans, to whom they were often related by marriage and with whom they were allied as often as they were at war with them. The Byzantines even imitated Turkish dress.

Three emperors made pitiful tours of the European courts to beg for help but got none; one was arrested for debt on his way home. Some emperors tried to patch up the old quarrel between the Greek and Latin churches; but the people, stirred to fanatical hatred by their priests, repudiated these concordats so violently that the emperors had to give in. As the Grand Duke Lucas Notaras, who served the last emperor, put it: "Better the turban of the Turk in Constantinople than the tiara of the Pope!"[31]

The Serbs occupied most of Greece, while in Asia Minor a new power arose: the Osmanli Turks. The nomad chieftain Ertoğrul led his clan from the Asian steppes into northwestern Anatolia before they had even been converted to Islâm. After his death, the growing tribe took its name from his son Osman,[32] a resolute young fellow who settled an argument in tribal council with his aged uncle Dündar by snatching up his crossbow and shooting the nonagenarian dead.

134. Nineteenth-century İstanbul: Inner Court of the Mosque of Sultan Osman (Nurosmaniye Camii). (From Robert Walsh: *The Turkish Empire Illustrated*, Lon.: 1842.)

The Osmanlis expanded at the expense of the Byzantines to the west and the Seljuks to the east, partly by war and partly by treaties, purchase, and marriage. By 1340, the Osmanlis had taken over all the Byzantine possessions in Asia Minor. During a dynastic struggle in the 1350s, the usurping emperor John VI Cantacuzenus[33] gave the Turks a fortress on the European side of the Bosporus in return for military help from Osman's son Orhan, to whom he married his daughter.

Thenceforward the Osmanlis steadily expanded their European foothold. The Empire was practically reduced to Constantinople itself, and a largely depopulated Constantinople at that. The Turks crushed a united Balkan army at the Maritza in 1363, the Serbs at Kossova in 1389, and an army of Crusaders from Western Europe, under Sigismund of Hungary, at Nicopolis in 1396. The temporary conquest of Asia Minor by Timur the Tatar, who captured Sultan Beyazit I, briefly interrupted the process.

In 1453, the cruel, treacherous, jovial, accomplished, and brilliant young Mehmet II resolved to end this little infidel enclave. He had followed the standard Osmanli practice of killing off his brothers as soon as he took office, lest one should dispute the throne with him.

One of his successors, Mehmet III, did away with nineteen brothers thus.

Mehmet assembled the world's most powerful artillery, including the biggest cannon of the age; for the Osmanlis then led the world in military science. Constantine XI Dragases made a heroic stand. He had his 4,973 Byzantines; about 3,000 volunteers from the West, mostly Italians and Spaniards; and Mehmet's surviving brother Orhan with his Turkish bodyguard. The Westerners were commanded by the Genoese admiral Giovanni Giustiniani—whose surname, by a curious coincidence, is Italian for "Justinian."

Mehmet brought nearly 100,000 Turks to the fray. Despite the disparity in numbers, the city held out for forty days. Then a bullet smashed Giustiniani's hand. Although the admiral had been fighting heroically, he lost his nerve and retired to a ship. He was followed by his 700 Genoese and died of his wound soon after. The Turks found a door left unlocked and unguarded after a sortie and poured in, and it was all over. Constantine Dragases fell fighting. The non-combatants huddled in churches, awaiting the miracle their priests had promised them. Mehmet told his troops they might do as they liked with these people; they killed all those too young or too old for their purposes and made slaves of the rest. Mehmet's brother Orhan was slain upon capture.

When Mehmet entered the city, he paused in awe at the entrance to Hagia Sophia. Inside, he found a Turk chopping up the floor with an ax and asked:

"Why are you doing that?"

"For the Faith," replied the soldier.

The sultan hit the man. "You have enough by pillaging and enslaving the city!" he cried. "The buildings are mine!"[34]

Mehmet had the mosaics whitewashed to conform to the Muslim tabu on images and turned the church into a mosque, adding minarets at the corners. The Turkish Republic has made the building into a museum and, by taking the whitewash off the mosaics, has at least conjured up a ghost of its ancient splendor.

Mehmet demanded of Grand Duke Notaras—he who had preferred the Turkish turban to the papal miter—that he give him his adolescent son as a catamite; for the Turks were even more given to pederasty than the Greeks. When Notaras demurred, Mehmet used the heads of the duke and his family as dinner-table decorations.

Eight years later, Mehmet called upon Trebizond on the Black Sea, which had its own "Roman emperor," to surrender. As usual, he promised immunity but had the emperor and all his family killed as soon as he got them into his power. During the rest of his reign, when not smiting the infidel, Mehmet occupied himself with studying Greek philosophy and building schools, mosques, hospitals, libraries, and other good works.

On Turkish tongues, "Constantinople" became "İstanbul,"[35] and so it has remained. One explanation calls "İstanbul" a simple corruption of "Konstantinopolis"; another less plausibly derives it from the Greek *eis tên polin*, "to the city."

Many Greeks fled to the West. Scholars took the surviving manuscripts of classical writings with them and thus touched off the classical movement in the Renaissance. Others fled to Russia, where they profoundly influenced the evolution of the Grand Duchy of Muscovy into the Russian Empire. It was then that Russians began to speak of Moscow as the "Third Rome." One might say that the Roman Empire never really fell; it is alive and well in the Soviet Union.

Many more Greeks remained in or moved to İstanbul, some to be converted to Islâm, others to enter the service of the Turks while clinging to their own ethnos. Under their guidance, the Turks copied the Byzantine bureaucratic organization.

Within the next two centuries, İstanbul became the capital of an empire every bit as large as Justinian's. The Osmanlis had conquered the Balkans, subdued most of Hungary, and twice besieged Vienna. The Tatar khans of the northern Black Sea coast and the deys, beys, and pashas of the North African states owed fealty to the sultan.

Much of the Turks' success was due to the *yeniçeri*[36] or Janissaries. This was a corps of infantry, made up of men who had been recruited as boys from the subject Christian peoples, converted, and given long, intensive training. For a while they were the world's most advanced soldiery. They wore uniforms, marched in step, and fired muskets by volleys when European powers still depended mainly on armored knights clattering around on plow horses with sword and lance. The bureaucracy was recruited by a similar system. In Egypt, a similar corps of slave-soldiery was called the *mamlûk*.

Later, the Janissaries became a nuisance. The sultans relaxed the rule barring the corps to the sons of Muslims, so that nepotism became rife. The Janissaries became wedded to obsolete military methods and, like Rome's Praetorian Guard, ousted or killed sultans who did not please them. In 1826, when they refused to be modernized, the reigning sultan massacred the lot.

The other factor was genetic luck, like that which gave Egypt three brilliant kings at the start of the Ptolemaic Dynasty. The first ten Osmanli sultans, from Osman to Süleyman I, were all men of outstanding ability and energy. They were not all pleasant persons. The predecessor of Süleyman I, Selim the Grim, ordered the instant execution of anybody who said anything to him that implied the

135. Nineteenth-century İstanbul: Armoury Bazaar (Kapalı Çarşı). (From J. M. Pardoe and W. H. Bartlett: *The Beauties of the Bosphorus*, Lon.: 1839.)

slightest criticism or opposition. When seven of his grand viziers had perished thus, it became a humorous curse in Turkey to say: "May you become Selim's vizier!" But, as Gibbon remarked: "Of a master who never forgives, the orders are seldom disobeyed,"[37] and under Grim Selim the Turkish Empire more than doubled in area.

Süleyman I was called "the Magnificent" by Europeans for his wealth but "the Lawgiver" by Turks for his justice. A tall, thin, stooped, reserved man, he was comparatively humane. Of those close to him, the only ones he had killed were his two older sons (suspected of plotting) and two viziers, one his long-time friend and associate Ibrahim. It was said that these executions were at the behest of Süleyman's favorite concubine, a charming Russian girl whom the Turks called Hürrem and the Europeans, Roxelana. She wanted the throne for her younger son and the viziership for her son-in-law. For many years Süleyman was devoted to her with un-Turkish constancy; she even persuaded him, against Osmanli custom, to marry her.

Despite some lapses and blunders, Süleyman was a giant in an age of political giants—Emperor Charles V, François I of France, Henry VIII of England, Martin Luther in Germany, and Akbar in India. He was so punctilious in justice and so tolerant of different creeds that Christian peasants migrated from adjoining kingdoms into the Turkish

136. Ordu Caddesi ("Army Avenue") in modern Istanbul. The broken columns in the foreground are remains of a marble arch of Theodosius I (+IV); the domed building is the Ottoman Turkish bath of Patrona Halil; the large building beyond the bath is the History and Geography Building of Istanbul University. (Courtesy of Henry Angelo-Castrillon.)

Empire, sure that there they would get a better deal. In standards of civilization, Süleyman's empire compared favorably with Western Europe, then embroiled in the paroxysms of the Reformation and the great witch-burning. In 1540, a geographer from the court of François I, Nicolas de Nicolay, said in describing the mosque of Mehmet II:

All around the mosque, one finds dwellings for the Imam and the ulemas, in addition to which one also sees 200 more houses with lead-covered domes, for visitors of all nations and all religions. Travelers passing through the city may, with their servants, put up at these houses without cost. Outside the walls of the mosque are 150 houses reserved for the poor of the city. To the wretches who take refuge in these quarters are daily distributed one akçe [a small silver coin] and a sufficiency of bread. Since, however, many of the poor dislike this kind of life, many of the houses remain vacant, and the money thus saved is distributed among the hospitals of the city.[38]

Then the law of averages caught up with Osman's dynasty. After Süleyman I came twenty-six inferior sultans. Some were scoundrels, some half-wits, some weaklings manipulated by the women of their harems. Some were mere mediocrities who became villains under the pressure of their position. As the Byzantine historian Psellus remarked:

> In the case of a private citizen, his own nature, plus a good start in life, may be sufficient to ensure virtuous behaviour, for the simple reason that he is not over-much troubled by outside affairs, nor do external events have any effect on his private disposition. How different it is with an emperor, whose private life is never, even in its most intimate detail, allowed respite from trouble! Consider how brief are the moments when the sea is calm and peaceful, and how at other times it is swollen, or lashed by waves . . . An emperor's life is like that. If he seeks recreation, at once he incurs the displeasure of the critics. If he gives rein to kindly sentiments, he is accused of ignorance, and when he rouses himself to show interest, they blame him for being meddlesome. If he defends himself or takes blunt reprisals, everyone levels abuse at his "wrath" or his "quick temper." And as for trying to do anything in secret—Athos would be more likely to hide itself from human gaze than an emperor's deeds to escape the notice of his subjects. No wonder then that no sovereign's life has been blameless.[39]

The parade of sorry sultans began with Roxelana's favorite son, Selim II, whose character is shown by his nickname of Selim the Sot. In his reign, the Turkish naval hegemony of the Mediterranean was broken by the great naval battle of Lepanto, where in 1570 the Turkish fleet was shattered by the combined Italian and Spanish fleets under Don John of Austria. Although soon afterwards the Christian fleets dispersed and the Turks made good their losses, the Turkish navy was no longer greatly feared.

The land empire coasted under its own momentum for another two centuries. At the second siege of Vienna, in 1683, the Turks were picturesquely routed by an army of Polish knights in anachronistic plate armor, with huge artificial wings sprouting from the backs of their cuirasses.

For the next two and a half centuries, the Osmanli frontiers, like those of Byzantium earlier, retreated step by step with occasional rallies. The Austrian and Russian empires nibbled away at the weakening Sultanate. The Turks were often saved less by their own efforts than by some bizarre blunder on the part of an Austrian commander, or by the plagues, caused by the filthy habits of the common muzhik, that from time to time swept a victorious Russian army. The Turks vented their frustration on the subject peoples. This oppression culminated in the genocide of the Armenians in the 1890s and 1910s. As an Armenian whose father had lived there told me:

"In those days, if the local Turk called at your house, you had to give him dinner; and if he didn't like the food, he pulled out his gun and shot you dead."

At this time, Turkish rule over non-Turks got the name of the world's worst. Even after Turkey was stripped of its empire in 1918, memories of its rule in the Balkans left a residue of bloodthirsty hatred, which has not disappeared even yet.

After 1453, aside from a few fires and earthquakes, no more major devastations visited İstanbul. Most of the monuments that survived 1204 and 1453 (only a fraction of those that once stood there) are still in place. The sultans adorned the city with mosques, fountains, and other structures in sensuous Islamic style, with intricate geometrical decorations.

The most striking Turkish contributions to İstanbul's décor are the several mosques built by the architect Sinan Ağa under Süleyman I and Selim II. Sinan, whose forebears were Christian Turks, had come up through the bureaucracy. His masterpiece was the Sultan Süleyman Mosque,[40] between the Aqueduct of Valens and the Golden Horn. One need not be an architect, however, to see that Sinan closely followed the design of Hagia Sophia.

Early in +XVII, another Turkish architect built an even grander mosque, facing Hagia Sophia across a park. This is the Sultan Ahmet Mosque,[41] called the "Blue Mosque" from the color of its interior tiles. Still, it is essentially an enlarged and elaborated Hagia Sophia.

Besides the many mosques, the sultans adorned İstanbul with numerous other structures: kiosks, fountains, gates, and palaces. On the hill at the eastern end of the peninsula, a vast complex of palaces gradually took the place of the ruined Byzantine palaces. This complex, the Topkapı Saray or Palace of the Cannon Gate, is now a museum. Here one can see a dazzling exhibition of oriental art.

The first three courtyards through which one passed had ornamental entrances: the Bab-i-Hümayun or Gate of Felicity, the Bab-üs-Selam or Gate of Peace, and the Bab-üs-Saade or Gate of Happiness. To pass unauthorized through the Gate of Happiness meant instant death. The executioner plied his trade at the Gate of Peace, with a faucet to wash the blood off his hands. At the Gate of Felicity were exhibited the heads of malefactors; after a disturbance in 1658, 500 heads were put on display at once.

Other palaces rose elsewhere. The vizer had his own, the ornamental gate to which was called the Bab-i-Ali or Exalted Gate. Since all European diplomats passed through it in doing business with the Turkish government, they came to use "Sublime Porte" (that is, Exalted Gate) as a synonym for that government. In +XIX, when the Turks were spasmodically trying to catch up with Europe, several sultans built palaces, heavily ornamented in European baroque style, here and there along the shores of the Bosporus.

İstanbul, however, was never quite the same after 1453. With some exaggeration, an early twentieth-century historian wrote:

> To the Turks the capture of Constantinople was a crowning mercy and yet a fatal blow. Constantinople had been the tutor and polisher of the Turks. So long as the Ottomans could draw science, learning, philosophy, art, and tolerance from a living fountain of civilization in the heart of their dominions, so long had the Ottomans not only brute force but intellectual power. So long as the Ottoman Empire had in Constantinople a free port, a market, a center of world finance, a pool of gold, an exchange, so long did the Ottomans never lack for money and financial support. Muhammad [Mehmet] was a great statesman; the moment he entered Constantinople he endeavoured to stay the damage his ambition had done; he supported the patriarch, he conciliated the Greeks, he did all he could to continue Constantinople the city of the Emperors. When he took Trebizond in 1463 he passed on the Greek population to reinforce the depleted quarters of Constantinople; but the fatal step had been taken; Constantinople the city of the Sultans was Constantinople no more; the markets died away, the culture and civilization fled, the complex finance faded from sight; and the Turks had lost their governors and their support. On the other hand, the corruptions of Byzantium remained, the bureaucracy, the eunuchs, the palace guards, the spies, the bribers, go-betweens—all these the Ottomans took over, and all these survived in luxuriant life. The Turks, in taking Stambul, let slip a treasure and gained a pestilence . . .[42]

After the revolution of 1920, İstanbul ceased even to be the capital, which was transferred to Ankara on the bleak Anatolian plateau. But İstanbul is still a big, bustling Mediterranean port and a fascinating repository of the monuments and memories of successive civilizations. It has the curious distinction of possessing Europe's oldest subway, a short funicular line running up the slope of Beyoğlu from the water-front.

The climate is notoriously windy, and in winter it can get quite cold. When I was there, in February, a howling wind from the Russian steppes brought whirling snow and nearly froze me to death. The Turks impress one as short, stocky, swarthy, dark (with a few blonds), broad-headed, and square-faced. Many wear mustaches. They also strike one as a sober, reserved, taciturn, dour, dignified, and often melancholy folk—or perhaps they only seem that way in contrast to their volatile, garrulous, humorous, charming Greek and Arab neighbors.

In any case, I hope to get back there someday. Like Rome, İstanbul is not a place whose wonders can be exhausted in one visit, or even in several.

XVI

FAREWELL TO ANCIENT CITIES

TIME IN ITS IRRESISTIBLE AND CEASELESS FLOW
CARRIES ALONG ALL CREATED THINGS, AND DROWNS
THEM IN THE DEPTHS OF OBSCURITY, NO MATTER IF
THEY BE QUITE UNWORTHY OF MENTION, OR MOST
NOTEWORTHY AND IMPORTANT, AND THUS, AS THE
TRAGEDIAN SAYS, "HE BRINGS FROM THE DARKNESS
ALL THINGS TO THE BIRTH, AND ALL THINGS BORN
ENVELOPS IN THE NIGHT."[1]

Comnena

W HAT have we learned in our survey? First, let us not go off half-cocked by trying to apply, in a crude and literal way, the lessons of ancient city life to the problems of today. While it may be true that people, en masse, always behave the same way other things being equal, the other things never are quite equal. City life has greatly changed over the millennia. Where the ancient urbanite worried whether the walls and ditches around his city would keep out the Huns, we worry about suburban sprawl and mass transportation. Where he cursed as he waded ankle-deep in the mud of an unpaved street, we curse when the city is buried under a blanket of corroding smog. To make the right allowances for changes in conditions, and so to infer just how differently people will behave in the future as compared with the past would call for that Divine Wisdom after which Justinian named his church.

It does not *necessarily* follow, for example, that because the disarmament policy of Constantine X helped to destroy the Byzantine Empire, we should arm to the teeth with the latest continent-busting weapons; or that, because Rome's policy of giving free bread to its citizens proved harmful but at the same time an inescapable political trap, we should abolish all poor relief. Circumstances alter cases.

Neither, on the other hand, can the lessons of Rome and Byzantium be brushed aside as irrelevant. The people are much the same as they were, and there is no reason to doubt that their actions will be as implacably motivated by self-interest in the future as in the past; that a person or group receiving special favors from a government will try to get more favors without limit; and that a government will take advantage of a neighbor's weakness as surely as the Turks took advantage of Byzantium.

Some features of city life have changed but little. From the beginning of the urban revolution, the city has been the nurse of the arts and sciences. Nearly all inventions and discoveries have been made by city men. The proximity of many creative minds speeds up the generation of ideas, for these people interact, pass thoughts back and forth among themselves, and combine them in new permutations.

Hence the city has been the source of progress and change. Change need not be progressive. The urbanite, dreading boredom and having acquired a taste for change for its own sake, demands change whether it be of permanent value or not. Non-progressive changes we call fads and fashions. Whereas peasant villagers dress up for a holiday in the same traditional costumes for centuries at a stretch, city people seem always to have been subject to ephemeral fashions in dress, coiffure, speech, amusements, and personal possessions and furnishings.

For example, the Athenian young blood of Alkibiades' time made an affectation of tacking the ending -*kos* (f. -*kê*, n. -*kon*) on all adjectives whether they needed it or not: an exact parallel to our "biggish," "warmish," and so on. Cicero ridiculed the young sports of his Rome for wearing togas large enough for sails. Half a millennium later, young Constantinopolitans were dressing like Huns. Their objective, we may infer, was the same as that of modern collegians who assume the appearance (minus the sombreros and six-shooters) of Mexican bandits of the Pancho Villa era, or motorcycle gangs who affect Nazi trappings. They seek to alarm and antagonize their elders (or those outside their in-group) by looking like ruffians of a peculiarly depraved and desperate sort—to "bug the squares" as contemporary jargon has it.

Being a source of progress and change, the city has also been the nursery of crime, since one of the deterrents to crime is a rigid, unchanging social milieu ruled by immemorial custom, such as a pre-industrial peasant village affords. Besides, the city on the one hand offers greater temptations to criminals and on the other hand extends them the protection of anonymity, since the evildoer can easily lose himself in a crowd of strangers. It is not surprising, then, that crime is a concomitant of city life. Much the same reasoning applies to corruption.

Finally, the metropolis—the populous capital of a great state—performed both constructive and destructive functions in the lives of these states. As the empire expanded, the capital city was materially enriched by plunder, by tribute, and by the commerce that the concentration of people set in motion. Because it furnished people, not yet demilitarized, and ideas for the conquest and exploitation of other lands, the city helped the growth of the empire. It also fostered it by acting as a melting pot in which the distinctive peculiarities of the peoples making up the empire were homogenized and disappeared. One source of strife—man's deep-rooted xenophobia—was thus abated. The dialect of the capital city became the "official" form of the national language, which everyone in the empire could understand, even if he could not speak it.

At the same time, the city was spiritually enriched by the development of the arts, the sciences, and other intellectual activities, which resulted from the concentration of brains and talents.

So the city became a magnet drawing countrymen, because they found the city more interesting—more fun—to live in. They grumbled about its shortcomings and often found their hopes for fame and fortune delusive; but they seldom went back to the farm. The satirist Juvenal was certainly caustic enough about life in Imperial Rome, but Juvenal stayed in Rome except for a brief exile in Egypt. When the sentence was lifted, he hastened back to Rome.

On the other hand, the countless petty frustrations and irritations of being jammed with hundreds of thousands of other human beings in a confined space built up a diffuse and widespread charge of resentment. When this charge became high enough, any complaint, however trivial, could touch off an explosion in the form of rioting. The urbanites got rid of their internal tensions by an orgy of fighting, looting, arson, vandalism, and murder. Any division among the people—whether between rich and poor, or between different races, creeds, cultures, tongues, or even sporting factions, served as a pretext for internecine strife. The Nika Sedition in Constantinople is a classic case with many obvious modern parallels, such as London's Protestant-Catholic Gordon riots of 1780, New York's Civil War draft riots, or the American Negro riots of recent years. It may be noted that after Belisarius' massacre of the racing fans, Constantinople was quiet for many years.

The allure of the city, however, thinned the rural population. Because of high infant mortality, populations did not expand so swiftly as they do now to make up losses. Since the peasantry furnished the best soldiers, this urbanization diminished the empire's military might. The descendants of the peasants who moved to the city were soon demilitarized.

That the peasant (with individual exceptions) made a better soldier than the urbanite is easy to understand. The farmer (or hunter, fisherman, trapper, herder, or other professional outdoorsman) was used to being out in all weathers. He was inured to physical hardships. He was well muscled from hard physical labor. In most cases, his life had been so hard that the army, with its regular meals and simple drills, seemed luxurious.

The city man, on the other hand, found his military service a dreadful hardship. His service interrupted his career or ruined the business he had been trying to build up. A sedentary occupation had often left him too flabby to wear armor, march, dig, and fight. The city had sharpened his wits but had not given him the hard-bitten, fatalistic courage he needed to stand in a line of spearmen and meet a cavalry charge without flinching. These differences between the country soldier and the city soldier have not entirely disappeared.

While the great city was skimming off the country's best soldierly material and neutralizing it, its wealth and glitter were drawing the greedy glances of covetous neighbors. Its treasures attracted the invader, as Waset-Thebes drew Esarhaddon, Persepolis drew Alexander, and Rome drew Alaric. Sometimes a ruler could buy off the menace; but he who has been bribed will soon be back for more.

So, you see, the city is by no means all good or all bad. It has mixed effects. It has helped to raise up great empires and then helped to cause their downfall. It fosters science and progress; but it nurtures crime and corruption, too. It makes men thoughtful and wise—and also physically weak and cowardly.

But then, without the city, there would never have been a civilization in the first place. Writing and reckoning would not have been invented, since a primitive peasant village gets along perfectly well without them. And then this book would never have been written. Whether that would be a good thing or a bad is not for me to say.

NOTES

ABBREVIATIONS

CAH=Cambridge Ancient History
EB=Encyclopaedia Britannica
GRBM=Dictionary of Greek and Roman Biography
    and Mythology
KJV=King James Version (of the Bible)
RSV=Revised Standard Version (ditto)

INTRODUCTION
    1. Rudyard Kipling: *Cities and Thrones and Powers*.
    2. See Chapters IV, VIII, and IX, on Troy, Angkor Wat, and Tikal
respectively, in my wife's and my *Ancient Ruins and Archaeology*.

Chapter I, THE COMING OF THE CITY
    1. Lord Dunsany: *The Madness of Andelsprutz*.
    2. A mold of sorts appears to have been used at Tell Halaf a thousand
years or so earlier but to have been abandoned.

Chapter II, THEBES OF THE HUNDRED GATES
    1. Percy Bysshe Shelley: *Ozymandias*.
    2. Jeremiah xlvi, 25; Ezekiel xxx, 14f.; Nahum iii, 8.
    3. Or Amun, Amen; Wêset, Wêsi; Epet.
    4. *Iliad*, IX ll. 380–87.
    5. In the local dialect, al-Uqṣur.
    6. Egyptian, Ḥat-nen-nesut or Ḥenen-seten; modern Arabic, Ahnâs.

7. Egyptian, Khnumu; mod. Arabic, Ashmûnayn.

8. CAH, vol. III, p. 271. The original besieger was Tefnakhte of Saïs; besieged, Pefnefdibast of Herakleopolis.

9. Or Hajjaj. The Arabic letter *gîm* (or *jîm*) stands for a sound pronounced in northern Egypt like the *g* of "go" but in most other dialects of Arabic like the *g* of "gem."

10. For Karnak, the desirable volume of Baedeker is *Egypt and the Sûdân* (Leipzig, 1929).

11. Or Akhenaten, &c., meaning "Aton is satisfied."

12. Carter (1963), pp. 98f.

13. From Arabic Qubṭ, which comes from Greek Aigyptos ("Egypt"), which comes from He-ku-Ptaḥ, the original name for Memphis.

14. Or Montu-, -hetep, &c.

15. Egyptian, Ḥiqu-khasut or Ḥiqshôs.

16. Egyptian, Het-uart or Howari.

17. CAH, vol. II, p. 104.

18. For those who wonder what sounds are meant by the symbols used in transliterating Egyptian and Semitic words, here are the main ones. *Kh* is the unvoiced velar fricative, like the *ch* of German *ach*. *Ḥ* is the unvoiced uvular fricative, between *kh* and the ordinary *h* as in "hat." Ordinary *h* is sounded even when it is not followed by a vowel, as in Ahnâs, Allâh. *K* and *q* are sounded like the initial sounds of "keep" and "cool" respectively; they count as different sound-units ("phonemes") in these languages. ' represents a light cough; ', a voiced sound made by jerking the Adam's apple up and down. The "emphatics" *ṣ* and *ṭ* are too complicated to explain here, but the two *s*-sounds can be approximated by sounding *s* and *ṣ* like the s's of "geese" and (with exaggerated loudness) "goose" respectively.

19. Or Nofretete, &c.

20. Egyptian, On; mod. Arabic, al-Maṭariyya.

21. Mod. Tell el-Amarna or (Arabic) Tall al-Amârinah.

22. Or Abdu-Heba.

23. Or Harmhab.

24. Egyptian, Ṣân; the biblical Zoan.

25. Or Psamtik; Greek, Psammetichos.

26. Egyptian, Ṣai; mod. Arabic, Ṣa al-Hagar.

Chapter III, JERUSALEM THE GOLDEN

1. Rudyard Kipling: *The Merchantmen*.

2. Exodus iii, 8.

3. Egyptian, Swenet; Greek, Syênê. Elephantinê was called Yêb in Aramaic. The colony is believed to have been set up either by Psamtek I (r. −663 to −609) or by Psamtek II (r. −593 to −588). See CAH, vol. VI, pp. 143, 180.

4. Genesis xi, 7.

5. Deuteronomy xx, 16f.

6. It is uncertain whether the town was also known as "Jebus," although this name occurs in Judges xix, 10 and 1 Chronicles xi, 4, and in the form

"Jebusi" in Joshua xxviii, 16. "Jebus" may have been an eponymous ancestor of the Jebusites, or their name for the district, or both.

7. Joshua x, 26.

8. Hebrew, Şiyôn (or Tsiyôn).

9. Hebrew, Shâ'ûl.

10. Joshua x, 13; 2 Samuel i, 18; spelled "Jashar" in the RSV.

11. RSV, 2 Samuel xxi, 19; Hebrew, Elḥânân. The translators of the King James Version inserted "the brother of" before "Goliath," to make the tale consistent with the David-and-Goliath story and because 1 Chronicles xx, 5, written long after the event, said: "Elhanan the son of Jair slew Lahmi the brother of Goliath the Gittite." The otherwise unknown Lahmi may be an error for "Bethlehemite" (spelled respectively LḤMY and BTLḤMY in unpointed Hebrew). It is probable (though not certain) that the account in 1 Chronicles is garbled, that 2 Samuel correctly gives Goliath's slayer as Elhanan, and that the slingstone story was made up out of whole cloth by some glorifier of David. I would not put it past David to have advanced the claim himself.

12. 1 Samuel xxvii, 9.

13. 2 Samuel iii, 28f. 1 Chronicles ii, 15f. (followed by Josephus in *Jewish Antiquities*, VII, i, 3) makes Joab David's nephew, on the ground that Zeruiah was Joab's mother and David's sister. This is not impossible; but the first nine chapters of 1 Chronicles comprise a voluminous genealogy, compiled after the Return from Babylon to attest and preserve the racial purity of the returning Jews. It is probably about as trustworthy as some of the *Mayflower* genealogies whipped up by genealogists of the less meticulous sort for American clients with a lust for a distinguished lineage.

14. 2 Samuel ix, 1, 3. The name of Mephiba'al is given as "Mephibosheth" in the Bible, but this is a case of later Yahvist editing. By the time the Books of Samuel were given their final form, the word *ba'al*, which originally meant simply "lord," had come to mean one of the gods of the heathen. To avoid writing this tabued word, the scribes substituted *bosheth*, "shame," wherever *ba'al* appeared in the names. The incident of Mephiba'al appears *before* the hanging of the seven sons of Saul (2 Samuel xxi, 6–9) but there is good reason to think that this is one of the confusions of sequence common in these books.

15. For another explanation of the remark about lame and blind men (2 Samuel v, 6) advanced by the Israeli soldier-archaeologist Yigael Yadin, see Kollek and Pearlman, pp. 28, 30.

16. 2 Samuel xxiv, 24. The sum would be very roughly the equivalent in modern money of $500 to $1,000. 1 Chronicles xxi, 25, which calls the Jebusite Ornan, says the price was 600 shekels of gold. This would be the equivalent of $30,000 to $60,000—an incredible price, but the sort of thing to be expected in Chronicles. This book also gives an account—probably much exaggerated—of the work done by David in planning the Temple and gathering materials for it.

17. The Bible calls this king Hiram, but he was probably Hiram's father Abiba'al.

18. 1 Kings i, 39.

19. 1 Kings iv, 25.

20. Canaanitish, Aḥîrôm.

21. 1 Kings ix, 28; x, 22. The "Ophir" of the first reference is probably a destination in the southern part of the Red Sea—possibly Eritrea, the land of the Afara. The "Tarshish" of the second reference (spelled "Tharshish" in the KJV) was probably the civilized city or region ralled Tartessos, at the mouth of the Guadalquivir (ancient Baetis) River in southwestern Spain. Some, however, think it was Tarsus in Anatolia.

22. Josephus: *Jewish Antiquities*, VIII, v, 3; *Against Apion*, I, 17.

23. Arabic, Saba'; Latin, Sabaea, in what is now Yaman.

24. Parrot (1955) would (p. 26) place the *ulâm* inside the building. This would make the building 60 cubits long outside and 70 cubits long inside—a miracle indeed. As it is, the dimensions given for the *hêkhâl* and the *dĕbhîr* add up to 60 cubits, the same as the outside length, without allowing for the thickness of the walls. Evidently the measurements given in the Bible were not accurate.

25. Hebrew, *kĕrûbhîm*, pron. "ka-ROO-vim."

26. Because of some ambiguous remarks about Yahveh's throne in the sacred writings, some speculate that the *dĕbhîr* also contained an empty throne, or that the Ark had the form of a throne with the chest under the seat.

27. Hebrew, Ṣâdhôq (or Tsâdhôq).

28. 1 Kings xi, 5, 7; 2 Kings xii, 3.

29. 1 Kings ix, 20ff. says that Solomon conscripted, not the Israelites, but only the wretched remnants of the non-Israelite Canaanites left in the land. This sounds like a posthumous rehabilitation.

30. 1 Kings xii, 14. A "scorpion" was probably a leaded whip.

31. 2 Kings xxiii, 4.

32. For a broader discussion of the Lost Ten Tribes cult, see Chapter VI of Willy Ley's and my book, *Lands Beyond*.

33. Akkadian, Nabu-kudurri-uṣur. The spelling "Nebuchadrezzar" is used in Jeremiah and Ezekiel; the more familiar but less authentic "Nebuchadnezzar," probably due to a copyist's error, in 2 Kings and Daniel. Like the CAH, I prefer the former.

34. Persian, Artakhshathra. Either Artaxerxes I, who reigned −464 to −424, or Artaxerxes II, −404 to −358; it is uncertain which.

35. Africa, p. 43.

36. Gibbon, vol. I, p. 69.

Chapter IV, NINEVEH, THE BLOODY CITY

1. George Gordon, Lord Byron: *The Destruction of Sennacherib*.

2. Diodorus, II, i–xxviii; Photius, pp. 110–20.

3. Xenophon: Anabasis, III, iv.

4. Sykes, p. 338. For details of Rich's Baghdadi residency, see Constance M. Alexander: *Baghdad in Bygone Days* (Lon.:1928).

5. Akkadian (or Assyro-Babylonian), Idiklat, "swiftness"; Arabic, Dijla.

6. Akkadian, Purat, "river"; Arabic, Furat.

7. Or Kuyunjik, Kouyoundjik; Nebi Younis, Yunus, &c.

8. A. H. Layard: *A Popular Account of Discoveries at Nineveh* (1851), *apud* Deuel, p. 97.

9. Akkadian, Sharrukîn; "Sargon" (Isaiah xx, 1) is the Hebrew form. Sargon II took the name of a much earlier Assyrian king, not the Sargon (Shargali-shari) who was king of Sumer and Akkad in —XXIV. It is uncertain whether Sargon II was the brother of his predecessor or a usurper.

10. Akkadian, Tukulti-pal-Esarra; "Tiglath-pileser" is the biblical Hebrew form.

11. Pritchard, pp. 275–95; Champdor, p. 90; Finegan, p. 203; CAH, vol. III, p. 13.

12. Akkadian, Shulmanu-asharid.

13. Or Khosru; Greek, Chosroês.

14. Akkadian, Sin-akh-erîba; Hebrew, Sancherib; Greek, Senachêribos, Sanacharibos. "Sennacherib" is the Greek of the Septuagint.

15. The modern Khosr.

16. Jacobsen and Lloyd, p. 35.

17. *Ibid.*, p. 38.

18. 2 Kings xix, 35; Herodotus, II, 141.

19. Akkadian, Ashur-akh-iddina. "Ashur" was actually spelled Ashshur (or to be meticulous Aššur), either by itself or in names compounded with it, but it is uncertain whether the *sh* sound was actually doubled in pronunciation, as it is in, say, "push shot."

20. Finegan, p. 215.

21. CAH, vol. III, p. 127.

22. Nahum iii, 1, 7, 18.

Chapter V, TYRE IN THE MIDST OF THE SEA

1. James Elroy Flecker: *The Old Ships.*

2. Josephus: *Jewish Antiquities*, VIII, v, 3; *Against Apion*, I, 17f.

3. Suidas, *apud* GRBM, *s.v.* "Sanchuniathon."

4. Eusebius: *Praeparatio evangelica*, I, vi.

5. Herodotus, VII, 89.

6. Canaanitish, Gebal; mod. Arabic, Jabayl.

7. Several early, brief inscriptions found in Sinai and Palestine have been hailed as links between the Egyptian and the Phoenician systems, but the question is much disputed. See D. Diringer: *The Alphabet* (N.Y.: 1948), pp. 195–221.

8. Many centuries after the Hebrew and Arabic alphabets originally developed, scholars devised for them systems of "points"—that is, dots and dashes above or below the letters—to represent the vowels. But the points are still omitted from most writing and printing in these languages.

9. Fleming, p. 10.

10. Also Melkarth, Melqart, Melek-Qarth, &c.: Greek, Melikertes, usually identified with Herakles.

11. Canaanitish, Arvada; mod. Arabic, Ruâd.

12. Mod. Arabic, Ṣaidâ.

13. Strabo, XVI, ii, 23.

14. Pliny the Elder, XXXVI, lxv (190ff). See R. J. Forbes: *Studies in Ancient Technology* (Leiden:1957), vol. V, pp. 110–52.

15. Canaanitish, Gadir, "fortress."

16. Herodotus, IV, 196.

17. Canaanitish, Pumiyathôn.

18. Greek, Astartê; Hebrew, Ashtoreth.

19. Diodorus, XX, xiv, 5f.

20. Ezekiel xxvii, 3–7.

Chapter VI, BABYLON, THE GATE OF THE GODS

1. Robert E. Howard: *Babylon*, ll. 1–8. From *Always Comes Evening* (Sauk City: 1957), p. 70.

2. Lloyd (1947–55), p. 33.

3. Arabic, *tall*, pl. *tulûl*.

4. W. F. Ainsworth: *A Personal Narrative of the Euphrates Expedition* (1888)), vol. I, p. 390, *apud* Lloyd, *op. cit.*, pp. 104f.

5. Strabo, XV, iii, 10.

6. Or (later) Bâb-ilâni.

7. Isaiah xiii, 19ff.; xlvii, 10ff.; Jeremiah li, 37. The quotations from Isaiah, ostensibly written before the Babylonian Captivity, were probably written during it and interpolated into the earlier literature.

8. Revelation xiv, 8. The RSV makes this passage more intelligible by translating "the wine of the wrath of her fornication" as "the wine of her impure passion."

9. Alfred Duggan: *Besieger of Cities* (N.Y.: 1963–68), p. 18.

10. Herodotus, I, 178–83. Herodotos' "cubit" was about 20 inches; his "furlong" (*stadion*), about 607 feet; his "talent," about 66 pounds. The "brass" of the translator (Rawlinson) is properly bronze; brass was then a rare and newly discovered alloy.

11. Or Ḥammurabi; it is uncertain which guttural consonant the name began with.

12. King, vol. III, p. 14.

13. Pritchard, p. 270.

14. CAH, vol. I, p. 516. Dilbat was a town 20 miles south of Babylon.

15. Akkadian, Nabu-apal-uṣur.

16. Schneider (p. 69) estimates the population of Babylon at its peak as 300,000 to 400,000.

17. Koldewey, p. 46. See also Willy Ley: *Exotic Zoology* (N.Y.: 1959), Chap. IV.

18. L. Sprague de Camp: *The Dragon of the Ishtar Gate* (N.Y.: 1961), pp. 82f.

19. Or Ninmah.

20. Greek, *kremastos;* Latin, *pensilis.*

21. Diodorus, II, ix, 1ff.

22. Koldewey, p. 91. The Arabic word mentioned seems to be *dulâb*, meaning also "cupboard."

23. Or zikkurat; Akkadian, *ziqquratu*.

24. Lucian: *Of the Syrian Goddess*, 28f.

25. L. Sprague de Camp: *An Elephant for Aristotle* (N.Y.:1958), pp. 183f.

26. Aristophanes: *The Clouds*, ll. 961ff. (Edith Hamilton transl.).

27. Latin, Cidenas. See G. Sarton: *A History of Science* (Cambridge, Mass.: 1959), vol. I, pp. 444ff.

28. Jastrow, p. 360.

29. For a more detailed account of the origin and history of astrology, see my wife's and my *Spirits, Stars, and Spells* (N.Y.: 1966), Chap. II.

30. Arabic, Taymâ.

31. Akkadian, Bel-sarra-uṣur.

32. Persian, Kurush; Hebrew, Koresh; Greek, Kyros.

33. Arrian: *Anabasis*, III, xvi. See also *ibid.*, VII, xvii; Diodorus, II, ix, 8f.; and Strabo, XVI, i, 5.

34. From *Oh, Babylon, Lost Babylon*, an unpublished poem by Robert E. Howard.

Chapter VII, MEMPHIS OF THE WHITE WALL

1. Burton, vol. V, p. 106.

2. Herodotus, II, 99.

3. Greek, Phtha.

4. Greek, Manethôs or Manethôn.

5. Manetho, fr. 6, pp. 27, 29.

6. Also Mênas, Mênis, Meinis, Mên, or Mein.

7. Egyptian, Abodu; mod. Arabic, Arâbat al-Madfûna.

8. Or Ḥa-ka-Ptaḥ, Ḥet-, Ḥat-.

9. Greek, Phiops.

10. Or Men-nefer, -nefru; Hebrew, Noph or Moph. In +XIX the local Coptic population still called the district Memf.

11. For a more detailed account of the building of the pyramids, of the theories and controversies about them, and of the pseudo-scientific cults that have grown up around them, see my *The Ancient Engineers*, pp. 31–44; or the second chapter of my wife's and my *Ancient Ruins and Archaeology*.

12. *Maṣṭaba* is Arabic for "bench." These tombs are so called because they were shaped like the mud-brick benches made by Egyptian peasants in front of their huts.

13. Or Djoser, Tcheser, Zoser, Zeser, &c.; Greek, Tosorthos or Sesorthos.

14. Or Aiemhetep, I-em-Hotep, Yemhatpe, &c.; Greek, Imouthês.

15. Greek, Troia; mod. Arabic, Ṭura.

16. Or Snefru, Snofru; Greek, Soris.

17. Egyptian, Het-waret or Het-uart.

18. Or Senusret, Senwosret.

19. Hebrew, Tirhaqah; Greek, Etearchos, Tarakos, or Tarkos.

20. Egyptian, Niku or Nikau; Greek, Nikôs, Nechôs, Nekaus, Nechaôs, or Nechaô.

21. Meroitic, Tanwetamani.

22. This Necho is sometimes called "Necho II" on the assumption that his grandfather of the same name, who served as viceroy under Ashurbanipal, should be counted as "Necho I."

23. Herodotus, IV, 42.

24. *Ibid.*, II, 35f.

25. Diodorus Siculus, I, lxxxiii, 8f.

26. L. Sprague de Camp: *The Bronze God of Rhodes* (N.Y.: 1960), pp. 246–53.

27. Or Aprias, Ouaphrê; Egyptian, Uaḥibrê', Wehebrê, or Wahabra; Hebrew, Hophra.

28. Egyptian, Aḥmose or I'aḥmase.

29. Persian, Kambujiya. He is sometimes called Cambyses II because his grandfather, Cyrus' father, who had been king of the Persians when they were tributaries of the Medes, was also named Cambyses.

30. Greek, Psammenitos; erroneously called Amyrtaios by Ktesias. Amyrtaios was a lieutenant of Inarôs who, after the capture of Inarôs, carried on the struggle against the Persians for a while but then vanished from history.

31. Herodotus, III, 1.

32. Photius, LXII, 8–11.

33. Greek, Dareios or Dareiaios; Persian, Darayavahush or Dareyavosh.

34. Persian, Khshayarsha.

35. Persian, Hakhamanish.

36. Egyptian, Ienheru or Ienharoû.

37. Nectanebo; Egyptian, Nekhtharḥab or Nekht-har-hebi.

38. He named it Fusṭâṭ, and in time Cairo engulfed it.

Chapter VIII, VIOLET-CROWNED ATHENS

1. John Milton: *Paradise Regained*, IV, 237–46.

2. Originally known as the New Hekatompedon of Athena Polias; later called the Parthenon ("Place of the Maidens") from the name of the treasure chamber at the west end.

3. Or (Latinized) Piraeus; in Anglicized pronunciation, pigh-REE-us; in mod. Greek pron., PEE-ray-efs.

4. Thucydides, I, 140.

5. See, e.g., Aristophanes' *Thesmophoriazusae.*

6. Actually, the original walls diverged, forming a triangle that included the shores of the Bay of Phaleron. Since it soon transpired that an invader could easily land on the shores of the bay and advance upon Athens between the walls, a third wall was built, close and parallel to the original North or Peiraic Wall, and the South or Phaleric Wall was allowed to decay.

7. Thucydides, II, 63.

8. "Let the good of the people be the highest law," Cicero: *Of the Laws*, III, 3.

9. Xenophon: *Hellenica*, I, vii.

10. Aristophanes: *The Clouds*, ll. 170f.

11. Greek, Platon, a nickname from *platys*, "broad." His real name was Aristokles.

12. Cicero: *The Republic*, I, x (15).

13. Diogenes Laërtius, II, iii, 8.

14. Thucydides, II, 37–41.

15. *Ibid.*, I, 70.

16. Gibbon, vol. II, p. 184.

17. CAH, vol. V, p. 263.

18. Thucydides, III, 82f.

19. Gibbon, vol. II, p. 179.

20. H. G. Wells: *The Outline of History* (N.Y.: 1920), vol. II, p. 382. The wording differs in later editions.

21. Thucydides, I, 22.

Chapter IX, SYRACUSE AND ARETHOUSA'S FOUNTAIN

1. Pausanias, V, vii, 3.

2. Cicero: *In Verrem*, IV, 52f.

3. Or Plemmyrium; now respectively the Cape of St. Pangaia and the Peninsula della Maddalena. The bay between them is still called the Porto Grande.

4. Herodotus, VII, 165.

5. *Ibid.*, VII, 162.

6. Or *gamoroi*.

7. Thucydides, V, 105.

8. The original, from the introduction to Hegel's *Philosophy of History*, reads: "Peoples and governments have never learned anything from history, or acted on principles deduced from it."

9. Schneider, p. 118.

10. Diodorus, XIV, xli, 3f.

11. *Ibid.*, *loc. cit.* and xlii, 2.

12. *Ibid.*, XIV, 1, 4.

13. Plutarch: *Sayings of Kings and Commanders: Archidamos Son of Agesilaos*.

14. See the discussion in Finley, pp. 75–80.

15. Russell, pp. 90–94. A misprint in Russell's book says "Aegesta" for "Segesta." The account of Agathokles' death is from Diodorus, XXI, xvi. Justin's less melodramatic narrative (XXIII, ii) suggests that Agathokles died, not from a poisoned toothpick—the kind of poison story to which ancient writers, ignorant of the true limitations of poisons, were addicted—but more prosaically from cancer.

16. *Ibid.*, pp. 95f.

17. Vitruvius, IX, Pref., 9–12.

18. Diodorus, XXVI, xviii; Pappus, VIII (ed. Ver Ecke, pp. 836f.). For a slightly different version, see Plutarch: *Marcellus*, xiv, 7 (306).

19. Polybius. VIII, 7; Plutarch: *Marcellus*, xv–xvii. Polybius says cranes; Plutarch, catapults. For technical reasons (see my *The Ancient Engineers*, p. 162) cranes are more likely.

20. Diodorus, XXVI, xviii.

21. Or Geôrgiôs Maniakês.

Chapter X, CARTHAGE AND THE FAITHLESS HERO

1. Edgar Allan Poe: *The City in the Sea*. ll. 24–29.

2. Polybius, I, 67.

3. *Ibid.*, I, 66.

4. *Ibid.*, I, 67.

5. *Ibid.*, I, 68.

6. *Ibid.*, I, 69. These names are variously spelled (in Greek, Latinized Greek, or Latin) Barkas or Barca; Geskon, Gesco, Gisgo, or Gisco; Spondios or Spendius; and Mathôs or Matho. "Barca" is probably a nickname meaning "lightning."

7. *Ibid.*, I, 70.

8. Cornelius Nepos: *Hannibal*, 2. Cornelius calls the god "Jupiter," but he probably meant Ba'al Hammon, the head of the Carthaginian pantheon.

9. Warmington, p. 164.

10. Flaubert: *Salammbo*, Everyman's Library ed., 1931, p. 36.

11. *Ibid.*, pp. 96f.

12. See Rhys Carpenter: *Beyond the Pillars of Heracles* (N.Y.: 1966), Chapter III.

13. Charles-Picard, p. 253.

14. Flaubert, *op. cit.*, pp. 64f.

15. Other dates, given by Appian, Eusebius, Livius, Justin, and Velleius Paterculus, work out to −1234, −1214, −846, −825, and −809 respectively.

16. Justin, XVIII, viii, 5.

17. *Ibid.*, XVIII, viii, 6.

18. For further discussion of the falls of Troy, see my wife's and my *Ancient Ruins and Archaeology* (N.Y.: 1964), Chapter IV.

19. L. Sprague de Camp: *The Arrows of Hercules* (N.Y., 1965), pp. 125ff.

20. Plutarch: *Praecepta gerendae reipublicae* (in *Moralia*), III, 6.

21. Flaubert, pp. 97f.

22. De Camp: *op. cit.*, pp. 139–43.

23. For use of elephants in this war, see my *Elephant* (N.Y.: 1964), pp. 120f.

24. Plutarch: *Flaminius*, xxi; Livius, XXXV, 14.

25. Polybius, XXXIX, 5; *Iliad*, VI, 448.

26. Or Genseric; Greek, Gizerikos.

Chapter XI, *ALEXANDRIA AND THE DARKHOUSE*

1. Theocritus: *Adoniazusae* (*Idyll Fifteen*), in Moses Hadas: *The Greek Poets* (N.Y.: 1953), p. 339.

2. Also spelled Alexandreia, -ea.

3. *Odyssey*, IV, 355 *sqq*. The name "Pharos" probably comes from the same source as "pharaoh."

4. Some scholars argue that Homer meant, not the distance to the coast, but the distance to the Canopic mouth of the Nile, twelve miles to the east.

5. Or Soma.

6. *Hê Alexandreia têi pros Aigyptôi.*

7. W. H. Davenport Adams: *Lighthouses and Lightships* (Lon.: 1870), p. 14. See also de Camp: "The 'Darkhouse' of Alexandria," in *Technology and Culture*, VI, 3 (Sum. 1965), pp. 423–27.

8. Abu Abdallah Muḥammad ibn-Muḥammad ibn-'Abdallah ibn-Idrîs. "Idrîs" was the name of his great-grandfather.

9. Idrîsi, III, iv (ed. Dozy, pp. 166f.).

10. Forster (p. 147) says that an earthquake brought down the uppermost part of the lighthouse about 1100. If Idrîsi saw the tower before this happened, his figures might be partly reconciled with those of ibn-ash-Shaykh, who measured the tower when it was actually lower than it had been a century before. I doubt, however, if the tower ever exceeded 600 feet, as Idrîsi's figures indicate.

11. Heliodorus, pp. 1f. See also *Three Greek Romances* (Garden City, N.Y.: 1953), also translated by Dr. Moses Hadas.

12. Lucretius, I, 101: "Such are the crimes to which religion leads."

13. Greek, *mouseion.*

14. Some reckon this king as Ptolemaios VIII. It depends upon whether his nephew, who as a boy was proclaimed king but was almost immediately overthrown and killed on his uncle's orders, should be counted as Ptolemaios VII.

15. For a fictional version of these voyages, see my novel *The Golden Wind* (Garden City, N.Y.: 1969).

16. Heron: *Pneumatics*, xxi.

17. For further discussion of this point, see de Camp: "The Landlocked Indian Ocean," in *Fantasy and Science Fiction*, XXXVI, 6 (Jun. 1969), pp. 34–40.

18. Or Sarapis.

19. Greek, Serapeion, Sar-.

20. For various stories of the establishment of this cult, see Tacitus: *History*, IV, 83.

21. Hippolytus: *The Refutation of All Heresies*, IV, xxxv.

22. Will Durant: *Caesar and Christ* (N.Y.: 1944), p. 608.

23. Pliny the Younger, X, 34.

24. One plethron=100 feet.

25. De Camp: *The Golden Wind*, pp. 16ff., 22f. For possible arrangements of the oars in Philopator's fortier, see Lionel Casson: "The Super-Gal-

leys of the Hellenistic Age," in *The Mariner's Mirror*, LV, 2 (1969), pp. 185–94.

26. De Camp, *op. cit.*, pp. 57f. The details are from Athenaeus: *Deipnosophistae*, V, 198f. *sqq*.

27. Bevan, p. 139.

28. Or XII, if Physkon's nephew be counted as Ptolemy VII.

Chapter XII, ANURÂDHAPURA AND THE ROC'S EGG

1. Pan Chao: *The Ruined City*, in *Poems of Solitude*, transl. by Jerome Ch'ên and Michael Bullock (N.Y.: 1960).

2. Burton, vol. VI, pp. 15ff.

3. Marco Polo, (Everyman's Library ed. 1908–58), ch. XXXVI, p. 393. Polo's memoir was dictated in Italian, written in French, and then translated freely into several languages. The existing versions vary a good deal and at best give only the general sense of Polo's words. See Willy Ley: "Scheherazade's Island," in *Galaxy Science Fiction*, XXIV, 6 (Aug. 1966), pp. 45–155.

4. Depending on the meaning of "pace," this would be about 125 or 250 feet.

5. Or dâgoba, dâgäba. In transliterated Sinhalese, the letters â, ä (or æ) and *a* stand respectively for the vowels (approximately) of "calm," "cat," and "cut." As in French, Hindi, and Japanese, there is practically no stress accent.

6. Pron. "T'HOO-pa," "CHAY-TEE-ya," with only a very light stress on the capitalized syllables. In the languages of India and Ceylon, digraphs like *th, kh*, and *bh* stand for the corresponding sounds in words like "hothouse," "thickhead," "abhor," &c.

7. Or Aśoka, Açoka, Asoka.

8. Or Ruwanwæli, Ruanweli, &c. Like Hindi, Sinhalese has a sound between English *v* and *w* (somewhat like *b* in Spanish *haber*), represented sometimes by one letter and sometimes by the other. Anurâdhapura is pron. "UN-OOR-AHD-ha-POOR-a."

9. *Periplus*, 61.

10. Burton, vol. VI, p. 14.

11. Pron. "lung-kah." Claudius Ptolemaeus rendered Siṃhala as "Simoundou" and "Salike."

12. Sanskrit, *bhikṣu*, pron. "b'hik-shoo." In Sanskrit, the sounds transliterated as *ṣ* and *ś* were separate, the latter being like *ch* in German *ich;* but in mod. Hindi both have become like English *sh*. See Sunti Kumar Chatterji: "The Pronunciation of Sanskrit," in *Le Maître Phonétique*, No. 97 (Jan.–Jun., 1952), pp. 2–9.

13. Pron. "MUH-HAH-VUNH-sa." The letter *ṃ* means that the preceding vowel is nasalized, as many vowels are in French.

14. Or *Cûlavaṃsa*, pron. "CHOO-la-VUNH-sa." In the transliteration of Indian and Ceylonese names, *c* is sometimes used for a sound close to English *ch*. In transliterating words from these languages, I should personally like to represent the sounds of *ch* and *sh*, as do my learned colleagues, by single

letters, e.g. *c* and *ç;* but I fear my editor would have a fit and some of my readers would be confused.

15. Mahânâma, p. 116.

16. *Ibid.,* VI, 47 (p. 54). Since he writes in Pâli, the author calls nirvâna *nibbâna.*

17. In the languages of India and Ceylon, *t* and *d* stand for the sounds of these letters in "get this," "width"; *ṭ* and *ḍ* for the initial consonants of "try," "dry." Sanskrit and Pâli also distinguish *ṇ, l* from *n, l;* but, since these distinctions have disappeared from modern Hindi and Sinhalese and would be inaudible to a Western ear anyway, I shall ignore them.

18. Mahânâma, X, 66–83 (pp. 73f.).

19. Or Śâkyas, Sakyas.

20. H. G. Wells: *The Outline of History* (Garden City, N.Y.: 1931), p. 394.

21. Sanskrit, Sthaviravâdin.

22. Or Candragupta, pron. "chun-drug-oop-tuh."

23. Mahânâma, XVIII, 47ff. (p. 126). Claudius Ptolemaeus calls Anurâdhapura "Anurogrammum Regio," obviously from Anurâdhagama.

24. *Ibid.,* XX, 3–6 (p. 136). In what looks like scribal confusion, the author mentions two Indian kings: "Asoka, king of Avanti" (western Madhya Pradesh), the father of Mahinda, reigning in Ujjenî (mod. Ujjain); and "Emperor Dhammâsoka" (translatable as "Pious Ashoka"), ruling most of India from Pâṭaliputra (Pâli, Pâṭaliputta). The two rulers are probably one and the same man; Mahânâma probably pieced together two accounts from mutually inconsistent sources.

25. Burtt, p. 71.

26. Or Cola.

27. Or Duṭṭagâmanî; Sinhalese, Duṭugämanu.

28. Mahânâma, XXV, 52–74 (pp. 174f.).

29. *Ibid.,* XXIX, 2–9 (pp. 191f.).

30. *Ibid.,* XXIX, 23–27 (pp. 192f.).

31. *Ibid.,* XXIX, 57–61 (pp. 195f.).

32. Pliny the Elder, VI, xxiv (84f.).

33. Comhaire and Cahnman, p. 55.

34. Or Kâśyapa.

35. Or Mugalan.

Chapter XIII, ROME, THE CITY OF ALL TIME

1. Henry Wadsworth Longfellow: *Michael Angelo,* III, 4.

2. Since the younger Pliny's uncle (Pliny the Younger, VI, xvi) and his aunt (Juvenal, XII, xif.) are both described as fat, it is likely that the nephew inherited the trait.

3. Martial, IX, xviii.

4. Ammianus, XVI, x, 13f.

5. Davis (1959), pp. 7ff.

6. Modern *pozzuolana,* Pozzuoli.

7. Suetonius: *Augustus*, xxviii.

8. Being a fourth-declension noun, the nominative plural of *domus* is *domûs*.

9. Strabo, V, iii, 7; Seneca: *De ira*, III, xxxv, 5; *De beneficiis*, VI, xv, 7; Juvenal, III, 190–202.

10. For a more detailed account of the Tiber bridges, see my *The Ancient Engineers*, pp. 191–94, 379.

11. Juvenal, III, 60–64.

12. *Ibid.*, X, 80.

13. Charles Galton Darwin: *The Next Million Years* (N.Y.: 1953), pp. 170f.

14. H. G. Wells: *The Outline of History* (Garden City, N.Y.: 1931), p. 451. Current opinion classes Neanderthal man as merely a race of *Homo sapiens* and not as another species. The idea that he was a squat, shambling oaf with "misshapen hairy paws" and "a chinless, bestial face" was based upon one of the first Neanderthal skeletons found, which happened to be that of an arthritic old man. Most were stocky men of medium height, whose brows beetled and whose foreheads and chins receded no more than those of millions of living men.

15. Cicero: *Ad familiares*, VII, 1.

16. Polybius, XXXI, XXV, 3–8; Arnold Toynbee: *A Study of History* (Lon.: 1934–39), vol. IV, pp. 505–12.

17. Quoted from an unidentified source by Basil Davenport, in *The Roman Reader* (N.Y.: 1951–59), p. 479.

18. Pliny the Younger, VII, 5.

19. Seneca: *De clementia*, I, xxiv, 1.

20. Juvenal, III, ll. 243–47.

21. Pliny the Younger, II, xi.

22. Martial, VI, xxxv.

Chapter XIV, PĀṬALIPUTRA AND THE MILLION GODS

1. Carl Sandburg: *Four Preludes on Playthings in the Wind.*

2. Or Candragupta Maurya (pron. "chun-drug-oop-tuh mor-yuh," with even stress). In Sanskrit, the sounds represented by the digraphs *ai, au* were diphthongs something like the vowels of English "high," "how." In modern Hindi, the letters represent simple vowels like those of "hair," "haul." Otherwise, rules for pronouncing words from Sanskrit or Hindi are about the same as those from Pâli or Sinhalese.

3. Pron. "pah-tul-ip-oot-ruh"; it has also been called Pushpura and Kusumpura.

4. Arrian: *Indica*, 10. Megasthenes actually gave the dimensions of the city in stadia or furlongs, each stadion being about one-eighth of a mile. The Erannoboas is presumably the Son, one of several affluents that join the Ganges in this region.

5. Strabo, XV, i, 36.

6. Edwardes, p. 43.

7. *Ramâyâna*, II, 57; *apud* Basham, p. 86.

8. Or *Arthaśâstra*, *Arthaçâstra*, pron. "urt-hush-ah-struh."

9. Pron. "kaw-til-yuh"; also spelled Kauṭalya.

10. Hadas, p. 266; Edwardes, p. 50.

11. Or brâhmanas.

12. Or kṣatriyas, pron. "kshut-re-yuhs."

13. Or vaiśyas, pron. "vesh-yuhs."

14. Or śûdras, sudras.

15. Or canḍâlas, pron. "chun-dah-luhs."

16. Or cakravartin, -ti, pron. "chuk-ruv-ur-ti(n)."

17. Saletore, p. 176.

18. Or Puṣyamitra Śunga, Sunga.

19. Or Śakas, Sakas; Greek, Sakai.

20. Or Kuṣânas, Kushans.

21. Or Kaniṣka.

22. Or Kâśî.

23. Basham, pp. 203f.

24. Mookerji, p. 62.

25. *Kâma*="love, lust, passion"; *sûtra*="seam" (cf. "suture") or "handbook."

26. Vâtsyâyana, p. 209.

27. *Ibid.*, pp. 47f.

28. Aubrey Menen: *Dead Man in the Silver Market* (N.Y.: 1953), p. 22.

29. Or *caturanga*, pron. "chut-oo-ung-guh." For the history of chess, see Edward Falkener: *Games Ancient and Oriental and How to Play Them* (Lon.: 1892; N.Y.: 1961); Comnena, XII, vi.

30. Or yakṣî, pron. "yuk-shee."

31. Translation of the inscription on the Iron Pillar, on a nearby plaque; courtesy of the Maharajkumar Virendrasingh.

32. Lord Dunsany: *While the Sirens Slept* (Lon.: 1944), p. 140. See also Willy Ley: "The Iron Pillar of Delhi," in *Galaxy Science Fiction*, VIII, 1 (Apr. 1954), pp. 75f.

33. Or Deogadh.

34. Or *śikhara, sikhara*.

35. *Odyssey*, XII, ll. 109f.

36. I hope no reader infers from this that I believe in the literal truth of Plato's Atlantis story. For my views, see the first chapter of *Ancient Ruins and Archaeology*.

37. Or Śiva, Siva.

38. Or Viṣnu.

39. Basham, pp. 309f.

40. Vâtsyâyana, p. 172.

41. Saletore, p. 215.

42. Or śakti, sakti.

43. Or Taksásilâ.

44. Or Mihirakula.

45. Or Harṣavardhana.

46. N. Y. *Times*, 22 Dec. 1968, p. 14.

47. As Arthur Koestler ("Mahatma Gandhi—the Yogi and the Commissar," in the New York *Times Magazine*, 5 Oct. 1969) expresses it (p. 117): a "twilight air of unreality, muddleheadedness and sanctimonious evasion of vital issues."

48. Letter from the Dowager Lady Dunsany, 18 Oct. 1963; quoted by permission.

Chapter XV, CONSTANTINOPLE AND THE HOLY WISDOM

1. Gilbert Keith Chesterton: *Lepanto*, ll. 1–6.

2. Diener, p. 212.

3. E.g., J. Everetts Haley: *A Texan Looks at Lyndon* (*A Study in Illegitimate Power*) (Canyon, Tex.: Palo Duro Pr., 1964).

4. Procopius: *History of the Wars*, I, xxiv.

5. Or Andronikos Komnênos.

6. Gibbon, vol. II, p. 143.

7. Pratt, p. 61.

8. *Ibid.*, pp. 65f.; quoted from G. P. Baker: *Justinian*.

9. "Romania" was revived, in the form Rômania (sometimes spelled Rumania) in 1866 for the newly united land of the Vlachs and Moldavians, peoples of mixed Dacian, Roman, and Slavic descent, speaking a Romance language. Now the Republica Populara Româna, or People's Roman Republic. The last Byzantine emperor was actually urged by some of his supporters to change his title to "king of the Hellenes," but nothing came of this.

10. In Byzantine and mod. Greek, pron. "ah-YEE-ah so-FEE-ah."

11. EB, *s.v.* "Vladimir, St."

12. William Butler Yeats: *Sailing to Byzantium*.

13. Or Basilius, Basileios.

14. Or Theophanto, Theophania.

15. Or Nikêphoros Phôkas.

16. Or Iôannês Tzimiskês.

17. Psellus, I, 4.

18. Hearsey, p. 29.

19. Gibbon, vol. I, p. 145.

20. *Ibid.*, vol. II, p. 520.

21. Diener, p. 167.

22. Comnena, X, i (p. 235).

23. *Ibid.*, XIX, vii (p. 380).

24. Diehl, p. 99.

25. *Ibid.*, pp. 104f.

26. Comnena, X, ix (p. 258).

27. Or Konstantinos Doukas. According to another system of reckoning, this Constantine should be Constantine XI, one of his predecessors, a usurper who reigned only momentarily, being counted as Constantine VIII.

28. Psellus, X, iii, 18.

29. Or Alexios Komnenos, Alexis.

30. Comnena, XIV, iv (pp. 372f.).

31. Eversley, p. 77; Gibbon, vol. II, p. 1339.

32. Probably a combination of the Arabic 'Uthman and a Turkish name like Otman. "Osmanli" is often rendered as "Ottoman."

33. Or Iôannês Kantakouzênos, Cantacuzene.

34. Gibbon, vol. II, p. 1355; J. A. Miller: *Master Builders of Sixty Centuries* (N.Y.: 1938), p. 109.

35. Pron. "is-tahn-bool," with an even stress accent.

36. Pron. "yen-ee-cheh-ree," meaning "new soldiers."

37. Gibbon, vol. II, p. 1330.

38. Gülersoy, p. 158.

39. Psellus, VI, iii, 28.

40. Turkish, Süleymaniye Camii, pron. "sü-lay-mah-nee-yeh jah-mee-ee."

41. Turkish, Sultan Ahmet Camii, pron. "sool-tahn ah-h'met jah-mee-ee."

42. Sykes, pp. 290f. Different sources give different dates for the fall of Trebizond, from 1460 to 1463.

Chapter XVI, FAREWELL TO ANCIENT CITIES

1. Comnena: Preface, i. The "tragedian" is Sophocles, and the quotation is from his *Ajax*.

BIBLIOGRAPHY

Standard reference works used in writing this book but not listed separately below include the Bible (King James and Revised Standard versions); the Cambridge Ancient History; the Cambridge History of India; the Encyclopaedia Britannica (14th Edition, 1932); La Grande Encyclopédie; the Oxford Classical Dictionary; the Pauly and Wissowa Realenzyklopädie der Klassischen Altertumswissenschaft; William Smith's Dictionary of Greek and Roman Biography and Mythology and Dictionary of Greek and Roman Geography; and the following classical authors, most of them in Loeb Classical Library editions but some in other versions: Ammianus Marcellinus, Appian, Aristophanes, Aristotle, Arrian, Athenaeus of Naucratis, Caesar, Cicero, Dio Cassius, Diodorus Siculus, Diogenes Laërtius, Eusebius, Frontinus, Herodotus, Heron, Hippolytus, Josephus, Justin, Juvenal, Livy, Lucan, Lucian, Manetho, Martial, Cornelius Nepos, Pappus, Pausanias, *Periplus of the Erythraean Sea*, Petronius, Philo, Philostratus, Plato, Pliny the Elder, Pliny the Younger, Plotinus, Plutarch, Polybius, Procopius, Claudius Ptolemy, Seneca, Spartianus, Strabo, Suetonius, Suidas, Tacitus, Theocritus, Thucydides, Velleius Paterculus, Virgil, Vitruvius, and Xenophon.

AFRICA, THOMAS W.: *Rome of the Caesars*, N.Y.: John Wiley & Sons, Inc., 1965.

ALBA, DUKE OF: "The Pharos of Alexandria," in *Proceedings of the British Academy*, XIX (1933), pp. 277–92.

ANDREWS, A.: *The Greek Tyrants*, N.Y.: Harper & Row, Pubs., 1956–63.

ASHBY, THOMAS: *The Aqueducts of Rome*, Oxf.: Clarendon Pr., 1935.

ASIMOV, ISAAC: *Asimov's Guide to the Bible*, Garden City, N.Y.: Doubleday & Co., Inc., 1968–69.

AUBOYER, JEANNINE: *La Vie Quotidienne dans l'Inde Ancienne (environ IIe S. avant J.-C.–VIIe S.)*, Paris: Librairie Hachette, 1961.

BAEDEKER, KARL: *Egypt and the Sûdân*, Leipzig: Karl Baedeker, 1929.

———: *Palestine and Syria*, Leipzig: Karl Baedeker, 1912.

———: *Southern Italy and Sicily*, Leipzig: Karl Baedeker, 1930.

BAILEY, CYRIL (ed.): *The Legacy of Rome*, Oxf.: Clarendon Pr., 1923.

BANERJI, R. D.: *The Age of the Imperial Guptas*, Benares: Benares Hindu University, 1933.

BASHAM, A. L.: *The Wonder That Was India*, N.Y.: Grove Pr., Inc., 1954.

BELL, H. IDRIS: *Egypt from Alexander the Great to the Arab Conquest*, Oxf.: Clarendon Pr., 1948.

BEVAN, EDWYN: *A History of Egypt Under the Ptolemaic Dynasty*, Lon.: Methuen & Co., Ltd., 1927.

BOTSFORD, G. W., and E. G. SIHLER (eds.): *Hellenic Civilization*, N.Y.: Columbia Univ. Pr., 1915.

BOWRA, C. MAURICE: *The Greek Experience*, N.Y.: Mentor Books, 1957–59.

BROWN, PERCY: *Indian Architecture (Buddhist and Hindu Periods)*, Bombay: D. B. Taraporevala Sons & Co., Ltd., 1942.

BURTON, RICHARD F. (transl.): *The Book of the Thousand Nights and a Night*, Lon.: Burton Club, 1886, 17 vols.

BURTT, E. A. (ed.): *The Teachings of the Compassionate Buddha*, N.Y.: The New American Library of World Literature, Inc., 1955.

BURY, J. B.: *A History of Greece (to the Death of Alexander the Great)*, N.Y.: Modern Lib., Inc., 1900–37.

BURY, J. B., et al.: *The Hellenistic Age*, Cambridge: Cambridge Univ. Pr., 1925.

CARCOPINO, JÉRÔME: *Daily Life in Ancient Rome*, New Haven: Yale Univ. Pr., 1940.

CARTER, HOWARD, and A. C. MACE: *The Tomb of Tut-Ankh-Amen*, Lon.: Cassell & Co., Ltd., 1923; N.Y.: Cooper Square Pubs., Inc., 1963.

CARY, M. J., and T. J. HAARHOFF: *Life and Thought in the Greek and Roman World*, Lon.: Methuen & Co., Ltd. (University Paperbacks), 1940–61.

CHAMPDOR, ALBERT: *Babylon*, Lon.: Elek Books, Ltd., 1958.

CHARLES-PICARD, GILBERT and COLETTE: *Daily Life in Carthage (at the Time of Hannibal)*, N.Y.: The Macmillan Co., Pubs., 1961.

COKE, RICHARD: *Baghdad, City of Peace*, Lon.: Thornton Butterworth, 1927–35.

COLLAS, PERICLES: *A Concise Guide to Athens*, Athens: C. Cacoulides, n.d.

———: *A Concise Guide to the Acropolis of Athens*, Athens: C. Cacoulides, n.d.

COMHAIRE, JEAN, and WERNER J. CAHNMAN: *How Cities Grew*, Madison, N.J.: Florham Park Pr., 1959.

COMNENA, ANNA: *The Alexiad of the Princess Anna Comnena*, Lon.: Routledge & Kegan Paul, Ltd., 1928–67.

CONTENAU, GEORGES: *Everyday Life in Babylon and Assyria*, Lon.: Edward Arnold Ltd., 1954.

COTTRELL, LEONARD: *Lost Cities*, N.Y.: Rinehart & Co., Inc., 1957.

DAVIS, WILLIAM STEARNS: *A Day in Old Athens*, Boston: Allyn & Bacon, Inc., 1914–42; N.Y.: Biblo & Tannen, Inc., n.d.

———: *A Day in Old Rome*, Boston: Allyn & Bacon, Inc., 1925; N.Y.: Biblo & Tannen, Inc., 1959.

DEUEL, LEO (ed.): *The Treasures of Time,* N.Y.: World Pub. Co. and Avon Books, 1961.

DIEHL, CHARLES: *Byzantium: Greatness and Decline,* New Brunswick, N.J.: Rutgers Univ. Pr., 1957.

DIENER, BERTHA: *Imperial Byzantium,* Boston: Little, Brown & Co., 1938.

EDWARDES, MICHAEL: *A History of India,* N.Y.: Farrar, Straus & Co., 1961.

ELGOOD, P. G.: *Later Dynasties of Egypt,* Oxf.: Basil Blackwell, 1951.

EVERSLEY, LORD: *The Turkish Empire,* N.Y.: Dodd, Mead & Co., 1917.

FAIRSERVIS, WALTER A., JR.: *The Ancient Kingdoms of the Nile,* N.Y.: Thomas Y. Crowell Co., 1962.

FINEGAN, JACK: *Light from the Ancient Past (the Archaeological Background of Judaism and Christianity),* Princeton: Princeton Univ. Pr., 1946–59.

FINLEY, M. I.: *Aspects of Antiquity (Discoveries and Controversies),* N.Y.: Viking Pr., Inc., 1968.

FLACELIÈRE, ROBERT: *La Vie Quotidienne en Grèce au Siècle de Périclès,* Paris: Librairie Hachette, 1959.

FLEMING, WALLACE B.: *The History of Tyre,* N.Y.: Columbia Univ. Pr., 1915.

FORSTER, E. M.: *Alexandria (A History and a Guide),* Garden City, N.Y.: Anchor Books, 1922–66.

FREEMAN, EDWARD A.: *The Story of Sicily,* N.Y.: G. P. Putnam's Sons, 1892.

FUSTEL DE COULANGES, N. D.: *The Ancient City,* Garden City, N.Y.: Doubleday & Co., Inc., n.d.

GIBBON, EDWARD: *The Decline and Fall of the Roman Empire,* N.Y.: Modern Lib., Inc., n.d., 2 vols.

GLANVILLE, S. R. K. (ed.): *The Legacy of Egypt,* Oxf.: Clarendon Pr., 1942.

GORDON, CYRUS H.: *Introduction to Old Testament Times,* Ventnor, N.J.: Ventnor Pub., 1953.

GRAVES, ROBERT: "It Was a Stable World," in *Occupation: Writer,* N.Y.: Grosset & Dunlap, Inc., 1950, pp. 234–43.

GREEN, PETER: *Essays in Antiquity,* Cleveland, World Pub. Co., 1960.

———: *Armada from Athens,* Garden City, N.Y.: Doubleday & Co., Inc., 1970.

Guide to the Patna Museum (Stone Sculptures, Bronzes and Terracottas), Patna: Govt. Printing, 1955.

GUIDO, MARGARET: *Syracuse (A Handbook to Its History and Principal Monuments),* Lon.: Max Parrish & Co., Ltd., 1958.

GÜLERSOY, ÇELIK: *Un Guide d'Istanbul,* Istanbul: Istanbul Marbaas, 1966.

HADAS, MOSES: *Hellenistic Culture,* N.Y.: Columbia Univ. Pr., 1959.

HALLIDAY, WILLIAM REGINALD: *The Growth of the City State,* Liverpool: Hodder & Stoughton, 1923.

HAMILTON, EDITH: *The Echo of Greece,* N.Y.: W. W. Norton & Co., Inc., Pubs., 1957.

———, *The Greek Way,* N.Y.: Mentor Books, 1948–61.

———, *The Roman Way,* N.Y.: Mentor Books, 1932–57.

HAMLIN, TALBOT: *Architecture Through the Ages,* N.Y.: G. P. Putnam's Sons, 1940–53.

HARDEN, DONALD: *The Phoenicians,* Lon.: Thames and Hudson, Ltd., 1962.

HAVERFIELD, F.: *Ancient Town-Planning*, Oxf.: Clarendon Pr., 1913.

HAYES, WILLIAM C.: "Daily Life in Ancient Egypt," in *National Geographic Magazine*, LXXX, 4 (Oct. 1941), p. 419.

HEARSEY, JOHN E. N.: *City of Constantine, 324–1453*, Lon.: John Murray, Pubs., Ltd., 1963.

HELIODORUS: *An Ethiopian Romance*, Ann Arbor: Univ. of Michigan Pr., 1957.

HIORNS, FREDERICK R.: *Town-Building in History*, Lon.: George G. Harrap & Co., Ltd., Pubs., 1956.

HITTI, PHILIP D.: *History of Syria*, Lon.: Macmillan & Co., Ltd., 1951.

———: *Lebanon in History*, Lon.: Macmillan & Co., Ltd., 1957.

IDRÎSI: *Description de l'Afrique et de l'Espagne, par Edrîsî* . . . Leyden: E. J. Brill, 1866.

Istanbul, with introd. by Fatma Laylâ Çambel and Ursula Meyer-Ravenstein, Garden City, N.Y.: Doubleday & Co., Inc., 1961.

JACOBSEN, THORKILD, and SETON LLOYD: *Sennacherib's Aqueduct at Jerwan*, Chi.: Univ. of Chicago Pr., 1935.

JASTROW, MORRIS: *The Religion of Babylonia and Assyria*, Boston: Ginn & Co., 1898.

JOGUET, PIERRE: *Macedonian Imperialism and the Hellenization of the East*, Lon.: Paul, Trench, Trubner & Co., 1928.

JOIN-LAMBERT, MICHEL: *Jerusalem*, Lon.: Elek Books, Ltd., 1958.

KENYON, KATHLEEN M.: "Ancient Jerusalem," in *Scientific American*, CCXIII, 1 (Jul. 1965), pp. 84–90.

———: "Biblical Jerusalem," in *Expedition*, V, 1, (Fall 1962), pp. 32–35.

———: *Jerusalem (Excavating 3000 Years of History)*, N.Y.: McGraw-Hill Book Co., Inc., 1967.

KING, L. W.: *The Letters and Inscriptions of Hammurabi, King of Babylon About B.C. 2200* . . . , Lon.: Luzac & Co., 1900, 3 vols.

KOLDEWEY, ROBERT: *The Excavations at Babylon*, Lon.: Macmillan & Co., Ltd., 1914.

KOLLEK, TEDDY, and MOSHE PEARLMAN: *Jerusalem: A History of Forty Centuries*, N.Y.: Random House, Inc., 1968.

KRAELING, CARL H., and ROBERT M. ADAMS (eds.): *City Invincible*, Chi.: Univ. of Chicago Pr., 1960.

LAYARD, SIR HENRY: *Early Adventures in Persia, Susiana, and Babylonia*, N.Y.: Longmans, Green & Co., 1887, 2 vols.

LECKY, W. E. H.: *History of the Rise and Influence of the Spirit of Rationalism in Europe*, N.Y.: D. Appleton & Co., 1866, 2 vols.

LEWIS, GEOFFREY: *Turkey*, N.Y.: Frederick A. Praeger, Inc., Pubs., 1960–65.

LIVINGSTONE, R. W. (ed.): *The Legacy of Greece*, Oxf.: Clarendon Pr., 1922.

LLOYD, SETON: *Foundations in the Dust (A Story of Mesopotamian Exploration)*, Harmondsworth, Eng.: Penguin Books, Ltd., 1947–55.

———: *Ruined Cities of Iraq*, Lon.: Humphrey Milford, 1942–45.

LONGRIGG, STEPHEN HEMSLEY, and FRANK STOAKES: *Iraq*, N.Y.: Frederick A. Praeger, Inc., Pubs., 1958.

MACLAGAN, MICHAEL: *The City of Constantine*, N.Y.: Frederick A. Praeger, Inc., Pubs., 1968.

MCNEILL, WILLIAM H.: *The Rise of the West*, Chi.: Univ. of Chicago Pr., 1963.

MACQUEEN, JAMES G.: *Babylon*, Lon.: Robert Hale, Ltd., 1964.

MAHAFFY, J. P.: *The Empire of the Ptolemies*, Lon.: Macmillan Co., 1895.

———: *Greek Life and Thought (from the Age of Alexander to the Roman Conquest)*, Lon.: Macmillan Co., 1887.

MAHÂNÂMA: *The Mahâvaṃsa or Great Chronicle of Ceylon*, Lon.: Pali Text Soc., 1964.

MENDIS, G. C.: *The Early History of Ceylon*, Calcutta: Y.M.C.A. Pub. House, 1932–46.

MONTET, PIERRE: *Everyday Life in Egypt*, N.Y.: St. Martin's Pr., Inc., 1958.

MOOKERJI, RADHAKUMUND: *The Gupta Empire*, Bombay: Hind Kitabs, 1947.

MORET, ALEXANDRE: *The Nile and Egyptian Civilization*, N.Y.: Alfred A. Knopf, 1927.

NICHOLAS, C. W., and S. PARANAVITANA: *A Concise History of Ceylon*, Colombo: Ceylon Univ. Pr., 1961.

OLMSTEAD, A. T.: *History of the Persian Empire*, Chi.: Univ. of Chicago Pr., 1948.

OMAN, SIR CHARLES: *A History of the Art of War in the Middle Ages*, Lon.: Methuen & Co., 1924, 2 vols.

OTTIN, MERRY: *Land of Emperors and Sultans*, N.Y.: Crown Pubs., Inc., 1962.

ÖZGÜÇ, TAHSIN: "An Assyrian Trading Outpost," in *Scientific American*, CCVIII, 2 (Feb. 1962), pp. 96–106.

PARROT, ANDRÉ: *Babylon and the Old Testament*, N.Y.: Philosophical Library, Inc., 1958.

———: *Discovering Buried Worlds*, N.Y.: Philosophical Library, Inc., 1955.

———: *Nineveh and the Old Testament*, N.Y.: Philosophical Library, Inc., 1955.

———: *The Temple of Jerusalem*, N.Y.: Philosophical Library, Inc., 1955.

———: *The Tower of Babel*, N.Y.: Philosophical Library, Inc., 1955.

PARSONS, EDWARD ALEXANDER: *The Alexandrian Library*, Lon.: Cleaver-Hume Pr., Ltd., 1952.

PEREIRA, MICHAEL: *Istanbul (Aspects of a City)*, Lon.: Geoffrey Bles, Ltd., 1968.

PETRIE, W. M. FLINDERS: *Memphis*, Lon.: British School of Archaeology in Egypt, 1909, vol. I.

PHOTIUS: *The Library of Photius*, vol. I, Lon.: Macmillan Co., 1920.

PICARD, GILBERT: *Carthage*, N.Y.: Frederick Ungar Pub. Co., 1965.

POIDEBARD, A.: *Un Grand Port Disparu: Tyr*, Paris: Libr. Orientaliste Paul Geuthner, 1939.

PRATT, FLETCHER: *The Battles That Changed History*, Garden City, N.Y.: Doubleday & Co., Inc., 1956.

PRITCHARD, JAMES B.: *Ancient Near Eastern Texts (Relating to the Old Testament)*, Princeton: Princeton Univ. Pr., 1950–55.

PSELLUS, MICHAEL: *Fourteen Byzantine Rulers* (*The Chronographia of Michael Psellus*), Harmondsworth: Penguin Books, Ltd., 1966.

PURI, B. N.: *Cities of Ancient India*, Meerut: Meenakshi Prakashan, 1966.

RICE, DAVID TALBOT: *The Byzantines*, N.Y.: Frederick A. Praeger, Inc., Pubs., 1962.

RIEFSTAHL, ELIZABETH: *Thebes in the Time of Amunhotep III*, Norman: Univ. of Oklahoma Pr., 1964.

RIVOIRA, G. T.: *Roman Architecture*, Oxf.: Clarendon Pr., 1925.

ROBINSON, C. E.: *The Days of Alkibiades*, Lon.: Edward Arnold & Co., 1925.

———: *Everyday Life in Ancient Greece*, Oxf.: Clarendon Pr., 1933–34.

ROBINSON, CHARLES ALEXANDER: *Athens in the Age of Pericles*, Norman: Univ. of Oklahoma Pr., 1959–63.

ROSTOVTZEFF, M. I.: *The Social and Economic History of the Hellenistic World*, Oxf.: Clarendon Pr., 1941, 3 vols.

ROWELL, HENRY THOMPSON: *Rome in the Augustan Age*, Norman: Univ. of Olahoma Pr., 1962.

RUNCIMAN, STEVEN: *Byzantine Civilization*, Cleveland: World Pub. Co., 1933–56.

RUSSELL, BERTRAND: *Power* (*A New Social Analysis*), N.Y.: W. W. Norton & Co., Inc., 1938.

SAGGS, H. W. F.: *The Greatness That Was Babylon*, N.Y.: Hawthorn Books, Inc., 1962.

SALETORE, RAJARAM NARAYAN: *Life in the Gupta Age*, Bombay: Popular Book Depot, 1943.

SANDYS, SIR JOHN EDWIN: *A Companion to Latin Studies*, Cambridge: Cambridge Univ. Pr., 1910–43.

SCHNEIDER, WOLF: *Babylon Is Everywhere*, Lon.: McGraw-Hill Pub. Co., Ltd., 1963.

SCHREIBER, HERMANN and GEORG SCHREIBER: *Vanished Cities*, N.Y.: Alfred A. Knopf, Inc., 1957.

SILVERBERG, ROBERT (ed.): *Great Adventures in Archaeology*, N.Y.: Dial Pr., Inc., 1964.

———: *Lost Cities and Vanished Civilizations*, Phila.: Chilton Book Co., 1962.

SJOBERG, GIDEON: *The Preindustrial City*, Glencoe, Ill.: Free Pr., 1960.

SPEISER, E. A., et al.: *Everyday Life in Ancient Times*, Wash.: National Geographic Soc., 1951–58.

SWANN, WIM: *Lost Cities of Asia*, N.Y.: G. P. Putnam's Sons, 1966.

SYKES, SIR MARK: *The Caliphs' Last Heritage*, Lon.: Macmillan Co., 1915.

TARN, W. W.: *The Greeks in Bactria and India*, Cambridge: Cambridge Univ. Pr., 1951–66.

———: *Hellenistic Civilization*, Lon.: Edward Arnold & Co., 1927.

TOYNBEE, ARNOLD (ed.): *Cities of Destiny*, N.Y.: McGraw-Hill Book Co., Inc., 1967.

VATSYAYANA: *Kama Sutra of Vatsyayana*, N.Y.: Medical Pr., 1961.

VAUX, ROLAND DE: *Ancient Israel*, Lon.: McGraw-Hill Pub. Co., Ltd., 1961.

WARMINGTON, B. H.: *Carthage*, Lon.: Robert Hale, Ltd., 1960.

WEBER, MAX: *The City*, Glencoe, Ill.: Free Pr., 1958.

WEERASOORIYA, HUBERT E.: *Voices in Stones* (*A Book on Anuradhapura*), Galle: Ruhunu Books, 1958.

WELLER, CHARLES HEALD: *Athens and Its Monuments*, N.Y.: Macmillan, 1913.

WHIBLEY, LEONARD: *A Companion to Greek Studies*, Cambridge: Cambridge Univ. Pr., 1906.

WILBER, DONALD N.: *The Land and the People of Ceylon*, Phila.: J. B. Lippincott Co., 1963.

WILSON, JOHN A.: *The Ancient Culture of Egypt*, Chi.: Univ. of Chicago Pr., 1951–59.

WYCHERLY, R. E.: *How the Greeks Built Their Cities*, Lon.: Macmillan & Co., Ltd., 1962; Garden City, N.Y.: Doubleday & Co., Inc., 1969.

INDEX